The Irish Revolution
(Volume I)
The Murdering Time
From The Land League To
The First Home Rule Bill

Michael J. F. McCarthy

Alpha Editions

This Edition Published in 2021

ISBN: 9789354418945

Design and Setting By
Alpha Editions
www.alphaedis.com
Email – info@alphaedis.com

AUTHOR'S NOTE.

THE author of this volume lived continuously in Ireland through all the events he narrates, and may claim to be himself a child and product of the Revolution of which he attempts to give a complete short history.

Besides carefully consulting Hansard's Parliamentary Debates and many contemporary Government publications, he has refreshed his memory by systematic reference to journalistic records, notably the files of the 'Freeman's Journal,' the Dublin 'Daily Express,' 'United Ireland,' 'The Nation' (Dublin), the 'Cork Examiner,' the 'Belfast Newsletter,' and 'The Times'—to all of which he owns his indebtedness.

He desires also to acknowledge much assistance received from well-known works dealing with the subject from special standpoints, particularly Mr Barry O'Brien's able and sympathetic 'Life of Parnell,' Viscount Morley's official 'Life of Gladstone,' Sir Wemyss Reid's 'Life of Forster,' Mr T. P. O'Connor's 'Life of Lord Beaconsfield' and semiofficial 'Parnell Movement,' Mr Davitt's 'Fall of

Feudalism,' P. J. P. Tynan's 'Irish Invincibles and their Times,' Le Caron's 'Twenty-five Years in the Secret Service,' and Mr F. H. O'Donnell's 'Irish Parliamentary Party.'

If the book have any merit, and whatever be its shortcomings, he has kept one aim before him stead-fastly in writing it—namely, to tell the truth, so far as his experience and study enable him to do so, uninfluenced by creed or party feeling.

October 1912.

CONTENTS.

CONTENTS

PART III.—THROUGH MURDER TO VICTORY.

PART IV.—TRIUMPH AND DEFEAT OF PARNELL.

ILLUSTRATIONS.

PART I.

ON THE THRESHOLD OF THE REVOLUTION

CHAPTER I.

Our district of Ireland was as peaceful as the ideal Arcadia in the spring of 1877. The farmers had had many years of prosperity, the competition for land was keen, and if a tenant was ejected for not paying his rent, another eagerly took his place. When a farm was about to be given up, numbers of farmers would go to the estate office and tender for it, the landlord or agent having the delicate but pleasant task of deciding between the claimants; and, though there was usually a consensus of opinion as to who ought to get the vacant farm, the landlord's right to give it to whomsoever he willed was admitted, and his decision accepted as final. Shopkeepers were also anxious for land, most of them being farmers' sons, and longing for the fresh air of the fields; and, when a farmer was in difficulty, some shopkeeper to whom he owed money was often the first to make an offer to the landlord.

The open competition for land and the peaceful state of the country at this time, when we were on the threshold of the revolution, are both illustrated, I think, by the following incident. In March 1877 my father got possession of a fertile farm of two hundred acres, surrendered by a tenant who was heavily in arrear with his rent, and for which there had been an unusually large number of applicants. On the day my father got possession I accompanied him as an interested spectator. It was a fine day with a blue-and-white sky and a fresh breeze laden with the scent of the sea and of furze blossoms. The tenant, who was a distant relative of ours, met us in the farmyard and greeted us in soft, sorrowful Irish tones. We had frequently visited him in his prosperity, and his wife asked us to come in and rest, but my father declined the offer, for he found the meeting a severe trial.

The sub-agent requested the farmer's wife to put out the fire, and, as she did so, she began to cry aloud, while he, stamping the embers, said in a kindly tone that the world was full of trouble, and what could not be cured had to be endured. Her husband was standing petrified in the yard, while she, with a child in her arms, was being helped out of the house. The sub-agent locked the door and gave formal possession to my father, who then returned the key to the farmer's wife, telling her to remain in the house as long as she wished. Then we went off to the nearest field, where the sub-agent placed a handful of rich brown earth in my father's hand, saying, " I give you possession of this farm and wish you every luck with it." There were four cottages occupied by labourers, in each of which the fire had to be extinguished, the occupants put out, the door locked, and the key handed over to my father, who immediately gave it back to the woman of the house and told her to re-enter. All this could not have been more peaceably carried out in England itself. How different it would have been two years afterwards!

My father had another farm of smaller size a few miles away which came to him by inheritance, besides a small holding in the outskirts of the town. He did not live on either farm, but at his place of business in the town, and was just the class of man who would have been denounced as a "land-grabber" two years afterwards. Having got possession, a question arose as to how the new farm was to be tilled for the current year. Our men and horses were only sufficient for the land we already had, and the season was getting late. But as soon as it was known that my father had got the new farm, he was overwhelmed with offers of help from farmers of his acquaintance, who sent men, horses, harrows, ploughs, and grubbers, and in a short time prepared about forty acres for corn and other crops. The cheerfulness with which they came to the aid of a friend without any promise of reward is worthy of record as showing how naturally generous is the Irish disposition. Many even brought food with them, not wishing to put us to trouble, though of course we had ample provision for them. These friends were not relations, except one or two, though our connections were so numerous that I had one or more relatives amongst the farmers on all the principal estates, and in whatever direction I went for twelve or fifteen miles I was sure to find many a cousin.

The former tenant sat by the fence all day, smoking in the sunshine, inspecting the busy scene, and occasionally tendering advice. He had the customary six months equity of redemption—that is to say, if within that time he paid the landlord, he could claim reinstatement. We knew he could not raise so much money, but his labourers, whom we had taken over, kept saying positively that he would get the farm back, loyally hoping, or professing to hope, that he would achieve the impossible. When the end of the time for redemption was coming near, and just after we had drawn the hay and some of the corn into the haggard, we were aroused one night by the police, and told that there was a fire at the new farm. I sprang out of bed, hurriedly dressed, and rushed out with my father and a servant boy into the chilly darkness, expecting a possible enemy behind every bush along the lonely road. When we had gone about three-quarters of a mile and reached the top of a hill, we saw the horizon gory with flames—a thrilling sight for onlookers who knew that what was being consumed was their own property.

We hastened on, and, arriving out of breath, found that the fire was confined to the end rick at the corner of the haggard. Our labourers were in the haggard dashing water on the flames. The former tenant was also there, but retreated on seeing us, and did not reappear. We found it hard to think he had committed the outrage, and preferred to believe that some enthusiastic friend of his may have been guilty. Our men told us that, when they arrived, the wind was blowing the fire in towards the other ricks, and if it had not changed soon afterwards, nothing could have saved the rest of the haggard, and it is probable that the stables, barns, and cowhouses, which formed one side of the haggard, might also have been burned.

My father had insured the haggard and buildings on the suggestion of his bank manager, who was also an insurance agent. It had been an easy matter till then to effect such insurance, as agrarian outrages were infrequent; but soon after this it was impossible. When it was known that we were insured, the friends of the former tenant spread a report that we set fire to the rick in order to get the insurance; but we took no notice of the slander, and remained on friendly terms with our predecessor, who stayed on until his six months were expired, when we gave him an open hint that we required the house, and he left. After that we had no further outrage. The people had not been " educated " and aroused, as they were soon destined to be, when the Land League came to our district.

Viscount Midleton, the landlord of our town and its immediate neighbourhood, was an absentee. The founder of the family, Alan Brodrick, was Lord Chanceller of Ireland in the reign of George I., and got a peerage in 1715. The ruins of two houses in which his successors lived were to be seen at different sides of the town—both beautifully situated, one on the sloping shore of Ballyanon Bay in the estuary of Midleton River; the other, of more recent date, at Cahirmone, an inland park in which stood and still stands, defying the ravages of time, a well-preserved square Geraldine castle picturesquely placed in the rich valley of the rushing Dungourney River. Before my time the estate had been a large one, but much of it had been alienated by one of the previous owners. Midleton, then, never saw Lord Midleton except when he came over for a week at Easter with some of his children and stayed at the local hotel. He called on one or two of his tenants with whom he had business, went for walks and drives in the district, went to church (where, of course, he was not seen by the Catholic people), and then departed for his home in London or Godalming.

The Longfield estate, of which my father was a tenant for his new farm, was much larger than the Midleton, and was then in the hands of trustees, the heir being a minor. Young Mr Longfield lived with his sisters at Castlemary, about four miles from Midleton, in a very unpretentious way. He was considered wealthy, and at the time of his birth, I heard the old people say, there had been great rejoicings, as he was an only son and had a number of sisters older than himself. We used to see him and his sisters going to the hunt on horseback, but they took no notice of the tenants whom they did not know personally. Neither did the agent live on the property, but on the Great Island near Queenstown, across the East Ferry, some four or five miles from Castlemary, and he was never seen except when he came twice a-year to a house in Midleton or Ballinacurra to receive rents.

The Longfield estate was by no means harshly managed, its owners being generous, kindly people for those who knew them, but unhappily their tenants did not know them. Of the Midleton estate the same might be said, for, though the agent lived in the town, the tenants had no friendly communication with him. This unsocial arrangement was universal in Ireland, the exceptions to it only proving the rule.

Captain Smith-Barry, owner of a small estate, whose beautiful place on Ballyedmond Hill dominated the wide valley of Midleton, was the nearest resident landlord. There was a considerable estate at Shanagarry, originally bestowed upon William Penn, and the landlords of which were descendants of Penn who lived in America. The landlord of the Ponsonby estate near Youghal, some fourteen miles away, was an absentee, and his agent lived in Midleton, being the only Catholic agent in our district. This estate was destined to achieve an unenviable notoriety in the coming revolution, but it was as peaceable in 1877 as the Midleton or Longfield properties. The estate on which my mother's people had their farms, north of Midleton, was orginally part of the Midleton estate, but was now owned by Mr MacBride, a Scotsman, who lived in Scotland. And when, just before the foundation of the Land League, his son came to live on the estate, he came with the announcement that he was about to raise the rent of my aunt's husband so as to force him to give up his farm, the landlord intending to take the house and plantations as a residence and demesne. Though the Land Act of 1870 had extended the Ulster custom to the whole of Ireland, and a landlord could not evict a tenant now without compensation, except for non-payment of rent, there was nothing to prevent a landlord from raising the rent and so getting rid of a tenant without being liable for compensation.

There was one nobleman resident near Midleton, the Earl of Shannon, the founder of whose family was a Mr Boyle, Speaker of the Irish House of Commons in the middle of the eighteenth century. The property contained a castle and demesne in which the owner now lived in much magnificence, being the master of the United Hunt, then recently formed by uniting two pre-existing packs of foxhounds. Lord Shannon kept the kennels at his place at Castlemartyr, and, for some years before the Land League, he spent a great deal of money there, keeping a large stud of hunters as well as two packs of hounds, and hunting three days a-week. He used to drive in great state to the meet, where his hunter was waiting him, and when the distance was considerable the hounds went in a covered van. He was a bad horse-man and never faced a fence, so that he was con-stantly to be met galloping along the road enquiring of passers-by if they had seen the hounds, and accom-panied by a number of obsequious horsemen who pre-ferred his lordship's company to that of the hounds. For some years before Lord Shannon brought the kennels to Castlemartyr, my mother's brother had kept a pack of harriers at his place, Clonmult, about four miles from Castlemartyr, and the rivalry between him and Lord Shannon deserves mention as showing the ambitious spirit of the Catholic farmers.

The Clonmult Harriers, built up by my uncle from his boyhood, hunted two days a-week and held an annual race-meeting at the end of each season, being supported by some Catholic merchants and well-to-do shopkeepers and a few Protestant landed gentry, but the main expense falling on my uncle, who was more passionately devoted to hunting than any of the Nationalist leaders were to politics. When the Earl of Shannon set up his great establishment, many of my uncle's supporters, dazzled by its magnificence, deserted the Clonmult Harriers. But my uncle was undaunted and continued to hunt twice a-week.

Lord Shannon showed the greatest hostility to him and tried to crush him by various devices. There is never much love lost between a master of foxhounds and a master of harriers in the same country, but here the enmity was intensified by the natural antipathy of the Catholic tenant-farmer to the Protestant landlord. Lord Shannon considered him-self an Englishman, and spoke and acted in that exaggerated English style which those who only know Englishmen in England cannot realise. My uncle used to hunt outlying foxes in the glens or furze brakes of the farmers who gave him permission to enter their lands. These farmers were now warned by their landlords to prohibit him from entering, and were offered rents for the sole use of their coverts by Lord Shannon, but not one of them prohibited my uncle or accepted money from the United Hunt. My uncle's landlord was also approached, but refused to interfere. Letters were continually appearing in 'The Field,' 'Land and Water,' and other sporting papers, charging my uncle with surreptitiously drawing the preserved coverts of the United Hunt—which he never did. He would hunt an outlying fox till he killed or earthed him, no matter where he went—he used to say he would follow him into Lord Shannon's drawing-room—but he was too good a sportsman to poach on the enemy's preserves.

His answer to Lord Shannon's attempts to crush him was to give up hare-hunting and take to fox-hunting, breeding a pack of Irish foxhounds as large as the English hounds of the United Hunt. He started fox-hunting openly, only drawing his friends' coverts, but hunting his foxes through the coverts of the United Hunt, where the friendly covert-keepers often stopped the earths to oblige him, and soon he had better sport and longer runs than Lord Shannon. When the sporting papers gave an account of one of his long runs, their columns were usually deluged with letters of protest and denunciation of my uncle's conduct.

Lord Shannon had to retire from the mastership, and his successors, after carrying on the fight for

a few years, offered to take my uncle's hounds into
the United Hunt and let him hunt them himself
one day a-week. Great was the astonishment and
disdain of the large, fashionable fields at seeing their
own master and huntsman superseded once a-week,
and the command taken by a tall farmer in a coat
of Lincoln green instead of the orthodox scarlet.
This arrangement did not work satisfactorily, and,
after a season, the country was divided, my uncle
getting all that part of it in his own neighbourhood.
His joy at having an abundance of foxes, and being
able to enter in his own right the great preserves
from which he had been so long excluded, may be
better imagined than described. His hunting was
never stopped during the worst days of the Land
League, and it was largely due to Edmund
Fitzgerald's popularity that the United Hunt was
also allowed to hunt in its own part of the country.

The landlords spent their time, as far as the people
knew, entirely in amusement, half the year being
given over to fox-hunting. A meet of the hounds
gave the country people their only chance of seeing
what their rulers behaved like in the society of their
own class. It seemed like a vision of a higher world
where toil and trouble were unknown to see the
ladies, all smiles, mounted on good horses and arrayed
in perfectly-cut riding-habits, or sitting gracefully
in carriages, holding *levées* and receiving compliments
from men in scarlet, great landlords or dashing young
officers from the nearest barracks, riding the best
Irish hunters that could be bought for money,
attended by a plentiful supply of liveried coachmen,
footmen, and mounted grooms.

Some of the better-class farmers and shopkeepers

used to ride to hounds, but always with a feeling of revolt against the inferiority of their position. Many a young farmer, astride his ungroomed colt, with cracked bridle and saddle, rusty bit and stirrups, felt poignantly that he had no portion in David, no inheritance in the son of Jesse—a situation unintelligible to those whom he envied. Yet so keen was the love of sport that, when some local sportsman rode into Midleton on a winter's evening with the news that they had hunted a fox twenty miles and killed him in the open, the town would talk of nothing else that night. And if, on such occasions, some young farmer or shopkeeper managed to see the finish on his own horse, everybody felt proud of him.

Nowhere, perhaps, was the estrangement between the tillers of the soil and their natural leaders more to be lamented than in the baronies of Imokilly and Barrymore. The peculiar beauty of the landscape around Midleton, the restful character of the views and fertility of the soil, show that nature meant it to be a peaceable and plenteous land full of homes and happy people. The town stands in a rich undulating plain about three miles wide from north to south, and thirty miles long from east to west. At the eastern extremity is ancient Youghal, picturesquely placed at the mouth of the Blackwater, one of the oldest boroughs in Ireland, incorporated by King John in 1209. There the first Franciscan monastery in Ireland was founded by a Fitzgerald in 1224, and a Dominican friary by another Fitzgerald in 1269. There Roger Mortimer landed in 1317. There Walter Raleigh lived and smoked his pipe in his home at Myrtle Grove, which is still standing. There the Earl of Cork held out for the King in

1641, while his son, Lord Broghill, fought for the Parliament. At the western end of the plain is Cork, the island city, one of the most beautiful and beautifully-placed towns in the world, capital of the Kingdom of the MacCarthys in the days before Strongbow came to Ireland.

Midleton, so called in English because it is almost equidistant from Cork and Youghal, stands at the junction of the Midleton and Dungourney Rivers, and at the head of a lovely estuary which, if it were in England or Scotland, would have been long since immortalised in prose and verse, and would be a perennial haunt of tourists. There are many Middle Towns and Middletons in Ireland, England, and America; but our town, the Gaelic name of which is Monasthir, is the only one spelled with a single "d." Half a mile down the estuary is the port, Ballinacurra, and the charming waterway, now widening, now narrowing and ever deepening, runs a meandering course for nearly twenty miles between steep hills and gentle slopes, woods and pastures, with many a cape, bay, and island, to the mouth of Queenstown Harbour, known in Irish as the Cove of Cork.

Beginning with Ballyedmond House on the hill north of Midleton and ending with Mr Penrose Fitzgerald's house at Corkbeg Island, picturesque residences stand at frequent intervals, commanding the fairest views, and occupied by wealthy people who were at this time mostly landlords, and all, save one, persons whose ancestors had exercised their undoubted right to join the Reformed Church after the Reformation. At the Midleton side of East Ferry, a lovely strait which separates Great Island

from the mainland, the estuary expands into a kind
of lake in which are the Brown Islands, and beyond
them, between the main estuary of the Lee and the
Midleton estuary, is Fota Island, the residence of Mr
Arthur Hugh Smith-Barry (now Lord Barrymore),
one of the largest landowners in Ireland, and destined
to figure prominently in the approaching revolution.
High up on the hills or nestling in the valleys, behind
this front of prosperity and loyalty to the English connection, lived the Catholic farmers and labourers in their
thousands who adhered to the faith of pre-Reformation times. They seldom or never set eyes upon this
beauteous scene, and were so busy in the struggle for
life as to be almost incapable of enjoying it.

The same state of things prevailed along the shores
of the central estuary of the Lee from Cork to
Queenstown. The great majority of the magnificent
residences fronting the water, the most delightful of
their kind in the British Isles, on the wooded heights
of Glanmire, Montenotte, Tivoli, and Dunkettle, on
Little Island and Great Island, and on the opposite
shore at Ballintemple, Blackrock, Passage and Monks-
town, were the property of members of the Reformed
Church, while behind on the hills were the farmers
and labourers devoted to the old religion, as they
fondly called it. In the city itself the majority of
the wealthiest men were Protestants; and the mass
of the people, being Catholics, believed in their hearts
that religion was the surest test by which one might
know an Irishman from a foreigner.

This veneer of affluence and loyalty to England,
masking a people worm-eaten with discontent and
seething with revolt against what they called foreign
supremacy, was typical of the state of all Ireland,

except the north-east, at this time when we were on the threshold of the revolution. It must not be supposed that those who believed in the Reformation had any legal privileges as compared with those who disbelieved in it or that they lived in idleness. On the contrary, except the landlords, who had no need to labour, they were very hard - working, had no privileges whatever, and set an admirable example to the country.

This was not always so, and the disestablishment of the Church was so recent that old times were not forgotten. Relics of the riotous living which too often prevailed in the days of Protestant ascendancy still remained—days when it must be admitted that Catholics were no more virtuous than Protestants. There was still a man or woman to be found here and there who was the illegitimate offspring — or " caper," as it was called — of some local landlord. Indeed, at the time of which I write, there lived near Midleton two Protestant young men, gentlemen farmers dwelling in separate houses in the same town-land, who kept a number of courtesans between them ; and peasants, holding their breath in astonishment, saw the young women in gaily-coloured dresses and uncovered heads disporting themselves on the roads or in the fields when their masters were from home. Neither the frowns of society nor the remonstrance of the parson had any influence over these young men, and the parish priest did not yet feel his posi-tion secure enough to denounce the offenders. Their conduct was quite exceptional, and is only worthy of mention as being redolent of a former generation who sowed the wind of pleasure which the present generation was to reap as a whirlwind of revolution.

The Catholics had ample opportunities of amassing wealth before the coming of the Land League. But experience in our neighbourhood went to show that they had not the same knack of keeping money as the Protestants, and I have found the same all over Ireland. In Midleton the trade was chiefly in their hands. The two corn merchants, one of whom was very rich, were Catholics. So were the owners of the distillery, a rich family named Murphy. The maltster and the flour miller were Protestants, but just at this time the miller, who lived in great state, got broken and a Catholic took his place. All the shopkeepers were Catholic, and before my time one of them, a draper, having made a great deal of money, went in for building, planning an ambitious new street which has not yet been finished, leaving his children two farms with such a quantity of house property that they gave up their shop, after which they lost the farms and most of the house property and fell into poor circumstances. One of the daughters was the Reverend Mother, or Head, of Midleton Convent for over a generation. One of the sons became a barrister and ultimately Governor of various colonies, owing his preferment to his intimacy with John Pope Hennessy, a Kerry man, who got returned for King's County as the first Catholic Conservative in Parliament, and was a favourite of Benjamin Disraeli. The career of this Catholic shopkeeper's son brought home to the minds of many of his more intelligent fellow-townsmen some of the advantages of the wider sphere opened up by the much-abused connection with England.

CHAPTER II.

LAND, SCHOOLS, AND RELIGION.

It is not fair to blame the landlords for the social estrangement between them and their tenants. The landlords as a body were Protestants and the tenants Catholics, and this generic difference ought never to be passed over in examining the causes of the Irish revolution. In our district there was not one considerable landowner who was a Catholic, and I only remember one Catholic land agent. There were at this time 120 landowners in Ireland, each of whose estates had a rateable valuation of £10,000 a-year and upwards, the valuation being, almost invariably, much less than the rental: The Duke of Abercorn, £35,802; Lord Annaly, £13,752; Earl Annesley, £29,204; Earl of Antrim, £20,837; Mervyn Archdall, £16,991; Earl of Arran, £10,112; Lord Ashtown, £15,343; Earl of Bandon, £19,215; Earl of Bantry, £14,561; W. P. Barker, £10,810; Arthur Hugh Smith-Barry, £32,412; Marquis of Bath, £19,651; Sir H. W. Becher, £10,528; Earl of Belmore, £10,970; Earl of Bessborough, £21,006; Sir R. Gore Booth, £16,774; Sir Victor Brook, £15,288; Sir H. H. Bruce, £11,397; Henry Bruen, £17,385; Earl of Caledon, £19,754; Lord Carberry, £10,515; Lord Carew, £11,566; Earl of Carysfort, £25,921;

Earl of Castlestuart, £11,768; Lord Castletown, £14,151; Earl of Charlemont, £25,634; Representatives of the Earl of Charleville, £10,052; Lady Margaret Charteris, £11,635; Earl of Clancarty, £11,724; Marquis of Clanricarde, £20,836; Colonel Clements, £12,957; Lord Clermont, £15,262; Viscount Clifden, £20,793; Lord Clonbrock, £11,442; Earl of Clonmell, £13,738; Maxwell Close, £13,441; Representatives of Thomas Connolly, £12,611; Marquis Conyngham, £32,644; Colonel Cooper, £11,548; Sir Algernon Coote, £18,007; Earl of Cork, £12,249; Earl of Courtown, £11,361; Earl of Darnley, £18,186; Earl of Dartrey, £18,338; Henry De Stafford O'Brien, £13,515; Earl of Devon, £14,512; Duke of Devonshire, £34,326; Lord Digby, £12,745; Viscount Dillon, £19,231; Marquis of Donegall, £18,372; Viscount Doneraile, £13,738; Marquis of Downshire, £91,522; Drapers Company of London, £14,859; Marquis of Drogheda, £10,466; Earl of Dufferin, £16,000; Earl of Dunraven, £10,937; Lord Dunsandle, £17,393; Earl of Egmont, £13,594; Marquis of Ely, £23,151; Earl of Enniskillen, £18,795; Earl of Erne, £23,804; Lord Farnham, £20,938; Earl Fitzwilliam, £47,699; Colonel Forde, £15,404; Earl of Gosford, £17,934; Lord Greville, £15,705; Lord Harlech, £10,821; Marquis of Headfort, £19,201; H. A. Herbert, £10,547; Lord A. E. Hill-Trevor, £11,811; Anne Adèle Hope, £10,333; Lord Inchiquin, £11,681; Arthur MacMurrough Kavanagh, £15,138; Earl of Kenmare, £34,473; Lord Kilmorey, £13,708; Colonel King-Harman, £40,105; Earl of Lanesborough, £11,579; Marquis of Lansdowne, £31,536; Lord Leconfield, £20,519; Duke of Leinster, £47,646; Earl of Leitrim, £10,000; Sir John

Leslie, £20,344 ; Viscount Lismore, £16,354 ; Earl of
Listowel, £16,151 ; Marquis of Londonderry, £37,211 ;
Earl of Longford, £15,485 ; Earl of Lucan, £12,940 ;
John Madden, £12,190 ; Duke of Manchester, £17,164 ;
Lord Massereene, £15,000 ; Lord Massy, £11,689 ;
Mercers Company of London, £11,640 ; James Lennox
Naper, £15,581 ; Lord O'Neill, £44,947 ; Marquis of
Ormonde, £15,611 ; Rev. A. H. Pakenham, £15,601 ;
Sir Roger Palmer, £20,560 ; Allan Pollok, £12,727 ;
Lord Powerscourt, £15,267 ; Lord Rathdonnell,
£14,422 ; Earl of Roden, £11,208 ; Earl of Rosse,
£10,461 ; Lord Rossmore, £13,427 ; Salters Company
of London, £17,263 ; Earl of Shannon, £12,319 ; Eve-
lyn P. Shirley, £20,744 ; Marquis of Sligo, £16,157 ;
Alexander J. R. Stewart, £15,655 ; Lord Stuart de
Decies, £11,463 ; Lord Templemore, £15,080 ; Viscount Templetown, £17,551 ; Rt. Hon. W. F. Tighe,
£11,474 ; Chas. Tottenham, £12,284 ; Colonel Van-
deleur, £11,216 ; Lord Ventry, £17,067 ; Sir Wm.
Verner, £10,675 ; Sir Richard Wallace, £74,189 ;
Hon. C. B. Wandesforde, £14,256 ; Marquis of Waterford, £32,325 ; Earl of Wicklow, £15,581 ; Owen
Wynne, £14,091.

With the exception of the Earl of Kenmare, I do
not recognise a single Catholic name in this list.
There may be one, or perhaps two, others ; but, if
there be, it does not affect the principle that the
landlords, as a body, were Protestants. The total
number of landowners, great and small, was 68,750,
the yearly valuation of the land £13,420,000, and
the estimated rental between £18,000,000 and
£20,000,000.

There was no religious bitterness at this time ; but
the priesthood, in the exercise of what they believed

to be their duty, dissuaded Catholics from social or philanthropic co-operation with Protestants, and this especially applied to landlords and tenants, lest the landlords should use their influence to proselytise the tenants.

The priests were, according to their own ideas, true Irishmen and sympathetic with their flocks; and were always telling the people that the next world was of more importance than this, and the life after death more worthy of attention than the life here. Their chief concern with politics up to this was to get a Catholic University under the management of the Bishops, and to acquire complete control over the elementary schools. They made every parliamentary candidate promise to support denominational education, and the people acquiesced without understanding the issue at stake. In Midleton the P.P. ruled with a rod of iron, and the Catholic who dared to take any social or political step without his consent was regarded as a kind of outlaw.

There was no public elementary school in Midleton. The Parish Priest, Father Fitzpatrick, would not allow it. But about the time I was born, the Christian Brothers had opened large elementary schools in the town, capable of holding five hundred pupils, the cost of erecting the schools and monastery and providing a yearly stipend for the monks being cheerfully subscribed by the townspeople and the well-to-do farmers. There was also a Presentation Convent with equally large elementary schools for girls. The objection to the national, or state-supported, elementary schools was that statues, holy pictures, and crucifixes were forbidden in them. These emblems were liberally displayed in the

Christian Brothers' Schools, for they accepted no grant from the Government, their principle being that it would be an iniquity to take money on condition of giving up the sacred emblems of the Catholic faith.

Now the Parish Priest had grown jealous of the Brothers and was not on speaking terms with them, because, as they dressed precisely like priests, the people paid the same deference to them as to the priests, the men taking off their hats, the women curtseying. The Parish Priest was never tired of telling the people that the Brothers were not clergymen, but only "pious laics"; and, when he met them, he would cut them, while they would humbly salute him by raising their hats. The Brothers used to tell us at school that the Parish Priest had no authority over them, and they refused him liberty to inspect their schools, which were never entered by a priest. They were most pious, and went to early morning mass daily at the Convent, where they confessed to the nun's chaplain and received the sacrament.

There was no Catholic secondary school in Midleton, and the Parish Priest would not help to provide one. He brought a slovenly old man into the town, whom he called "a classical teacher," and asked our fathers to send us to his lodgings to learn Latin and Greek, but none of the better-class parishioners obeyed. My father sent me to the Vincentian School at Cork, thirteen miles away, and I went there every morning by train and returned in the evening. The Diocesan Seminary, owned by the Bishop, was at Fermoy, twenty miles away by the nearest road and fifty miles by train. Catholic parents, wishing to give their sons a higher education under the auspices of the Church, had to send them either to Cork or to Fermoy.

There was (and is still) in Midleton a Protestant
school, Midleton College, endowed by Lady Elizabeth
Villiers, Countess of Orkney, in the reign of William
and Mary, and originally intended as a free school for
the district, as the name of the street leading to it—
Free School Lane—clearly proved. It was at this
time a most prosperous boarding-school, attended by
the sons of landlords, professional men, and other well-
to-do Protestants from all parts of Ireland,—three of
its most famous *alumni* being the famous John
Philpot Curran; Chief Baron Yelverton (created
Viscount Avonmore), Grattan's right-hand man in 1782,
but a supporter of the Union in 1800 ; and Isaac Butt.

My father decided to send me to Midleton College
in 1877, after three years' trial of the Vincentian
Seminary, having always said that Protestant education was better than Catholic, and that the Irish
Catholics would have got no education but for the
Protestants. Some other townspeople also sent their
sons, so that there were eight or ten Catholic day-boys
including myself. Because of this, all our fathers,
but especially mine, were in the black books with
Father Fitzpatrick, who was a most autocratic man,
and veiled allusions of a disparaging character from
the altar were a common experience. The agent of
the Ponsonby estate, who was a Catholic, was one of
those who sent his sons to Midleton College at this
time, and one of them, Mr Edward O'Farrell, is now
Assistant Under-Secretary for Ireland. The Parish
Priest made it very unpleasant for us, and obstructed
my father whenever he could do so ; but the presence
of so many Catholics, in spite of his displeasure,
showed the considerable leaven of independence in
the town.

One result of my going to Midleton College was that I got an opportunity of hearing the British as well as the Irish side of the age-long dispute between Ireland and England. At the Christian Brothers and the Vincentians, I had heard the Irish, or the Rebels', side. Now I heard the English or the Loyalist side. I therefore acquired a habit of impartiality in regard to Irish politics which prevented me from going wholly with the party of Authority or the party of Revolt, and enabled me to think dispassionately of things which my relatives and many Catholic companions could only speak of in terms of indignation and violent partisanship. While I remained a Catholic and a Nationalist—though this latter word was not known in Ireland at the time I write of—I realised that there was much to be said for the English and the Union with England. And while my sympathy was with the cause of the tenants against the landlords, I saw that there was much to be said for the landlords, and that, far from being inhuman tyrants, they were human beings like ourselves trying to do their best according to their lights. I also had opportunities of hearing both the Protestant and Catholic sides of the religious controversy, and came to realise that Protestants might be very good people, even better than many of the Catholics whom we had been taught to look on as the elect. These matters I may be pardoned for mentioning for the sake of the light they throw upon life in the South of Ireland just before the revolution.

At this time the people had practically no voice in the management of public affairs, but were beginning to assert themselves in the corporations, township boards, and boards of guardians. The Grand Jurors, who did the work now done by County Councils, were chiefly landlords nominated by the sheriff, who was himself always a landlord nominated by the Judge of Assize from three names submitted by the sheriff of the preceding year. There were very few Catholics in the Grand Jury. There were some, and my aunt's husband was one of them. But there was not one Catholic magistrate in our district, except the stipendiary, and not one Protestant on the bench who took the popular side in politics. The Irish farmers and their relatives, the shopkeepers, did not accept this order of things in the same spirit as the Saxons accepted subjection from the Normans in England. In Irish the Saxons were always called "creepers"—a fact which I only mention to show the difference between the two subject peoples. The Normans never conquered the Irish so thoroughly as they conquered the Saxons. Our Norman conquerors were comparatively few in number and became sympathetic with the native Irish with whom they intermarried. Many of their descendants were now Catholics and Nationalists in our neighbourhood, bearing such well-known names as Cogan, Fitzgerald, Barry, Roche, Power (De La Poer), Colbert, Burke (De Burgh), Beausang, and many others.

The primeval Irish, of whom the McCarthys are the chief example in county Cork, never regarded themselves as slaves. Under the Brehon laws the land was the common property of the tribe, and the Chief, or Tanist, was the elected trustee of the commune. The slave could always rise to the position of a free labourer, and the poorest regarded himself as a blood relative to his Chief. This spirit was not crushed out by the Normans, under whom the old

Irish customs continued, and the old Irish families enjoyed a large amount of liberty. The Elizabethan settlement at the end of the sixteenth century—affecting most of Munster and the whole county Cork—and the Jacobean, Cromwellian, and Williamite settlements of the seventeenth, though they pressed so hardly on the native Irish, did not succeed in crushing them out or in making them forget that they were the original proprietors of the soil.

The teaching in the Catholic schools and the preaching in the Catholic chapels prevented the people from forgetting the past, and, after the lapse of centuries, they still regarded those who monopolised the Government and the land as the descendants of plunderers, invaders, and usurpers. Every landlord was looked upon as the heir or assignee of some English planter who had wrongfully seized land belonging to a native family. I have travelled a good deal in the rural districts of England since the time of which I am now writing, and I have never found this spirit anywhere amongst the Saxon peasantry, who accept subjection and inferiority as fate, and inherit no legacy of idealism and discontent; living only for the present, while the Irishman lives in the past and the future.

My mother's people, the Fitzgeralds of Clonmult, who traced their pedigree back to the Norman invasion without a flaw, were more Irish than the McCarthys, and forgot that they had ever come into the country as strangers so recently as the twelfth century. Their lands had been divided amongst the sons and grandsons and finally alienated, but there was a large colony of them in the district in the first half of the nineteenth century. They had lost the freehold of the land in the eighteenth century under the penal laws, and it had passed to Protestants; but, in 1877, three distinct families still remained in the neighbourhood, each occupying a large farm. They were first cousins, children of brothers, and their farms represented what their grandfather alone had held in his day. But the lands of the grandfather were only a small portion of what his ancestors had held, which, we were always told, covered many square miles of country. The other farmers of the district had a great respect for the Fitzgeralds, but they did not pay the lords of the soil the deference so willingly paid them by farmers in England.

Despite the internal feeling of revolt and growing outward independence of the farmers, landlords were still regarded with awe and saluted with humility by the majority of their tenants. The memory of old Mountifort Longfield of Castlemary still sent a shiver through the frames of his tenantry. His property extended for miles along the public road near Cloyne, and we used to hear how in the old days, when the tenants saw or heard he was coming, they would drive their cattle or poultry out of sight lest he should think they were thriving and raise their rents, their prayer being that he might take no notice of them, or their houses, or their fields. They feared to keep the fences and gates in repair for the same reason, and the best farms had the most slovenly appearance from the road. One tenant who had coloured his house, trimmed his hedges, and cultivated a flower-garden by the roadside, was once congratulated on his good taste by the landlord; but, when he next went to pay his rent, he was warned that it was to be increased by several shillings an acre. Old Mr Longfield, who was the first in our part of the country to erect a Turkish bath in his house, was reported to have died by suffocation or heart failure in his bath, and his end was popularly regarded as a visitation of providence. I do not remember him, but as his successors were liberal and even generous landlords, the popular opinion was probably based on want of knowledge of the real man.

But while the Catholic farmers found themselves cut off from the good things enjoyed by the landlords, and had to console themselves with the thought that the tables would be turned in the next world, they too had their festivities—eating and drinking, marrying and giving in marriage, rafters groaning with the weight of home-cured bacon, tables with roast fowl, potatoes, hams, and whisky. The farmer who preceded us on our new farm was the scion of a numerous family of farmers, several of whom were ruined by their own extravagance—one of them being nicknamed "The Lord,"—and their lavish style of living was proverbial. Their name was Smithwick, and my Fitzgerald grandfather had married one of them. Besides their fine place which my father took over, there were three other farms hard by which they had to give up.

South of Midleton, between Cloyne and the sea, there was a colony of Protestant farmers named Smith, and, as my stepmother's people had their farms in this district, also on the Longfield estate, I knew them all. There were six families, each having a large well-worked farm at the time I write of. The colony was originally English, but the present generation became so blended in with their Irish neighbours that there was the greatest harmony in the district, and their presence was a distinct gain. My stepmother's people were Wigmores, originally Welsh, and our branch of them had become Catholics. Between the Smiths and their well-to-do Catholic neighbours there was a great deal of pleasant social intercourse, visiting between the womenfolk, dinner-parties and dances. One of these Smiths kept a pack of harriers and was a bosom friend of my uncle, Edmund Fitzgerald,—the affection between the Protestant and the Catholic farmer, living sixteen miles apart, being unique, and showing how useful sport is in promoting harmony. None of the Smiths joined the Land League, though their rents were the same as their neighbours'. When one of them got broken by the bad times, he just sold out his chattels and went with his family to Australia. They were on the best of terms with the Parish Priest of Cloyne, though strict attendants at the Protestant church; and the Church of Ireland rectors at Cloyne and Ballycotton were liked and respected by the Catholics of the whole district. One of the Protestant Wigmores, an elderly lady who lived with her Catholic relative, was regularly visited by the rector of Ballycotton, whose sons I knew at Midleton College, and the rector often met the Parish Priest, the meeting always giving rise to much good humour.

It is a great mistake to think that Irish farmers did not make money under the landlord system, and there are many in Ireland convinced that if the revolution had not gone to such extremes, Ireland would be a pleasanter country, and no less prosperous, under the dual ownership system than under peasant proprietary. No English farmstead could excel the neatness and comfort of my uncle's place, for instance, as handed down to him by his father who died in the famine of 1847, of fever taken from the poor people whom he was visiting with relief. Well-trimmed, thick beech hedges, ten feet high, surrounded two orchards planted with such a variety of apple-trees as I have never met elsewhere. There was an enclosed garden besides, and all the out-offices, stabling, cow-houses, coach-house, piggeries and hen-houses, were in admirable order, with an archway entrance from the road to the farmyard. My aunt's husband, on two hundred acres for which he paid the full value in rent, was even better set up and lived in affluence. The cheap labour no doubt had much to do with the farmers' prosperity in the seventies, the labourers getting very low wages and being fed on potatoes, or home-made cake, with occasionally salt herring and onion sauce, called dip, the beverages being skimmed milk, tea or coffee, and on Sundays bacon and cabbage for dinner.

The only superior caste the farmers venerated were the priests, and the Sunday Mass was the greatest event of the week. How the people crowded to Mass! What a scene of bustle there was at the chapel gate, where two or more labourers, very fresh in limp white collars and Sunday frieze, stood with collecting-boxes, into which everybody had to put at least a halfpenny. Sometimes the Parish Priest or one of his curates would stand with them, and often put a man or a woman back who did not happen to have the necessary coin—though such defaulters were always admitted when the rest of the congregation had passed in.

All that fox-hunting and other diversions were to

the landlords during the week, the farmers and labourers found in their Mass on Sundays. It was a relaxation as well as a comfort, never failing to create a sensation, and always bringing the relief associated with duty done. Those who attended first Mass, at eight o'clock or half-past, came home with an appetite for breakfast and a disposition to spend the day pleasantly. Those who went to second Mass at noon spent some time in gossip afterwards, and brought home an appetite for early dinner. In rural districts there was only one Mass, at ten or eleven o'clock, and the men spent the morning afterwards discussing the affairs of the district at the village cross-roads, while the women gossiped in the houses of their friends.

The richer class of Catholics at this time seemed to have almost lost the sense of nationality which was so strong in their poorer brethren, whose chief glory was, like the Athenians, that they were au-tochthonous, or, in other words, had sprung from the soil of Ireland, and had never come in as strangers. Where the rich Catholics were landlords or agents, they copied the English in everything, and, though they went to Mass, were almost as completely separated from the bulk of their fellow-Catholics as the Protestants, who were indeed far more Irish and patriotic. These well-to-do Catholics were neither fish nor flesh. The dominant Protestants kept them out of all real power. The Nationalists detested them. And they were thrown back, as it were, upon the hierarchy, who made much of them, and often got them elected members of Parliament, thus enabling many of them to get well-paid Government posts for themselves and their relatives; so that at this time a member of Parliament was generally regarded as a man qualifying for a Government office.

Sunday afternoon and evening were devoted to luxurious idleness — and nowhere is the *dolce far niente* so keenly appreciated as in Ireland. The men played bowling matches, the bowlers, usually four in number, being accompanied by a crowd of spectators. The course was over some miles of public road, the stakes being won by the pair of bowlers who covered the distance first. There was also dancing at the cross-roads, and card-playing in the labourers' houses. Dancing was looked upon as a fine art, or a display of skill, as well as an excuse for coming together, the peculiar Irish steps—jigs, hornpipes, and reels—being strenuous muscular exercise as well as a pastime, in which the boy or girl who held out the longest got the most applause.

Fair days were regarded as festivals. Long-deferred purchases were then made, and it used to be the custom for young people to ask for a "faireen," or a present in honour of the fair. It is interesting to note that the Irish word for fair, *oenach*, was the name of the assemblies held at the courts of the Irish kings in pre-Norman days. In 1877 almost every parish had its fair, which, at most, only came once a quarter, often only once in six months, and sometimes only once a year. But these small fairs in our neighbourhood were then being fast superseded by a monthly fair in Midleton, where previously there were only four fairs in the year. This change, which was going on all over Ireland, put a stop to much parochial sociability, while the habit of going into the larger towns once a month enabled the farmers to combine more effectively for political purposes, and prepared the way for the success of the revolution.

But the chief cause of the impending revolution was the personal estrangement between landlord and tenant. Admitting that religion acted as a great separating force, this estrangement ought not to have gone so far if the landlords were as concerned for their moral duties as for their legal rights. There were scores of farms in our neighbourhood on which not merely the landlord, but even the agent, had never set foot within living memory. All repairs to fences, gates, and houses were done, or, as in too many cases, left undone, by the tenants; and things had come to such a pass that a visit from the landlord or agent would have been not only feared but resented. If the agents were Catholics or men of the middle class, this could never have happened. But the landlords on all considerable properties selected agents from their own class of society—often younger sons of landlords—and thus it came about that the agent, instead of being a connecting link, was usually as isolated from the tenants as his principal.

CHAPTER III.

IRISH POLITICS IN . 1877.

NOTHING was further from men's minds in our part
of Ireland, in 1877, than the thought that we were
on the eve of a revolution which, without an armed
rising, would overthrow the landlords, put all parliamentary representation and municipal government
into the hands of the people, and bring a Dublin
Parliament within bounds of possibility.

The open door in politics was well illustrated by
the election for the city of Cork in 1876, caused by
the death of Mr Joseph Ronayne, M.P., brother of
my aunt's husband. "Honest Joe Ronayne," as he
was called, had made a fortune as an engineer in
California, and on his return became Home Rule
member for Cork. In 1874 he had uttered these
words, which may be said to be the origin of the
policy of Obstruction : "Let us interfere in English
legislation ; let us show them that, if we are not
strong enough to get our own work done, we are
strong enough to prevent them from getting theirs."
There were three candidates for his seat—John Daly,
a Home Ruler ; Denny Lane, a Nationalist ; and
William Goulding, a Conservative. Daly was a
self-made draper and a Catholic. Goulding was
a manufacturing chemist and a Protestant. Lane

was a Catholic, a writer of lyrics, an archæologist, secretary of the Cork Gas Company, and a successful starch manufacturer—a friend of "Father Prout," and also of Joe Ronayne, whose sister married Martin Mahony of Blarney Tweed fame, a brother of Prout's. Lane posed as a more extreme Nationalist than Daly, and, owing to the split in the Nationalist vote, William Goulding, who called himself a "Liberal Conservative"—a cult much affected then in Ireland—was triumphant.

The return of a Conservative Government in 1874 had given the landlords fresh security and increased courage after the set-back they had received from Mr Gladstone's disestablishment of the Church of Ireland and passage of the Land Act in 1870. From 1874 to 1879 they were perhaps at the zenith of their power, and had probably reached the climax in 1877, just when they were on the eve of being utterly overthrown. It was only a small minority of reading farmers who were interested in the obstructive policy which had begun in Parliament. Mr Parnell was little known in the south, except amongst political experts like Joseph Ronayne, who wanted to revive the struggle for national independence, the names of O'Donnell and Biggar being more often in men's mouths. The great majority did not understand obstruction, while the better classes, agreeing with Mr Butt, derided it as absurd and impracticable.

Mr Isaac Butt, the nominal leader of the Home Rule Party, was a Protestant, but he worked in complete harmony with Cardinal Cullen, who lived beside him in Eccles Street, then a fashionable residential quarter of Dublin. The word "Nationalist" had not yet been adopted, and, when first used by some young men in our locality, was received with disfavour. Home Rule had become a platonic passion, a continuation of the Repeal Movement of Daniel O'Connell, whom middle-aged men had seen or heard of from their fathers, and whose time-honoured policy they thought should not wholly die. Isaac Butt was not a genuine leader of the people, nor his party genuine popular representatives, being redolent of the old ascendancy days, with some exceptions, and speaking down to an unintelligent proletariate whom they deemed as unworthy as incapable of serious thought. Home Rule, thus propounded, did not touch the heart of the people, and was nothing more than a pious aspiration. And as yet, when the new policy of obstruction was mentioned and explained, it was usually received with laughter. To stop all business in the House of Commons until the Government consented to give Home Rule appealed to the play-boy character of the Irish.

It was in 1877 that the Obstructionists attracted world-wide attention; and in the last days of July, when the session was drawing to a close, Sir Stafford Northcote, the Government leader, proposed resolutions enabling the House to deal with them in future. He was supported by the Liberals, including Mr W. E. Forster, a name then unfamiliar to Irishmen in general; and even Mr Butt, their titular leader, repudiated the Obstructionists, saying of Mr O'Donnell, "If he represented my country—and he does not represent my country—I would retire from Irish politics as from a vulgar brawl." The O'Donoghue also disputed "the right of the Obstructionists to speak for the Irish nation." But the Obstructionists persisted in dividing the House, and kept it sitting from 4 P.M. until after 6 P.M. the next day, twenty-six and a half hours, the longest sitting recorded up to that time. On that memorable day Mr Parnell was supported by Mr Edmund Dwyer Gray, Mr Kirk, Captain Nolan, and Mr O'Connor Power, as well as by his colleagues, Biggar and O'Donnell, while his sister, Fanny Parnell, sat in the gallery all the time; but, in the thirteen divisions on their motions for adjournment, they never mustered more than five votes.

After this Mr Parnell became the most important Irishman in Parliament, and in order to understand the revolution it is essential to become acquainted with his history and character. On his father's side he was English, the founder of the family in the reign of James I. being a draper of Congleton in Cheshire, whose sons sided with Cromwell and the Parliament in the next reign. One of those sons, Thomas, migrated to Ireland after the Restoration, purchased a property there, and had two sons. One, called after himself, was a well-known poet, friend of Pope, Swift, and Bolingbroke, and was also Archdeacon of Clogher in the Church of Ireland. The other, John, became a judge of the Irish King's Bench. John's son was the famous Sir John Parnell, friend and colleague of Henry Grattan, and was appointed Irish Chancellor of the Exchequer in 1788. Having opposed the Union, and declared prophetically, " We shall recover our rights by constitutional means," he became a member of the United Parliament at Westminster. Sir John's elder son, Sir Henry Parnell, was an eminent parliamentarian and financier, became

Secretary for War in the Grey Ministry of 1830, was created Baron Congleton in 1841, and committed suicide in the following year.

Sir John's younger son, William, remained in Ireland, where he succeeded to a property at Avondale, in county Wicklow, which had been given to his father by an admirer named Hayes. William Parnell was M.P. for Wicklow and a friend of the poet Thomas Moore, who, while on a visit to Avondale, where the Avonmore and Avonbeg join to form the Avoca River, wrote that immortal lyric, "The Meeting of the Waters," the sentiment of the last verse of which is so singularly inapplicable to the hero of the Irish Revolution :—

> " Sweet vale of Avoca ! how calm could I rest
> In thy bosom of shade, with the friends I love best,
> Where the storms that we feel in this cold world should cease,
> And our hearts, like thy waters, be mingled in peace."

John Henry Parnell, son of William, succeeded to the property at Avondale in 1821, visited the United States in 1834, and there married Miss Delia Tudor Stewart, daughter of a distinguished American naval commander who fought in the war against England, and descendant of a Protestant Ulster evicted tenant who had emigrated to America in the eighteenth century. Charles Stewart Parnell, born in 1846, was the younger son of this marriage, one of a family of five sons and six daughters, being descended on his father's side from statesmen, legislators, and men of property who were also Cromwellians and Liberals, and on his mother's side from evicted tenants, rebels, and republicans. His mother had a rooted hatred of England and the English which she instilled into her son. "The English are hated in America for their grasping policy," she would say. "They want us all to think they are so goody-goody. They are simply thieves."

Charles Stewart Parnell, as a youth, was a typical Anglo-Irishman in many respects, being of dare-devil temperament, always ready to decide the merits of a question by a fight. In his hatred of England he sympathised with the Fenians, for whose paper in Dublin, directed by Charles Kickham and others, his sister Fanny wrote contributions. His mother openly supported the Fenians and preached rebellion to the Earl of Carlisle, Liberal Lord-Lieutenant of Ireland in 1867, the result being that a night raid for arms and treasonable correspondence was made by the police upon her house in Temple Street, Dublin, where she then lived, and a sword belonging to Charles, who was an officer in the Wicklow militia, was seized and carried off.

Great amnesty meetings to procure the release of the Fenian prisoners were held in Dublin in 1868, at which Isaac Butt was the chief orator, and out of them grew the Home Rule movement started by Butt and his friends two years afterwards. Charles had gone to school in England, and was then at Magdalene College, Cambridge, from which he was "sent down" in 1869, when he was twenty-three, for assaulting a tradesman, who brought an action against him and recovered twenty guineas damages. Parnell was sitting late at night in the road outside the railway station, where he had just partaken of sherry and champagne, with a college chum standing over him, when the tradesman came over to inquire what the matter was. Whereupon Parnell sprang to his feet and rewarded his curiosity by an unmerciful pommelling.

Parnell's elder brother, John Howard Parnell, went to the States and settled in Alabama, where Charles visited him in 1871. John took Charles to see the Governor, and, after the interview, Charles said : " You see that fellow despises us because we are Irish. But the Irish can make themselves felt everywhere if they are only self-reliant and stick to each other. Where has he come from ? And yet he despises the Irish !" Shortly afterwards John took him to see a house he was building for an Irishman named Ryan, who found fault with it in Charles's presence. " It is too good for you," said Charles contemptuously. " You're a liar," retorted Ryan. Whereupon Parnell took off his coat, and John had the greatest difficulty in preventing a fight. These incidents show how very Irish he was, despite his English breeding and characteristics, and help us to understand the unsuspected bond of sympathy between him and his Celtic followers. He had no respect for laws or rules or conventions, which he only regarded as binding on others but not on himself. Being High Sheriff of Wicklow in 1874, and wishing to stand for Parliament at the general election of that year, though he knew a Sheriff was disqualified, he took the unusual step of petitioning the Lord-Lieutenant to relieve him of his office. The petition being refused, he stood later in the year as a Home Ruler for county Dublin and was defeated. Although he proved an apparently hopeless failure as a speaker, his personality, backed by his family history, impressed the Home Rule League so favourably that, on the death of John Martin, the '48 leader, in April 1875, Parnell was elected in his place as member for county Meath.

The day he entered the House of Commons he listened calmly to Joseph Biggar, a retired Belfast trader and member of the Supreme Council of the Irish Republican Brotherhood, making a four-hours' speech in obstruction of an Irish Coercion Bill. Parnell's maiden speech was weak and halting, as judged by the then standard of oratory, but it contained these characteristic words: "Why should Ireland be treated as a geographical fragment of England? Ireland is not a geographical fragment. She is a nation." At the beginning of the session of 1876, Sir Michael Hicks-Beach, then Chief Secretary for Ireland, made a speech ridiculing Home Rule, in which he said that Home Rule could not liberate " the Manchester murderers." Parnell objected to the word "murderers," and Beach said "he regretted there was an honourable member in the House who would apologise for murder." The House jeered at Parnell and called on him to withdraw. Whereupon he arose and said with icy deliberation: "I wish to say as publicly as I can that I do not believe, and never shall believe, that any murder was committed in Manchester." The Chief Secretary was dumb, and the House set its wits to work to interpret the oracle delivered by the new Irishman, who at once became the idol of the Fenians in Ireland, Great Britain, and America.

The year 1876 being the centenary of American Independence, a Fenian meeting was held at Harold's Cross, near Dublin, at which an address of congratulation to the United States was read and carried with acclamation—Mr O'Connor Power and Mr Parnell being deputed to go to America and present it to President Grant. They saw Grant in New York, but he said that international etiquette required that such an address should be presented through the British Ambassador. The delegates refused to do this and Parnell at once came home, but the address was ultimately accepted by Congress over Grant's head.

On reaching Liverpool, Parnell made a speech in which he said : "I have lately seen in the city of New York a review of the militia, in which five or six thousand armed and trained men took part, at least half of them being veterans of the war. They marched past with firm step and armed with improved weapons. If in Ireland we could ever have under Home Rule such a national militia, they would be able to protect the interests of Ireland as a nation, while they would never wish to trespass on the integrity of the English Empire. It is a foolish want of confidence that prevents the English Government from trusting Ireland. They know that Ireland is determined to be an armed nation, and they fear to see her so, for they remember how a section of the Irish people in 1782, with arms in their hands, wrung from England legislative independence. Without a full measure of Home Rule no Irishman will ever rest content."

This utterance, so different from Isaac Butt's or even Joseph Biggar's style, captured the hearts of the Fenians. In the House he soon became Biggar's leader in the game of obstruction, mastering the rules by breaking them, and becoming leader of the Obstructionists by "sheer tenacity." "My opinion on obstruction," he said, "is that it should be like the action of a bayonet, short, sharp, and decisive."

Butt disowned him, saying: "I am not responsible for the member for Meath, and cannot control him. I have, however, a duty to discharge to Ireland, and I think I shall discharge it best when I say I disapprove entirely of his conduct." This created a breach not only between Butt and Parnell, but between Butt and the Fenians, and marked the end of Butt's influence in Irish politics. In dealing with the English, Butt was for conciliation. Parnell now proclaimed a policy of unwavering hostility. "Are the Irish people for making things convenient for Englishmen and advancing English interests?" he asked a Fenian gathering at Glasgow in May 1877. "If so, I will bow to their decision, but my constituents will have to get someone else to represent them."

In the July following, at Manchester, he said: "I do not believe in a policy of conciliation of English feelings or prejudices. Why was the English Church in Ireland disestablished? Why was some measure of protection given to the Irish tenants? It was because there was an explosion at Clerkenwell, and because a lock was shot off a prison van at Manchester. We will never gain anything from England unless we tread upon her toes; we will never gain a single sixpennyworth from her by conciliation." These were the pregnant words, almost unnoticed by the British public, but greedily devoured by the leaders of Irish political thought, with which Charles Stewart Parnell began the Irish Revolution ten years after the Fenian Rising had been suppressed.

In August a meeting was held at the Rotunda, Dublin, at which Butt and Parnell were present. "I care nothing for the English Parliament and its outcries," said Parnell, to the infinite chagrin of

Butt; "I care nothing for its existence, if that existence is to continue a source of tyranny and destruction to my country." His reward for this came on the first of September following, when the Home Rule Confederation of Great Britain, the directors of which were Fenians, elected him its president in the presence of Butt, who was deposed from the position. "There is one thing about Parnell on which we can rely," said a Fenian, "and that is his hatred of England. We feel that will last for ever!"

Eight days after this Parnell openly dissociated himself from Butt in a speech at Burslem, in which he said : "The followers of Mr Butt say we must behave as the English members behave; in fact, we must be Englishmen. We must go into English society and make ourselves agreeable, and not cause a ruffle on the smooth sea of parliamentary life, lest we forget our position as gentlemen and as members of the British House of Commons. Mr Biggar and myself, however, think that that is a wrong view to take, and that it is better for us always to remember that we are Irish representatives." At Greenock a fortnight later he said to a Fenian meeting : "We must carry out a vigorous and energetic policy in the House of Commons. If that be done, then I believe we have a power in Parliament of which few men have any notion." Two days afterwards in Meath he said : "I think that opposition to English rule is best which is most felt. O'Connell gained Catholic Emancipation outside the House of Commons. No amount of eloquence could achieve what the fear of an impending insurrection, what the Clerkenwell explosion and the shot into the police van achieved."

Parnell's aim, thus clearly announced, was to

conquer the House of Commons, the fountain of power, by obstruction within and by force and terrorism outside. He was prepared to take the responsibility for the violence inside the House; but, while he openly hounded the Fenians on to violence outside, he would not become a member of their organisation; so that he might be in a position to disclaim responsibility for what they did as the result of his incitement. The splendid and callous audacity with which this rebel programme was propounded as a " constitutional policy " struck the followers of Isaac Butt dumb, and caused sober English statesmen to regard its author as either an impracticable enthusiast or an ambitious wire-puller, unscrupulously bidding for Fenian support with no other object than to supplant his leader. But it was a true expression of Parnell's views, and it carried the general body of Fenians by storm.

CHAPTER IV.

THE FENIANS.

THE Fenians, who were in possession of the field before Mr Parnell arrived, were to be found all over the country, and were particularly numerous in Cork —their founder, John O'Mahony, having been a Cork man,—and not a few of them in our district being relatives of my own. There were also a great number of them in America, who had fled there after the rising of 1867. The Fenian movement in Ireland was an aftermath of the American Civil War, in which so many Irish-Americans fought,—one of my father's brothers being amongst those killed in battle on the Northern side,—but none of my father's people in America joined the Fenian Brotherhood. One of my American-born cousins on the mother's side came over in the *Jacknel*, the United States schooner which brought men and arms for the rising, and was tacking to and fro off the coast near Ballymacoda, about twelve miles from us. He so yearned to set eyes on the ancestral home of the Fitzgeralds that he came ashore contrary to orders, and on his way to Clonmult met the police patrol. He was arrested on suspicion, but my uncle persuaded a sporting Justice of Peace that the young American had only come to Ireland with the pious intention of visiting the tombs of his ancestors; and, having stayed unmolested at Clonmult for a short time, he returned to America.

He told my uncle that the disunion amongst the Fenians on board the *Jacknel* was appalling, and he was delighted to have got away from them. My uncle himself had the same tale of divided counsels and jealousy amongst Irish Fenians in his district. Though at first he helped in drilling the young men at night in the fields, he refused, because of the dissensions, to take the Fenian oath, which was: " I promise by the divine law of God to do all in my power to obey the laws of the Fenian Brotherhood, and to free and regenerate Ireland from the yoke of England. So help me God." On the day that the rising was fixed to take place he rejected all solicitations to join, and, taking out his harriers, went for a day's hunting. As he drew Dungourney Glen he was expecting to start a Fenian or a policeman from every brake instead of a hare, and found some of the rebels hiding in the furze bushes.

The actual rising was perhaps the least important part of the Fenian movement. The Fenians successfully rescued their Head Centre, James Stephens, from Richmond prison, Dublin, and smuggled him out of Ireland, though the Government offered £2000 for his recapture. I knew the Governor of the prison, Mr Marquis, in after years. He lived to a great old age, and stood as godfather to one of my first cousins. Indeed, Stephens and he were both living peaceably in Dublin twenty years after this time, the Fenian in Clontarf and his jailor in Kingstown. The Fenians in England made a daring attempt at rescuing two comrades, Kelly and Deasy,

from a prison van in Manchester six months after
the rising, killing an English policeman in broad
daylight. Three of them, who were hanged for this
exploit, were at this time venerated as national
heroes, Mr T. D. Sullivan having written the
Nationalist anthem, "God Save Ireland," in their
honour, and the anniversary of their death being
celebrated by great processions every winter. There
was not a Catholic schoolboy who did not sing "God
Save Ireland," and know that it was written in
honour of Allen, Larkin, and O'Brien, the "Manchester Martyrs," the "noble three" who died "high
upon the scaffold tree" with "God Save Ireland" for
their last words.

Though the rising was easily suppressed, the
Fenians remained. My earliest recollection is that
of being held up in my father's arms on the night
of the Midleton rising to see the Fenians in our
district marching through the Main Street. And,
though I was only three years old, I remember the
black figures of the men in a disorderly crowd on the
white road and the rifle-shots in the dark, by which
a policeman and a Fenian were killed close to our
house. At hearing the shots my father drew back
into the room and closed the shutters. On that
night, at Castlemartyr, a relative of my father named
Daly was killed by the police, and the anniversary
of his death was celebrated by processions.

The Fenians rejoiced at the appearance of a leader
so imbued with hatred of England as Parnell and
approved of his policy of obstruction. And he, for
his own purposes, tried to win their support, though
he was never a man for armed revolt, being quite
unprepared to lead a rebellion or use a rifle. The

JOSEPH GILLIS BIGGAR.

"Joseph Biggar was a peculiar character, one of those Belfast Catholics
who are sharpened by the Protestant atmosphere in which they live. . . .
He was in the House before Parnell, and felt none of the hero-worship
which younger members of the party now had for the Chief."—PAGE 453.

Fenians had the sympathy of all the Nationalists and ninety-nine out of a hundred Catholics. It may be said that the hierarchy condemned them, but it must be remembered that the censure was merely official, and the priests had brothers and cousins amongst the rebels. Fenianism was condemned because it was not successful, but, if it had been successful, it would have been blessed.

If Mr Parnell had condemned the physical force element he could have made no headway in Irish politics. He knew that a fight with a British army of occupation would be madness; but he evidently determined to use the force of the Fenians for his own ends in other ways than that for which the organisation was formed. The hope he held out to them was that, by getting a Dublin parliament, he would be able to make Ireland absolutely unprofitable to England from a commercial point of view by putting a high tariff on English imports, and that he could develop a standing army under the guise of Volunteers strong enough to wrest the complete independence of Ireland from England during the first serious war in which England might be engaged. There was no secrecy about this in Ireland, except in the newspapers and in the speeches of the politicians. The landlords and all who objected to living under the rule of the Irish majority knew it, and knew also that their salvation depended on maintaining the connection with England. The lay Catholics did not meditate the persecution of the Loyalists, but they meant to make them eat humble pie and sink to the position they were entitled to on a counting of heads.

Mr Parnell had to show results from constitutional agitation, and, in his desperate eagerness to do this, developed the line of attack commenced by Biggar (who was a Fenian), and which was tantamount to a physical force movement in the British Parliament, wearing out his opponents by sheer violence. From the first he tried to be of service to the Fenians, who had been necessarily inarticulate, because their methods did not bear talking about ; and most of his speeches were meant to give voice to Fenian ideals in constitutional phraseology ; his policy being, in fact, one of talking, backed up, on occasion, by a certain amount of slaying. The Fenians, pleased at his avowed hatred of England, hoped, under cover of the talking campaign, to strike another blow on the lines of the rising of 1867. But Parnell's success demolished that hope, inasmuch as reading and talking gave a sufficient outlet to the feelings of the rising generation, and the Land League and National League destroyed their need for secret societies.

The reorganisation of the Royal Irish Constabulary and the great military garrison kept in the country made an armed rebellion hopeless. The Arms Act, soon to be passed along with Mr Forster's Coercion Act, and to be renewed by Mr Morley in 1886, was destined to make it almost impossible for a Nationalist to have a gun during the revolution now at hand. The result was that the physical force men, who approved of slaying, found other outlets for their energy, and formed small secret societies for the killing of obnoxious individuals to forward the constitutional agitation. While those who entered into this ignoble scheme believed it to be justified by the impossibility of carrying out the more honourable policy of armed rebellion, it was only the dregs of the original Fenians who joined these murder societies.

In Connaught, where the most murders of this kind
were destined to be committed, the original Fenians
had little influence—all the manly outbreaks in 1867
taking place in Leinster and Munster, at Tallaght,
Kilmallock, Caherciveen, Midleton, Killarney,
Drogheda, Waterford, and other places. In our
district the Fenians, as a rule, held aloof from the
Land Agitation, believing, much as they sympathised
with Parnell, that, like O'Connell and Butt, he would
fail to win the complete independence of Ireland from
England—which, as I have already said, was not
merely what the Fenians themselves aimed at, but
what ninety-nine out of a hundred Irish Catholics
looked upon as the proper goal of any national
movement.

The young people, distracted by the conflicting
views of Fenians and Home Rulers, looked with a
great longing to the United States of America, and it
was a burning question with all boys and girls
whether they should stay at home or emigrate. When
there were several sons in a small farmer's family,
it was a recognised thing that one or more should
seek his fortune in America. The servant boys and
girls were all anxious to go, and nothing but the want
of the passage money prevented them. Most of them
had relatives in the States, who sent letters and frequently money to help the old people, or to assist
younger brothers, sisters, nephews and nieces to cross
the Atlantic. The larger farmers disliked emigration,
because it lessened their supply of cheap labour, and
their sons looked on it as a resource for persons
beneath them, though many of them also had to go.
Those who went and succeeded became altered men
and women, and rarely, if ever, returned, but their

letters told of a land of liberty, equality, fraternity, and wealth. My uncles and aunts on my father's and mother's side went and never came back again, and of their scores of children and grandchildren born in America I never saw one. Some of those who failed and came back brought the message that at home one could get an even greater reward for a given amount of industry than in the States, and, if the message was not literally true, it enshrined the salient fact that the Irish at home were unhappy because they did not do with all their might the work their right hands found to do — the yearning to leave Ireland and make money abroad making them discontented.

Although the population in 1877 was well over five millions, or almost 180 to the square mile—a million more than it is to-day—middle-aged people could remember when it was eight millions, or nearly 300 to the square mile, and they pointed to the ruined cottages to be seen everywhere, telling of a diminishing race. On the side of the hill above our new farm at Geyragh was a large tract divided into hundred-acre fields, and worked like a great English farm by the landlord. The old men in the neighbourhood remembered when it was inhabited by a colony of small cottiers who had been evicted at the time of the famine, and whose descendants were either dead or gone to America, leaving no trace behind them. The present poverty of the son of the landlord who evicted them was regarded as a visitation of providence. Decadent towns and villages everywhere told of vanished trades and of the hundreds of thousands of craftsmen in Ireland before the famine of 1847 and the advent of English manufactures.

But, despite a decreasing population, Ireland was a busy agricultural country in 1877. On all sides the trade in cattle, pigs, sheep, horses, corn, and butter went on without cessation, poultry and wool being also relied upon for a share of the year's revenue—the poultry being the *peculium* of the farmers' wives or daughters. In our district, where the land was especially suitable for barley, there was a distillery, and the Cork brewers also came to buy the corn for malting. The price of all kinds of grain was then very high, compared with what was soon to be the rule, yet vast fortunes were made by the manufacture of whisky and porter, the times being so good that all were spending money freely as well as making it. On many farms the butter paid the rent, Cork butter then fetching the highest price in the English market; the Cork butter merchants being very rich men who made a regular trade of advancing money to the farmers on the security of future deliveries of butter. Farmers were continually backing bills for one another; and on fair-days they were to be seen in groups of three or four going sheepishly into the bank with their hats in their hands, as if it were a church, to sign their names or their marks. One bank manager (he belonged to the Munster Bank) told me many years after that his orders then were never to lend money at less than ten per cent, or to pay more than one per cent for a deposit, even if it were ten thousand pounds to be left undrawn for a year. He said he often got 50 or 60 per cent on bills for small amounts and rarely made a bad debt; and, if his directors only knew how to invest the profits the branches made, the shareholders would be millionaires. But the Munster Bank was then doing very well, paying ten per cent on its ordinary shares, and we were all very proud of it as the only Cork institution of the kind.

While our side of the country was so peaceable in 1877, despite the strong leaven of Fenians, there was a perennial bitterness in Connaught amongst the small cottiers in the regions since officially called "the congested districts." And in the county Roscommon one of those small secret societies to which I have referred murdered a landlord named Young on his own estate this year. The murder had been a particularly daring one, having been spoken of for months before as a public service which ought to be performed; and after its committal, a farmer, who told the police that he had seen a suspicious person loitering in the neighbourhood, had his house burned down over his head the same night. Just at the time that Mr Parnell was outraging parliamentary decorum at Westminster, the Grand Jury of Roscommon, with a view to punishing the locality, voted £4000 as compensation to Mr Young's widow—the largest amount of money ever awarded in a like case. When I visited Castlerea a quarter of a century after the date of which I am writing, to get information about the quarrel between Lord De Freyne and his tenants, I said to a gentleman who was telling me something of the neighbourhood that I had heard the people there were so cowardly that they would be afraid to fire a gun. "They shot my father dead in his own avenue just outside the town," he replied. It was Mr Young's son I was speaking to.

Mr Parnell dare not specifically condemn such a murder as this, though he was free to speak against "crime" in general terms; for, if he did, his position would be untenable. He had little knowledge of

Connaught at this time, and no foreboding of the prophets so soon destined to arise there; and when that knowledge came, he deliberately worked on co-ordinate lines with the perpetrators of agrarian out-rage, using their achievements to advance his own cause, yet not holding himself responsible for what they did. The student of Irish affairs soon discovers there was no strict line of cleavage between the men who believed in agitation by talk and the men who believed in dealing out death to the enemies of Ireland. They were Irishmen of the same class, with but one objective, namely, the making of Ireland an independent nation free to act out her own ideals.

The peaceful condition of the eastern side of Ireland was well illustrated by the reception given to Mr Gladstone in November this year at Dublin, where he not only got the freedom of the city, but was followed by cheering crowds in the streets and held a regular *levée* at Kingsbridge station on his departure for the country seat of his host, Lord De Vesci, in the heart of Leinster. The Liberal leader paid no attention to Charles Stewart Parnell, his mind being full of the Bulgarian atrocities. He fondly thought that the Irish question had been settled by the Disestablish-ment Act of 1869 and the Land Act of 1870, and that his business in Irish politics henceforth would be confined to resting on the laurels won by those statutes.

CHAPTER V.

FAILURE OF THE CROPS.   SLAYING OF LORD LEITRIM.
DEATH   OF   PIUS   IX.   AND   CARDINAL   CULLEN.
UNION OF FENIANS AND CONSTITUTIONALISTS.

JUST before Christmas in 1877, a Fenian prisoner
named Michael Davitt was released on ticket-of-leave,
after seven years' penal servitude, and came to Ireland.
Three more widely known Fenians, Sergeant McCarthy,
Corporal Chambers, and J. P. O'Brien, were also released and came to Dublin on January 5th, 1878.
Mr Parnell met them early in the morning at Kingstown, accompanied them to the city and invited them
to breakfast at Morrison's Hotel.   Sergeant McCarthy
dropped dead in the coffee-room, and his death was
ascribed to his ill-treatment in prison.   Parnell was
deeply impressed by this tragedy, which drew public
attention to the union between him and the Fenians,
and excited widespread sympathy for the Fenians
themselves.   Some say that Parnell wished to join
the Fenians, but that they refused to admit him, fearing to let him know the poverty of their organisation
at that time.   Others say, and this is more probable,
that he refused to join the Fenian Brotherhood when
asked, his reply being: "I think I can do good with
the parliamentary machine.   But I do not want to
break up your movement.   I want it to go on.

Collect arms, do everything you are doing, but let the open movement have a chance too. We can help each other, but I can be of more use in the open movement." For this reason Kickham and other leading Fenians were dead against having anything to do with Parnell or the parliamentarians.

Soon after Sergeant McCarthy's death, Butt presided over a conference at Dublin, and once again said his policy was "to get liberal-minded Englishmen fairly to consider how they would redress the grievances of Irish misgovernment." Parnell, who was present, said the Englishmen to be found in the House of Commons were not "fair-minded," but were "party politicians who considered the interests of political organisation paramount beyond every other consideration." He added ominously : "If I refrain from asking the country to-day to adopt any particular line of action, it is because I am young and can wait, and because the country can also wait."

In the summer of 1878, a sudden check came to the prosperity of Irish farmers, caused by a fall in the price of cattle, a bad season and shortage of crops. The blow came as silently as blight on a potato-field, and it stunned the people as if it were a dynamite explosion. The general run of Irish farmers had nothing laid by for the rainy day, and were gifted with little resourcefulness for striking out a new line. I vividly remember seeing the deep wrinkles on my father's forehead when I came on him by surprise and noticed for the first time how grey his hair was getting, but he was afraid to speak of his anxiety, though we all saw the meagre produce of our costly new farm as compared with the preceding year. Before 1877 I had often heard my father say farming was so profitable that rent did not matter. He now felt the disappointment keenly, but had no intention of backing out of his bargain. He was paying £2 an acre for the new two hundred acres, a very high rent in our district, and, as he was spending more than he made in buying stock, he withdrew money from investments to pay the landlord. He disapproved of physical force, the guiding principle of his life being that a man should pay what he owed, and in this happily he was not exceptional in Midleton.

At the other side of Ireland, where the physical force men had organised the small secret societies I have mentioned, rent was not now considered in the light of a just debt. A notice of eviction was taken rather as "a sentence of death," to use Mr Gladstone's description of it not long after in Parliament, and the man who passed the sentence was himself adjudged worthy of death—"give as you get" being a favourite Irish precept. This was the line taken with the Earl of Leitrim by his tenants in county Donegal this year. Lord Leitrim was a bachelor, and known as a generous man to the poor, but very strict in his dealings with his tenants, making no secret of his distrust of them, and letting it be known that he always carried arms in anticipation of an attack on his life. Landlord and tenants were separated by a wall of caste and sectarian prejudice—he did not know them, nor they him. He had recently evicted many, and was said to be contemplating the eviction of eighty more. One day in April this year, when he was driving, fully armed, in company with his clerk to visit his solicitor, his valet following in a tax-cart about a mile behind, he was shot dead on the lonely road by some invisible persons. Then the assassins deliberately killed the clerk and driver, so that there might be no living witness against them; and the valet, coming on the scene soon afterwards, found the three bodies lying in a pool of blood. When the news of this tragedy in the north-west came to us in the south-east, much horror was expressed, but there was also secret jubilation amongst a certain section of the farmers, while the physical force men were openly elated. Even the hard-headed and law-abiding—not excluding a few Scotch and other Protestant tenants in our district,—seeing that there was no possibility of our being implicated, did not hesitate to say the murder "would help to lower rents."

Two months before the slaying of Lord Leitrim, Pope Pius IX. had died, and the altered position of his successor, Leo XIII., had not a little influence in bringing about the revolution in Ireland. Pius, who had known what it was to be a temporal ruler, had wielded an autocratic power over the Irish ecclesiastics through his *protégé*, Cardinal Cullen, the first cardinal given to Ireland. But henceforth Leo XIII., sobered by the changed conditions under which he ascended the papal throne, acquiesced in rather than dictated the policy of the Irish hierarchy. Nor did the death of Pius IX. come alone. Cullen, who up to this time virtually had the Irish Catholic ecclesiastics under his thumb, was seventy-five years old, and died in October; and the death of the ultramontane Cardinal, following close upon that of the Pope, left the Irish hierarchy without a leader. Cullen's place was taken by Edward M'Cabe, parish priest of Kingstown, a home-bred Irish priest, with none of the dignity or statesmanlike ability of his predecessor, who had spent most of his early life in Rome. Cullen used to keep Butt and the Home Rulers in leading-strings; but M'Cabe, having no personal magnetism, and small influence on public opinion, was unequal to such a task, and the Roman hierarchy lost the unquestioned predominance they had so long owed to Cullen's zeal and commanding personality. Thus the way was cleared in an important particular for the new political *régime* which was already beginning to assume solid shape.

In August 1878, when the failure of the harvest was indisputable, Michael Davitt went to America, and there, in conjunction with John Devoy, an American Fenian, put forth a new Fenian programme in which "the land of Ireland was to be made the basis of Irish nationality." This was endorsed by a public meeting in New York, and the result of it was an approach by the Fenians to the Constitutionalists. Hitherto the only plank in the Fenian platform had been the destruction of English rule in Ireland by force of arms in the field. Now it was to include the acquisition of "the land for the people." As Parnell had included the use of physical force in his "constitutional" programme, so now the Fenians included an agitation for Land Reform in their programme of rebellion. Davitt brought the Fenians into the "constitutional" movement, Parnell brought the parliamentarians into the movement of rebellion and homicide.

The American Fenians wanted to have a treaty with Parnell, and cabled to him asking him not to couple his demand for Home Rule with the main-

tenance of the integrity of the British Empire, and
a number of other things; but Parnell ignored their
messages and went his own way. He continued to
attack Butt, saying: "He wants to please the English. But you may be sure that when we are pleas-
ing the English we are not winning. We must not
care for English opinion. We must go right on in
the way Ireland wants." Hitherto, though he had
been able to reach the Irish in Great Britain through
the Home Rule Confederation, he had no means of
getting at the masses of the Irish people, because
a large meeting in Ireland was almost impossible,
except under the auspices of Butt and the Home
Rule League. The agricultural distress was now to
give him the opportunity he wanted. A meeting was
organised for him in Tralee in November 1878, at
which he said that "nothing short of a revolution
would bring about a change in the landlords," and
urged "the establishment of a tribunal for fixing
rents and creating a peasant proprietary." After
the meeting a friend said to him: "It will take an
earthquake to settle the land question." Parnell's
reply was: "Then we must have the earthquake!"

The disestablishment of the Church in 1870 had
removed an obstacle to the revolution which was to
change the landlords. But there were two less-
known statutes passed by the Conservative Government in 1878 which also helped the revolution, and
have done much to shape the national character.
The Intermediate Education Act gave a million from
the Church Surplus Fund in trust to certain commissioners for exhibitions and prizes to students and
result-fees to teachers, and ordered examinations to
be held at convenient centres all over the country,

beginning in 1879. This new departure excited intense interest in the scholastic world, especially in the Catholic secondary schools, which, having no endowments, regarded the money as a State subvention. The headmaster of Midleton College, having given us a glowing account of the measure, decided that I should be one of those to compete for an exhibition. The social effects of the Sunday Closing Act, also passed in 1878, were most remarkable all over the country, and helped the revolution in a way which I shall describe afterwards. Henceforth the public-houses, instead of being open from 2 to 9 P.M., were shut all day on Sundays, except in the cities of Dublin, Belfast, Cork, Limerick, and Waterford, where they were allowed to open from 2 to 7 P.M. The effect on our town was magical. There used to be at this time a veal market in the city of Cork on Mondays, and the farmers from our district used to bring their fatted calves in carts into Midleton on Sunday evenings, and there rest themselves and feed their horses before starting for Cork, the string of carts sometimes reaching the entire length of the street. People taking fat pigs, fowl, apples, or other commodities to Cork, used to join the caravan for company's sake, with the result that there was always a concourse of people in our town on Sunday evenings in spring and summer, the drivers of the carts remaining in or about the open public-houses, which used to be full of drinking parties, singing, arguing, and making much noise, the songs from the tap-rooms mingling with the crying of the calves.

At nine o'clock, when the public-houses closed, the drivers would get into their carts, and the entire cavalcade would start for Cork, thirteen miles away, leaving the town in a silence which seemed all the greater because of the previous commotion. Many of the drivers, heavy with drink, used to sleep in the carts on the road, trusting to one or two wakeful men to lead the way. It was a weird experience to encounter this curious procession out on the lonely road at dead of night, the horses swinging along without guidance, most of the calves and men fast asleep, a wakeful calf sometimes emitting an almost human cry, a horse occasionally straggling aside to snatch a mouthful of grass from the fence, and throwing the whole cortége into confusion. After the Sunday Closing Act all this ceased, and arrests for drunkenness, as well as faction fights and battles between the police and drinking parties, which used to be a common spectacle on Sunday nights, were seen no more.

CHAPTER VI.

THE DISTRESSFUL YEAR 1879. DEATH OF ISAAC BUTT. FOUNDATION OF THE LAND LEAGUE.

IN January 1879, John Devoy came to Ireland along with Michael Davitt, their object being to set the " Land for the People " agitation going by the force of the Fenians. They had many interviews with Parnell, but he would not join the Fenians. He assured Devoy of his sympathy, but asked the American Fenians, who called themselves the Clanna-Gael, to give him time " to work the parliamentary machine."

A meeting of the supreme council of the Fenian Society, or Irish Republican Brotherhood, of which Davitt as well as Biggar were members, was held at Paris, and, mainly through Kickham's influence, it firmly vetoed the project of joining in a land agitation. But a resolution was agreed to that " the officers of the organisation should be left free to take part in the open movement if they felt so disposed—such officers to be held responsible for acts or words deemed to be injurious to the revolutionary cause." Devoy then returned to the States to win Fenian aid for an Irish land agitation, while Davitt remained in Ireland to carry on the propaganda in the chief battle-ground at home. All this, however, would have been mere wire-pulling and of little practical interest, but for the failure of the harvest and the fall in the price of stock, which made the farmers a willing prey to the agitators.

While Devoy and Davitt and Parnell were thus devising their schemes for the emancipation of Ireland from all partnership with Great Britain, Isaac Butt was dying, and speculation was rife as to who would succeed him in the leadership of the Home Rulers. Mr Parnell had not yet " arrived," and, during Butt's illness, Mr Shaw, our county member, who lived in Cork, took the chair at the party meetings. But that the " advanced" section were becoming dominant was proved in April, when Lord Robert Montagu was formally expelled for having written to the news-papers in denunciation of Biggar and the obstructive policy. The presence of such a man as Lord Robert Montagu shows how essentially Butt's party differed from the Nationalist party of the revolution.

Mr Butt died on May 5th, and while it may be said of him that he was the ablest Irish politician since Daniel O'Connell, he was a mere amateur compared with Parnell. Ineffective as Butt was, however, he was now succeeded by a man in every respect his inferior; for Shaw was to Butt as McCabe was to Cullen. Thus again the way was opened for the new man with the new policy of plain-speaking—the man who was to use talk like a sword or a gun, and who would show the world that straight talking was the quickest road to victory in Parliament as straight shooting was in the field of battle. A crisis was alone wanting to call this man to his proper place, and this now arrived with appalling suddenness.

The year 1879 was the most distressful since the

great famine of 1847. Live stock were unsaleable and crops were almost a total failure. All the familiar avenues of money-making for farmers were closed as by an edict of omnipotence. On April 20th Davitt held his first meeting at Irishtown in county Mayo, to propound his policy of "the land for the people," and for many weeks following enormous meetings were held in Connaught, the vague reports of which were like the moaning of wounded beasts struck down by the thunderbolt and protesting against the injustice of Heaven. The chief promoters of these meetings were a Mr Killen, a barrister and professor of political economy in Dublin, and Michael Davitt, then only known to the public as an ex-Fenian liberated from penal servitude on ticket-of-leave. Davitt had only one arm, having lost the other when working as a mill-hand in Lancashire, whither he had emigrated at five years of age with his father and the rest of his family when they had been evicted from their little farm. He had lived mostly in England, and now on returning to Ireland, as the "hungry" months of summer proceeded and it was obvious that the crops were going to be a disastrous failure, found the materials for a great agitation ready to his hand.

Of all places in Ireland, Connaught was the best adapted for this purpose, not only because the people were poorer and more ignorant than elsewhere, but because of the presence of large numbers of those migratory labourers, known as harvesters, who go to England yearly to save the English hay and corn and return for the winter to their native place, being carried at a low rate by the railways and shipped in large crowds in the steamers like cattle. These men came back to Connaught discontented at the beginning of each winter, having tasted a higher standard of living in a country where they saw no class so downtrodden and despised as they felt themselves to be in their native land, and, having made enough money in England to support them during the winter, had little else to do in the long nights but to plot against their landlords and the authorities—as they believed, for their own and Ireland's benefit. Their motives were not necessarily bad, but, being very ignorant, they saw no way of remedying their grievances except by outrages like the murder of Mr Young. They formed local secret societies and fomented rebellion everywhere amongst their home-keeping relatives, so that, when Michael Davitt came to Mayo, he found his fellow-countrymen seething with sedition.

Realising that an honest appeal to arms would only result in butchery, with no prospect of success for the rebels, Davitt undertook to show his friends a road to liberty and prosperity more effective than the policy of isolated murders. This was the time-honoured device of organised agitation, which had almost become a lost art since the death of O'Connell, but which was now to be revived with such an accompaniment of murder and violence and followed by such a revolution as no man then foresaw. Davitt's immediate object was to compel landlords to forego their rents in consequence of the failure of the crops and the fall in the price of live stock, but his ultimate goal was "The Land for the People." Mr O'Connor Power, one of the Connaught Home Rule members, a young man of great eloquence whom many expected to succeed Butt, put the new policy in a nutshell when he said that "the Irish land question meant the restoration of the land to the people." Mr Davitt said they were confronted with two alternatives, "either the extermination of the people, or the extermination of the exterminators," and thus put his policy in a nutshell : "I believe rent for land under any circumstances, prosperous times or hard times, is an unjust and immoral tax on the industry of the people. Landlordism, as an institution, is an open conspiracy against the wellbeing of the people. Not one of them ever puts a hand to a plough or a foot to a spade."

A great meeting was arranged to be held at Westport on June 7th, and to this Davitt invited Parnell. Archbishop MacHale of Tuam, the diocesan of Westport, officially condemned the meeting, but the Government, probably because of this, did not interfere. Parnell hesitated to identify himself openly with Davitt, knowing the Fenianism behind the scenes of which the outside public was quite unsuspicious. The Archbishop, who was regarded as a great patriot and lovingly spoken of as "John of Tuam, the Lion of the West," sent an intimation to Parnell not to come. But Parnell went, and delivered his first incendiary speech on the land question. "You must show the landlords," he said, "that you intend to keep a firm grip of your homesteads and lands. You must not allow yourselves to be dispossessed as you were in 1847. I should be deceiving you if I told you that there was any use in relying upon the exertions of the Irish members of Parliament. If your members were determined and resolute they could help you, but I am afraid they won't. I hope I may be wrong, and that you may rely on the constitutional action of your representatives in this sore time of your need and trial ; but above all things remember that God helps him who helps himself." This depreciation of parliamentary action pleased the Fenians, and urged them on to take the law into their own hands without waiting for constitutional reform.

After this speech Parnell went back to the House of Commons, and by persistent obstruction succeeded in getting flogging in the army abolished, except in cases where the alternative punishment was death. When all the other opponents of "the cat" would have given way he stood firm, and to him must be assigned the credit of the reform.

The doctrines about land and landlords enunciated by Davitt and his friends soon spread into our part of the country, the young farmers openly applauding them and looking forward to the time when there would be no rent. Mr Thomas Brennan, one of the eloquent and able young Fenian leaders of the infant Land League, used to give harrowing pictures of the poverty of the small farmers in Connaught, dilating on the oppression and cruelty of evictions and the sufferings inflicted on ill-fed mothers, emaciated children, and hard-working fathers ; while on the other side of the picture he painted in equally eloquent terms the idleness, luxury, and heartlessness of the landlords. Brennan did more perhaps than any man at the beginning to excite pity, awaken sentiment, and arouse fury on the land question. About the genuineness of the distress there was no doubt, though there may well be a sharp difference of opinion as to the method of meeting it adopted by the agitators. Out of 17,000 sheep exposed for sale this year at Banagher September fair—one of the great sheep markets of Ireland situated on the Connaught border—only 2000 were sold ! At the preceding year's fair, not an exceptionally good one, out of 19,000 sheep entered for sale, 17,000 had been sold.

At midsummer 1879, the first examinations were held under the Intermediate Education Act, our centre being at Cork, whither I went to stay at a friend's house, and there made my first acquaintance with 'Alice in Wonderland,' then a great novelty in Ireland, but the humour of which was unintelligible to me then and since, owing perhaps to the manner in which it was brought to my notice. When taking a last look at my books in my bedroom, a girl of the house, about my own age, used to tease me from the landing below by singing about the soup and other things, but especially—

"Twinkle, twinkle, little bat,
How I wonder what you're at,
Up above the world so high,
Like a tea-tray in the sky!"

A priest in soutane and biretta acted as superintendent at the examination—he is now an archdeacon and parish priest of my native town—and the boys from Midleton College, being all Protestants except myself, were greatly amused at his dress, calling the biretta "that funny three-cornered bandbox." When I got home and told how I had done my papers, Dr Moore predicted that I would get an exhibition; but, when the results came out in autumn, I did not appear in the list of exhibitioners, to his chagrin and mine. I had only taken up four subjects—classics, English, French, and mathematics; while the students from other schools, especially the Catholic, had taken up not only all my subjects, but Spanish, Italian, political economy, Irish, and others more abstruse, and as the exhibitions were awarded on the aggregate of marks,

the exhibitions went to those who took the most
subjects. The effect of this Act on Irish education has
been to produce men with a smattering of everything,
but no deep knowledge of anything. It is only right
to add, however, that some exceedingly brilliant
scholars won exhibitions that first year when I failed.

In July a vacancy occurred in the borough of Ennis,
and the Liberal candidate was Mr William (afterwards
Judge) O'Brien, Q.C., a Catholic lawyer born in Midleton who had attended Midleton College as a day boy.
The Bishops and priests were in favour of O'Brien,
and Mr Shaw agreed with them. Parnell determined
to put forward a man of his own, Lysaght Finnigan,
one of the most eloquent speakers I ever heard.
Parnell went to Ennis, and did all in his power for
Finnigan against the priests, with the unexpected
result that Finnigan was elected. It was a turning-
point in Parnell's career. "If Ennis had been lost,"
he said afterwards, " I would have retired from public
life, for it would have satisfied me that the priests
were supreme in Irish politics."

About this time a party meeting was held to consider the Government's Irish University Bill, which
proposed to dissolve the non-sectarian Queen's University, established by Sir Robert Peél in 1847, and
create a new Royal University to be governed, not by
the Crown directly, but by a Senate nominated by the
Crown. It was understood that half the members of
this Senate were to be Catholics nominated after
consultation with the Irish hierarchy. Cardinal
McCabe favoured this arrangement, and Edmund
Dwyer Gray, member for Tipperary and owner of ' The
Freeman,' the Nationalist daily paper, as the spokes-
man of the hierarchy, urged the party to accept the

Bill. Parnell was for rejecting it, and said they should demand from the Government a full Roman Catholic University, such as the Bishops wanted, under the entire control of the hierarchy. While prepared to oppose the hierarchy on the land question, he would yield to them on education, for he knew the Irish laity would not assert their claim to control education, and, as his object was to gain support from all parties in Ireland, he declared for the whole educational platform of the Bishops. But Parnell's advice was rejected. Gray carried the party with him, and the University Bill became law.

Mr Parnell returned to Ireland after the adjournment of Parliament, and at the end of August he said at a great meeting in Limerick, which Butt used to represent in Parliament: "It is the duty of the tenants to pay no rent until they get a reduction." He dwelt on the moderation of this policy, and prophesied that, if the landlords refused to take advantage of it, they would be beaten to their knees, and would be coming to the tenants in a few years begging for the fair value of their land so that they might give up landlordism and find another way of living. The difference between his speeches and those of Butt and the others was their simplicity and candour. He had no trick of oratory, and aimed at the simplest expression of the simplest thought. O'Connell and Butt were men who had been trained on a diet of Demosthenes and Cicero, and were professional talkers. If Parnell's mind was trained on anything, it was on a sceptical study of the English Bible. Such simple injunctions as " Keep a firm grip of your homesteads " and " Pay no rent until you get a reduction " rang through the land like a tocsin, and came tripping from every tongue in our district.

At this stage he was preaching compromise, while Davitt was preaching extermination, and I have often thought that if any considerable section of the landlords had then sided with him, the revolution might not have gone to such extremes. He had the ideal of a Dublin parliament clearly before him, in which he was to play the part of a second Henry Grattan; and I think Parnell at this stage would have liked to see the Irish landlords, as the richest class in the country, properly represented in the wished-for parliament in College Green, and wielding the influence there to which their birth, culture, and responsibility entitled them. When Alderman Redmond, of Waterford, asked him in 1882 what he would do with the landlords after Home Rule, his reply was : " I would treat them fairly and honestly. I would encourage them to live quietly among their own people. I would give them a fair share of parliamentary honours, and I would make them happy in their own country, which they are not at present."

Parnell's point of view must never be forgotten. It was as an Anglo-Irish Protestant that he hated England as represented by the Castle system in Ireland. He was not fired by that desire for revenge on the English planters and English Protestants which animated the Catholic Irishmen who gathered round him. His position resembled that of George Washington rather than of Daniel O'Connell; and, while he developed into one of those English who " became more Irish than the Irish themselves," his Irishism was not devotion to the old creed which for the majority of Irishmen is the most important essential of patriotism, but detestation of English interference with Anglo-Irish management of Ireland. As he said to his brother when at school in England : "These English despise us because we are Irish ; but we must stand up to them. That's the way to treat an Englishman—stand up to him !" The interfering Englishman from England was his *bête noire*.

Davitt and his friends, on the contrary, had as their ideal the abolition of rent and landlordism, hating the leisured class who would have been preserved by Parnell's policy of compromise. And while Parnell's advice to ask for reductions of rent was taken up everywhere, many of the people at his meetings thought it too moderate, and used to interrupt him with cries of "Lead will settle it," "More lead," "Lots of lead," and "Give them an ounce of lead." He never encouraged murder or outrage in any of his speeches, his aim at first being rather to direct hostility against English government in Ireland, of which Irish landlordism was one of the offshoots. But it would have been impossible for him to adopt a puritanical attitude towards the physical force men who were there before him and had a right to their opinions.

The first glimpse which we got of Mr Parnell was at a meeting in the Cork Corn Exchange at this time. I was present and distinctly remember the secondary position he occupied as compared with men like Chevalier O'Clery and Frank Hugh O'Donnell. Mr Shaw, who was in the chair, represented capitalism, being chairman of the Munster Bank and largely concerned in those speculations which not many years afterwards were the cause of its stoppage. Mr Butt had also represented capitalism in a professional form, being a successful barrister, accustomed to work for high fees and in sympathy with the wealthier classes of the community. The same may be said of O'Connell himself. These men and their colleagues regarded the Irish people as Horace viewed the Roman mob—farmers and shopkeepers being for them lower intelligences to be used and kept at a distance.

Mr Parnell inaugurated a new *régime*, and, despite the back seat given to him by the promoters of the meeting that day, I remember my uncle and others regretting that he was not the leader instead of Shaw. He had many peculiar qualifications wanting in his predecessors. He was an Anglo-Irish aristocrat, yet he had little money and no respect for the makers of money. His estate was impoverished, yet, like an Irishman, he scorned to devote his energies to developing its mineral resources or working hard at a profession. Being an American and a Republican on his mother's side, it was not natural for him to treat the people as lower intelligences to be spoken down to or cajoled. In all his speeches from the first he gave the people of his best, and helped to raise them to see things from his point of view. The old *régime* went in for managing and humouring. Parnell told them the plain unvarnished truth, and used the same language in speaking to the humblest as to the most cultured audience. If this new movement had fallen under the control of a leader like Butt, or even like O'Connell, there would have been no revolution to record in Ireland. It was Parnell who destroyed the old-time respect of the people for mere titles and positions, causing them to regard Viceroys, Chief Secretaries, and Cabinet Ministers as common men to be judged solely on their merits.

It is due to Parnell that the new school of Nationalism,
which was now to become practically effective through
the Land League, started with equality of man as one
of its fundamental axioms and an utter disrespect for
formality and established political authority.

The Irish farmers still needed a great deal of civilising, and the rough state of the human soil in which
the seeds of Parnell's simple philosophy fell was proved
in a shocking way by an outrage committed in county
Cork this year. A farmer and his sister-in-law, coming
from market near Kanturk on a June evening, were
attacked with a billhook by a neighbouring farmer, a
relative of theirs, almost hacked to pieces, and left for
dead on the road, though when discovered they were
still alive and were successfully removed to hospital.
As this outburst of savagery attracted great notice in
England, I think it right to record that it created a
feeling of horror in our district.

An unfortunate incident at Lurgan tended to
exasperate the people against the authorities on religious grounds this year, as it happened on the
15th of August, when Ulster Catholics turn out in
procession to celebrate the Assumption of the
Blessed Virgin, as a counterblast to the Protestant
celebration of the victory at the Boyne on the
12th of July. The police interfered to prevent a
collision with the Orangemen, and killed a boy and
wounded many persons. For this the Nationalists
held the Chief Secretary responsible, and "Jimmy"
Lowther, as he was called, came in for a great deal
of abuse.

In September, Mr Parnell addressed great meetings
at Tipperary, a town destined to become famous in
the later stages of the revolution, and at Navan in

his own constituency, at both of which peasant proprietary and national independence were demanded;
but at Navan a special vote of thanks was passed to
him for his great exertions on behalf of the national
cause. These vast meetings finally marked him out
as the man to lead the new movement, and, at a conference at the Imperial Hotel, Dublin, on October 21st,
when Davitt's Connaught Society was launched as the
Irish National Land League, Parnell was unanimously
elected president, the treasurers being Joseph Biggar
and Patrick Egan, both Fenians, and the secretaries
Michael Davitt and Thomas Brennan, also Fenians.
Parnell was now at the head of the Nationalist
organisations in Ireland and Great Britain, and it
was a foregone conclusion that he would soon become
leader of the parliamentary party. The conference
requested its new president to go to America for the
purpose of getting money for the agitation, and this
mission resulted in making him absolute dictator in
the whole field of Irish politics.

The Government now seemed to realise that a new
political situation had arisen, and decided to make an
effort to suppress the revolutionaries. They had their
eye on Davitt for some time; and, in November, after
the Land League had developed from a local to a
national organisation, they arrested him along with
Killen and a man named Daly, proprietor of 'The Mayo
Telegraph,' on a charge of sedition. But they did not
see their way to proceed with the prosecution, and the
accused were liberated on bail, Mr Lowther contenting
himself with "proclaiming" the Land League counties,
so as to make the possession of firearms and the holding of meetings without the consent of the Government illegal.

That the Land League and the Away from England movement were yet far from holding the field, to the exclusion of all other interests, was well illustrated by the enthusiasm with which the centenary of the national poet, Thomas Moore—whom so many of the revolutionaries and Away-from-Englanders now regard as a backslider—was celebrated in Dublin, crowds of people flocking to the festival from all parts of Ireland. Neither did the Nationalists as yet assert any claim to political dictatorship. In the county where Lord Leitrim had been murdered, for instance, neither the Land League nor the Home Rule League was strong enough to start a candidate, and that large Catholic constituency still enjoyed the privilege of selecting its member from one or other of the great British parties—an Englishman, Mr Thomas Lea, being returned at the end of this year as a Liberal for county Donegal by a majority of 700 over a Conservative opponent.

During the winter of 1879 there was hunger in the houses of the poor—a state of things from which our district had been exempt for over thirty years. Hearing it said that a labourer, whom I knew, had no food for himself or his family, I asked in a fit of youthful indignation whether those who were lamenting his case had taken him some. Knowing that he would not beg or go into the poorhouse, and that it might be a week before the Vincent de Paul Society would hear of his case, I seized as many loaves of bread as I could carry and went to his home, where I found him comatose before a fireless hearth with his large infant family around him, while his wife on a stool in a corner was suckling a baby at her breast. Their faces were all grey with hunger, and

when I laid the bread on the table they stared in
silent amazement, but showed no anxiety to eat.
Nor did I wait to see what they would do, fearing
lest my self-control should give way.   Rushing home,
I found a basket with some meat, tea, sugar, butter,
and milk ready for my poor friends, to whom I made
a second trip with very new sensations, this being my
first mission of charity.

The newspapers and the politicians were now calling on the Government to start relief works, and
warning Lord Beaconsfield that, if he did not do so,
the same consequences would ensue as in 1847.   The
Government estimated the falling off in the principal
crops, as compared with 1878, at £10,000,000, of
which the potatoes accounted for £6,000,000, but the
authorities were disposed to minimise rather than
exaggerate, and the true loss would be nearer to
£15,000,000.   The Duchess of Marlborough, wife of
the Lord-Lieutenant, started a Relief Fund at the
Castle, for which she appealed for subscriptions in
Ireland and England, but those who thought that
this generous effort would meet the emergency knew
nothing of Mr Parnell and the new men who were
about to take advantage of the distress to begin a
root-and-branch revolution in Ireland.   Just before
Christmas, when the distress was at its height, and
those who remembered the famine of 1847 were
prophesying the worst, Mr Parnell took the decisive
step which lifted him above all the Irish members,
and at a single bound raised him to a political
dictatorship.   With his mother's American blood
throbbing in his veins, he set out for her country
across the Atlantic, taking young John Dillon as his
companion, and attended by his private secretary,

Mr Timothy Healy, whom nobody thought worthy
of notice at the time. He had employed Healy
because, as the nephew of A. M. Sullivan, Healy
would keep his master in touch with what was then
the most advanced section of constitutional Nationalists. Parnell went to America as president of the
Land League ostensibly for funds to relieve Irish
distress, but in reality to get money for, and perfect
his control of, the political machine in Ireland, with
which he hoped to overthrow the system of English
government and substitute a College Green parliament in which he meant to play the part of constitutional dictator.

PART II.

OLD LAND LEAGUE DAYS

CHAPTER VII.

Mr Edmund Dwyer Gray, M.P., took office as Lord
Mayor of Dublin on the first of January 1880.   His
newspaper, 'The Freeman's Journal,' had always been
on the popular side since its foundation, more than
a century before, and always under Protestant
direction, first under Lucas and his successors, and
latterly under Mr Gray's father, Sir John Gray, a
medical doctor who procured for Dublin its excellent
supply of Vartry water.   As the power of the
Catholic hierarchy was waxing greater year by
year, and it grew increasingly difficult for a leader
of popular thought to be outside the Catholic Church,
Edmund Dwyer Gray, having married a Catholic
wife, had become a Catholic.   And now, young, able,
and self - confident, whatever public honours the
Catholic party in Dublin had in their gift were at
the convert's disposal.   He belonged to the "safe"
section of the Home Rule party, being entirely in
accord with the Catholic hierarchy whose patronage
he courted for himself and his paper, yet remained
in close touch with the Protestants because of his
birth and breeding.   The breach between the Mansion
House and the Castle which occurred in his year of
office, and has never since been healed, was not of

his seeking; but, when it came, he made the most of it for himself politically and financially.

On New Year's Day he announced that the Corporation, as " representing the Government in a small way," proposed to spend £200,000 in public works for the relief of distress; and, on January 2nd, he held a citizens' meeting at the Mansion House at which Cardinal McCabe was represented, and the famous Archbishop Trench of the Church of Ireland was present. Sir Arthur Guinness (now Lord Ardilaun), who was then one of the members for the city of Dublin, and many Home Rule members, as well as leading citizens of all creeds and politics, attended; and a Mansion House Distress Fund was started—the Lord Mayor at the same time praising the Duchess of Marlborough's fund, and saying that " all idea of rivalry was to be dismissed." This new fund brought Mr and Mrs Dwyer Gray into extraordinary prominence, and the keen rivalry between Mrs Gray, who was a very ambitious woman, and the Duchess not only caused unpleasantness between the ladies, but had not a little to say to the very unfortunate act of public policy which broke off the hospitable relations hitherto existing between the Viceroy and the Lord Mayor.

On January 20th Gray presided over a meeting of the Home Rule members in the City Hall, at which a resolution was passed condemning the Government for not starting relief works to give employment to the starving people, Sir Patrick O'Brien taunting the Cabinet with taking shelter behind the petticoats of the Duchess of Marlborough. Another resolution was proposed by The O'Donoghue, M.P. for Tralee, and seconded by Mr O'Connor Power, M.P. for

Mayo : " That we tender our sympathy and promise all legitimate support to the gallant peasantry of the West now struggling to retain possession of their homes ; and protest against their being driven forth to starve for non-payment of rents fixed under a system which constitutes the landlord the absolute owner of the soil, and confers upon him the power of exacting whatever rent he pleases, such system being carried out in defiance of the repeated protests of the Irish people solemnly delivered through their representatives in Parliament."

Gray, under the inspiration of his wife, meant to make his year of office a great social success, and had asked the Lord-Lieutenant to attend the inaugural banquet at the Mansion House, leaving it to his Excellency to fix the date. The Lord-Lieutenant had accepted the invitation, and the function was to take place on February 3rd. Gray, now fearing to give offence to the Duke of Marlborough by a resolution which, though not mentioning the Land League, practically approved its policy, refused to put the motion from the chair. " I am not prepared to give the peasantry of the West any tangible support in their struggle," he said, " so far as it has assumed the aspect of a physical struggle. I am not prepared to risk my own life, or to encourage them in their resistance to the law. The resolution may be read by any ignorant man as such an encouragement, and, as I am not prepared myself to engage in such a struggle, I am not prepared to encourage them."

Mr Shaw, the nominal leader of the party and chairman of the Munster Bank, said " there was a natural antipathy to a bailiff or process-server. He felt it himself ; and when he saw one of those fellows prowling about, he felt inclined to take the linch-pin out of his car. To select this time of suffering for the scattering broadcast of ejectment processes was outrageous, and the employment of the police in such a service extremely improper." The meeting adjourned, and, on its resumption next day, the resolution was altered by omitting the words "of the West," so as to make it apply to all Ireland. Gray hoped that, as the Land League was confined to the West, his prospects of social triumph would not be imperilled by such a general resolution, which, on being put to the meeting, was unanimously passed.

This illustrates how wide was the gulf separating Gray and 'The Freeman' at this juncture from Parnell and Davitt. The members who supported the resolution to which Gray objected were men of means and good social standing who worked with the Liberals, and their object was not so much to encourage the Land League as to embarrass the Conservative Government. Biggar is said to have inspired the resolution, putting the respectabilities forward as stalking horses to win public support for the Fenian policy. In this he succeeded beyond his most sanguine expectations.

Four days after the resolution was passed, the Duke of Marlborough wrote to Gray, saying: "I observe that in your official capacity as Lord Mayor you presided at a public meeting in the City Hall at which resolutions were passed in relation to the opposition in the West of Ireland to the enforcement of the law and to the means which Her Majesty's Government have taken for the relief of the distress. I regret that the character of the resolutions will prevent me having the honour of dining at the

Mansion House on the 3rd of next month, as it would not be in my power either to ignore them when they have received your official sanction, or to observe upon them while accepting your lordship's hospitality."

Gray, stunned by this letter, hurriedly called the Corporation together. He said " he did not regard it as a personal slight, but as a slight to the citizens of Dublin, and his Grace had been led by ill-advisers to write it." There was to be a *levée* at the Castle next day, and Gray had arranged to go in state with the principal members of the Corporation. Would he go? He could not resist the temptation. He would go, " because, as Lord Mayor, he represented all the citizens, and his Grace was the representative of Her Majesty." So far removed was the leader of the Dublin Home Rulers from Parnell's revolutionary movement at this stage! He would abandon the banquet and give the money for the relief of the poor. He believed "the ostensible motive was not the real motive" of the letter. The Duke must have advised the Cabinet to take adequate measures to deal with the distress, and his advice had not been taken. Under such circumstances he was ashamed to come to the Mansion House and speak to the toast of "The Lord-Lieutenant and Prosperity to Ireland." Gray pointed out that the resolution sympathising with the peasantry had been amended so as to apply to the whole country and not merely to the West, and therefore was not in favour of the methods of the Land League. It was a humble, temperate, loyal speech, and was endorsed by corporators of all politics present, including Sir John Barrington, Gray's Conservative predecessor at the Mansion House.

'The Times,' commenting on the incident, wisely said it was "unfortunate" that the "abstract Lord-Lieutenant" could not dine with the "abstract Lord Mayor," irrespective of party politics, and pointed out how the Prime Minister never refused an invitation to the Guildhall, whatever might be the Lord Mayor of London's politics.

On that day a notice appeared in all the London papers that "there was no connection between the Duchess of Marlborough's fund and the Mansion House fund," and asking that subscriptions for the Duchess's fund "should be forwarded to her Grace or to the London Mansion House." The starting of the rival distress fund was Gray's (or Mrs Gray's) unpardonable offence, the speech of Sir Patrick O'Brien at the meeting of the Home Rule members was the barbed shaft which called forth the Duke's letter. Gray went to the *levée* in state next day, accompanied by his chaplain, Canon Daniel, and made his obeisance to the representative of Her Majesty.

Two days afterwards the Duchess and her lady friends held a meeting at the Castle, at which her son, Lord Randolph Churchill, as usual read all the minutes and correspondence relating to the fund. She made a political speech which will illustrate the commanding position she held in the Irish Government. " Even the present charity," she said, " is not to escape Mr Parnell's misrepresentations. But I cannot be surprised that he, who slandered our gracious Queen and dared to say her Majesty's purse was shut while her people were starving, should give utterance to the unjust assertion about me that the Government had suggested my effort, meaning, I suppose, that his Grace and the Chief Secretary had sheltered themselves behind the ladies of Ireland!" Such misrepresentation and the starting of other funds had interfered with their subscriptions.

On the same day the impotence of the Duke of Marlborough and Mr Lowther was proved, when Gray and a deputation from the Mansion House fund waited on them to ask the Government to supply seed potatoes to the distressed districts. The only answer the two English heads of the "Irish" Government could give to this modest and reasonable request was that they "would lay the whole facts before the Government, but could not say what the decision in England would be!"

That evening the Lord Mayor and Lady Mayoress, uninfluenced by the Duchess's reference to Parnell and the Duke's cold reception of the deputation, attended the drawing-room at the Castle in state. But, however anxious the Grays may have been to keep up their connection with viceregal society, the official relations between the Castle and the Mansion House, hitherto invariably friendly, were broken; and the Irish Government by its own act got out of touch with the chief centre of Nationalist social life in the Irish capital at a most crucial time. Biggar and the Fenians were delighted, not merely at the snub administered to Gray, but because of the fresh impetus which the incident gave to the new revolutionary movement.

Gray was a man whom a far-seeing Viceroy might have used against Parnell with telling effect. When Parnell first thought of standing for Parliament in 1874, he had waited on Gray at 'The Freeman' office; and Gray, neither then nor since, saw anything wonderful in the haughty young Wicklow squire who seemed such a prodigy to the peasant politicians of the Land League.

Meantime Parnell and Dillon had arrived at New York on January 2nd, and got a public reception from the Irish. Mr Parnell took the lead from the start, Dillon's *rôle* being only that of a foil or picturesque background to his leader, who at once told the Americans that his real object was to "take advantage of the opportunity offered by the distress" to make war on the English Government in Ireland and the land system which it fostered. James Gordon Bennett's paper, the 'New York Herald,' invited Parnell to join its committee for the relief of Irish distress, but, to the astonishment of the New Yorkers, he refused, saying, "If you want to help us, help to destroy the system which produces famine."

He disparaged the relief fund of the Duchess of Marlborough, which, he said, only helped tenants who paid their rents and distressed landowners. The Irish Attorney-General (Edward Gibson) had just been dilating in Dublin on the pecuniary distress of the landowners. The 'Herald' published a long letter from Arthur MacMorrough Kavanagh giving the landlords' side of the dispute, to which Parnell replied by citing the case of the barony of Farren in county Monaghan, as given in Mr Trench's 'Realities of Irish Life.' The rent in 1606 was only £250 a-year. The rent in 1880 was £80,000! "The added value," said Parnell, "has been the work of the tenants. Not anything that the landlord has done has added one penny to the value of the property."

He condemned the Mansion House relief fund, as well as the Duchess of Marlborough's, and checked the flow of American subscriptions to both. He had come to America to get all the money he could for political organisation. He was willing to take money for the relief of distress, and promised to keep it separate from money received for political purposes, but he depreciated charity. "No charity that can be given by America," he said, " will avail to prevent Irish distress. That must be the duty of the British Government, and we must see that we shame that Government into a sense of its obligations."

The Irish in the States, who till then were held in slight esteem, received the attractive young ambassadors from the people of the old land—Parnell fair as a Viking, Dillon dark as a Spaniard, both tall, stately, and handsome—with unbounded pride and enthusiasm. John Dillon's father had been in the '48 movement, and spent a period of exile in America, after which, having been elected member for Tipperary, he entered into an alliance with the English Radical party, and at the moment of his death, a short time before this, had organised a complimentary banquet to John Bright in Dublin. Mr Parnell, in alliance with the Fenians, was now to change this policy of friendship with English Liberalism into a steady antipathy to all things English, as represented by the existing system of government in Ireland. At Brooklyn he said : " We desire to restrain this movement within the strict letter of the law, but it is impossible to suppose that the great cause can be won without shedding a drop of blood. Although decimated by famine and pestilence, or slaughtered in ineffectual resistance to the armed power of England, yet the heart of our country remains, the courage of our race is unquenched."

The Irish-Americans, whose contempt for England had not been mitigated by contact with dominant Americans of the type of Parnell's mother, were charmed beyond measure with Charles Stewart Parnell, the young leader who spoke burning words of patriotism with the calm deliberation of an Anglo-American, and was admired and understood in the States as no Irishman or Englishman was ever admired or understood before.   The Clan-na-Gael and all American Fenians welcomed him with open arms, and he returned their confidence by such plain fearless speech as they had never heard from a politician.   " A true revolutionary movement," he said on landing at New York, "should in my opinion partake both of a constitutional and illegal character. It should be both an open and a secret organisation, using the constitution for its own purposes, but also taking advantage of its secret combination."   His progress through the States was one triumphal procession. Military guards met him at every town, and salvoes of artillery announced that he had arrived or departed. At Cleveland, on January 26, he said : " It has given me great pleasure during my visit to the cities of this country to see the armed regiments of Irishmen who have frequently turned out to escort us ; and when I saw some of those gallant men to-day, who are even now in this hall, I thought that each one of them must wish with Sarsfield of old, when dying upon a foreign battlefield, *Oh that I could carry these arms for Ireland !*   Well, it may come some day or other." Such language amazed even the American politicians, who, seeing the enormous influence he wielded over the Irish-American voters, threw themselves at his feet, and publicly invited him to Washington to address the United States Congress—he being the fourth to whom this privilege had been accorded, Lafayette and Kossuth being two of the three previously invited. Many of the State congresses also asked him to address them on the sufferings of Ireland caused by English misgovernment.

His words were so plain and direct that they confounded those Englishmen at home who believed Machiavellism to be an essential element of politics. At Buffalo he said : " Ireland has a right to separate nationality, and, if it were possible to gain this, every Irishman's blood should be shed in defence of his country." At Cincinnatti, on February 23rd, he said : " When we have undermined English misgovernment, we have paved the way for Ireland to take her place amongst the nations of the earth. And let us not forget that that is the ultimate goal at which all we Irishmen aim. None of us, whether we be in America or in Ireland, or wherever we may be, will be satisfied until we have destroyed the last link that keeps Ireland bound to England." For many years after those words were spoken English public men and leaders of thought kept demanding what he meant, as if it could possibly have been more plainly put. Fearing to accept it as what it was, namely, the simplest statement of every patriotic Home Ruler's political aim, they seemed to be always trying to make him unsay it, as if his unsaying would ever make Irish Nationalists unthink it or prevent them from working to achieve it.

Taking his private secretary, Timothy Healy, along with him, he crossed the Canadian border and addressed immense meetings at Toronto and Montreal. On returning to New York he founded the Irish

National Land League of America. The 69th Regiment turned out in full strength to see him off, and stood drawn up on the quay saluting as the tender moved away—Parnell bareheaded on the bridge and "looking like a king."

It is no exaggeration to say that this tour of Parnell's in the States is one of the most important landmarks in the modern history of Ireland, and perhaps the true starting-point of the Irish revolution. His great personality and his simple, candid speeches created a new public opinion in America, focussed the attention not merely of the English-speaking world but of foreign countries on the condition of Ireland, and raised the dispute between Irish landlords and tenants from the level of a sordid quarrel to a political issue of the first magnitude and world-wide interest. His visit to America was the beginning of an impeachment of British government in Ireland, and the court asked to hear evidence and pronounce sentence was no longer the British House of Commons, but the United States of America and the world at large.

CHAPTER VIII.

PARNELL'S RETURN AND THE GENERAL ELECTION OF 1880.

THOUGH Parnell's triumph gave no pleasure to the Catholic hierarchy and priesthood, who resented so abrupt a departure from time-honoured methods, it sent a delirious thrill through Catholic Ireland. Men, women, and children felt fired by this new assurance that their kith and kin in America were at one with them as a body politic ; and the money—£40,000, the largest sum ever collected by an Irish politician in one tour—which Parnell brought home for the alleviation of the distress and other objects, was the least significant part of an incident which set the pulses of Nationalism beating boisterously all over the island. "The Americans sent me back with this message," he said, "that for the future you must not expect one cent for charity, but millions to break the land system." The Fenians gave him their subscriptions for "lead," the Irish-American labourers and servant girls gave him their dollars "for bread." He accepted the lead money and the bread money and admitted it openly, telling us, when he came home, how at one American meeting an admirer gave him twenty-five dollars, saying that five were for bread and twenty for lead. He employed the money as seemed best to himself when he returned to Ireland.

While Parnell and Davitt were using the distress to increase their popularity, and set the revolution going, the Catholic ecclesiastics brought themselves into evidence, as if to remind the people of the allegiance due to the Church. At the beginning of January miraculous appearances of the Virgin Mary and other heavenly personages at the parish chapel of Knock, in county Mayo, were reported in the 'Tuam News,' and greatly stimulated the faith of the believing masses, who flocked to Knock from all parts of Connaught, where the Land League was most successful, and the new shrine became a formidable counter-attraction to the new prophets. When in September the apparitions occurred again, people from all parts of Ireland made pilgrimages to the spot, excursion trains being run to the nearest railway station in great numbers, and the chapel was full of people night and day waiting expectantly for a fresh apparition and hoping to be cured of their ailments. In our district, far as it was from Knock, bottles of water containing a solution of mortar from the wall of the chapel were used as medicine, and also applied externally to cuts, bruises, sprains, and sores. Some of us had our doubts, but we had perforce to keep them to ourselves, when miraculous cures were cited for our edification.

The dazzling accounts of Mr Parnell's progress in America seemed to confound the Duke of Marlborough and Mr James Lowther, and it was announced, on January 16th, that the Government had definitely decided to abandon a second prosecution for sedition commenced against Davitt, Killen, and Brennan, whereupon there was universal rejoicing, and the three leaders threw themselves into the agitation with renewed energy. The farmers were panic-stricken,

MICHAEL DAVITT.

"We are confronted with two alternatives, either the extermination of the people or the extermination of the exterminators. I believe rent for land under any circumstances, prosperous times or hard times, is an unjust and immoral tax on the industry of the people."—PAGE 68.

but, so far, except in Connaught, they did not make war on the amenities of civilised life. Hunting, the chief pastime of the landlords and a mainstay of the horse-breeding industry, was still allowed, and Ireland as yet enjoyed world-wide fame as a hunting country. Knowing nothing of the disturbance which was brewing, the Empress of Austria arrived in Dublin for a month's hunting in February, and when, four days afterwards, she was thrown from her horse with the Ward staghounds, happily without serious injury, every farmer in the land felt sorry for her—especially my uncle, one of whose hunters she afterwards bought at a high figure, naming the horse " Clonmult," and keeping him in the imperial stud for many years.

Mr Parnell was still in America when Parliament met. Sir Stafford Northcote, leader of the House, admitted the calamitous failure of the principal crops. The Government, however, would not start relief works, but proposed a Relief of Distress Bill, advancing money to Boards of Guardians and other bodies on exceptionally favourable terms for such relief works as they might consider advisable. The Home Rule members denounced the Bill as worthless, and Mr David Plunket, defending it, spoke scathingly of Mr Parnell for having forbidden the Americans to subscribe for the relief of Irish distress on the grounds that the money would find its way to distressed landlords. "To the agitator," said Mr Plunket, " the present distress seems a good occasion to exasperate the people and to make them as little as possible ready or patient to endure their sufferings." So little sympathy had the Liberals with the Home Rulers that they refused to vote for the Irish amendment, which was defeated by 216 to 66.

The Government, having been six years in office, suddenly decided to dissolve Parliament on March 8th, and the importance they attached to the Irish question was shown by the fact that Lord Beaconsfield's manifesto took the form of a letter to the Lord-Lieutenant, in which he accused the Liberals of intending to tamper with the Union, though he cited no evidence to prove the charge. He referred to the Home Rulers as "a portion of Ireland's population attempting to sever the constitutional tie which unites it to Great Britain in that bond which has favoured the power and prosperity of both." This manifesto, which gave the Land Leaguers unfeigned pleasure because of the attention it attracted to Ireland, had been preceded by a policy of appeasing the Catholic hierarchy. The Intermediate Education Act and the University Act, under which the Royal University of Ireland was established by charter this year, were in the nature of distinct endowments for the schools and colleges of the Jesuits and other religious orders, male and female, the Government hoping to undermine the power of the Parnellites by attaching the hierarchy and priesthood to its side. The sudden decision to dissolve was no doubt influenced by a desire to take Mr Parnell by surprise and bring on the elections while he was out of the country, before he could make arrangements for a plan of campaign.

Four days after Lord Beaconsfield's letter, Mr Gladstone retorted that "those who injured the Union were the party who maintained an alien church and unjust land laws," whereas his policy was "to bind the three nations together by liberal and equal laws." Instead of legislative separation, he professed a desire for closer union; but we in Ireland knew that the statutes he had then recently passed, instead of " binding the three nations together," had brought Mr Parnell appreciably nearer to the "last link." Lord Hartington, the titular leader of the Liberal party, said that " Home Rule was impractic-able," and the demand for it "should be met by firm resistance combined with equal laws and in-stitutions."

Lord Hartington had a heavier stake in Ireland than any of the Liberals and all but a few of the Con-servatives. The estate of his father, the Duke of Devonshire, around Lismore, with a rental of over £40,000 a-year, was only a dozen miles away from us, " the Duke's tenants," some of whom were relatives of mine, being always spoken of with envy because of the reasonable rents, fixity of tenure, and generosity of the landlord. Indeed they at first refused to join the Land League, and never became active in the agita-tion. One of the engines on our railway between Cork and Youghal was named the " Hartington," which as a schoolboy I had more than once driven when the driver honoured me with permission to join him on the foot-plate. Besides helping to build our line, the Duke of Devonshire had built at his own cost a line from Lismore to Fermoy, bringing his estate into direct communication with Cork and Waterford, and, if the majority of Irish landlords were like him, there would have been no Land Agitation.

Mr Parnell returned from America on March 21st, and received a national ovation at Queenstown, depu-tations from Dublin, Cork, and the surrounding towns, including our own, going to welcome him home. In-numerable addresses were presented, mostly couched in terms of fulsome adulation. That of the head Land

League, for instance, said that "he fled across the water like another Perseus to save the Andromeda of nations from the political monster now threatening her with national destruction." Mr Parnell listened with inimitable gravity to this preposterous language, but had no sympathy with it; for never was there an Irish leader more completely devoid of sentiment. When Mr A. M. Sullivan informed him that the Home Rule Confederation of Great Britain, of which Mr Parnell was president, had been working for the Liberals and against the Conservatives during his absence in America, and that the Irish vote had turned from thirty to forty constituencies in favour of Mr Gladstone, Mr Parnell's reply was: "It would have been infinitely better for Ireland to keep the Conservatives in power, as Lord Beaconsfield would infallibly bring England into some disastrous European complications, the occurrence of which would be the signal for concessions to Ireland far far beyond anything Gladstone can ever conceive."

A section of the Fenians in their address said it was "the firm belief of the intelligent manhood of the country that it was utterly futile to seek for any practical national good through the means of parliamentary representation," and that "the Nationalists of the country" had determined to take no part in the elections. Parnell heard and said nothing, but threw himself at once into the work of the elections then in full swing. It was publicly understood that he had come home to play the part of political dictator. Edmund Dwyer Gray and 'The Freeman' were against him, but the people, tired of the old men and oblivious of the wire-pulling behind the scenes, encouraged him everywhere. He was at a great disadvantage, owing to the unexpectedness of the dissolution, but he put forward as many of his friends as possible, mostly new and unknown men entirely dependent on himself. With such a party in his mind, his need of money was pressing; but wealth in a candidate was only welcomed when accompanied by subservience. His own particular candidates had no visible means of support except politics, but the mob was for them, and the poorer they were the more they were trusted—poverty combined with eloquence being the chief qualification.

He was admirably adapted for the *rôle* of dictator, and from the first he played it to the manner born. There being great difficulty in getting trustworthy men, he stood himself by request in three constituencies, Meath, Mayo, and Cork city. On March 29th, he wrote a letter to one of the electors of county Louth saying he would regard the election of Mr Philip Callan, the sitting member for that constituency, as " a political discredit to the country." This Mr Philip Callan was a local man and well-connected, but so inextricably bound up with the licensed trade organisation that he was known as " the publicans' man " in Parliament. His opponent was Mr A. M. Sullivan, proprietor of ' The Nation ' and a supporter of Parnell's, a county Cork man and one of the ablest and most eloquent Home Rulers, as well as an uncompromising temperance advocate who had been mainly instrumental in passing the Sunday Closing Act. In thus defying the brewers, distillers, and publicans, who were then so powerful in Ireland, Mr Parnell showed a moral courage even greater than he had displayed in America; but, despite his condemnation, Callan was elected, and the licensed trade claimed the credit of a victory over the new dictator.

Fresh from his unprecedented triumph in America, Parnell's word was received as law in many quarters. The city of Cork had been represented by Mr Goulding, a Protestant Conservative to whom I have referred, and Mr Nick Dan Murphy, a Catholic Home Ruler and member of the family which owned the distillery at Midleton. John Daly, the prosperous Catholic draper and ex-Mayor of Cork, who had been unsuccessful in 1876, now stood in the hope of defeating Goulding. But Denny Lane did not come forward, as politics were becoming too hot for the poetical secretary to the Cork Gas Company, who had a marvellous knack of making and keeping money. Goulding's agent, remembering how his principal owed his election in 1876 to a split in the National vote, offered a well-known Cork Fenian £50 to pay the sheriff's costs and a free gift of £200 to fight the election, if he would nominate an extreme Nationalist against Daly. The Fenian, disapproving of Daly, agreed, but stipulated that he was not to give the name of his candidate, and was to get the money at once. The cash was handed over. A paper nominating Parnell was hurriedly filled up, two of the assenting burgesses being priests, Father John O'Mahony and Father Denis McCarthy, and Parnell was nominated at the last moment. This contest was watched with greater interest than any other, though the public were ignorant of the circumstances under which Parnell had come forward. Parnell at once came to Cork, and was informed that he owed his nomination to the Tories, but he accepted the money and fought the election, coupling Daly's name with his own and asking the electors to put out the Catholic Whig as well as the Protestant Tory. The general opinion was that Parnell would only get enough of votes to keep out Daly and put in Goulding, while Murphy's seat was deemed absolutely safe. Imagine then the enthusiasm with which we heard the news that Parnell and Daly had both been returned! Our joy was as great as the chagrin of Bishop Delaney, the Whig prelate of Cork, at the defeat of Nick Dan Murphy, whose family had been raised to prosperity by Bishop Murphy, a predecessor of Delaney's who had regularly acted as banker for the Catholics of Cork. There were public rejoicings in our town that night. The brass band turned out, tar barrels were lit and fiery speeches made, which was the usual way of celebrating a popular triumph. Parnell's election for Cork sealed the doom of Mr Shaw as chairman of the Home Rule party.

Our constituency, the county Cork, had so far been represented by Mr Shaw and Colonel Colthurst. Shaw, who was a Methodist, was willing to compromise with Parnell; but Colthurst, an English Catholic, relying on the support of the Bishops, refused to conciliate the new dictator. Colthurst was genial, gentlemanlike, and elderly, with no liking for extremes, and was one of the many Anglican converts to Catholicism in the decades following the conversion of Newman and Manning. Having come to Ireland with testimonials from Cardinal Manning, he had been received with open arms by the Bishops and priests of county Cork, and, through their influence, was elected our member after the death of Mr McCarthy Downing and in opposition to his own nephew, Sir George Colthurst of Blarney, a local landlord and a Protestant, who stood as a Conservative.

Mr Parnell had brought with him to Cork a county

Dublin farmer named Kettle, one of the secretaries of the Land League, and now nominated him for the county against Colthurst, Mr Shaw being allowed a walk-over, probably because Parnell could not get a candidate to oppose him. The parish priests of the county, from Bantry to Youghal, supported Colthurst. The Bishops collectively issued a letter in support of him and Shaw. The farmers and shopkeepers who believed in Parnell supported Kettle, and it was well that they had little regard for persons, because Kettle was a most unattractive candidate, an indifferent speaker, and always suffering from severe hoarseness. But, in spite of these drawbacks, the crowd used to cheer wildly when they saw him with half his body projecting at an angle of forty-five degrees from the upper window of some hotel or public-house, gesticulating and opening his mouth very wide, but failing to make himself heard.

At Midleton fair I saw one of the leading farmers of our district, an enormous man named Buckley, speaking from a cart for Kettle, while Father Fitzpatrick was speaking for Colthurst from a pig-crib lower down the street. Buckley's landlord, Captain Smith-Barry, and Miss Smith-Barry chanced to pass by, and, stopping on the outskirts of the crowd, Smith-Barry burst into laughter, and pointing with his stick, said in a loud voice, "Look at Paddy Buckley! Look at Paddy Buckley!" The crowd near the Captain grew confused, and Buckley, taken aback, ceased speaking; but, smothering his resentment, he took off his hat to Miss Smith-Barry, and, when the Captain passed on, proceeded with his speech without referring to the interruption. This Patrick Buckley was a cousin of mine, and not long afterwards wanted to force my father to make a match between myself and his daughter, whom I never saw, she and I being in our teens. Twelve months after this, if Captain Smith-Barry had dared to act as he did that day, he would have been stoned, and Buckley, instead of saluting, would have denounced him — so quickly did what seemed child's play develop into a life-and-death struggle.

The friends of the priests did not resort to violence in county Cork against Parnell, but they did in other places. At Enniscorthy, for instance, where he went to speak for John Barry and Garret Byrne, his nominees for the county Wexford, the platform was stormed, Parnell was struck in the face with a rotten egg, his clothes were torn, and he had to fly for shelter to his hotel without getting a hearing. ' The Freeman,' which was his bitter opponent all through the elections, had more influence in Leinster than in Munster or Connaught.

It was at this election that the people got the first opportunity of hearing their own friends speak with authority as political guides. The farmers recognised in Kettle one of themselves, a man earning his living by the sweat of his brow, or at all events by the production of live stock and crops ; while they saw in Colonel Colthurst a fine gentleman who had never and would never " put hand to plough or foot to spade." The Colonel's speech was soft and musical, his appearance well-groomed, his manners attractive, and his smile bewitching. I remember how he kissed my youngest brother, three years old, when he came with Father Fitzpatrick to canvass my father, who, expecting the visit, was not at home. At the previous contest he voted for Colonel Colthurst, but now he plumped for Kettle, who made no house-to-house canvass, perhaps because he compared so unfavourably with his opponent, being rough, coarse, hoarse, and unable to smile. Nor were any of the Land League orators who came to help him ever known to smile—their politics being grim and serious, a matter of life and death.

Amongst those orators was James J. O'Kelly, who is still a member of Mr Redmond's party, looking very warlike and speaking in a deliberate American way which deeply impressed the crowd ; also Mr Lysaght Finnigan with his eloquent sentences, sonorous voice and appropriate gestures, whom none of the new men excelled in oratory, except perhaps Mr Thomas Sexton, then standing for Sligo, whose successes were chiefly in Parliament and not at large open-air meetings. At that election Finnigan was re-elected for Ennis, and O'Kelly for Roscommon, being two of the new men whom Parnell forced into the old party, and they came to us with the prestige of conquerors. There were also many orators from Cork, where a school of popular rhetoric was fast growing up, but Mr Parnell himself did not come to Midleton. The Land League's time, however, was not yet come in our county ; Mr Shaw headed the poll with 5354 votes, mainly through the influence of the Munster Bank ; the power of the parish priests secured 3581 votes for Colonel Colthurst, and Kettle received 3430.

The political education our district got from that contest changed its attitude not merely to the land-lords, but to the world in general. Besides the utter revolt against landlord influence, there was a new-born independence of ecclesiastical dictation in politics which led many of us to hope that a day of still wider mental emancipation was in store. Although Kettle was not elected, the high poll recorded for him, almost equal to Colthurst's, was regarded as a moral victory. Parnell was already secure of the mastery, and we regarded ourselves as conquerors. Tales of triumph came in from many quarters ; band, tar barrel, and speechifying in the evening became the rule rather than the exception. It was felt that there must be another Land Act, and the farmers began to look forward to a Bill legalising " the three F's," that is, giving them Fair Rent, Fixity of Tenure, and Free Sale. They scarcely expected so much; that was their *summum bonum*. They had no expectation of getting Home Rule, and paid scant heed to what Parnell said in America on that subject. It was only the Fenian leaven that cherished the Nationalist ideal over and above the immediate profit from a new Land Act. They, however, did not speak of turning out the Bank of Ireland to make room for a parliament in College Green, but of starting an Irish Republic. They called themselves Nationalists, while the farmers called themselves Land Leaguers.

CHAPTER IX.

PARNELL BECOMES LEADER OF THE HOME RULE PARTY.

THE Home Rule Party in 1879, immediately after Butt's death, consisted of the following members : Joseph Biggar, R. P. Blennerhassett, Sir George Bowyer, Dr John Brady, Maurice Brooks, George E. Browne, George L. Bryan, Philip Callan, Eugene Collins, Colonel Colthurst, Lord Francis Conyngham, Edmund Dease, J. Delahunty, Kenelm Digby, Nicholas Ennis, George Errington, Charles J. Fay, J. Lysaght Finnigan, Charles French, Daniel F. Gabbett, E. Dwyer Gray, Colonel King-Harman, Mitchell Henry, G. H. Kirk, H. O. Lewis, John George MacCarthy, Justin McCarthy, Sir Joseph McKenna, J. P. O'Gorman Mahon, Patrick Martin, C. H. Meldon, Lord Robert Montagu, Arthur Moore, George Morris, N. D. Murphy, Major Nolan, Sir Patrick O'Brien, Major O'Beirne, W. R. O'Byrne, Chevalier O'Clery, The O'Conor Don, Denis M. O'Conor, Frank Hugh O'Donnell, The O'Donoghue, Major O'Gorman, Dr O'Leary, R. O'Shaughnessy, W. H. O'Sullivan, Charles Stewart Parnell, J. O'Connor Power, Richard Power, W. A. Redmond, William Shaw, Edward Sheil, Serjeant David Sherlock, P. J. Smyth, A. M. Sullivan, E. J. Synan, and Dr M. F. Ward.

Of these fifty-nine men there were only six—

Biggar, Finnigan, Justin McCarthy, Parnell, O'Connor Power, and A. M. Sullivan—who were really permeated with the Nationalist spirit, and in actual touch with those Fenians who pulled the wires of the Nationalist movement. All the rest were as harmless from a Government point of view as an equal number of English Conservatives — being landowners, like Colonel King-Harman; professional men, like Dr O'Leary and Serjeant Sherlock; merchants like Maurice Brooks; retired military officers; and persons of substance with settled incomes of one kind or other.

After the General Election of 1880, the number of nominal Home Rulers was only increased by three; but the number of Home Rulers prepared to follow Parnell's lead, and therefore (though many of them did not know it) to act in concert with the Fenian wire-pullers, was increased from five to twenty-six— that is, over five-fold, as the result of the exertions of Parnell and the Land League. Of these twenty-six stalwarts, twenty-one were new men : John Barry, Garrett Byrne, Dr Commins, W. J. Corbet, John Daly, Charles Dawson, John Dillon, H. J. Gill, T. M. Healy, Richard Lalor, James Leahy, Edmund Leamy, J. C. McCoan, E. Mulhallum Marum, Rev. Isaac Nelson, Arthur O'Connor, T. P. O'Connor, James O'Kelly, Captain O'Shea, T. Sexton, and T. D. Sullivan. Captain O'Shea, who took the place of Lord Francis Conyngham in Clare, was politically unknown in Ireland, and assuredly Mr Parnell had no premonition of the fatal influence this new recruit was destined to have on Irish politics. There were seven other new men returned on whom Parnell could only rely if he proved he could succeed without them.

These were : A. H. Bellingham, J. A. Blake, Sir R. Blennerhassett, D. H. Macfarlane, R. H. Metge, B. Molloy, and J. F. Smithwick. Of the thirty-three members of the old party who were re-elected, Parnell could only count on the six stalwarts I have mentioned, and perhaps one or two others like W. H. O'Sullivan and F. H. O'Donnell.

But the victory now was not to be decided by a mere counting of heads. Parnell's men had a fixed purpose and a leader who knew his mind and theirs ; whereas the Shawites were not prepared to put party before individual interests. When the members met before the opening of Parliament on April 29th, each side hesitated to put the question of leadership to the vote, and it was postponed till the next meeting. Mr Parnell having chosen to sit for Cork, gave Meath to A. M. Sullivan and Mayo to the Rev. Isaac Nelson, a Nonconformist minister, whose selection proves how completely the Catholic hierarchy were out of the movement up to this stage. In the middle of May the party met at Dublin to appoint a leader, forty-one members being present and nineteen absent, and Parnell was elected by a majority of 23 to 18. Those who voted for Parnell were : Barry, Biggar, Byrne, Commins, Corbet, Daly, Dawson, Finnigan, Gill, Lalor, Leahy, Leamy, McCarthy, McCoan, O'Gorman Mahon, Mulhallum Marum, A. O'Connor, T. P. O'Connor, O'Kelly, Captain O'Shea, W. H. O'Sullivan, T. Sexton, T. D. Sullivan. The eighteen who voted for Shaw were : J. A. Blake, Brooks, Callan, Colthurst, Errington, Fay, Foley, Gabbett, Gray, McFarlane, McKenna, Martin, Meldon, Sir P. O'Brien, R. Power, Smithwick, P. J. Smyth, Synan. Foley, member for New Ross, was rather a Liberal than a Home Ruler, and when he ceased to be a member later in the year his seat was given to Mr John Redmond, son of Mr W. A. Redmond who was not re-elected.

Before the dissolution the Conservatives had a majority of 34 over Liberals and Home Rulers combined. The new House was officially classified as consisting of 349 Liberals, 243 Conservatives, and 60 Home Rulers, giving the Liberals a majority of 46 over Conservatives and Home Rulers combined. But, as nearly a score of Shawites would vote Liberal, Mr Gladstone could count on a majority of from 60 to 65.

It cannot be said that Parnell was popular with the majority of the party he now led, but all bowed to him because of his influence over the mass of the people outside the Whig and Fenian wire-pullers. The ordinary farmer believed Parnell could wring legislation from the Government to reduce rents and stop evictions, and he did not believe this of any other man. One of Parnell's first decisions was that he would never sit on the Government side of the House, but always on the Opposition side, to show that, as Irish leader, he had no affinity with either English party. Shaw and his friends now sat with the Liberal Government, as had been the custom under Butt, while Parnell and his friends sat with the Conservatives; and in this the Bishops and 'The Freeman' supported Shaw. Parnell's position was that he would always help any Opposition to put out any Government unless the Government were pledged to Home Rule. Though he did not command the balance of power, it was obvious that if he became master of the entire existing Home Rule party's sixty seats, and captured 20 or 25 other Irish seats from Liberals and

Conservatives, he would become arbiter of the House of Commons and could make and unmake Governments at will. Never since 1833 had either British party a sufficient majority over the other to enable it to carry on the Government without the aid of the Irish vote.

Parnell would have done far better at the elections if the dissolution had not been sprung on him while he was in the States. But he determined to make his following as formidable as possible, and now caused it to be distinctly understood that no follower of his was to accept office from any Government. Instead of being place-hunters, as all previous Irish parties were, they were to scorn the patronage of the Government. And henceforth in Nationalist Ireland "place-hunter" and "Castle hack" became titles of ignominy and shame. Better the dollars of the Irish servant girls of the States than the sovereigns of the British Treasury!

Michael Davitt now went to America and there formed a firm alliance with Patrick Ford of 'The Irish World,' by whom a large sum of money was collected and transmitted to the Land League in Dublin from time to time, to be used as Parnell thought fit for advancing the agitation secretly or openly. Parnell and Davitt at this time were each thirty-three years of age. A third man, named James Carey, who was even then evolving his schemes for helping the revolution entirely unknown to the public, was also thirty-three. Edmund Dwyer Gray was thirty-four. And Joseph Biggar was fifty-two.

Mr Gladstone, having become Prime Minister, appointed Earl Cowper Lord-Lieutenant and Mr

W. E. Forster Chief Secretary. Mr Forster was in the Cabinet but the Lord-Lieutenant was not; and the main responsibility of Irish Government devolved on Forster, of whom the Irish people knew nothing save that he was another English stranger come to make another muddle at Dublin Castle. The well-informed knew he was a Nonconformist, and largely responsible for the School Boards and undenomi-national elementary education in England, which did not make him welcome to a hierarchy whose platform was denominational education with the schools under ecclesiastical control. The people had high hopes of Mr Gladstone, remembering his recent visit to Dublin, his disestablishment of the Church, and his Land Act of 1870 which gave the tenant a right to compensation if evicted for any cause except non-payment of rent. But this general election had so altered their view of affairs that they looked rather to Parnell now than to the Government. Indeed the historical distinction of the general election of 1880 is that it brought Mr Parnell into power. Two months before the dissolution, Mr Gibson (now Lord Ashbourne), then Conservative Attorney-General, had prophesied that "the next Liberal ministry would be led by Mr Gladstone and driven by Mr Parnell."

The Duchess of Marlborough, before her withdrawal from Dublin, announced that her relief fund amounted to £112,484, of which she had expended £32,295 on seed potatoes and £60,882 on clothes, food, and other relief. The rival fund organised by Edmund Dwyer Gray and his wife at the Mansion House reached the total of £143,000, of which £110,000 had been expended in various forms of relief up to that date. The Mansion House Fund, despite Mr Parnell's disapproval, was an effort at self-help and advanced the revolution by making the Mansion House and the Lord Mayor a centre of social influence for the Nationalists.

A commission was now appointed to inquire into the Irish land question, Lord Bessborough being chairman and Mr Shaw one of the members; but the Parnellites denounced it on the grounds that it was composed of "landlords' men." And, when Mr P. J. Smyth, M.P., said it was foolish not to give it a fair trial, he was denounced as a traitor. The Government, yielding to Mr Parnell, introduced a Compensation for Disturbance Bill, originally promoted by Mr O'Connor Power, enabling tenants evicted for non-payment of rent to claim compensation from the landlords. Having passed the House of Commons, it was thrown out by the Lords, to whom, on this account, Mr Gladstone attributed all the subsequent disturbance. Mr T. P. O'Connor voiced Irish indignation by setting down a motion for the abolition of the hereditary chamber. But, even if the Bill had passed, I do not believe it would have prevented trouble, for any compensation evicted tenants might have claimed would have been overbalanced by their debt to the landlord.

The Conservatives now threw in their lot unreservedly with the landlords, Sir Stafford Northcote denouncing "the three F's"—fixity of tenure, free sale, and fair rent—as "fraud, force, and folly." Griffith's Valuation, that is, the valuation fixed by the Government for rating purposes, was now adopted by the Land League as the proper standard of rent, and tenants asked for reductions bringing their rents down to that figure. Mr T. D. Sullivan, one of the

new Parnellite members, was then writing a series of
verses called "Land League Lays" in 'The Nation,'
which the people were singing everywhere to old
Irish airs. The chorus of one of these, called
"Griffith's Valuation," ran :—

> "That's the word to say,
>   Down with confiscation,
> Not a cent we'll pay
>   But Griffith's Valuation."

Not far from my uncle's house, where I used often
to go in the holidays, many farmers and labourers
were wont to congregate every evening in the large
kitchen of the blacksmith's house which was open to
all comers. Cards were always being played at one
or more tables, and all the politicians and gossips of
the locality were to be found there discussing the
latest news of the fight between landlord and tenant.
I took a great interest in hearing what they said, and
I well remember the evening a young farmer rushed
into the house with that week's 'Nation,' which had
just arrived, and read aloud T. D. Sullivan's song
about Griffith's Valuation, amidst the applause of the
whole party, all the young men present learning the
words by heart afterwards and singing them.

The old Home Rulers were still against Parnell in
many places, and, where they held power, showed
their hostility. When his admirers in the Limerick
Corporation, for instance, proposed, on the first of
July, to confer the freedom of the city upon him,
the moderate party in the "City of the Violated
Treaty" strongly objected, and Mr Ambrose Hall,
a well-known Limerick merchant, said that Mr
Parnell had demoralised the Irish farmers by his
doctrines—an opinion held by many staunch Home

Rulers who admitted the justice of the farmers claims. The public, who filled the gallery of the city hall, raised an uproar at this, forced their way into the chamber, assaulted the opposing members, and broke up the meeting.

Towards the end of the session in August, in a debate arising out of Mr T. P. O'Connor's motion for abolishing the House of Lords, the first collision took place between Mr Forster and the Parnellites. The sturdy old Quaker charged Mr John Dillon with cowardice in inciting others to crime while he himself kept out of the grip of the law ; Dillon retorted in a characteristic speech ; and there was an angry scene. Parnell was waiting for the Government to declare its land policy, the Land League was growing fast, and events were happening which soon forced pious Liberals to gather up their skirts lest they should catch the contagion of crime which, to quote Mr Gladstone, dogged its steps.

At this moment an appalling murder took place, of which I heard a great deal when I entered Trinity College two months later. A undergraduate of Trinity, Mr Charles Boyd, or Charlie Boyd as he was called, when driving with his father on August 8th, near their home at New Ross, was shot dead by a party of disguised men. His father was a landlord, and the general conviction was that the assassins, in aiming at the father, had slain the son. Four tenants were arrested on suspicion, but no motive could be traced to them, as their relations with Mr Boyd were friendly, and they were released.

Just at the time of young Boyd's murder, the 'New York Herald' created a sensation by publishing details of the Irish Republican Brotherhood, or

Fenian Society, which it stated had 36,000 members in Ireland, and 12,000 in Great Britain—all pledged to achieve the independence of Ireland by physical force. At the same moment we, in county Cork, had the possibility of an armed insurrection brought home to us by a robbery of arms from a ship in Passage Docks, on the night of August 11th. On her way to America, with a quantity of guns amongst her cargo, she had put in for repairs, and a party of disguised men boarded her, locked up the captain and revenue officer, and, having taken forty-two of the guns, went quietly over the ship's side and rowed in their boat down the river. Neither the captain, nor the revenue officer, nor the crew of twenty - three men who were on board, gave any alarm, or took any steps to prevent the robbery or capture of the robbers. Loyalists ascribed this to the widespread feeling of terror then existing in Ireland. The Cork Land League passed a resolution denouncing the robbery, and expressing their belief that it was committed " by persons who desire to see a renewal of the Coercion Acts, and to give the Government good value for its secret service money." The Fenians were mysterious and smiled.

A fortnight later, when we were in the midst of the unfruitful harvest, we were shocked by the murder, not of a landlord by a tenant, but of one tenant by another, arising out of a quarrel between two half-brothers named Power, occupants of a small joint farm in county Mayo, about the boundaries of their portions. There was one of those joint farms on our bounds at Geyragh—the only survival in our district of what used to be a general custom. It was occupied by an uncle and nephew, each field belong-

ing to both parties. The whole farm belonged originally to the uncle's father, who had left it in common
to his two sons, giving each a share of each field.
And there were big stones to indicate which part
belonged to one and which to the other. It was
out of primitive arrangements like this, so conducive
to disputes, that the worship of Terminus originated
amongst the Romans; but no quarrel ever arose on
the joint farm near us, whose occupants were most
respectable and united. The Powers having quar-
relled, the younger brother, Kevin, summoned the
elder for assault. Soon afterwards they met in the
fields, and the elder brother, George, who happened
to be carrying a scythe, attacked Kevin, cut off his
head, and carried his savagery so far as to mutilate
the body. The act is worth mentioning, as it illustrates the fierce land hunger amongst the peasantry,
and how the wild justice of revenge was indifferently
directed against their own class and the landlords.

The word "boycotting" was not yet invented, but
the practice was, the first case which attracted general attention occurring in county Cork this summer.
Mr Bence Jones, a Protestant landlord near Bantry,
and director of the Munster Bank, had a dispute
with his tenants, and they decided to bring him to
reason by getting the public to refuse to deal with
him. The Cork cattle-dealers, who were enthusiastic
Land Leaguers, refused to buy Jones's cattle. Wherever he sent them, they came back unsold. At
length he decided to export them to England, and
put them secretly on board a cross-channel steamer
at Cork. But when the dealers heard they were on
board they refused to allow their cattle to be shipped,
and the company had either to put Jones's cattle

ashore, or let their steamer go almost empty, and be boycotted afterwards.

Jones's beasts were evicted, and he sent them to Dublin by rail, in the hope that they might pass unobserved in the stream of cattle continually leaving Dublin. But the emissaries of the Land League followed them, and warned the steamship companies. The London and North-Western Railway Company and the Dublin Steam-packet Company, both managed on old-fashioned business lines, divided the cross-channel cattle trade between them, and, after consultation, braved the Land League, and each took half the cattle to England. A year later, so strong had the Land League grown, that it is doubtful if even these companies would have accepted boycotted stock, and obnoxious persons had to send cattle to England *viâ* Belfast.

The treatment of this Cork landlord was only what Mr Parnell had publicly prescribed for those who broke the Land League law. On this as on every other subject his words as usual were so simple that he who ran might read and understand. At Ennis on September 19th, he said : " Keep a firm grip of your homesteads. . . . If 500,000 farmers strike against 10,000 landlords, I should like to see where they would get police and soldiers enough to make them pay. Now what are you to do with a man who bids for a farm from which his neighbour has been evicted ? " There were loud cries of " Shoot him ! " But Parnell continued : " I wish to point out to you a very much better way, a more Christian and more charitable way, which will give the lost sinner an opportunity of repenting. You must show him when you meet him on the roadside, in the

streets of the town, at the shop counter, in the
fair and market, and even in the place of worship,
by leaving him severely alone, by putting him into
a moral coventry, by isolating him from his kind
as if he were a leper of old—you must show him
your detestation of the crime he has committed, and
you may depend upon it there will be no man so
full of avarice, so lost to shame, as to dare the public
opinion of all right-thinking men, and to transgress
your unwritten code of laws."

There was a calculating and practical purpose in
everything he said, in striking contrast to the words
of all other political leaders of his day.   He was not,
like O'Connell and Butt, under the thumb of the
hierarchy.   Neither had he any business or profession to attend to, save that of politics, being
single-minded in this that he had no other objective than to acquire the government of Ireland
for himself and his obedient followers, to use it, as
he hoped, for the benefit of the people.   As the
most active of his lieutenants were as single-minded
as himself, he had not to cater for conflicting interests in his own party.   Unlike Mr Gladstone, he
was distracted by no side-issues, but concentrated
all his energies on one purpose, avoiding oratory as
if it were the plague, and never putting the land
question or Home Rule before the people except as
a matter of business.   He had to get money for his
organisation, convinced that money was power, but
he always told the people that in giving him money
they were going to make more money for themselves,
and, unlike other Irish leaders, he never expressed
any gratitude for subscriptions.

Three days after the Ennis meeting the persecution

of Captain Boycott began in county Mayo, and six
days after the meeting a murder occurred in the
same county, which created consternation in Ireland
and England, and changed the whole current of
Liberal feeling towards Parnell and the Land League.
On that day Lord Mountmorres was slain as he was
returning to his house, Ebor Hall, from a meeting
of magistrates at Clonbur in county Mayo. The
masterly manner in which this murder was done
showed the strong hand of a resolute secret society,
for, when his body was found at a place called
Rutheen, half a mile from his home, there was
evidence showing that he had been killed by a
volley of rifle bullets. Fenian authorities say that
Mountmorres and Lord Leitrim were both slain for
seducing, or trying to seduce, the daughters of some
of their tenants. But whether their offence was the
assertion of their right to rent, or of the *droit du
seigneur*, their assassination was equally abhorrent
to the law-abiding.

Within a fortnight of the Mountmorres murder,
that is, early in October, a hundred landlords and
land agents, almost all Conservatives, waited on the
Liberal Lord-Lieutenant and Chief Secretary at the
Castle to ask for protection for their lives and property, alleging that a reign of terror existed in the
country, and begging the Government to obtain
special parliamentary powers to curb the growing
lawlessness. In the discussion which arose in England about the "problem" presented to the Liberal
Government by such murders as those of Charles
Boyd and Lord Mountmorres, Lord Randolph
Churchill gave it as his unsolicited opinion that
the Irish problem was best described by the word

"Bosh," inasmuch as the agitation only wanted to be put down by a proper use of the existing law. This was to some extent a sound judgment, for the expectation of new coercive Acts causes negligence in administering the ordinary law, and has always been a disturbing force in Irish politics.

Almost while the landlords were asking for coercion, Mr Parnell declared at Kilkenny that the partnership between landlords and tenants was proved to be impossible. "One of them must go," he said in his usual simple way; "it is more easy to remove the few than the many." At Longford soon afterwards, he said to the people: "The extreme limit of our demands when the time comes must be measured by your exertions this winter"—which was an open inducement to the farmers to agitate during the winter, so that the Government might be forced to bring in a good Land Bill even if it were accompanied by a Coercion Bill.

The agitation was now proceeding with amazing energy, gigantic meetings being held every Sunday within a radius of ten or twenty miles of us, to which we sent official deputations and numbers of volunteers, the young farmers and labourers thronging to hear the orators as they would go to a circus. The entire system of keeping Sunday was changed. Bowling and dancing ceased. Those about to attend a distant meeting would attend first Mass, or, if they left before that, would hear Mass at the place of meeting, and, having spent the day out, would come home in the evening very excited and often under the influence of drink. On every occasion the place of assembly was given over to violent discussion, skylarking, and drinking. The police used to attend in force, even when they did not object to the meeting, their presence helping to prevent violence. Police note-takers also used to attend, and prosecutions often followed the speeches; but the police reporter's presence was always resented, the organisers refusing to admit him to the platform, the newspaper reporters refusing to stand or sit near him, and he had to be protected by police on the ground.

The Sunday Closing Act had the result, not foreseen by its promoters, of helping the land agitation. As the great majority at each meeting lived on the spot, they could not be served with drink at the public-houses, and the drinking was necessarily confined to the minority who were *bona-fide* travellers, that is to say, had slept three miles away on the preceding night. The result was that the vast majority were compulsorily sober, and the meetings were more effective than they would have been if held when the public-houses were open to all comers on Sundays. The agitation also gained by the fact that numbers travelled over three miles to the League meetings, because of their desire to qualify as *bona-fide* travellers, so as to get drink. Those who promoted the Sunday Closing Act were, if we except Mr A. M. Sullivan and one or two others, Protestant temperance reformers identified with the unpopular side in politics, but they rejoiced at having made Ireland more sober, even though the increased mental activity benefited their political opponents. Mr A. M. Sullivan used to say that "Ireland sober was Ireland free."

Ireland, however, was still far from the sober freedom longed for by Mr Sullivan. Drinking was the rule everywhere that men or women met. The farmers, who came into fair and market fresh, clean, and bright-looking at early morning, would all go home "disguised in liquor," and totally different men in the evening. Some were quiet, others noisy. But the case of the quiet men seemed the more pitiable of the two. They would drink all day after their business was over, and, when they could not take any more, they would stagger home on foot, if they lived near the town, "blind" drunk, recognising nobody. When their homes were far away they used to be driven from town, lying helpless in their carts. The wives, who rarely drank, patiently accepted this arrangement as a dispensation of providence, and took charge of the money. Of course there were many men who did not get drunk, but all took more or less liquor. If it were not for the amount of drink taken by so many of those prominent in the revolutionary movement, the results achieved could have been obtained without all the attendant strife, bloodshed, and suffering.

CHAPTER X.

EVERY Sunday in October there were great Land
League demonstrations addressed by Mr Parnell or
his chief lieutenants. On October 3rd there were
seventeen huge meetings, Mr Parnell himself addressing one at Cork, at which 30,000 people were present.
A deputation went from our town and I was amongst
the crowd who witnessed his triumph that day. Leaving the train at Blarney, he drove to Cork, so as to
come in by the Western Road. As he entered the
city, accompanied by a great procession and a vast
concourse of people, a remarkable incident occurred.
Seated in the carriage with him were Timothy
Cronin and John O'Brien, secretary and treasurer
of the Cork Land League, who had got the resolution passed condemning the robbery of arms at
Passage, O'Brien being a Midleton man and Cronin
a frequent visitor to our town, the first a draper
and the second a butter merchant. A group of
armed Fenians stopped the procession, dragged Cronin
and O'Brien from the carriage, and forbade them, on
pain of death, to take any part in the demonstration !
The procession then went on its way along the quays

and principal streets, with innumerable bands and
banners, Parnell receiving such an ovation as any
conqueror returning from a victorious campaign might
well have envied. All the windows were full and
many of the house-tops; and he went slowly along,
standing in his carriage and bowing to the people,
through miles of houses which seemed alive with
human faces and fluttering handkerchiefs waved by
enthusiastic girls, the thoroughfares being packed
with men cheering themselves hoarse. It was such
an outpouring of human sympathy as might well
turn a man's head. I saw him the recipient of many
other such public welcomes, but never again so
instinct with power, so redolent of victory, as he was
that day, when his graceful figure and aristocratic
features reminded one of a Greek god come to take
part in a festival organised by his votaries.

The hierarchy resented this adulation almost amounting, as I heard a parish priest say, to impious deifica-
tion; and, on October 10th, Cardinal McCabe issued
a pastoral in which, after pointing out that the
Government had shown its readiness to redress the
wrongs of the country, he pronounced the claim of
the Land League to be unjust, and denounced not
only those who committed agrarian murders, but also
those who failed to express their abhorrence of those
murders, which was interpreted as a scarcely veiled
allusion to Mr Parnell.

Six days after the pastoral, Mr Hutchinson, a landlord who lived near Skibbereen in county Cork, was
fired at as he was driving home from town. He
escaped with his life, but his driver was shot dead.
A few days later, at Blarney, four miles from Cork,
thirty disguised and armed men went to the house of
a farmer named Daly who had recently taken a farm

surrendered by a man named Murphy ; and, placing a book in Daly's hand, commanded him to swear that he would give up the land. Daly refused, and, though they threatened to take his life and fired shots over his head, persisted in the refusal. They did not go to extremities, but went off to Murphy's house and drove him in one of their cars to the farm, where they put him formally in possession, and drove all Daly's cattle off. Murphy said afterwards he was unwilling to retain the land, as he had given it up voluntarily to attend to other business. I give this as an instance of how the law of the Land League was now being enforced near us ; and not a day passed without cases like this in many parts of the country.

Parnell, with his usual prescience, foresaw that the Government at the Castle would soon be bound to do something to stop the agitation, and, speaking at Galway on October 24th, he said : " If they persecute the leaders of this movement, it is not because they want to preserve the lives of one or two landlords. Much the English Government care about the lives of one or two landlords ! It will be because behind this movement lies a more dangerous movement to their hold on Ireland—because they know that if they fail in upholding landlordism in Ireland, their power to misrule Ireland will go too. I wish to see the tenant farmers prosperous, but, large and important as this class of tenant farmers is, constituting with their wives and families the majority of the people of the country, I would not have taken off my coat and gone to this work if I had not known that we were laying the foundation in this movement for the regeneration of our legislative independence. Push on, then, towards this goal ; extend your organisation, and let every tenant farmer, while he keeps a grip on his holding, recognise also the great truth that he is serving his country and helping to break down English misrule in Ireland."

Bands of young men were now roaming by night over the country as in the time of the Whiteboys and Peep-o'-Day Boys. Grim practical jokes were played, as well as serious outrages such as burnings, maiming of cattle, firing into dwelling-houses, and not a few homicides. It was a common practice to dig a grave before the door of an evicting landlord, or to drag a landgrabber from his bed and fire a volley over his head in his own kitchen, while threatening letters were distributed in shoals.

After Parnell's Galway speech, the Government took serious action against the leaders of the Land League, and, on November 2nd, criminal informations were filed against Mr Parnell and thirteen of his colleagues—Joseph Biggar, M. Boyton, T. Brennan, John Dillon, Patrick Egan, Joseph Gordon, Matthew Harris, J. W. Nally, Malachi O'Sullivan, Thomas Sexton, P. J. Sheridan, T. D. Sullivan, and J. W. Walsh. The fourteen men thus prosecuted were, with Michael Davitt, the most active leaders of the Land League up to that date, and their names are classical in the history of the movement. In the action thus brought against them they were technically called "traversers," and the word was on all lips in Ireland while the prosecution lasted. The Attorney-General who led the prosecution was Mr Hugh Law, and, curious to relate, his son is now a member of Mr Redmond's party. The indictment against them consisted of nineteen counts, the chief of which was conspiring to prevent the payment of rents, the letting of vacant farms, and the due execution of legal processes, thereby creating ill-will between different classes of Her Majesty's subjects. Indignation meetings were held all over the country, and the Government "persecution" only increased public sympathy and admiration for the "traversers," who were now martyrs as well as heroes.

After the general election a branch of the Land League had been started in our town, the hard times driving the farmers to seek safety by falling into line with the rest of the country. The reports of Mr Parnell's and other speeches, and the doings of the League branches in other parts of Ireland, caused the newspapers to be read by ten people for the one who had read them before. And, as the younger generation educated in the National schools were very impressionable and ready to accept all printed matter which chimed in with their own ideals as more or less inspired, the daily or weekly newspaper leaped into the place occupied by the Bible in Great Britain. Every statement of the Land League leaders was accepted as Gospel truth by the people. The newspaper was their evangel, Mr Parnell their saviour, and his lieutenants their apostles. Print thus became for the first time an actuality for the Catholic peasants and part of their everyday life, speaking to them in a thrilling, palpitating language, intelligible—and there lay the marvel—yet different from anything previously known, for it enabled them to hear their friends at a distance talking to them in accents of power about the wondrous works of the Land League in regaining for them the independence filched from their ancestors.

I was not only present at the meeting at which our branch was founded, but composed the first report of the proceedings. It was held in the billiard-room of a public-house, and it was very hard to get enough of farmers to make a start. The owner of the house had been manager for a well-to-do young shopkeeper, a cousin of mine, who, having been connected with the Fenians, had to fly to America after the rising. This young Fenian's case illustrates the respectable class from which the rebels were drawn in our district. He had in his own right the largest ironmongery, seed, and guano stores in the town; and his elder brother, the first Catholic solicitor in our district, had not only the best practice in Midleton but was also coroner for the East Riding. The brothers belonged to the Moore family, which held many good farms from different landlords. The people spoke of Coroner Moore as reverently as if he were a priest, and he had great influence amongst them. The girls of one branch of the Moores were the only farmer's daughters who rode on horseback and wore riding costumes, being on that account considered partially mad by the farmers' wives and daughters, though they were as rational as their critics. The ex-Fenian, having come home, was now managing his own business, assisted by another ex-Fenian, an equally respectable man who had stood in the dock with comrades who had been sentenced to death and reprieved—the ordeal of his own trial and hearing sentence passed on his friends leaving an indelible imprint on his face, and determining him to take no part in politics but to devote all his spare time to religious observances.

The man in whose house the Land League was started had a good appearance and fluent address, and was the husband of a woman of much refinement. He spoke in the impressive American style, then very common in Ireland owing to the number of returned

Fenians, and acquired much influence as a political "boss." Farmers who could not say half-a-dozen English words in public to save their lives, but could speak volubly in Irish, regarded him as a conjurer or magician, while they held him in slight esteem as a man of business. He had mooted the idea of starting the branch, and for some years it brought a great deal of money to his house, which became the head centre of district politics; but in the end, like so many of the Land Leaguers, he lost both health and business.

It was market day, the streets being crowded with people, and I enthusiastically joined a group of canvassers going up and down, to and fro, urging farmers to come to the meeting. Most of them shrugged their shoulders, making various excuses, preferring to be with us in spirit and remain where they were, promising to drink health and long life to us. When the meeting at length assembled, the company were as awkward and nervous as a lot of horses promiscuously driven into a barn. My uncle, who feared lest he should be asked to become president, suddenly proposed my father, who was lifted bodily into the chair with loud applause. He said truly that the honour came upon him by surprise; he could not compliment them on their selection; he would leave the speechifying to more eloquent men, and would try to pour oil on the troubled waters and remember that speech was silver but silence was gold.

He sat down amid cheers, his audience deeming the few words he had spoken, especially the proverbs, as a marvellous achievement. The owner of the house was appointed secretary, and delighted the farmers by assuring them that they were the most down-trodden and, up to that moment, the most spiritless and good-for-nothing people in Ireland; but that henceforth, as members of a branch of the Land League, they would be a terror to tyrants and play a noble part in restoring Ireland to the position she once held as "first flower of the earth and first gem of the sea." Though it seemed like play, it was really an epoch-making incident, typical of what was then happening all over Ireland. I felt it epoch-making, not because of any prophetic instinct, but because I was of an age and hopeful disposition to which everything seemed epoch-making in the best sense of that much-abused word. None of us had any prevision of the extraordinary things which were to follow, for my father in particular and for the district in general, from the branch then started.

As it may not prove uninteresting to the reader to hear something of the dilemma in which an Irish Catholic youth found himself thirty years ago, I may be pardoned perhaps for referring to the trouble I had this year in deciding what profession I should adopt. My father desired me to be a solicitor. "You will have nothing to do," he would say, "but to take an office, put your name in the window and sit down inside. Somebody will soon pass the way and give you a case. Then it will be your own fault if you don't make your fortune." He never went to law himself, and believed that, if lawyers were excluded from Parliament, the law would be simple and the world happy. Yet he was most anxious to see me a practising solicitor in his own town.

I was drawn in three different directions. I loved the free life of the country on foot and in saddle, my experience of farming so far being confined to inspecting, criticising, and breaking-in a colt occasionally, a most fascinating pastime. I had a keen appreciation of literature and some ability in Latin and Greek, being now the head boy in the classical side at Midleton College, where I had got all the available prizes for classics. The headmaster, Doctor Thomas Moore, urged me to enter Trinity College, try for a high place at entrance, take the Midleton exhibition there and try to get one of the Junior University exhibitions in my first term; then read for a sizarship, and go in for a scholarship in my second year; all of which, in Doctor Moore's opinion, I was bound to get. After that, he said, my academic career was assured. "Instead of costing your father a lot of money and throwing yourself away by becoming a country attorney, you will have the whole world before you, a moderatorship or even a fellowship in Trinity, or a post in the first division of the Civil Service, or something in Oxford or Cambridge."

I went in for the Intermediate examination again in the summer of 1880, with the same result as in 1879, namely, honours and very high marks in the limited number of subjects I took up, but failure to secure an exhibition on my total. There was a special class in our school for boys preparing for the solicitors' apprentices' examination, and, in a disappointed mood one day, I joined it without asking the headmaster's leave. Seeing me in the class soon afterwards, as he passed through, he was surprised and displeased, exclaiming: "What are you fooling your time away here for, sir?" I answered that I had made up my mind to be a solicitor. He said nothing and went away; but a few days afterwards he called on my father and explained his views as to what I ought to do, with the result that my father consented to my entering Trinity

College. I entered Trinity in October 1880, and in my first term more than realised all Doctor Moore's expectations, which was a satisfaction to him after the Intermediate failure, and a victory for me.

It is a custom at Trinity College that the students presenting themselves for entrance are entertained at breakfast in the hall on the morning of the entrance examination. The College regulation says : " Every person desirous of becoming a student in arts must at his entrance place himself under the tuition of one of the tutor fellows who receive pupils. The collegiate interests of the pupil are under the guardianship of his tutor." I entered under Professor Mahaffy, who was at that time one of the popular tutors ; but the most popular tutor was Professor Gray, who could not take all the students who wanted to enter under him. On the morning of my entrance about a dozen of us assembled at Mahaffy's rooms, and after some conversation he took us across the square to the dining hall. I had never seen any of the students who assembled that morning for breakfast under their different tutors, and it would be a bootless task now to endeavour to trace what has become of them. Some are distinguished men, but the majority have disappeared from public view. Professor Mahaffy happily is still alive, as are also not a few other Junior Fellows of that date, including Dr Traill, the present Provost. But the Senior Fellows of that day are all dead—Galbraith and Sammy Haughton, the Home Rule Fellows, and John Kells Ingram, the Liberal Fellow, who wrote " Who fears to speak of Ninety-eight ? " against whose appointment to the provostship soon after the Fellows presented a memorial to Mr Gladstone. I often heard Dr Galbraith, attended by his inseparable satellite, Joshua Nunn, the college solicitor, discussing politics at Miss Thomson's tea-shop (now Harrison's) in Westmoreland Street. This old comrade of Butt did not approve of Parnell and the Land League. "You are in rebellion," he had said to Parnell in 1878. " Yes, but in justifiable rebellion," replied Parnell, who believed that laws were only made to be obeyed by other people, not by himself.

Mahaffy sat with us at breakfast, which was a very hospitable meal, and kept the conversation going gaily all the time. We had been studying the campaign of the Carthagenian general, Hamilcar, in Sicily ; and Mahaffy, sipping the admirable coffee, said he wondered what Hamilcar had to drink on the top of Mount Hercte when he was besieged by the Romans. One of the students, a Munster Catholic, said wittily that he supposed Hamilcar drank "mountain dew," which is an Irish name for potheen, or illicit whisky. Mr Mahaffy laughed heartily, and doubtless told the story at the Viceregal Lodge at his next visit. Mr Mahaffy was called "the general" at that time, because he was said to have dubbed himself "the best generally educated man in Europe." He had just been to Greece, and had returned with the news that the King of Greece was "the nicest king he knew." Almost as I write these lines, thirty-two years after that entrance day, Dr Mahaffy is hob-nobbing with the same King of Greece at Athens. The student who amused us that morning had a curious career, first becoming a lawyer and then a priest, and, alas, developing a taste for "mountain dew" which led him to an early grave.

All through this October readers of the newspapers had been constantly hearing of a Captain Boycott, agent for the Earl of Erne's property in Mayo, and also farming on his own account at his place near Lough Mask. The Erne tenantry refused to pay unless they got reductions, as Mr Parnell had advised them, and Boycott sent a bailiff in September to serve them with notice to quit for the following March. The tenants raised a hue and cry, and hunted the bailiff to his house, where they besieged him. Then they warned all Boycott's servants to leave his employment ; warned the local shopkeepers not to sell him any goods ; warned the blacksmith and other tradesmen not to work for him. Even the laundress refused to wash his clothes, the postboy to carry his letters, and bearers of telegrams were waylaid and the messages taken from them. This was a literal carrying out of Parnell's advice that obnoxious persons should not be shot but " shunned as if they were lepers of old."

Major Edward Saunderson, Captain Somerset Maxwell, Colonel Lloyd, and other Loyalists collected funds from the Ulster landowners and organised a corps of five hundred armed Orangemen to march to Boycott's assistance. Although Saunderson was then a Liberal, having sat for county Cavan as a Liberal in the Parliament of 1868-74, Mr Forster warned him that he would not allow so large a body of armed Orangemen to go from Ulster into Connaught for fear it would cause a civil war. He would, however, allow as many men as Boycott wanted for the saving of his crops, which were in danger of being lost.

Fifty Orangemen went with Saunderson and his friends, but the Government sent several regiments of infantry and cavalry, and even artillery, and hundreds of police, to protect the " emergency men," as they were called. The Land Leaguers played practical jokes on the invaders, and there were several false alarms, but no opposition was given to the saving of Boycott's crops, and after a fortnight's sojourn the emergency men returned home on the 26th of November.

Twenty years after this incident, when Colonel Saunderson was leader of the Irish Unionists, he talked it over with me at Castle Saunderson, and it was his opinion that if Forster had allowed the five hundred to go in the first instance, so large a force, coming spontaneously to the relief of a land agent, would have proved to the Mayo Land Leaguers that the Loyalists were able and determined to defend their friends, and the demonstration would have given the Land League a set-back at its place of origin. But a few men, coming under the protection of a large force of soldiers and police, gave the Mayo peasants the impression that the landlords were entirely dependent on the British Government. Captain Boycott wrote to Mr Gladstone asking for compensation, but the request was peremptorily re- fused. And inasmuch as, when the emergency men left Mayo, Boycott and his family elected to go with them, the affair was a moral victory for the Land League, and proved that Parnell's policy of " isolating " a breaker of the Land League law was more efficacious than murder.

Parnell had now become so important in the national life that, when he shaved off his beard about this time, it caused as much discussion as the shaving of the Kaiser's moustache would cause in Germany to-day. Lord Cowper's opinion of him at this stage is instructive : " He had no second, no one at all near him. I should say the next man to him was Davitt, but a long way off. We thought Mr Healy clever, but he did not trouble us much. Mr Dillon used to go about making speeches, but our view of him was that somehow he was always putting his foot in it. Our attention was concentrated on Parnell. We did not think he was instigating outrages. We thought he connived at them. We believed he would stop at nothing to gain his end, and we believed his end was separation. I think he was very English. He had neither the virtues nor the vices of an Irishman. His very passion was English, his coolness was English, his reserve was English."

That he was English and American is true, but that he was "more Irish than the Irish themselves" is also true. For no man then in Ireland so delighted in taking the hardest and straightest road to his ideal goal, and none so rigorously condemned the English arts of accommodation and compromise.

CHAPTER XI.

DOINGS OF THE MIDLETON LAND LEAGUE.   CARRYING
THE LAND WAR INTO ULSTER.

WHILE the emergency men were at Boycott's,
Henry Wheeler, son of a land agent, was brutally
murdered on November 12th near Limerick Junction
in the county Tipperary.   Six months earlier, near
the scene of this murder, the Sheriff and Resident
Magistrate, with a large force of police, went to carry
out an eviction.   The farmer to be evicted held a
large farm, and owed £750 for something over a
year's rent, most of the farmers here being well-to-do,
and the land, perhaps, the most fertile in Ireland.
When the officers of the law came near the farmstead
they found the house barricaded with felled trees, and
the tenant's wife, speaking from an upper window,
threatened them with violence if they proceeded
farther.   When they tried to effect an entry they
were beaten off with pitchforks, molten lead, boiling
water, and stones.   Returning to the charge, they
battered down the door and found twenty-three men
inside armed with hatchets and scythes, of whom ten
escaped and thirteen were arrested.

These murders, outrages, and resistance to the law
made Home Rulers of many timid Radicals in England, while in Ireland they gave new life to the

physical force men. All human sympathy was frozen up, the only point of view from which a murder was regarded being its effect on the progress of the revolution. Irishmen who protested against shocking public opinion in England were met by Parnell's dictum that nothing was to be lost but much gained by that operation. Colonel Gordon, then only known to fame as Chinese Gordon, visited Ireland at this time and wrote in the newspapers that the antipathy between landlords and tenants could not be bridged over, that the people in the west were worse off than the Chinese, Indians, or Anatolians, and suggesting that the Government should buy eleven of the worst counties and manage them as a Crown estate. But even if this were done it would not dispose of men like the Traversers or the physical force party behind them.

The Traversers applied for a postponement of their trial on December 4th, and Lord Chief-Justice May, refusing the application, made some remarks which were considered prejudicial. Whereupon Mr Dillon denounced him as " a cowardly liar and an ermined ruffian "; but the judge took no notice of the attack until the day of trial three weeks afterwards. May was one of those old-fashioned Tories who seemed stunned by the audacity of the new politicians. Seeing their party out of power, such men used to become almost apoplectic when they had to allude to the revolution which they saw in progress.

A brief account of the doings of our branch of the Land League will indicate the social changes which incensed men like Chief-Justice May. When the branch had been some time established, the committee decided to interfere in other matters besides agrarian disputes. My father did not approve of this, but he yielded to the majority and saw no reason to retire from the chairmanship. First they resolved that Colonel Roche, a country gentleman who had long been chairman of the Guardians, should be set aside in favour of a tenant farmer. The Board of Guardians was the one public body in which land-lords, farmers, and shopkeepers met together—the Grand Juries being almost entirely composed of land-lords. There was a large percentage of *ex officio* Guardians, mostly landlords appointed by the Local Government Board, but these were now outvoted, and "a man of the people" put into the chair for the first time. It was afterwards decided to depose the chair-man of the Town Commissioners, a wealthy Catholic merchant who rode to hounds, owned race-horses, and kept a carriage and pair with liveried servants for his wife. He was not extreme enough for the Land Leaguers, though his interests were identical with those of the farmers; and accordingly a shopkeeper was elected in his place. The Land League of course remained the supreme authority over both bodies. It is only the bare truth to say that this meant a revo-lution in Midleton, and there was great elation over both popular victories. As the names of streets were being changed all over Ireland, George Streets and William Streets becoming Brian Boru, Wolfe Tone, or Parnell Streets, we named a new bridge in a new road, constructed to give employment during the winter of 1879, John Dillon Bridge.

But the most daring revolution attempted by our branch was in connection with the monthly fair. The conduct of Lord Midleton displeased the committee. It was not that he was an evicting landlord, for I do not remember a single eviction on his estate—it was

simply that they wanted to bring him down because
he was an absentee whose existence they regarded
as an offence which " smelled to Heaven." The
Midleton property was not a large one, the income
then, including town rents, being said to be only
£6000 a-year. When there were only four fairs in
the year, Lord Midleton used to farm out the tolls
to a townsman, who paid him a lump sum and made
a considerable profit over; but, when the monthly
fairs were established, he determined to become his
own collector. The toll-farmer used to have men at
the four roads leading out of the town collecting tolls
on all animals sold, so that it was the buyer who paid,
unless otherwise arranged, and unsold animals were
allowed home free. When the monthly fairs were
established, Lord Midleton compelled all cattle to be
driven into an enclosed green and demanded tolls at
entry, so that cattle had to be paid for whether sold
or not. To effect this he got the police to prevent
farmers from standing their cattle on the streets, as
had been the immemorial custom. But, in any case,
the dealers favoured the new arrangement, because
it was more orderly and relieved them of liability for
tolls, and it became established just before the Land
League, when the people were quiescent.

The branch now passed a resolution that Lord
Midleton's fair green was to be boycotted, and the
cattle-dealers, being enthusiastic Land Leaguers,
joined in making the decree effective. At the first
fair after this decision, as the people drove their
cattle into the town, they were told not to go into
the fair green but to stand them on the streets. The
gentlemen-farmers and other non-Land Leaguers went
into the fair green, but no dealer followed them in,

and they took their stock home unsold. There was great rejoicing after the first fair held in this fashion, the dealers being in high good humour and the farmers well satisfied with having escaped tolls and scored off the absentee. This procedure was followed for a number of fairs, and Lord Midleton once again called the police to his assistance. The constables took the names of parties standing cattle in the street, but, as everybody was equally guilty, I do not remember that any one was actually proceeded against.

Nor was this all. Lord Midleton kept the only public weighing-machine, and did a large business in weighing hay, straw, corn, and other commodities. The branch now purchased and set up a public weighing-machine of its own ; and Lord Midleton's machine, which used to be so busy that he kept a man specially to attend to it, then became rusty and grass-covered and the man had no employment. The Land League machine, on the other hand, fixed in the Secretary's yard, was kept busy, and I have seen people waiting in a *queue* to get their stuff weighed, and paying a fee for every transaction. Any one who used Lord Midleton's machine was warned, and, if he offended again, was boycotted. These were some of the notable signs of the power of the Land League in our district, and it was so all over Ireland, except in the north-east.

The storm of agitation passing over the country was naturally a serious detriment to business. The Danes were taking advantage of our troubles to deprive us of our pre-eminence in the butter and bacon trade of the United Kingdom. The bad times due to the importation of foreign meat, then a new and disturbing feature in British agriculture, bad weather, poor harvests, and cheap grain which scarcely paid for its tillage, owing partly to inferior quality and partly to the importation of foreign grain, instead of rousing the farmers to fresh effort, only made them more distracted and listless. The landlords continued to demand full rents; the tenants, acting on Mr Parnell's advice, refused to pay more than Griffith's valuation and got large abatements in many cases. But these individual gains were of little moment when compared with the national loss caused by the general neglect of business.

It must not be imagined that, while the tenants were thus carrying on the war, the landlords, on their part, were inactive. No less than 2110 families, making a total of 10,657 individuals, were evicted, or, as Mr Gladstone put it, " sentenced to death," in this eventful year 1880, as compared with 6239 individuals in 1879, 4679 in 1878, and 2177 in 1877. The number of emigrants was 95,857 as against 47,364 in 1879, the great increase, more than double, being a proof of the bitter reality of the distress. The young people were losing hope, and many entire families who could afford it also emigrated. Since 1851 the number of emigrants had been 2,637,187, most of whom had gone to the United States, where every one that was successful acted like a magnet to draw one or more relatives out of Ireland. The number of outrages, which was only 236 in 1877, was 2590 in 1880. During the ten months from March, when Parnell returned from the States, till the end of the year, there were seven murders, twenty-one cases of firing at persons, and sixty-two cases of firing into dwellings reported by the police.

CARDINAL McCABE.

"Cullen used to keep Butt and the Home Rulers in leading strings, but McCabe, having no personal magnetism and small influence on public opinion, was unequal to such a task."—PAGE 60.

The Head Land League, by way of counterblast to the Boycott relief expedition, issued an address to the people of Ulster on December 7th, hoping to win recruits by putting the Land League programme before the farmers of the north. They kept Home Rule entirely in the background, and described the Land League as "a struggle pure and simple between the tenants and their friends on the one side and the landlords, Protestant and Catholic, and their supporters on the other"; and assured the Ulster farmers that the question of religion did not enter into the dispute, which indeed seemed quite true up to that time, appealing for proof to the recent elections, in which they said "Catholic gentlemen of the staunchest type and oldest families were unseated solely on account of their not being sufficiently advanced on the question of Land Reform."

It was a curious coincidence that on the day after the issue of the address, December 8th, James Mulholland, a bailiff, was shot dead near Cookstown in county Tyrone, in the middle of Ulster, when he was on his way to serve an ejectment, which was the first proof the public had that the principles of the Land League had penetrated into the heart of the Protestant north-east. Cookstown, it is but right to add, is a neighbourhood in which Protestants and Catholics are about equal in numbers. After this there were many Land League meetings in Ulster, at all of which the pecuniary profits to be made by the Land Agitation were continually explained, while Home Rule was hardly ever mentioned.

On the day of the Cookstown murder, Mr Parnell received the freedom of the city of Waterford, whose citizens are proud to call it the *Urbs Intacta*, his speech, as usual, being simple and sensible.   He advised the Nationalist ratepayers to take an active interest in local government, and advocated the substitution of bodies of elected ratepayers for the unrepresentative, sheriff-nominated Grand Juries—a reform which has since been accomplished.   He prophesied that "self-government would be fully restored to the Irish people in five or six years"—a prophecy which was realised in a sense, because exactly five years and four months from that date Mr Gladstone introduced his first Home Rule Bill. Mr Parnell's private secretary, Mr T. M. Healy, and Mr J. W. Walsh, one of the Traversers, were tried at Cork assizes a week after this for having "intimidated" a farmer who had taken land from which another had been evicted.   Healy and Walsh were only putting Mr Parnell's policy about land-grabbers into practice, and the jury found them not guilty, at which there were public rejoicings in Cork.

The Irish Parliamentary Party, as it was now called, met and re-elected Mr Parnell as its sessional leader on December 27th, the day before the trial of the Traversers began at Dublin, and also formally resolved to sit on the Opposition side of the House, irrespective of what English party might compose the Government, this resolution and the refusal to take office being the corner-stones of Parnell's power in the House of Commons.   If either party proposed anything advantageous to Ireland it was to be supported, but it was clearly understood that Irish support was never to be given except in return for a price.   Mr Parnell, more than any other Irish leader, taught the Irish people to expect payment on the nail in politics, and that is why the Land Agitation

was more selfish and successful than any of its predecessors, every step being calculated with an eye to
resultant profit.

When Mr Parnell and his fellow-traversers were
arraigned in court on December 28th, Lord Chief-
Justice May announced that he would take no part
in the trial owing to the "misconstruction" which
had been put upon his remarks by Mr Dillon; and the
trial proceeded before Judge Fitzgerald and Judge
Barry (a Midleton College man), both Roman Catholics
and most able lawyers. The Lord Chief-Justice's
retirement was acclaimed as another victory for the
Land League, and there was great difficulty in getting a jury to try the case. Numbers of Dublin
jurors refused to attend, preferring to pay a fine, or
even run the risk of imprisonment, rather than incur
the greater danger of being called upon to pronounce
a verdict on the Uncrowned King and his colleagues.
After a certain number of jurors had been "challenged"
by the Crown and others ordered to "stand by" by
the Traversers, there were just twelve men left, and
with these the trial began.

CHAPTER XII.

FORSTER'S COERCION ACT.   IMPRISONMENT OF DAVITT.
THE LADIES' LAND LEAGUE.   ARCHBISHOP CROKE.

AT the opening of 1881, the hopes of the Loyalists
were revived at seeing Alderman Moyers, a Conservative and Protestant, installed as Lord Mayor of
Dublin in succession to Mr Gray. The State trials,
as they were called, were proceeding in the city.
Enormous crowds used to escort Mr Parnell and his
fellow-traversers to court every morning, and accompany them to the Land League office in the evening.
When Parliament opened on January 7th, and the
members of Parliament left for Westminster, the
public lost interest in the trials, which ended, on
January 25th, in a disagreement of the jury. Judge
Fitzgerald said in his charge that the Land League
was an illegal association, but the Government took
no action and the League continued to gain in
numbers and strength all through the spring and
summer. Two jurors were against and ten in favour
of acquittal, and the Loyalist party deemed it a
victory to have secured a disagreement.

In Parliament Mr Forster gave notice that he would
introduce a Coercion Bill. Mr Gladstone a little
later, having declared that "with fatal and painful
precision the steps of crime dogged the steps of the

Land League," claimed precedence for the measure over all other business, including a promised Land Bill. Mr Parnell, fresh from Dublin, entreated the House not to allow itself to be made once more "the catspaw of landlords." Mr Forster said the number of outrages in 1880 was 600 in excess of the largest number in any year since 1844; but, on being pressed, admitted that 1327 were threatening letters. He said the Government considered the situation so serious that they had increased the number of troops in Ireland from 19,000 to 26,000.

Amongst those who supported Mr Parnell against coercion was Charles Russell, an Irishman, destined afterwards to be the first Roman Catholic Lord Chief-Justice of England in modern times, who then represented Dundalk as a Liberal. Mr Parnell won the approval of all sections of Home Rulers by his speech against the Coercion Bill. Even The O'Donoghue, who had disowned his obstructive policy and used to be counted as a Liberal, said he had united all his countrymen. Mr Litton, K.C., Liberal member for county Tyrone, approved of the programme of the Land League while he condemned its methods.

The Conservatives united against Parnell with the Government, but fifty-seven members followed him into the lobby. Out of 102 Irish members present, he carried forty-eight Home Rulers and three Liberals with him, and caused twenty-nine Liberals to abstain from voting, thus influencing eighty Irish votes, which was so far his greatest achievement as leader.

Mr Forster, in moving the first reading of his Protection of Life and Property Bill, said "the Land League was supreme and there was a real reign of terror over the whole country"; and asked for power "to arrest *mauvais sujets* and keep them in prison in order that they might be prevented from tyrannising over their neighbours." The essence of the measure was a suspension of the Habeas Corpus Act, giving the executive the power of arrest without legal trial, on the ground that juries were refusing to convict popular offenders. Dr Lyons, the Liberal who had ousted Sir Arthur Guinness from the representation of the city of Dublin, moved that the Bill be postponed until after the introduction of the Land Bill. This was seconded by Mr Givan, Liberal member for county Tyrone, but was defeated. Then began the open war between Parnell and the Liberal Government. Next day the Parnellites began a course of vehement obstruction, with an all-night sitting lasting for twenty-two continuous hours. In consequence of this Mr Shaw and fifteen of his friends seceded from the Nationalist Party and refused to follow Parnell's leadership.

Mr Gladstone had now a difficult part to play in Ireland. So great was the distrust of him entertained by Irish Protestants that, when Dr Humphrey Lloyd, the distinguished Provost of Trinity College, died on January 17th, the Fellows took an extraordinary step to prevent the possible appointment of Dr Ingram, the Liberal Fellow to whom I have referred, to the princely position with its stipend of £3000 a-year and the splendid Provost's House. The post is in the gift of the Premier, but the Fellows at once selected as their Head Dr Jellett (a Midleton College man), then Senior Lecturer, and forwarded a memorial to Mr Gladstone informing him of their choice and protesting against the appointment of any other person. Mr Gladstone yielded and gave the post to "the stern and unbending Tory."

Mr Michael Davitt, on February 2nd, fiercely attacked " the renegades who had abandoned Mr Parnell in the face of the enemy"; and Mr Forster, wishing to encourage the Shawites, had Davitt arrested next day at Dublin, taken to England, and lodged in a convict prison to complete his sentence of penal servitude. This method of procedure was more severe and disgraceful than the trial for sedition formerly commenced against him, having moreover the advantage of rendering a fresh trial unnecessary. Many of the landlords thought the Land League, thus deprived of its founder, would speedily collapse in the west where it was strongest, but in this hope they were deceived. Mr Davitt became a martyr as well as a hero, and all over Ireland the ballad-mongers at the fairs and markets used to sing: "Although poor Michael Davitt is now in convict jail, his heart is with poor, dear old Ireland still!" The movement was now independent of the leaders, resting on the double basis of fallen prices and aroused ambitions.

On the day after Davitt's arrest, Mr Dillon refused to give way to Mr Gladstone when called on by the Speaker, and was suspended. Mr Gladstone then moved a resolution giving the majority of the House power to declare any specific business "urgent," and giving the Speaker absolute power to regulate and end the debate as he thought fit when urgency had been declared. Parnell rose and moved that Gladstone be no longer heard! The Speaker refused to put the motion. Parnell insisted and was suspended. Then 32 Irish members refused to leave the House for the division on Gladstone's motion, and they were all suspended and removed by the Sergeant-at-arms.

The Coercion Act became law on March 2nd, 1881,

and was to continue till September 30th, 1882, the hope being that before that time the promised Land Bill would have ended the agitation. Mr John Dillon said in the House on March 3rd that if reasonable methods failed, the old forcible methods must be resorted to. Sir William Harcourt, the Home Secretary, charged Mr Dillon with having, under the privilege of Parliament, advised Irish farmers to shoot those who attempted to evict them ; whereupon Mr Edmund Dwyer Gray and Mr M'Coan dissociated themselves from Mr Dillon. Mr Timothy Healy, defending Mr Dillon, twice called Sir William Harcourt a liar, and was suspended by a majority of 233 to 15.

Meantime there was keen speculation amongst landlords and tenants as to what further concessions were to be given in the forthcoming Land Bill. Lord Dufferin, before returning to his embassy at St Petersburg in January, sent a note to the Bessborough Commission declaring his opposition to the three F's, but advocating the forced sale of encumbered estates, the lending by the Government to the tenants on such estates of money to buy their farms at the market value, and the appointment of an impartial tribunal to fix fair rents. This was the first suggestion from the landlords that the State should assume the right to fix the rent of land.

The leaders of the Land League continued to preach their fascinating gospel. Mr Thomas Brennan said the Land League was founded on the political economy of John Stuart Mill and the moral teaching of the Bible ; and at Carlow, on March 20th, in company with Mr E. D. Gray, said that the child born yesterday in the lowliest house there had as much right to the land as the wealthiest landlord. On the same day at Woodford Mr Dillon denounced the man who took an evicted farm as "a traitor, a swindler, and a robber with whom no honest man or his children could deal."

The Arms Bill, having proceeded simultaneously with the Coercion Bill, became law on March 21st, and proved a trump card for the Government in coping with the revolution, as it made it practically impossible for a Nationalist to get a licence to carry a gun, and thus reduced the death-roll of the Land War. During the first half of this year there were continual frays at evictions and process-servings. At one of these encounters, near Gurteen in county Mayo, when a process-server was attacked, the people killed a policeman and the police killed two young farmers, members of the Land League. And soon afterwards at Kiltimagh, in the same county, at a similar disturbance, the police killed a farmer's daughter and wounded another girl. This excited the passions of the Land Leaguers to white heat, and their verbal and printed denunciations of the Government passed all bounds. A public funeral of enormous dimensions was given to the two Land Leaguers killed at Gurteen, at which Mr John Dillon preached the funeral oration, saying: "May their blood and the curses of their children be on the heads of Forster and Gladstone who refused to hearken to our repeated warnings!"

On the passage of the Coercion Act, Miss Anna Parnell started the Ladies' Land League and became its first president—the idea being that, if the leaders were thrown into jail, the work might be carried on by women. It was the first time that the Catholic women of Ireland had been asked to join a political organisation. Cardinal McCabe, in whose diocese the Ladies' League was started, at once denounced it as "immodest and wicked"; but Archbishop Croke came to its rescue, determined that the hierarchy should not be left out of this new female movement, as it had been left out of the Land League. Soon after this Mr Parnell, accompanied by Mr James O'Kelly, visited Paris, whither Mr Patrick Egan, the Fenian Treasurer of the Land League, had removed all his books and funds for safe-keeping. They called on M. Rochefort and Victor Hugo in order to distract the attention of the newspapers from their real business, but they did not succeed in getting Hugo to make any declaration in their favour.

The Archbishop of Cashel's defence of the Ladies' Land League was a most important event. It was not for love of the British Government that the high ecclesiastics opposed the Land League, but rather because it originated with men who were not sufficiently submissive to their authority. Cardinal McCabe had several times pronounced against it, and the great majority of the bishops hesitated to oppose one who was in such close touch with Rome, believing that he knew what was best for their order. The result was that the hierarchy and priesthood had now for nearly two years found themselves flouted every Sunday by the Land League, in whose great meetings and triumphs they had no part. Our parish priest, Father Fitzpatrick, under whom Dr Croke once served as curate, continuously disparaged the Land League from the altar, and made more than one personal attack on my father. He discouraged the meetings, but nevertheless they were held, and those who attended had a glorious feeling that they were defying an authority of which hitherto they had been so much afraid.

Archbishop Croke actually saved the situation for his order; and, as the Catholic laity had been so used to ecclesiastical leadership that it gave them an uncanny feeling to be deprived of it, Croke's adhesion was accepted with gratitude and he became a popular idol and formidable rival to Mr Parnell. The bishop who thus brought the Land League within the net of ecclesiastical polity was a county Cork man, a native of Mallow, which, as well as Midleton, is in the diocese of Cloyne. He was a tall and strongly-built man, with what readers of 'Punch' are trained to regard as an "Irish" face—that is to say, short nose, long upper lip, and cheek-bones of great width and prominence. He was warm-hearted, generous and impulsive, but could be very tyrannical when it suited his purpose, as I knew from the sufferings of some friends in Thurles. I saw something of him as a child, when he was parish priest of Doneraile, where my stepmother's people lived, and was soon to meet him again. He was a distinguished theologian, having spent three years as professor in the Irish College at Rome and four years in New Zealand as Bishop of Auckland before he got the rich archdiocese of Cashel in 1875.

Not long after this he took another epoch-making step by preaching a crusade for reviving the old Irish field games, especially hurling or hockey, and becoming patron of the Gaelic Athletic Association, which, though it was not at first perceived, became a serious rival to the National League. I heard many priests say that those games prevented the young men from thinking about politics and economics, with the possibility that they might go on to think about Church government and religion. The hurling matches being always held on Sundays clashed with the political meetings, and often, when a political demonstration was announced, the young men were engaged for a hurling or football match—the crowds at these Sunday matches being proportionately as large as at Saturday football matches in Great Britain. Though the political leaders refrained from disapproval, they perceived the object, or at any rate the probable result, of Dr Croke's policy and were by no means rejoiced.

Mr Parnell and the Land League were now supreme in three and a half of the four provinces. When a farm became vacant the man who made an offer for it did so at the risk of his life, unless he had got the sanction of the local branch of the League, which, in too many cases, was obtainable by favouritism and bribery. Vacant land was to be found on all sides, which many would have gladly taken but for the ban of the League, under whose patronage evicted tenants became a scourge and a terror to the country. Solvent men feared not merely to take new land but to pay their rent for what they held, and the estrangement between owners and occupiers had so widened and deepened that it was dangerous to be seen speaking courteously to a landlord or agent. Such was the revolution which had come about in the space of three years.

CHAPTER XIII.

PERSONAL REMINISCENCES. THE BOYCOTTING OF
OURSELVES.

THE Midleton branch of the League resolved, in
accordance with Parnell's policy, that the tenants
on each estate should combine and refuse to pay
their rents unless they got substantial reductions.
My father had the rent ready to pay, and nothing
would have given him greater pleasure than to pay
it ; but he was bound by the decision of the Longfield tenants not to pay unless they got a reduction
bringing the rents almost down to Griffith's valuation. He got the customary notice that the agent
would attend to receive the half-year's rent ; the
agent came ; the tenants asked timidly for the reduction agreed upon ; and the reply was that the
application could only be considered if the rents were
first paid in full. The tenants then left without
paying, the agent went home empty-handed — an
unprecedented occurrence over which there was much
jubilation — and my father and his fellow-tenants
remained true to their combination, though almost
all of them could have paid.

One day in March, between Patrick's Day and
Lady's Day, my father went to Cork to a meeting
of the city Land League. While in Dublin I had

visited the headquarters branch in Upper Sackville Street—the drawing-room floor of Number 39, having the painted figure of a large nigger, the sign of the ground-floor tobacconist, between the windows—with feelings somewhat resembling those of a pious Moslem entering the shrine of Mahomet at Mecca. But while my sympathies were with my kith and kin, I never ceased to see the landlord, Protestant, and British side of the case. I was now supposed to be reading at home for an examination; but, instead of poring over classics, I was constantly out with some harriers I had recently acquired, and on this particular day I was walking through the fields in search of the cowboy to run a drag. Standing on a fence, I noticed at a distance two strange men apparently looking for somebody, and thought they were dealers come to buy cattle.

As I hurried towards them, I perceived something sinister and shady in them which I did not like. I asked what they wanted, and they replied by asking who I was. When I told them, they handed me a writ setting forth that judgment had been marked against my father for several hundred pounds, the amount of a half-year's rent and costs, and inquired if I was prepared to pay them. I had not more than a few shillings about me, and was completely staggered by the demand; but I bore myself as I thought befitted a man of means, who always carried several hundred pounds about him, but would not condescend to produce it to suit the convenience of such vulgar fellows, and, having a general notion that the proper thing to do was not to accept service, I handed back the writ.

Just as I did so, I saw all the milch cows rush into

the yard followed by three villainous-looking men
with long sticks, and it dawned on me that our
cattle were being seized for non-payment of rent.
This was not only the first practical illustration of
the land war which I had, but it was the first on
our estate or within a radius of some miles. The
cows were trying to get into their accustomed stalls,
but the strange men were driving them back and forc-
ing them across the yard to a lane leading to the public
road. Our labourers refused to let the cows pass out.
The sheep-dogs were barking; my harriers, confined
in a barn, began to give tongue; the geese were
shrieking; some of the women in the yard were
crying aloud; all of which made an extraordinary
din in that usually quiet place.

The sheriff's bailiffs told our working-men that, if
they obstructed the officers of the law, they would be
sent to prison; but the men, with a traditional Irish
hatred of bailiffs, would not give way. Neither
would the women. Thereupon one of the bailiffs, putting his two fingers in his mouth, gave a loud whistle,
and in a few moments six men of the Royal Irish
Constabulary with rifles came trotting up the lane.
At this unexpected sight our men stood aside, and
the cattle were driven into the lane helter-skelter,
the constabulary men standing close by the fence to
let them pass.

I knew father was pledged not to pay the rent, but
I thought it would be well to let him know what
was happening. I ran to the stable, and, putting
the bridle on a roan mare that was already saddled,
brought her out, determined to ride into town and
telegraph to my father. The head bailiff caught the
mare's bridle, saying : " I seize this mare for the rent

along with the cattle." I declared the mare was
mine, and if he seized her it would be an illegal
act. It appears this was the best thing I could have
said, for there is nothing bailiffs fear so much as making a wrong seizure. He let the bridle go and I rode
down the lane ; but at the end of it two constabulary
men, who knew me well, blocked my way and said :
" We will not let you go into the town to create a
disturbance." I assured them I only meant to wire
to my father. They hesitated, I struck the mare and
dashed off, just as the sergeant cried, " Do not let
him go ! " They called after me to stop, but I rode
as if for my life, passing by the cattle and the
drovers. As I galloped along I told everybody I
knew that our cattle had been seized, and reached
Midleton telegraph office in ten minutes.

After consultation with some sapient Land Leaguers,
who said that my father was with the inner circle at
Cork, and whatever he might do on their advice
was sure to be right, I sent the following telegram :
" Cattle seized for rent and now on their way to
Cork." Cork was thirteen miles away, and I knew
that the landlord could not possibly sell the cattle
anywhere but there. When the telegram had gone,
I rode down the street intending to take the road
back towards Geyragh to see what was happening to
the cows, which must have suffered much at the
hands of the drovers. It was two o'clock, and the
men from the distillery, the corn stores and the flour
mills, were coming out to dinner. And it so happened
that just as the workmen reached the street, the
cattle appeared on the bridge followed by bailiffs
and constabulary men. If the constables had not
been there, the workmen might not have known

what was happening, but the sight of "the peelers" put them on the alert, and, inquiring to whom the cattle belonged, they at once—and, as far as I know, entirely on their own initiative—determined on a rescue. The distillery men in their white smocks surrounded the cattle; a mob including several women collected; there was a sharp tussle, and in the *melée* I saw a young constable's gun wrenched from him by a muscular virago. Then, with the relish of schoolboys playing a practical joke, the men drove the cows up the main street and down a by-street at galloping pace. The bailiffs, afraid to venture on without the constables, gave up the struggle, and the cattle, followed by a crowd of running men, disappeared into the country.

The excitement was intense, and if the incident was not altogether unprecedented in Midleton, nothing like it had occurred there since the constabulary had been reorganised. The town seemed in a state of revolution. Men and women were shaking with laughter everywhere. The police were jeered at and hooted, the bailiffs had to go into hiding and only escaped under cover of darkness. The cattle, driven by a circuitous road, arrived safely at the farm, this being, perhaps, one of the first cattle-drives, if not the first, which had taken place in the district. The object, however, was the opposite of that of more modern cattle-drives, which are always for the purpose of injuring the owner of the cattle, whereas in our case they drove the cattle as they thought to benefit us.

For the rest of the afternoon the townspeople, forgetting their proper business, took to promenading the main street, and preparations were made to give my father a public reception on his return. The victory over the police was what they prided themselves on ; but the countrymen, who began to flock in at twilight, attached most importance to the rescue of the cattle and the defeat of the landlord. The bandsmen decided to meet my father at the railway station and play him home, for on the arrival of the last train work would be over and the labourers free for the night. A tar-barrel was prepared—an indispensable adjunct of nocturnal celebrations—and it was settled that my father, accompanied by the principal members of the Land League, should walk after the band and be followed by the blazing tar-barrel on a stage borne on the shoulders of four labourers. Everybody was looking forward to a night of festivity, that is to say, marching, music, and speech-making, with rollicking and skylarking for the young people.

An immense crowd was waiting outside the station when the train arrived, and when the secretary and my father alighted they were surrounded by shopkeepers and farmers, who began shaking my father's hands until they almost broke his wrists. The secretary said it was a magnificent victory, and added that my father had paid the rent on the advice of the heads of the Cork Land League, who considered that in allowing the cattle to be seized he had carried out the programme of the League. The landlord having been put to trouble and expense and held up to public odium, there was no further object to be served by withholding the rent. As soon as the secretary had given his explanation several young men rushed out and conveyed the news to the crowd, who received it with consternation. The ringleaders said my father had played them false and nullified their victory by paying the rent. Inside the station we knew nothing of this, and as we passed through the throng my father continued to receive congratulations from the substantial farmers and shopkeepers, who were quite satisfied with the course taken. Many of them felt they might be in the same position any day, and agreed that it was right to pay when the landlord had been put to the trouble of seizing.

But the mob could not see it in this light. They had defied the law. They had defeated the sheriff and police. Their object was to keep the landlord out of his rent. They had a right to feel aggrieved. My father had not given them a fair game for their money. They said he was a traitor not only to them but to Ireland, and should be made an example of. They had no fellow-feeling for him, inasmuch as it was impossible that they should ever be in his place. Before we made our appearance outside the station the bandsmen had marched away with their instruments under their arms, and the tar-barrel was carried off unlighted. At first we could not understand what was going on, but soon people began to come up and cry out passionately that he should not have paid the rent. Others called him a coward, and said he had sold them in the moment of victory. The substantial farmers and shopkeepers began to drop away when they found how public opinion was trending, until at length he and I were left almost alone on our way home. Even the secretary deserted us. The crowd at first made no hostile demonstrations, but we felt— and it was an eerie feeling—that they were out of sympathy with us. Some of our relatives met us on the way down and played the part of Job's comforters, and as we walked along amidst the murmurings of the crowd we could hear the words " the rent is paid," always followed by exclamations of horror and disapproval.

When we reached home, and I shall never forget that walk, there were no people on the sidewalk in front of the house, while there was a great crowd at the opposite side of the street, and blocking the way on each side. The country relatives hastily got into their vehicles and made various excuses for leaving. A few honest labourers came up and asked my father for a full explanation, and when they got it they said he was not to blame, as he had obeyed the orders of the superior officers of the Land League. But it was impossible to make the crowd understand this, and it was rumoured that he had gone to Cork specially to pay the rent. But the fact that he had to buy a cheque and fill it in for the necessary amount at the sheriff's office, in company with some of the committee of the Cork Land League, showed clearly that he had no intention of paying the rent when he left home. The rule is that sheriffs will only accept cash in settlement of a judgment debt, and if he had intended to pay he would have brought cash with him, or at least his cheque-book. All this was explained, but the mob refused to believe it. Booing, hissing, groaning, and ribald cries began to be heard, and we thought it advisable to close all our shutters, which happily were of thick timber.

We had barely effected this, and were standing on the doorstep, when a fusilade of stones came crashing on the house from across the street. My father hastily shut the door, and I was locked out. I stood for some time at the door with a faithful friend of my own age in the middle of a vacant space, while stones kept whistling over our heads and all around us. In front of me were a number of women whose faces were demoniacal as they shrieked, cursed, spat, and shook their fists at me. The memory of the sight makes me ashamed of humanity. Behind them were the men with the stones. When I realised my danger, which was not until my friend aroused me, I took safety in the crowd, and for several hours experienced the unique and mortifying sensation of standing in a mob which was wrecking my home. The constabulary, acting on instructions, made no attempt to stop the attack ; they did not take names or threaten prosecution, or even walk to and fro to keep the mob moving. Their barrack was close at hand, and they had closed the iron shutters and posted themselves immediately in front of it. If the mob had thrown stones at the police station I believe it would have been dispersed at the point of the bayonet or by a discharge of blank cartridge, but all animosity against " the peelers " was forgotten in the greater hatred of my father. The brass band, in a side-street close by, played a selection of patriotic airs while our house was being stoned. I even saw young people dancing in the light of the street lamps near the band, while the stones continued to rattle like a shower of gigantic hailstones.

About ten o'clock, when the public-houses closed, the band moved off, the greater part of the crowd following it, and the respectable men, who had been looking on for hours at the most extraordinary scene ever witnessed in Midleton, went towards their own houses. I saw two of the priests, two bank managers, several bank clerks, solicitors, doctors, revenue officers, all the leading shopkeepers, and numbers of the neighbouring farmers. They, of course, took no part in the stoning, but stood in groups smoking their pipes and discussing the unprecedented situation. I overheard many of their remarks, and what seemed to astonish them most was that my father's house, of all men, should be subjected to such treatment, and I heard the words, not once but often : " That's what a man gets for serving his country ! " My father was considered cautious and law-abiding, and if it had been almost anybody else's house they seemed to think they could have understood it better.

When the band and the mob had gone the police ventured in front of our house, where fragments of glass lay thick and stones ankle-deep made a causeway over the thoroughfare. I knocked at the door, which was opened by my father, who told the Head Constable he expected the police would have protected him. The Head Constable retorted that when his men were in danger that day nobody came to their aid. I slipped into the house, and my father seemed to think I had deserted him in trouble, ignorant of the fact that he himself had locked me out. No damage had been done inside, though the shutters had been forced open in some rooms. My youngest brother, then a baby, was sleeping in one of them, and a large stone, almost as big as his head, crashed through and fell on the counterpane. He was removed still sleeping to a back room, and slept all through the attack. Some female visitors accused me of being the cause of all the trouble, because, if I had not sent the telegram, my father would not have known that the cattle had been seized, and therefore would not have paid the rent—to which I had no answer to make, except that the best Land League authorities of the town had approved of what I had done. My father was very much cut up, but full of righteous indignation, being grievously affected by his loss of public esteem.

The band marched up the street playing "God Save Ireland," and stopped in front of the secretary's house, where a crowd collected. Though the secretary unreservedly approved of paying the rent, he got an ovation when he appeared at his window and congratulated the people on the victory they had won over landlordism. He never said a word in justification of my father or in condemnation of the attack made upon him, but quoted a verse of the well-known Irish song : " Rogues and traitors stand aside, Faugh-a-ballagh ! "—which the mob construed as referring to my father. The band returned to its rooms when he had finished, but over a hundred men went off to the residence of a landlord outside the town and tore down the piers of his entrance-gate, acting on the instigation of an aggrieved tenant.

In the morning it would be impossible to exaggerate the poignancy of our grief and chagrin. Every face was pale and tense, and instead of the cheerful bustle of business which used to characterise the shop at that hour, there were only ghosts silently moving to and fro in a deserted ruin. The shop window had been protected by outer shutters, yet the glass had been broken, and as there was a keen March wind we had to keep the shutters closed in the shop as if there were somebody dead in the house. In the windows of the front rooms, which only had inside shutters, there was no glass left, and we had to light the gas as if it were night. I felt I would rather march up to a loaded cannon's mouth in battle than step outside the door in broad daylight, being at an age when a family catastrophe seems like the end of the world. I did not feel aggrieved or persecuted, but disgraced.

My father went out of doors, and stamping about amongst the stones and glass was looking up at the windows when a glazier, happening to pass by, said laughingly that the Land League was going to be as good for his trade as for the farmers—and my father, entering into the spirit of the joke, recalled how, when he was young, the glaziers used to go amongst the mob at election times whispering " Break the glass, boys ! " The glazier was a Protestant, one of a family of painters and glaziers—admirable people. He assumed we would apply for compensation to the Grand Jury, but my father shook his head, saying that as some of his townsfolk had chosen to inflict this injury on him, he was willing to bear the loss rather than transfer it to his fellow-ratepayers who were not guilty.

The glazier went off, having got an order to reglaze our windows, and other people passed by—a priest on his way to say early Mass at the convent, some devout shopkeepers and their wives following the priest, some farmers, artisans, and labourers. My father knew them all more or less, but they cut him dead or turned their heads away as they passed, which was the first symptom of boycotting. I was anxious to know whether the paper had any account of yesterday's occurrence, and I mustered up courage to go to the newsagent's, my cheeks tingling and my heart beating at the strange sensation of being disgraced in my native town. The newsagent was also a Protestant, a cheery woman liked by everybody.

From her I had bought my weekly copies of 'The Young Folk's Budget,' 'The Boys of England,' 'The

Boys' Standard,' 'The Young Men of Great Britain,' and other boy's papers, whose names I now forget, and my first copy of ' The Arabian Nights,' a stout volume of five hundred pages, in a thick yellow paper cover, a wonderful shilling's worth. I used to have an account with her, for at home they had no conception of the number of boys' papers I bought. So precious were they to me that I never threw them away, and my bedroom and a corner of the store-room were full of back numbers piled against the wall for reference to the exploits of Tim Pippin or Dick Daring. A movement had been going on for some time to prevent boys from reading those English papers, and to induce them to read A. M. Sullivan's papers, ' The Emerald ' and ' Young Ireland ' ; and ' The Shamrock,' a paper owned by the afterwards notorious Richard Piggott, and published in the same office from which Parnell's ' United Ireland ' was soon to be issued. ' The Shamrock ' had an everlasting farcical story called " Mick McQuaid," an imitation of Lover's style ; but I always felt, as a boy, that there was a note of unreality about those Dublin boys' papers as compared with the English papers, which, however faulty they might be, always urged boys on to deeds of intelligible courage, making every one who read them feel it his duty to do something for somebody else's good.

Mrs Dalton—whose maiden name was Jones, her parents being Welsh—seized me by both hands and denounced what she called " our shameful treatment." Some person whom she would not name had notified her that my father and his family were to be boycotted, and that she must not supply us with the newspaper. The tyrants of the Land League stooped to the pettiest persecution as well as the greatest.

My father had been a restraining influence on the branch, and the hostility to him did not spring from genuine displeasure at his having paid the rent, but from a long-standing desire to get rid of him because of his moderation. Mrs Dalton gave me the newspaper and asked me to come or send for it each morning, as she dared not let her messenger be seen serving it at our house. When I got home a servant boy was sweeping up the stones and glass into heaps like cairns under which our reputation lay dead and buried.

It was a most dismal breakfast party, and there was a bitter irony in the newspaper's account of the stand my father had made in refusing to pay his rent until his cattle were seized, and in the description of their rescue from the bailiffs and police. There was no mention of the attack on our house until the next day. When my father suggested that I should ride out to the farm, there was an unspoken fear in our minds that I should find our labourers on strike and in league with the boycotters. This fear proved unfounded. They were at their work, though they knew what had happened. My father used to sell almost all his milk in the town, and we expected the customers to refuse delivery. But people of the better class did not refuse, though they had been warned not to deal with us. The milk-women were asked to leave us, but they rejected the overtures made to them. Some of the customers yielded to the threats of the boycotters, but the milk-women, domestic servants, and labourers stood by us loyally.

Once I was on horseback and saw the harriers around me, I temporarily forgot what had occurred, and galloped gaily over the Rocky Road to the Cross of Geyragh. How it surprised me to find the sun

shining as brightly as ever and the sky gay with its
March blues and whites, as Homer, a black three-year-
old colt with a white star on his forehead, bounded
along with his peculiar billowy stride ! There was
something almost aggressively sympathetic in the
familiar fields and fences, the blossoming furze, the
frisking lambs, the comfortable cattle, and the shy
graceful colts. The country people I met spoke kindly
and expressed their regret, saying that it was a faction
in the town, backed up by certain extreme men aspir-
ing to absolute power in the branch, who had fomented
the attack upon us.

Finding everything well at the farm and the men
loyal, I saw no reason why I should not have a hunt,
and, making up a drag, I sent a cow-boy over the
fields with it trailing behind him, and, when he was
near the end of his round, put the harriers on. Words
cannot express the joy with which I heard the first
hound open on the scent, her note going to my heart
with a power never since equalled by any music. So
kind was nature whose " every prospect pleases," that
one even forgot that " only man is vile." Returning
in the evening after a day under the open sky, my
heart grew heavy as lead as I neared the town. I
expected to find the windows repaired, but I was disappointed. The glazier — who was the only person
except our own employees who had entered our house
that day—had been waited on and forbidden to put in
the glass, being warned that, as my father was now
boycotted, whoever should work for him, or buy from
him, or sell him, would also be boycotted according to
the Land League law. Obviously if the glass were
put in, it would be broken again, and it was decided
that, as there was to be a meeting of the Land League

on the next Saturday, it would be advisable to wait until after that portentous event.

Saturday, which was market day, always saw our place crowded with customers, but on this Saturday nobody entered our door. The town was full of people, and every passer-by stopped to look at our broken windows, but nobody came in. No priest, no acquaintance, no friend (except one chum of mine), came to offer us sympathy or inquire how we were. The Land League meeting was crowded to excess, and my father was not only removed from the presidency but expelled. The Secretary and our other whilom friends had not a word to say in his behalf, the entire conduct of the proceedings being usurped by two men who resided eight miles away and belonged to another branch. We were in dread of another and a worse attack on us after this, but no further action was taken.

Going to Mass on Sunday morning was a severe ordeal, but we all went, as we did not wish to add the guilt of mortal sin to our misfortunes. Neither Father Fitzpatrick at first Mass, nor the curate at second Mass, made any reference to what had occurred, and nobody spoke to us going or coming. From that day forward those two demagogues I have mentioned regularly attended the Midleton branch and dictated its policy, giving their advice, or rather issuing their commands, until they became a positive terror to the respectable townsfolk. They were both small in stature, one a publican, the other a farmer. The farmer ought to have been very well-to-do, having a large fertile farm at a reasonable rent, but he preferred the new *rôle* of boss, or tyrant, opened to him by the Land League, and left his farm to his workmen, with

the result that he had to surrender some years afterwards. The publican was an unusually intelligent
man, a fluent speaker, possessed by the most revolutionary ideas, and, if he had been in Paris at the
French Revolution, he would have shed blood as
remorselessly as Robespierre or Marat. The branch
met every Saturday, and the rush for early admission
now resembled what one sees at a popular London
theatre. The room was always crowded to excess, and
it was a privilege to be allowed in to hear cases tried,
the new law administered, and the new Gospel
preached by those two demagogues. The new chairman was a farmer whose chief qualification was his
handsome personal appearance—a fine type of abori-
ginal Irishman, tall, well-made, with a kindly expression and dignified presence. He sat silent in the
chair and listened to the demagogues while the affairs
of the district were being discussed.

Differences between farmers, between shopkeepers,
or between shopkeepers and farmers, or labourers and
employers, as well as between landlords and tenants,
were formally brought before the branch, argued *pro*
and *con*, and decisions given by vote as in the popular
assemblies in ancient Greek democracies, the law
being the law of the Land League and the latest
speeches of Mr Parnell and the other leaders, and
boycotting always the penalty of disobedience. To
the credit of our district, there were few outrages
on persons or cattle, but we lived in terror of them,
because of the reports from other places, as there
were constant threatenings, and not a few burnings.

At length our glass was put in, and my father
had to throw himself with redoubled energy into
farming, because his town business had been irre-

parably injured. The official boycott was kept up
against us, but we were not starved or driven from
the neighbourhood, as had been done elsewhere.
When my father met the two ruling demagogues,
whom he had known since they were children, they
crossed to the other side of the street, more out of
shame, I believe, than hatred. When it was known
that they were to attend a meeting of the branch,
people expected a new decree of boycotting, a fresh
embitterment of public opinion, a personal attack on
ourselves or some of the neighbours. The day they
did not attend, the whole town drew a breath of
relief.

The boycotting soon left my father in want of
money to pay working expenses. He had plenty
of live stock, but could not sell them, and he knew,
from the experience of Bence Jones and others, that
it would be futile to offer them at Midleton, or any
other fair. He also had corn for sale, but it would
be useless to offer it to the distillery or the merchants. He had a number of stall-fed cattle to the
sale of which he had been looking forward, and in
the ordinary course the local butchers would have
bought them, or we should have sold them at the
fair. He now decided to send some of them by night
to Cork market, and, as he dared not go with them,
he asked me to stay at the house of a relative at
Glountane on the night before, and go to Cork very
early to sell the cattle.

The project was kept secret until late in the evening, and about midnight five fat bullocks were liberated from the stall and driven down the lane by
which the sheriff's men had carried off our milch
cows not long before. Then the landlord and British

law were the tyrants, but now our oppressors were
our own people and Land League law. The cattle
were driven unnoticed into Midleton and through
the main street, my father seeing them go by from
his bedroom window, and having passed "the top
o' Cork Road" at the end of the town, got safely
out of the first danger zone on their way to Cork.
I told my cousin, with whom I spent the night, of
the trick to which we were resorting. He had a
good-sized farm, and had no trouble with his landlord, though he was an ardent Land Leaguer, and
said he would shoot all the landlords in one night
"if there was nobody but himself concerned." But
he also kept a small pack of harriers, and, as some
local gentry subscribed to his hunt and followed his
hounds, he had to temporise and try to reconcile
his duty to the Land League with his devotion to
hunting. It was from him I got the harriers which
gave me so much amusement.

His father, who was an invalid, was a very intelligent man, knowing Homer's 'Iliad' and 'Odyssey'
apparently by heart, and repeating sentences from
'Cobbett's Advice to Young Men' for my benefit.
He did not know Greek, having read Homer in a
translation, and he said he envied me because I knew
the immortal language. My ignorance of Homer
astonished him, for I had only read the first and
twenty-fourth books of the 'Iliad,' and none of the
'Odyssey.' To me they were mere task-work suggestive of Greek grammar, irregular verbs, and
archaic forms. To him Achilles, Agamemnon, Ajax,
Ulysses, Hector, Paris, Priam, and the others, were
all living people, as real as William Cobbett or his
landlord. His younger son was studying for the

priesthood at one of the theological seminaries, and they all spoke of him with that respectful reserve with which Irish Catholics speak of their clergy, regarding them as beings of a different nature from themselves. There were quite a number of elderly farmers at that time who were well acquainted with classical literature, and the taste for learning, characteristic of the Irish Catholics, induced many of the young men to become priests — for the priest was always the learned man amongst them.

Leaving the house before dawn I reached Cork market between six and seven, but failed to see our cattle, and, to my horror, I saw many dealers whose faces were familiar, and who, like most of their profession, were extreme Land Leaguers. As they took no notice of me I began to hope I had passed unobserved, and, after what seemed to me an age, I saw our bullocks trudging wearily up Market Lane preceded by a boy, and followed by our most faithful man, Jack Murphy, and a dog. I paid the tolls and they passed in, but, on their way to the pen, a dealer whom I had recognised shouted to the man : " Aren't you McCarthy of Midleton's man ? " Jack made no reply. The dealer then shouted : " Aren't these McCarthy's cattle ? " Jack answered : " They're anybody's cattle that buys 'em. They're not sold yet." The dealer looked at me, and I remembered a time when, with youthful liberality, I had given him a bargain. I offered him my hand, and looked yearningly at him as if he were a long-lost brother. He seemed to remember our last deal, and, winking at me, whispered : " I will say nothing. I never sold the pass on a friend yet."

When the bullocks were in their pen, dealers came

to handle them and ask the price. They were really worth about £18 apiece, but my father had told me not to ask more than £16, hoping to tempt a buyer. I therefore asked £16, was offered £14, consented to split the difference at £15, and the cattle were sold. The buyer was marking them with his scissors when some other dealers shouted out : " They're boycotted, they belong to McCarthy ! " I shall never forget his answer. " Look here," he said, " I am after buying them blessed bullocks and putting my mark on 'em, and if they belonged to the Divil himself out of hell I would not go back on my word for all the Land Laiguers in Ireland ! " He was a staunch Land Leaguer and in a large way of business, and the others opened their eyes in wonder and went off. He paid me. I gave him a half-sovereign for luck and rejoiced at the success with which we had run the blockade. But my delight was feeble compared with that of Jack Murphy, whom I now treated to the best breakfast that could be procured in Cork for a man of his class. As we meant to run the blockade again, we had to keep the exploit secret. Many other artifices had to be used to get rid of stock and procure ready money. More cattle were sold, and some young horses we also got rid of by stealth, always selling at a sacrifice.

CHAPTER XIV.

PASSAGE OF THE LAND ACT.

"JUSTICE, sir, is to be our guide," said Mr Gladstone, introducing the Land Bill on April 7th, 1881. "It has been said that love is stronger than death; and so justice is stronger than popular excitement, than the passions of the moment, even than the grudges, the resentments, and the sad traditions of the past. Walking in that path, we cannot err; guided by that light—that divine light—we are safe."

Such language contrasted strangely with the calculating, business-like talk of Mr Parnell, who regarded this measure, which was in itself a revolution, as entirely due to himself and the Land League rather than to any sense of justice on the part of the British Government. In the duel which now ensued between Gladstone and Parnell the Irish leader went into the contest as a matter of life and death, and was backed up at home by a struggling people with a genuine grievance; whereas the English leader was in politics mainly as a distraction for his intellect, and the prosperous people behind him took only a limited interest in the public issues at stake.

Distinguished and able as Gladstone was he was utterly at fault in the combat with Mr Parnell. If it were a mere war of words he would have won the day against the greatest of Ireland's orators, but Parnell spoke deeds, as it were, his utterances being usually followed by practical injury to his opponents, such as a murder, an outrage, a combination to withhold rents, or some increase of activity in his political organisation. Mr Gladstone's words were not followed by resolute action consistently directed against his opponent. He could never ascertain how far he was supported by the people he was supposed to represent, and always had to retreat soon after taking what seemed a decided line, leaving the last state of those who depended on him in Ireland worse than the first. The action he was now taking in introducing the Land Bill was, to the Loyalist mind, a retreat from the position taken up in the Coercion Act; while from the Nationalist point of view the Land Bill, as a measure of conciliation, was nullified by the Coercion Act. I heard a farmer say that Gladstone's policy was " to cut a man's head and then give him a plaster."

The Shawites were in favour of the Land Bill, and ' The Freeman ' also received it favourably, which gave Mr Parnell no pleasure. One of the sections which was most discussed was that empowering the Government to help poor tenants to emigrate. Mr Parnell, in his first speech, said they should have assisted migration rather than emigration. If he had his way he would have bought out the rich grazing lands in Connaught and Meath and divided them amongst thousands of tenants from the congested districts. He told the House that nothing would settle the land question but peasant proprietary ; and his words were echoed by Mr John Redmond, who, having just retired on pension from a government clerkship, had been elected Parnellite member for New Ross. The landlords' distrust of the Bill was expressed by the Marquis of Lansdowne, then a Liberal peer, who asked that provision be made for landlords who pre-ferred to part with their estates rather than retain them under the novel conditions about to be imposed.

Parnell's chief fear was lest the success of the measure should make it impossible for him to achieve the object for which he had " taken off his coat," namely, a Dublin parliament; and he said at Newry, on April 23rd, that the Bill would " result in dis-appointment." The worth of the Land Bill would depend altogether on how the new courts would in-terpret their duties, and he felt that to praise the Bill while it remained an entirely unknown quantity would be impolitic. If he had expressed approval of it, the Land Courts might not have given as big re-ductions of rent as they did. On the night of the division on the second reading he denounced the Bill as " a miserable dole and a half remedy "; and he and thirty-five of his friends walked out of the House without voting. Twenty-four Home Rulers refused to follow him and voted for the Bill. Of the other Irish members, thirteen Conservatives and all the Liberals voted for the second reading, which was carried by a majority of two to one.

But this did not stop the anti-landlord campaign. Just after the second reading Mr Dillon, speaking at home, said that the farmers ought to " obstruct the levying of rack-rents by every device which their in-genuity could suggest." " Punish the man who assists the landlords to levy them," he went on. " I advise you to keep within the law, not because I respect the law, not because you respect the law, but because it

does not pay to allow the landlords to catch you outside the law." Mr Dillon was arrested the next day
at Portarlington, being one of the first suspects under
the Coercion Act. But retreat followed quickly on
the advance marked by this step, and he was liberated
almost immediately on the plea of ill-health, though
sturdy old Forster had little sympathy with an incendiary invalid who was always "putting his foot in
it." Boycotting at this time was so rife that even
strangers sojourning in Ireland were boycotted.
Lord Stanley of Alderney, then staying with Mrs
Macnamara of Ennistymon in county Clare, had
written to the English newspapers against the Land
League; and though there was no charge against his
hostess, threatening letters were sent informing her
that as long as she kept him in her house the local
artisans and tradesmen had orders not to work for her
or supply her with goods.

The Irish farmers did not foresee the extent to which
the Chief Secretary would use the power of imprisonment, without trial, conferred on him by the Coercion
Act. There had been a local and temporary Act
passed for county Westmeath some years before which
gave the same power, but no such general measure of
coercion as this had been devised in modern times.

One of the first suspects arrested was Father Sheehy,
Roman Catholic curate of Kilmallock, county Limerick,
brother of Mr David Sheehy, M.P., of Mr Redmond's
present party. Mr Forster apparently was bent on
showing that priests who broke the law were not to
escape the penalty inflicted on laymen. His Quaker
blood was aroused, perhaps, by the nickname of
"Buckshot," given to him because he had supplied
the constabulary with heavier ammunition than they

had previously used. Father Sheehy and Father Green, whom I afterwards knew as a curate at Dungourney, were the two first priests who publicly joined the Land League.

An incident occurred soon after this which caused much discussion, and shows how warmly the priesthood were taking up the Land League. At a town which the Catholics call Birr, its Irish name, and the Protestants call Parsonstown, derived from Parsons, the family name of the Earls of Rosse, the founder of whose family was a Lord Deputy in the reign of Charles I., there was a military station the Catholic soldiers at which used to attend Mass at the parish chapel with one of their officers. One Sunday the priest preached in favour of the Land League and recommended all present to join it; whereupon the officer, thinking it disloyal to listen to such language, stood up in the middle of the sermon and ordered his men out of church. They obeyed with soldierlike alacrity and marched out with great clattering of boots and bayonets. For this the Nationalist papers called for the officer's dismissal, but the authorities passed no censure on him.

The House of Commons having adjourned, Mr Parnell addressed a meeting in Hyde Park on Whit Sunday, and warned the Government that if coercion were applied recklessly fair rent would become no rent—a prophecy which, as we shall see, he afterwards tried to fulfil. The first inkling of the reign of terror which was before the country was given on July 10th, when a man, named P. T. Hickie, was charged at Bow Street, in London, with sending a letter threatening to assassinate Mr Forster. The defence was that it was meant to be a joke, but he was sent for trial and got fifteen months' hard labour.

During this summer, the farm labourers took con-
certed action to improve their position for the first
time. Long-suffering and loyal, they had been working for wretched wages, worse housing accommodation, and the coarsest food. If the farmers were
slaving to enrich the landlords, it was doubly true
that the labourers were slaving for the farmers. But
now, realising that the farmers were getting large
reductions, which the Land Bill was about to make
permanent or increase, besides making them independent of the landlords, the labourers began to
ask for better pay, and formed a Labourers' League.
Though the bulk of the crowd at most Land League
meetings was composed of labourers, the Nationalist
leaders did not seem to think them sufficiently intelligent to make it worth while to espouse their
cause. The labourers in our district demanded a rise
of wages. On many farms they actually struck, but
they chivalrously put forward their demands in the
idle time between the hay and corn harvests. There
were two kinds of labourers : one, called a " tenant,"
was married and lived rent free in a cottage belonging to the farmer ; the other, known as a "servant
boy," was unmarried and boarded in the farmer's
house. My father at once gave a rise of wages amounting, I think, only to a shilling a week, and increased
the quantity of tilled and manured land for potatoes,
and gave the grass of an additional sheep. If the
landlords had been in the same personal touch with
the farmers as the farmers were with the labourers,
the land agitation might have been as rationally
settled.

Lord Randolph Churchill moved the rejection of
the Land Bill on the ground that it was " the result
of revolutionary agitation, encouraged the repudiation

of contracts, diminished the security of property, and endangered the union of Great Britain and Ireland"; but his motion was negatived without a division, and the Bill passed its third reading by 220 to 14, receiving the royal assent on August 22nd. Mr A. M. Sullivan, differing from Mr Parnell, eloquently praised the Act and its author, Mr Gladstone. "As I sat there and listened to the words of the Premier," wrote Mr Sullivan, "I felt as if I had, after the cruel toils and privations of the desert, been at length vouchsafed a glimpse of the promised land. Seldom in the history of the world has the course of human legislation witnessed a more wise and elevated purpose than that proclaimed in every page of this scheme."

It was foreign to Parnell's nature to speak or feel in such a strain of sentimental exuberance. It was many generations since the iron of suffering had pierced the soul of his ancestors as it had pierced Mr Sullivan and his brothers in their childhood. A. M. Sullivan, commenting on Parnell's want of gratitude, said: "He knows better than any of us how to deal with the English. Many of us are inclined to be carried away by what we think a kindly or generous act. Parnell is never carried away by anything. He never dreams of giving the English credit for good intentions. It is not poor Isaac Butt they have to deal with or even O'Connell. Parnell is their master as well as ours." Mr Gladstone admitted in 1893 that, but for the Land League, the Land Act of 1881 would not have been passed.

CHAPTER XV.

PARNELL OBSTRUCTS THE LAND ACT. GLADSTONE
ARRESTS HIM AND SUPPRESSES THE LAND LEAGUE.

SPECULATION about the Land Act now became
feverish ; the farmers expecting great reductions ;
the landlords biding their time in fear ; the young
Catholic solicitors hoping to make fortunes. Briefly
what the Act did was to give the yearly tenants, who
had been subject to eviction at six months' notice and
formed the great majority of the Irish tenantry, fixity
of tenure and the right of free sale. It created new
Land Courts to which every yearly tenant could
apply to have a fair rent fixed, and, once he made his
application, the landlord could not evict him pending
the hearing. Thus the three F's, so lately denounced
as "fraud, force, and folly," became the law of the
land. Tenants could bring evidence that they were
paying more than the land was worth, landlords could
give testimony to the contrary.

When the court fixed the rent, the landlord had to
accept it, and it could not be altered for fifteen years,
and then only by the consent of the parties or another
judgment of the court. Either party, if dissatisfied
with the decision of the court of first instance, could
appeal to the Chief Land Commission, from which
there was an appeal to the Irish Court of Appeal, and

even to the House of Lords. Few cases went so far, the vast majority being settled at the first hearing. The leaseholders were excluded from the Act, and henceforth, instead of being an object of envy to yearly tenants, they were considered worse off.

The largest farmer on the Midleton estate, Michael Buckley of Ballyanon, whose brother has been already mentioned, was so disturbed at being excluded from the Land Courts by his lease that it was most painful to meet or speak to him at this time. He had a fine farm close to the town, with a good house and out-offices, built by a former Lord Midleton for a tenant named Moore, also my cousin, and one of the Moore family before mentioned, who was noted as the most extravagant farmer in our part of the barony of Imokilly at a time when extravagance was rampant. This Michael Buckley's brother was a Canon and parish priest of Cloyne, of whom his family were as proud as the Moores were of their Coroner. Canon Buckley prepared a genealogical tree tracing our branch of the Fitzgeralds, of whom my uncle was then the head, back to Adam. The pedigree to Maurice Fitzgerald who came to Ireland in 1172 was perfectly accurate, founded on original documents in my uncle's possession ; but how he got it from Maurice Fitzgerald to Milesius, King of Spain, and thence to Adam I do not know. The Buckleys kept it over the mantel in their drawing-room at Ballyanon, and to doubt its accuracy would have been deemed a reflection on the Canon.

In August 1881, Mr Parnell purchased the copyright, plant, and premises of certain Nationalist newspapers owned by Richard Piggott, whose career will be noticed in due course, and started in their stead ' United Ireland,' with Mr William O'Brien as editor. This was taken as a very unkindly act by A. M. Sullivan, whose papers had stood by Parnell when 'The Freeman' was denouncing him. But Parnell ignored the Sullivan faction; and the starting of 'United Ireland' brought Edmund Dwyer Gray to his knees, making 'The Freeman' the subservient mouthpiece of Parnell and the Land League. The new paper began by coercing the Land Courts to give large reductions of rent. "The spirit which cowed the tyrants in their rent offices," it wrote, "must be the spirit in which the Land Commission Courts are to be approached."

There was a by-election for county Tyrone on September 7th, caused by the appointment of Mr Litton, K.C., as one of the three Chief Land Commissioners—the other two being Mr Justice O'Hagan, nephew of the Lord Chancellor, and Mr Vernon, a land agent. Mr Litton lived near Cloyne, about two miles from each of our farms, at a nice place inherited from his uncle, a Master in Chancery who made money when court officials had innumerable perquisites, and spent a great deal of it on his model farm near us. There were three candidates for Tyrone —Mr Dickson, Liberal; Mr Knox, Conservative; and Harold Rylett, Unitarian minister, Parnellite. I had heard Mr Rylett speak in our constituency at the general election in favour of Kettle, and I rejoice to learn from a bitter personal attack which he made on myself in 'The Daily Chronicle' in March 1912 that he is still in the land of the living. His selection as a Parnellite candidate for Tyrone exemplifies how free the movement, so far, was from ecclesiastical influence. Dickson received 3168 votes, Knox 3084, and Rylett 900, the closeness of the Liberal and Conservative vote showing that the Parnellites held the balance of power and could return either a Liberal or Conservative at their will. Mr Gladstone did not view the result in this light, but wrote to Forster in a jubilant strain, saying he wished " to meet this remarkable discomfiture both of Parnell and the Tories with some initial act of clemency, in view especially of the coming election for Monaghan," and suggested "the release of the priest (Father Sheehy) as a beginning." "To reduce the following of Parnell," he added, " by drawing away from him all well-inclined men seems to me to be the key of Irish politics for the moment." Forster did not attach so much importance to the election, and reminded the Premier that Tyrone was in Ulster and outside Parnell's sphere of influence.

Our boycotting had by this time ceased, and there was such a revulsion of feeling, accompanied by regret, that, when the Head League requested our branch to send delegates to a convention at Dublin on September 14th, to consider the Land Act, my father was appointed one of them. This was the largest and most important convention ever held in Dublin, the attendance numbering nearly 9000. There have been many conventions since, but none so large or so definitely called for specific and urgent business affecting the whole island. All such gatherings are packed beforehand with men who will do as the leader tells them, and this was no exception. The Ulster delegates came to hear and not to speak, and sat silent when Mr Parnell proposed that the tenants should not apply to the Land Courts for the present, but that the Land League should select test cases in each district and be guided by the results as to whether they should use the Land Act. The Fenians and the American Land League were for rejecting the Act, while the Irish farmers as a body were for accepting it, and the course adopted by Parnell was intended to satisfy both sides. A resolution was also passed stating that it was not the fixing of rent, but its abolition, which was required. And, as a sop to the labourers, it was decided to add to the title of the Irish National Land League the words "and Labour and Industrial Union." Mr Parnell, fearing lest the Land Act would make the farmers indisposed to agitation, wanted to have the labourers, mechanics, and traders to fall back upon.

At this time there was a project afoot in Dublin for holding an International Exhibition in 1882. A guarantee fund of £20,000 had been subscribed in a few weeks, Earl Cowper heading the list with £500, and it was proposed that a member of the Royal family should open the exhibition. The Nationalists now refused to co-operate if the name of the Queen were associated in any way with the undertaking. Belfast, the chief centre of Irish manufacture, would not join unless the Queen were the patron. The subscribers to the guarantee fund withdrew their subscriptions, as it would be impossible to go on in the face of Nationalist opposition, and the scheme fell through. Mr Charles Dawson, M.P., who was the chief Nationalist member of the committee, then started a project for a "National" Exhibition for the encouragement of Irish, in preference to British and foreign, manufactures. This was warmly taken up by the Nationalists, and will be referred to again.

The passage of the Land Act had the effect of abolishing the Church Temporalities Commission,

which had issued its last report early in the year and
now made its exit from the stage. The amount of
money it had paid to the clergy of the disestablished
Church since 1870 for commutation of income was
£7,546,005 — the largest sums paid to individuals
being £111,867 to the Bishop of Derry; £93,045 to
the Archbishop of Dublin; and £88,442 to the Archbishop of Armagh. The amount in each case was
calculated at 3½ per cent on the probable life of the
incumbent. On the very day of the Land League
Convention, this Commission, the last trace of the
connection between Church and State in Ireland, was
dissolved and its duties transferred to the Chief Land
Commissioners, its demise synchronising with the
birth of a new era in Irish history.

In this September the populace of Dublin became
openly converted to the Land League—a fact largely
due to the success of the Convention. Of the city
members one was a Liberal, Dr Lyons, a Catholic
physician sitting on the Government side of the
House, and the other a Home Ruler, Mr Maurice
Brooks, a Protestant merchant. But Mr Parnell's
sway was now acknowledged by a spontaneous ovation
in which Lyons and Brooks had no share. The Chief
was met at Kingsbridge terminus, on his return from
the country, by an immense concourse with bands and
banners; his carriage was drawn amidst cheering
crowds along the quays and through Sackville Street
to the Land League offices, where speeches were delivered by himself and Mr Sexton. Forster was
greatly annoyed at the policy of testing the Land
Act and rejecting the Exhibition, as well as its endorsement by the Dublin populace; and, as the
annual gathering of the Liberal Federation was just

about to be held at Leeds, he wrote to Gladstone on September 26th saying : "I think you will do great good by denouncing Parnell's action and policy at Leeds."

Father Sheehy was now released from jail; and Mr Parnell, who was about to visit Cork, took the priest along with him. They got a wonderful reception, the Roman collar and black dress of the priest standing out conspicuously and distracting much attention from the Dictator. While the "Leader of the Irish Race" was undoubtedly a hero, the priest was not only a hero but a martyr, and his prominence meant that ecclesiastical influence had come to stay in the revolutionary movement. Bishop Delaney of Cork had not joined the movement, and never would, for he was one of the old Whigs; but men like Father Sheehy and Archbishop Croke more than safeguarded the interests of the ecclesiastical order.

Mr Gladstone was indignant at all this ingratitude, and, on October 7th, at Leeds, contrasted Parnell disparagingly with Daniel O'Connell, charging him with "inculcating discontent and covetous desires for other men's property," and "substituting for O'Connell's aim of friendship with England the new policy of hatred of England and everything English." He also accused Parnell of " assigning to landlords a bare rental of three millions, the prairie value of their land, in full compensation of the seventeen millions which the land produced." And, finally, ingratitude more strong than traitor's arms, "after doing everything he could to destroy the Land Bill, Parnell was urging the people of Ireland to test the Act, not to use it !" Mr Gladstone was angry with the Irish loyalists too, and contrasted their "sluggishness" with "the readiness with which in other countries loyal citizens would have rallied in support of the laws." Finally, he said that Mr Parnell "stood between the living and the dead, not like Aaron to stay the plague, but to spread the plague," and warned the Irish leader menacingly that "the resources of civilisation were not yet exhausted "—a broad hint that the Coercion Act lay in reserve.

Parnell replied in an unforgivable speech at Wexford on October 9th. "You have gained something by your exertions during the last twelve months," he said to the people, "but you have gained only a fraction of that to which you are entitled. And the Irishman who thinks he can now throw away his arms, just as Grattan disbanded the volunteers in 1783, will find to his sorrow and destruction when too late that he has placed himself in the power of the perfidious and cruel and relentless English enemy." Having said so much for England in general, he then turned to Mr Gladstone, the Englishman against whom he felt himself especially pitted : "It is a good sign that this masquerading knight-errant, this pretending champion of the rights of every other nation except those of the Irish nation, should be obliged to throw off the mask to-day and stand revealed as a man who, by his own utterances, is prepared to carry fire and sword into your homesteads, unless you humbly abase yourselves before him and the landlords of the country. . . . Those are very brave words that he uses, but they have a ring about them like the whistle of a schoolboy on his way through a churchyard at night to keep up his courage. He would have you believe he is not afraid of you because he has disarmed you. At

ARCHBISHOP CROKE.

"Archbishop Croke was the best friend the ecclesiastical order then had in Ireland, for he was saving the revolutionary movement from getting into permanent opposition to the Church and preventing political independence from developing into religious independence."—PAGE 323.

the beginning of this session he said something of this kind with regard to the Boers. He said he was going to put them down, but as soon as he discovered that they were able to shoot straighter than his own soldiers, he allowed those few men to put him and his Government down. I trust, as the result of this great movement, we shall see that as Gladstone by the Land Act of 1881 has eaten his own words, now those brave words of his will be scattered like chaff before the united and advancing determination of the Irish people to regain for themselves their lost land and their legislative independence."

Gladstone was stung by the bitterness of this attack, which no living man but Parnell could have delivered with such deadly effect. Forster wrote the same day to the Prime Minister: "Parnell's reply to you may be a treasonable outburst. If the lawyers clearly advise me to that effect, I do not think I can postpone immediate arrest on suspicion of treasonable practices." At that moment Richard Piggott, whom Parnell had bought out on generous terms, was offering to sell Forster information proving Parnell and the leading Land Leaguers guilty of treason and accomplices in murder; but the Chief Secretary refused to entertain the proposition. Lord Cowper was not in Ireland, and Forster went to England on the next day but one, having arranged with Sir Thomas Steele, Commander of the Forces and one of the Lords Justices doing duty in the absence of the Lord-Lieutenant, that if the Cabinet decided to arrest Parnell, he would wire the single word "Proceed."

On October 12th Steele got the wire to "proceed," and that evening Mr Parnell came from Avondale to

Dublin and put up as usual at Morrison's Hotel, telling the boots to call him at 8.30 next morning, as he intended to go to Naas by the 10.15 train from Kingsbridge. On the morning of the 13th the boots, coming to call him, said there were two gentlemen below waiting to see him. Parnell sent him back to get their names and business, and the man returned with the information that they were a superintendent and a constable of the Metropolitan Police. "Tell them I shall be dressed in half an hour, and will see them," replied Parnell. The boots went off with the message, but came back again to say that he had told them that Parnell was not staying in the hotel, and he advised the Uncrowned King to escape by the back of the house. Parnell refused, saying that the hotel was certain to be surrounded. The boots then went off and returned immediately with John Mallon, superintendent of detectives, and a constable in plain clothes, who respectfully served two warrants on Mr Parnell and asked him to submit quietly to arrest. Having finished his toilet, he went off with the policemen in a four-wheeled cab, which is of all vehicles the least noticeable. In College Green a number of uniformed constables seated on outside-cars drove in front of the cab; at Essex Quay a squadron of mounted police joined the procession in the rear; and in ten minutes Parnell was delivered into the custody of the governor of Kilmainham jail.

The arrest of Parnell was hailed with delight in England, where he was as detested as Paul Kruger was during the Boer War of 1899-1900. The biographer of Forster says it caused as much national rejoicing "as though it had been a signal victory gained by England over a hated and formidable enemy." It so

happened that Mr Gladstone was on the same day
presented with the freedom of the city of London,
and there was a scene of almost savage enthusiasm
in the Guildhall when he announced the arrest as
"the first step towards the vindication of the first
elements of political life and civilisation," and described Parnell as "the man who has made himself
prominent in the attempt to destroy the authority
of the law and substitute what would end in nothing
more or less than anarchical oppression exercised
upon the people of Ireland." A reporter from 'The
Freeman' contrived to interview Parnell in jail on
the day of his arrest, and the Chief's message to his
followers was: "I shall take it as evidence that the
people of Ireland are not doing their duty if I am
speedily released." There was universal grief and
anger in Catholic Ireland, but the remedy prescribed
by Parnell was to continue the war against landlordism and the English Government.

Morrison's Hotel, in which Gladstone's greatest
coup in his duel with Parnell took place, was an
old-fashioned hostelry at the corner of Dawson Street
and Nassau Street, overlooking the College Park,
where Mr Parnell and other Wicklow gentlemen used
to stay, because it was within easy distance of Westland Row and Hartcourt Street, the two stations for
county Wicklow. Whenever it was rumoured that
Parnell was in town, a crowd would invariably collect
before Morrison's and cheer until he showed himself.
Morrison's was knocked down ten or eleven years
ago to make way for the new building of the North
British Insurance Company which now stands on its
site.

Soon after Parnell's arrest, Thomas Sexton, James

O'Kelly, and John Dillon were quietly arrested and also conveyed to Kilmainham. The treasurer of the Land League, Patrick Egan, had escaped from Ireland with the documents and cash of the organisation, and was now safe in Paris, where he stayed during the troubled time which followed. He was a respectable Dublin Catholic merchant, and an intimate friend of A. M. Sullivan. He was a flour-miller by trade, and joint owner, with a man named O'Rourke, of a large mill at the Royal Canal bridge near Glasnevin Cemetery. O'Rourke, who was a bosom friend of Davitt's, carried on the business during Egan's absence, and I used to see him almost daily in the Chamber of Commerce, where he was pointed out as " Pat Egan's partner," and he seemed generally respected. Amongst others arrested, with a view to securing a fair trial for the Land Act, was William O'Brien, editor of ' United Ireland,' the paper itself being suppressed and its editions frequently confiscated by the police.

The first question on everybody's lips when Parnell's arrest was announced, was, " What is to be done now ? " The Land League promptly supplied the answer by promulgating on the next day its famous " No Rent Manifesto," calling on the farmers to pay no rent until Mr Parnell was released. It was signed by Parnell, Davitt, Egan, Dillon, Sexton, Brennan, and Kettle, and was discussed by the suspects in Kilmainham, who were allowed to meet together and talk politics freely—everything they said and did being, of course, known to the Government. Thus Parnell tried to fulfil his prophecy made in June, that if coercion was recklessly enforced, " fair rent would become no rent."

Forster and Gladstone waited a few days, and then, determined that their Land Act should get a chance, they issued in the name of the Lord-Lieutenant an official proclamation, on October 18th, suppressing the Land League as "an illegal and criminal association," at the same time making a further increase in the number of troops in Ireland. A great many people expected an armed outbreak, but for that the Fenians were not ready, and less honourable methods were devised for obtaining what Irishmen love to call "the wild justice of revenge." On October 19th, Archbishop Croke wrote to the newspapers denouncing and publicly dissociating himself from the No Rent Manifesto. Mr Gladstone, justifying his policy at Liverpool on October 27th, said that Mr Parnell and his party "were marching through rapine to the disintegration and dismemberment of the empire."

As for Parnell, he was by no means displeased with the enforced rest and seclusion at Kilmainham, where he was freed from the importunities of the Fenian wing of his revolutionary army. A new force had come into his life this year, and perhaps he also wished for time to think over it. He and Mrs O'Shea, wife of Captain William Henry O'Shea, a member of his own party, had fallen in love with each other, and the husband, on discovering the *liaison*, had challenged Parnell to a duel, which was only averted by the elaborate explanations of the wife. In the country outside, where he "bade the rest keep fighting," the war went on without him. Forster, writing to Gladstone in November, said, "I am sorry to say there is a turn for the worse. We have more secret outrages and attempts to murder. If we could get the country quiet, I should be anxious to leave Ireland. The best course for Ireland, as well as for myself, would be my replacement by some one not tarred by the coercion brush."

There were riots in Dublin on the nights following Parnell's arrest, and it was reported in the newspapers that there was a plot to assassinate Mr Forster; but the detective department said they knew all about it, and that the Chief Secretary's life was in no danger. The Nationalists in the Corporation proposed that the freedom of the city be conferred on Parnell and Dillon. The proposal was supported by Mr Gray, M.P., who was now a subservient Parnellite, Mr Dawson, M.P., and Mr Harry Gill, M.P.; but Mr Maurice Brooks, M.P., who had been twice Lord Mayor, led the opposition, and the motion was defeated by the casting vote of Lord Mayor Moyers. Gray resigned his seat in the Corporation as a protest against this; and, in consequence of Moyers' action, an arrangement for giving the lord mayoralty to a Nationalist and Conservative alternately was broken, and for over thirty years the Mansion House has been occupied by a Nationalist.

The old Home Rule League was now revived in Dublin and held meetings frequently, but it made no attempt to establish branches, nor did it receive any financial support or continue the organising work of the suppressed Land League.

CHAPTER XVI.

IMPRISONMENT OF MY FATHER.

WHEN the news of Mr Parnell's arrest arrived in our district it brought business to a standstill. Our labourers, who were digging potatoes, stopped work for a while, and I saw Jack Murphy shedding tears, though he had never seen the Uncrowned King, for Parnell never came to Midleton. Farmers left their fields to discuss the situation at the village cross-roads or in the streets of the town. Shopkeepers put up their shutters as for the death of a friend. Many expected an armed outbreak, but the Fenians knew that such a thing was impossible. The younger generation who had grown up since '67 were not Fenians, and not one man in a hundred possessed or knew how to use a gun. If a rebellion could have been carried through with shillelaghs, scythes, hatchets, or hurleys there would certainly have been one this winter. But fear of the gun prevented it.

We were all much grieved at the loss of Mr Parnell, for, knowing him only at a distance, each of us felt an intense personal attachment for him. When somebody congratulated my father on having been forced out of the chairmanship of the Land League because it saved him now from the possibility of arrest, he replied that he would gladly go to jail if by doing so he could release Mr Parnell. My father's successor was in hourly expectation of arrest, and for some days nothing else was spoken of when people met but imprisonments actual or anticipated.

On the third day after Mr Parnell's arrest my father came home from the farm in very good spirits, largely, I think, because the national calamity had caused the past to be entirely forgotten and old acquaintances were now willing to be friendly. We all went to bed that night as usual, and sleeping with customary soundness I was in a state of complete oblivion of the world when I heard a voice calling my name again and again. At length it became so definite and audible that I sat up in bed, conscious of surprise that a dream could be so wonderfully real. Then I heard the words, uttered in imploring tones : " Come down at once. Your father is arrested." And I saw my aunt in the room in her dressing-gown with a candle in her hand.

My first impression was that she had gone mad, and being still half-asleep I stared at her without speaking. " Get up at once," she said, " the police are in the house and taking your father off to jail." This decided me, even if she were mad, to do what she said. She left the room, I followed her, and, when I reached a turn in the stairs, to my utter bewilderment I saw an armed policeman with his helmet on and his gun resting before him posted on the landing. He allowed my aunt to pass, but he stopped me.

Having ascertained that the inspector of constabulary with other policemen was in the hall below, I rushed back to my bedroom and hastily dressed. I asked to be allowed into my father's room. The request was granted, and I stayed there while he went on with his toilet, my aunt crying and praying alternately and suggesting various things that he should take with him, while he was giving hasty instructions about business matters. The police knocked repeatedly, asking him to hurry up. I protested warmly, but it was of no avail.

They did not search the house or seize anything, knowing well that my father had nothing to fear, though Mr Forster considered him a suspect. They had got into the house by throwing pebbles at the bedroom window and saying that something had happened at our farm about which they wanted to see my father, and he, remembering the fire four years before, had gone downstairs, when they forced their way in and arrested him, it being the first time within living memory that he or any member of his family had been in the grip of the law.

The inspector, a well-bred but overbearing man, came into the bedroom and insisted on my father there and then coming with him. I looked at my watch and saw that it was four o'clock. My father went up to the nursery to kiss my younger brothers, who were asleep. He then bade us good-bye, my aunt continuing to cry as we followed the inspector and the constables downstairs. Outside it was dark and cold, and two outside-cars were waiting before the door—drivers and horses being strangers. There was a hail from the off-side of the first car, and I recognised the voice of the secretary. He too had been taken, and was seated with a policeman behind him, while on the near side were two other policemen, the driver sitting in the dickey in front. The second car was occupied by three policemen besides the driver, the vacant front place on the off side being for my father.

It was a heartrending moment. I did not know what action to take, but felt that I ought to do something. My father gave a cheery answer to the secretary's hail. The domestic servants were standing on the doorstep protesting that it was a shame and sobbing aloud. The town was buried in slumber, and, determined to awake it, I shouted that my father and the secretary were being arrested under the Coercion Act. My father and the secretary peremptorily ordered me to be silent. The inspector—a gigantic man who could have walked off with me under his arm—seized my throat and put his enormous hand over my mouth. Never had I been so roughly handled. He ordered the women indoors, and the constables hustled my father on to the side-car, where he sat quietly in front of the policeman. They did not handcuff him, as he gave his word that he would not try to escape. He knew the inspector and all the police, and had always been on the best of terms with them.

When he was seated the inspector gave the order and the first car started, but the horse which drew the second car refused to go, backing down the street and rearing. I shouted " Hurrah ! The horse is a Land Leaguer." The inspector struck me, and said that if I spoke again he would put me in the lock-up. He feared lest, if the townspeople were awakened, he would have to use firearms and there might possibly be loss of life. The second horse was at length induced to move, and went off with such a sudden plunge that he almost threw the occupants off the car. And so my father disappeared.

I asked the inspector where the suspects were being taken, but he refused to tell. We went back to the house and locked the door, but none of us went to bed. When day dawned and we went downstairs, I told the first person I met what had happened. The wife of the secretary had also told her friends, and in a few minutes the whole town was aware of it. From morning until night we held a constant levee of people coming to condole with us and to sing the praises of my father. The chairman and committee-men of the branch said they felt slighted at being passed over, and envied us the honour that had been conferred on us. I never heard greater flattery of any man than I heard that day about my father. "God's noblest handiwork is an honest man. Denis McCarthy was that and no mistake!" Such encomiums continued all through the day, as if my father had just been buried. Everybody expressed their sorrow for the treatment we had received in the spring, saying they always knew we did not deserve it, and had denounced those who boycotted us. In all this there was some consolation, for it meant that we were now completely rehabilitated in the esteem of our fellow-townsmen.

We felt my father's arrest keenly. He was a man who had never been a night from home, except at the recent Convention in Dublin, and, as he transacted all his own business, it seemed uncanny that he should not be at hand to advise and direct. Having ascertained that he was not in Cork jail we began to think that he had been taken to Kilmainham, but late in the evening a telegram came from the secretary that he and my father were in Limerick jail, and next morning this was confirmed by the Resident Magistrate, Mr Thomas Dennehy, a kindly scion of one of our old Catholic families, who was most popular and particularly friendly towards ourselves—a fact worth noting, because the R.M.'s soon became the most hated officials in Ireland.

He was a relative of Sir Thomas Dennehy, who was so long equerry and personal friend of Queen Victoria. When, twenty years after, I attended King Edward VII.'s coronation levee at Dublin Castle, Sir Thomas Dennehy, then recently retired, made his bow immediately before me, and I heard King Edward, who was seated on a dais with the Duke of Connaught standing beside him, say smilingly to the Duke : " There's old Dennehy." And the reply was : " Yes, isn't he looking well ? " Mr Dennehy proved a friend to us afterwards when my father had been longer in jail than we anticipated on the night of his arrest.

As our crops were still far from being saved, a good deal of potatoes remaining to be dug and corn to be garnered in both farms, there was a rush of offers of help, and similar scenes were enacted to those which took place four years before when we first took the large farm, except that it was now harvest and then it was spring. But what a revolution had taken place in the meantime ! Then the farmers were like children in their ignorance of politics. Now they had eaten of the tree of knowledge.

I went to see my father at Limerick jail. The secretary's wife had got from the Ladies' Land League a list of articles necessary to a suspect's comfort. My father set no value on such things, and would have thought it a mean thing not to be uncomfortable in prison. Nor would he ask for any relaxation from the rigours of imprisonment. The secretary, who was a fragile man, had at once gone into the infirmary. My father, doubtless, could have gone also, being far from robust and considerably older, but he would not do so, regarding illness as a kind of disgrace, and was therefore sleeping on a hard bed in solitary confinement and undergoing all the hardships of ordinary prison life, which were much greater at Limerick than Kilmainham. I had some difficulty in getting an interview with him, and, when I was admitted, the meeting was only for a short time, neither he nor I being able to say or do anything useful. A man with the strictest notions of integrity, he was naturally overcome at the thought that his son should find him in jail like a common malefactor. My eyes were full of tears, which, however, I managed to keep from falling. There was a warder present, and when he told us that the time was up, we separated almost without having said anything beyond mere conventional commonplaces. Having left the jail, I called on a friend who was manager of a large drapery house. He told me that he had supplied articles for many of the suspects, — various kinds of slippers, mufflers, soft hats, dressing-gowns, and spectacles of muffed glass because of the white walls. My father had made no complaint and had asked for nothing, but I gave my friend *carte blanche* to supply everything on the list and as much more as he thought necessary. I heard afterwards that my father refused to accept any of them.

While my father was in jail I gave up my college work and devoted myself entirely to the farms. I abandoned all idea of an academic career, which was a keen disappointment to many who had high hopes of my future success. But I found the adventurous outdoor life so much more congenial than the sedentary work of reading for examinations that I had no time for regrets.

Despite the continuance of outrages, two consequences of the arrest of the suspects must have given
intense satisfaction to Mr Gladstone. The solvent
tenants began everywhere to apply to the Land
Courts to have their rents fixed, and the scheme of
selecting test cases was not carried out. The first
application from the county Cork was from the Bantry
district, and it attracted universal attention because
the rent of the farm, 61 acres in extent, was £113, or
more than four times the Government valuation, which
was £27. The farmers feared lest the landlords would
proceed to evict them wholesale, as a Landlords'
Emergency Committee had been formed in Dublin,
and now another committee of Irish landlords in
London was established. The No Rent Manifesto
was also a failure, the only tenants who obeyed it
being those who could not pay. A visitor is said to
have asked Parnell in Kilmainham how the manifesto
was being obeyed, and his answer was : " All I can
say is that my own tenants are acting strictly up
to it."

But Parnell was not forgotten either by the
Nationalists at home or in London, where a mass
meeting of Irishmen was held in Hyde Park on
October 23rd and called for his release, the crowd
afterwards marching to the House of Commons, and
there shouting defiance to the British constitution.
Two days later, Mr Chamberlain at Liverpool said
that if the Irish agitation "had followed English
precedent, if its leaders had carried it on within the
spirit and letter of the law, there was no agitation
more deserving of sympathy and entitled to success.
Are we ready," he asked, "to consider the Union
itself as a standing grievance ? Are we prepared to

admit that the question of separation is an open one between us? Liberal and Radical as I profess to be, I say to Ireland what the Northerns said to the Southern States of America, 'The union must be preserved. Within its limits there is nothing you may not ask and hope.'"

That there was no limit to what an Irish Catholic might attain under the union was well exemplified by the career of Lord O'Hagan, or "Silken Thomas" as he was called at the Four Courts, whose retirement from the Lord Chancellorship on the 1st of November was interpreted as an expression of disapproval of the Government's policy. He was greatly venerated as the first Roman Catholic Chancellor since the Reformation and one of the ablest lawyers Ireland ever produced. His place was taken by Hugh Law, the Attorney-General. Every day now brought news of fresh arrests under the Coercion Act; but Mr Sexton, whom the Nationalists proudly called their "Silken Thomas," because of his eloquence, was released from Kilmainham on November 2nd on a medical certificate. There was no prospect of such relief for the hundreds of less known suspects; but neither their confinement nor the rush into the Land Courts affected the spread of Land League principles.

CHAPTER XVII.

THE women now took ostensible command of the
Nationalist movement in Ireland. The Ladies' Land
League, of which Miss Anna Parnell was president,
being the only Nationalist organisation, was liberally
supplied with funds from Paris and America. Anna
Parnell and her followers, like the modern suffragettes,
believed in strong measures ; and, construing Parnell's
incendiary speeches literally, gave the secret and
illegal side of the revolutionary movement their warm
support. Their funds did not come in subscriptions
from Irish Nationalists but in grants from Mr Egan
and the Fenian Land Leaguers, and the men who
paid the piper claimed the right to call the tune.
Nor were the ladies averse to this, for they thought
that Mr Parnell was as sincere as themselves when he
said his great movement could not be accomplished
"without shedding a drop of blood," and when he
urged his henchmen to do their duty by giving the
Government reason to keep him in Kilmainham for a
long time. Anna Parnell believed in avenging her
brother's arrest. The Land League Fenians behind
her meant to use their supremacy for wreaking a
bloody revenge upon the English enemy. Parnell's
parliamentary colleagues who were not in jail proved

to be men of little power, and were ignored alike by the ladies and the Fenians.

By a curious coincidence two women, Ellen Mac-Donogh and Mary Dean, were killed and many persons wounded near Belmullet in an affray with the police about a fortnight after Parnell's arrest, the first-named, a girl twenty-three years of age, being slain by a bayonet-thrust through the breast. Immediately after this the *régime* of the Ladies' Land League gal-vanised the secret side of the revolutionary movement into life in an extraordinary way in Dublin.

For several years previously the Dublin Fenians had been meeting at James Carey's house; Thomas Brennan acting as secretary to the centre until he got the lucrative post of secretary to the Land League. Carey himself acted as treasurer, and James O'Connor, who was now assistant editor of ' United Ireland,' was a leading member and often chairman of the meetings. The centre was chronically hard up, receiving nothing but the coppers of the artisans and labourers who attended. But it had been collecting and secreting some arms; and one of the members, suspected of informing, had been slain, or "executed," in the streets of Dublin—Carey being arrested as a suspect under the Coercion Act in connection with the murder. The value of this Dublin centre to the revolutionary movement was that it kept together a nucleus of men who professed to be willing to slay the enemies of Ireland, and it enabled leaders, like Mr Brennan, to lay hands upon those "executioners" when necessary.

Carey says that in November a man, calling himself "Mr Walsh," visited him and told him that a new body, to be called the Irish Invincibles Society, was to be started "to make history by removing all tyrants." Whether this was Walsh, Mr Parnell's fellow-traverser, who was indicted with Mr Healy in Cork, Carey does not say; but, so far, that Walsh was the only man of the name known in the Land League. The Invincibles were to be 250 in number, of whom 50 were to be in Dublin, and Carey says that Walsh named a committee of four — James Mullett, a publican of Lower Bridge Street; Edward McCaffrey, a vandriver of Peter Street; Daniel Curley, a carpenter of Gloucester Street; and James Carey himself, to control the society and select its members from the Fenians personally known to them. But, though its members were to be all Fenians, the society was not to be part of the Irish Republican Brotherhood.

Whether the Invincible Society was invented by Carey, or suggested to him by Walsh, is comparatively immaterial. The important point is that Carey then received fifty sovereigns to begin operations, and for six months afterwards money flowed in freely from outside sources for the purposes of the new society. Carey says that Walsh swore him in, the two men holding a penknife between them. The knife was the sacred symbol of the society. When an Invincible wanted to test a stranger he would take a penknife from his pocket and ask, " Do you see anything wrong with the knife ? " Whereupon the stranger, if an Invincible, would reply, " No, I see nothing wrong with it."

Gold and bank-notes were constantly given not merely to Carey but to Curley and the others by " Mr Walsh," by a certain " Captain McCafferty," and by a superior officer of the society whose only name was " Number One." Carey, while professing ignorance of the source of supply, says "they thought it was Land League money" which thus transformed their impecunious and futile Fenian "centre" into an engine of terror and destruction. Carey says he only selected one Invincible at the start, a man named Rinkle, but that Daniel Curley selected twenty and James Mullett selected Joseph Brady, a stonecutter twenty-three years of age and in the employment of the Corporation, who turned out to be the keystone of the Invincible arch. Of the thirty Invincibles—for the full complement of fifty was never reached—the event proved that there was no one but Brady capable of "making history by removing a tyrant." Many of the others could screw their courage up to slay an informer, but, in regard to the avowed object of the society, all they were able to do was to take what "they thought was Land League money," drink and swagger and boast while it lasted, and "arrange for the removal of a tyrant" at their secret meetings. Without this foolish, well-looking, good-humoured, insensate young Dubliner, with his enormous brute strength, the society could only have killed itself. Brady had the nerve to slay a man of the highest position, on whom he had never laid eyes before, who had done him no wrong, and against whom he had no personal grudge whatever. And Timothy Kelly, a mild and fragile-looking coachbuilder, twenty years old, was Brady's best assistant when the supreme crisis came. Such young fellows are indispensable to all murder societies, because they can be lashed into homicidal mania by the words of their designing seniors, and, when they have committed the crime by which others hope to profit, can be trusted to bear the punishment without betraying those who seduced them to their ruin.

The Invincibles were almost entirely skilled artisans, the few unskilled labourers connected with them being ordinary Fenians employed as auxiliaries or unofficially taken into confidence. Edmund McCaffrey, in whose house they usually met, and Joseph MacMahon were vandrivers. There were two clerks, Joseph Mullett and Patrick Whelan; one builder, James Carey, T.C.; five carpenters, Daniel Curley, Joseph Hanlon, Lawrence Hanlon, Daniel Delaney, and Thomas Martin; one stonecutter, Joseph Brady; two coachbuilders, Timothy Kelly and Peter Doyle; three tailors, Joseph Dwyer, Henry Rowles, and Joseph Poole; Peter Carey, a mason, and brother of James Carey; three shoemakers, Edward O'Brien, John Brennan, and William Moroney; two bricklayers, George and Joseph Smith; one publican, James Mullett; Michael Fagan, a blacksmith; two painters, Patrick Delaney and Thomas Devine; one gasfitter, Christopher Dowling; one compositor, John Martin; and Thomas Caffrey, whose brother, a milkman, served my house in Dublin for many years. The servants used to refer to him with pride as "the brother of an Invincible," and he was as innocent and presentable a young man as it would be possible to meet. Besides these and a few others, there were Michael Kavanagh, proprietor of a brown mare and an outside-car, and James Fitzharris, known as "Skin the Goat," owner of a horse and four-wheeled cab, who supplied the locomotion; Kavanagh being employed for speed, Fitzharris for secrecy. Kavanagh said he did not listen to the words of the oath, which Tim Kelly administered to him on a penknife, and only joined for the sake of the money to be earned by driving the Invincibles. Indeed it is clear that without "what they thought was Land League money" the Invincible Society would never have been born.

At the same time as the Invincible Society was started, Carey offered himself for election as councillor for the South Dock Ward in the Dublin Corporation; 'United Ireland' adopted him as the Nationalist candidate, and he was triumphantly returned at the November elections. The first "tyrants" selected for removal were Lord Cowper and Mr Forster, and the Invincibles began to prospect the Phœnix Park with the object of finding out how best to achieve their purpose. Carey and the others met not only "Mr Walsh," but also a priest calling himself "Father Murphy," at the Angel Hotel and elsewhere, and they all went together to examine the ground in the park. Carey knew the "priest," who was no other than P. J. Sheridan, Mr Parnell's fellow-traverser and paid organiser of the Land League, who, like Carey, having been arrested as a suspect and released, had apparently fled from Ireland, but was actually passing to and fro between Ireland and Paris, successfully evading the detectives in this most inviolable disguise.

"Father Murphy," Number One, Mr Walsh and the Invincibles dogged the steps of the Lord - Lieutenant and Chief Secretary—apparently without being observed by the detectives. Carey mooted the idea of taking a vacant house in Cork Hill at the entrance to the Upper Castle Yard and shooting Lord Cowper as he drove in or out; but the proposition was not adopted. Then Carey suggested the use of knives as more reliable than revolvers, and this was agreed to, Sheridan promising to get surgical knives, which he procured through an American doctor and left in a parcel at the London office of the Land League of

Great Britain, whose secretary, Frank Byrne, Carey knew as intimately as he knew Sheridan. A woman, said to have been Mrs Byrne, brought the knives, twelve in number, as well as a Winchester repeating rifle and revolvers, to Carey's house, making several journeys from England for the purpose.

While these things were happening in Dublin, a largely attended Land League Convention was held at Chicago towards the end of November, at which T. P. O'Connor, M.P., T. M. Healy, M.P., and Father Sheehy attended as the representatives of Parnell, and a considerable sum of money was raised for the work in Ireland.

Amidst all this excitement the Church once more attracted attention to the apparitions at Knock. There was then a Miss Cusack, member of a religious order at Kenmare, and well known under her *nom de plume* of " The Nun of Kenmare." She had been a Protestant, and, when she became a Catholic, her conversion was hailed as a great victory. At Kenmare she wrote many books, one being a voluminous 'History of Cork,' of which the priests induced almost every household to buy a copy. Miss Cusack visited Knock on November 21, announcing that she had been an invalid for nine years, but leaving the nature of her illness somewhat indefinite. She paid her first visit to the chapel on Saturday and attended Mass on Sunday, being carried on a couch to the altar rails to receive communion. But, just as the priest was approaching with the eucharist, she stood up dramatically and knelt at the rails like the other communicants, though the priest had come prepared to give her the sacrament in a recumbent posture. After Mass, she declared she had not received communion kneeling for nine years, and asserted that a miracle had been performed upon her. Mr E. D. Gray's papers published under sensational headings the details of this new miracle, which was accepted with implicit faith by pious Catholics all over Ireland and helped to make Knock a kind of Irish Lourdes. Not many years after this, Miss Cusack was so ungrateful as to revert to Protestantism, commencing a fresh career as an authoress and writing many books to expose Roman Catholicism as an imposture.

At the end of 1881, when nearly a thousand untried suspects, including my father, were languishing in jail, the Lord Mayor of London thought of opening a fund for distressed Irish landlords and the defence of property, but Mr Gladstone discouraged the project, feeling doubtless that, while he held so many farmers in durance, he could not identify himself with the landlords who had evicted that year 17,341 persons, as against 10,457 in 1880. He honestly hoped that, by keeping all those whom Forster called *mauvais sujets*, " village tyrants," and " dissolute ruffians " in prison, the Land Act would get a fair trial and stop the agitation to Ireland's advantage. But Forster, having no first - hand knowledge of Ireland, had arrested these men on the secret reports of local landlords or Constabulary officers,—we never found out who recommended my father's arrest,—and, while many of the suspects were rightly detained, injustice was done to so many by the wholesale arrests that the result was to intensify the anti-English sentiment encouraged by Mr Parnell. Nor was crime diminished, for, during the ten months from the passage of the Coercion Act to the end of 1881, there had been 20 murders, 63 cases of firing at persons, and 122 cases of firing into dwellings reported by the police—a total of 205 serious crimes, as compared with 90 in the same period in the preceding year.

The perpetrators of agrarian and semi - political crime were now undeniably stimulated to fresh zeal by what they deemed a laudable desire of avenging the imprisonment of the Chief. But it is to inspired wirepullers and societies, rather than to any spontaneous outburst of popular rage, that we must attribute the atrocious campaign of homicide and outrage which was to signalise the year 1882 and make it pre - eminently "the murdering time" of Parnell's revolutionary movement.

PART III.

THROUGH MURDER TO VICTORY

CHAPTER XVIII.

RELEASE OF MY FATHER. LORD MAYOR DAWSON.
LADY LAND LEAGUERS AND MOONLIGHTERS.
THE SLAYERS AT THEIR WORK.

AT the beginning of 1882, the condition of Ireland
was that of a country in a state of revolution suppressed by a large standing army and the imprisonment of national leaders whom no jury could be
trusted to find guilty of the illegalities for which they
had been arrested. There was no parallel for the
situation in any country possessing a popularly
elected Parliament. Nor did Ireland's troubled
history afford a precedent; for, when hundreds of
Fenians were under arrest fifteen years before, the
line was sharply drawn between the constitutional
and the illegal—the members of Parliament attending
to their duties undisturbed while the rebels were in
prison or in exile. Now that distinction was utterly
lost—so effectively had Mr Parnell carried out the
union of the open and secret sides of the revolutionary
movement.

The unimprisoned leaders were growing uneasy at
the long detention of the Chief, but could not make
overtures to the Government without loss of
popularity.. And the difficulty was to find an intermediary who would not compromise the Nationalist

cause. A conscientious scruple was said to be spread-
ing amongst the Radicals at the detention without
trial of so many respectable middle-class farmers and
traders ; but no reliance was to be placed on that.
Mr Forster believed what Joseph Cowen repudiated,
namely, that coercion was pacification. It is possible
that if Ireland were Russia and if Parnell and Davitt
could have been kept in jail for several years, and
all expression of opinion in the newspapers suppressed,
they might have found it impossible to revive the
agitation on their release, owing to the operation of
the Land Act. Ireland, however, was not Russia but
part of the United Kingdom, and Mr Gladstone was
no Czar, but a high-minded British statesman and a
lover of liberty. With such an opponent, the ultimate
victory of the revolution was bound to be all the greater
because of the stern measures employed against it.

We were growing alarmed at the length of time
my father was being kept in prison, the secretary
having been released on the plea of ill-health, after
two months spent almost entirely in the infirmary.
He had driven into Midleton at a late hour so as to
make his public reception more imposing—hundreds
of people walking out over a mile to meet his car,
accompanied by the brass band, and all marching back
together with band playing, banners flying, and tar-
barrels blazing. He spoke from his own window like
a conquering hero, saying that Mr Parnell would soon
have to be released, as crime could not be put down
without him, and that the suppression of the Land
League had in no way daunted the spirit of the
people.

After the speeches, the secretary took me aside and
told me privately that efforts ought to be made to

get my father out of jail, as he was in poor health but would never complain. I asked in surprise what efforts could be made. His reply was that a memorial, signed by some local magistrates, should be sent to the Government. It seemed to me like treason that any suspect should try to get free while Parnell was in jail, but the secretary assured me I need have no scruples, as this course had been taken already by the best advice and with success. I said my father would not approve of it. He said that neither my father nor the public need know anything about it. I went home with the extraordinary news, and, having considered it, we agreed that the plan should be tried. My father seemed likely to remain in jail indefinitely, utterly lost sight of amongst the hundreds of suspects, and if others had stooped to win liberty, why should we hesitate?

Next day I called on Mr Dennehy, the Resident Magistrate, and with his aid drew up a brief memorial informing the Lord-Lieutenant that my father, who was in ill-health, might now be released without danger to the peace of his district, and praying his excellency to order his liberation. There were no magistrates of popular views then, all being on the landlord side. The senior magistrate for the district, owner of a small property in Waterford but resident near Midleton—a man of loose morals, but careful about his health and an active adjudicator at petty sessions—refused to see us; and his butler handed back the memorial with the message that " those who put my father in jail should get him out, he would have nothing to do with it." We felt this keenly; but, when one remembers that the No Rent Manifesto was in force, one cannot blame a man whose income depended on rent for refusing to exert himself on behalf of a Land Leaguer.

When I called on Lord Midleton's agent, Mr Penrose Fitzgerald, the servant told me he was at dinner and could not be seen; but the agent, over-hearing me, came into the hall. He was dining in state, as carefully arrayed in evening dress as if he had grand company, though he was alone in a small room on the side of a street in a country town. He read the memorial and at once signed his name. Other magistrates also signed, and then the Resident Magistrate, having signed it, put it in a plain envelope, which he addressed to the Chief Secretary at Dublin Castle, telling me to throw it into the post office letter-box without a stamp. Some time after-wards, to our great joy, my father wrote stating that he was to be released on a certain day. He said he would not come home direct, because he wanted to avoid a public reception, and asked my aunt to meet him at Limerick. They went to Dublin for a week, returning without letting the public know the day of their arrival. One of the few things he told us was that it made him home-sick in his cell at night to hear conversation, laughter, singing, and music from the Governor's quarters when that official gave a party to his friends, who seemed to enjoy themselves thoroughly despite the many aching hearts inside stone walls and iron bars within earshot !

In January 1882, the Dublin Corporation got a Parnellite Lord Mayor in Mr Charles Dawson, M.P., and the freedom of the city was voted to Parnell and Dillon by a majority of 29 to 23 — the vote being now chiefly remarkable for the largeness of the minority. The Lord-Lieutenant and the Parnellite

Lord Mayor were, of course, at daggers drawn; and, when the Corporation asked that the prisoners might be released to receive the honour conferred on them, Lord Cowper refused the request.

It was in Dawson's years of office, 1882 and 1883, that the Mansion House came under genuine popular control. In Gray's year, the Nationalists had not established their power in Dublin. But now Mr Gray, who, as Lord Mayor, had been Loyalist and anti-Parnellite, was the obedient servant of Mr Parnell, whose most trivial word 'The Freeman' reported in leaded type. Mr Dawson fulfilled all the requirements of the new Irish democrats—a baker from Limerick doing well in Dublin, a typically clever young Catholic combining implicit belief in Catholic dogma with a certain assertion of political free thought. Like most of the new leaders, he took up special branches of political philanthropy, notably the improvement of artisans' dwellings, and was very busy organising the National Exhibition. The Mansion House was now a kind of rival to the Castle, the Lord Mayor's salary having been raised to the princely figure of £3000, with an allowance for a secretary; and Mr Dawson, as the first democratic Lord Mayor, did not underrate his own importance.

Every respectable ratepayer, and any Nationalist even if he were not a ratepayer, who could manage to appear in evening dress, felt he had a right to an invitation to at least one ball or banquet in Dawson Street; and a presentation to "the Lord and Lady Mayoress" was looked upon as the hall-mark of good Nationalist society by people who before this had deemed an invitation to the Mansion House as unattainable as the *entrée* to the Castle itself. At every festive meeting the Round Room was crowded to its utmost capacity, and the Dublin populace felt henceforth that they had some share in the good things from which they had been excluded. The richer class, who used to attend up to Mr Edmund Dwyer Gray's year, did not accept the invitations, and the Nationalists had the Mansion House to themselves. It was a rollicking time, and, ridiculous as was the behaviour of many of the guests, the functions gave them a sense of responsibility and had a civilising effect. White, the gigantic butler who had come to the Mansion House as a boy in the lord mayoralty of Daniel O'Connell, was indignant at the revolution. He said he put a decoy sixpence on the plate in the cloak-room at the end of a ball, and it was stolen. Nothing but Nationalism was spoken of; the great personages amongst the men being the new Parnellite members, who made but indifferent company and were looked askance at by the better-class Nationalists; and amongst the women the lady Land Leaguers attracted most attention.

The Ladies' Land League began 1882 with a programme of agitation like that of the latter-day Suffragettes, announcing its intention of holding meetings on New Year's Day all over Ireland. Miss Anna Parnell presided on that day at a large meeting in the Land League Rooms at Dublin, and alluded to her imprisoned brother as the Uncrowned King of Ireland; but her inflammatory speech, like those of ladies at other meetings, was ignored by the Government. Lord Cowper, asking for an increased power of summary jurisdiction, wrote to Mr Gladstone: "We know that women go about the country conveying messages and encouraging disaffection, and they distribute money in large quantities, both by hand and by letter." The fact was that the Ladies' Land League fell more under Fenian influence during Parnell's imprisonment than the Land League itself had ever fallen, and spent upwards of £70,000 in unexplained ways for revolutionary purposes.

Mr Forster, in order to justify his action in keeping the suspects in jail, published a return showing that the number of outrages had increased from 3505 in 1879 to 7788 in 1881. The increase in Munster was greatest, namely, from 950 to 3338, and was attributable to "moonlighting"— a dare-devil form of lawlessness which attracted a large class of young farmers and labourers, who would have broken out in open insurrection if they had arms and a martial leader. In the west of our county, and in Kerry, "Captain Moonlight" was intimidating farmers and others by midnight visits, seizing obnoxious persons and firing volleys over their heads, mutilating cattle, and burning houses and farm produce; so that his name became a household word, and "moonlighter" has taken its place in the English language. Early this year the police succeeded in arresting a man named Connell, on whose person were found many letters signed "Captain Moonlight," and, on his turning informer, over forty men were arrested in the Millstreet district of county Cork.

Connell went into hiding under police protection. Amongst other devices for the accommodation of such people, a large house at Clontarf, near Dublin, was used as an Informers' Home, and, on my walks to the sea-shore at Dollymount, I have often watched its inmates—dejected-looking men and women, sitting or walking aimlessly in the grounds, looking furtively

round them as if ashamed of being alive and expecting to be attacked. Mr Parnell said there was no
such individual as Captain Moonlight, but that the
outrages were committed by bands of young men
who could not get justice from the law; and, when
the outrages went on as before, Archbishop Croke
declared his belief that they were invented by the
police or grossly exaggerated.

A heinous crime was committed at the beginning
of this year, as to the genuineness of which there
could be no doubt. An elderly man named Huddy,
and his grandson, bailiffs on Lord Ardilaun's estate
in county Galway, were sent one day in January to
collect rents in a district known as Joyce's Country,
and they never returned. Lord Ardilaun and the
police made a vigorous search for them, and their
bodies were found at the bottom of Lough Mask.
They had been shot and tied up in sacks with stones
and sunk.

The Ladies' Land League in keeping alive the
revolutionary spirit was well seconded by 'The Irish
World' and 'United Ireland.' 'The Irish World,'
an American paper, had been declared illegal, and
all available copies seized by the police, after which
the editor, Patrick Ford, wrote : " Is a thick-headed,
shock-haired, leaden-hearted old reprobate like Forster
going to succeed in keeping out the light, or are we to
see Americans triumphant and defeating this hirsute
Forster ? " 'United Ireland' was also suppressed, and
a large quantity of it was confiscated at Liverpool on
February 3rd; but it was printed secretly and circu-
lated in defiance of the Government, changing its title
for a while to 'The Insuppressible.'

While the revolution was thus being helped on,

another link with the old Ireland before the Land
League was broken by the dissolution of the Queen's
University, established by Sir Robert Peel just before
O'Connell's death, in which so many Catholics had
been taking degrees despite the ban of the bishops
—its three colleges at Belfast, Cork, and Galway
being now absorbed into the new Royal University.
The Duke of Leinster presided as chancellor at its
last function in Dublin on the 1st of February, while
at the same time the students at Belfast were inter-
ring with mock solemnity the caps, gowns, and hoods
of a Master and Bachelor of Arts of the defunct
university.

When Parliament met on February 7th, the Speaker
read a letter from the Chief Secretary informing him
that Messrs Parnell, Sexton, Dillon, and O'Kelly had
been arrested, and that Mr Sexton had been released.
Mr Justin McCarthy, acting as temporary leader, protested against the continued imprisonment of the
suspects. Mr Forster justified his policy by assert-
ing that "landlords were collecting their rents;
farmers finding out that they had been misled by
the Land League; and juries doing their duty. The
signs of improvement, however, did not justify any
relaxation of vigilance by the release of prisoners."
Mr Sexton said "he believed every tenant who paid
his rent was enabling the general body of landlords
to continue the work of persecution and eviction."
The No Rent Manifesto was being disregarded, and
Mr Sexton, in the security of the House, thus gave
it an advertisement which in Ireland would have sent
him back to Kilmainham.

Almost red hot upon Sexton's declaration against
paying rent, young Patrick Freely was murdered

near Ballyhaunis, in county Mayo. His father, who had been a member of the Land League, had paid his rent, and on the night of February 23rd a party of men broke into his house. Failing to find the father, they dragged the son out of bed and gave him "vile usage" outside the dwelling. He escaped from them and returned to the house, into which they followed him and shot him dead.

On the night of Saturday 25th, the Invincibles made their presence felt in Dublin, the police finding a bacon-curer named Bernard Bailey lying dead in Skipper's Alley with two bullet wounds in his head. Two months before this, Bailey had a quarrel with a Fenian in whose house he lived, and had given information to the police which led to the discovery of a quantity of arms. Since then Bailey had been living under police protection, which had only been withdrawn a few days before his death. A week after the murder, James Mullett, one of the four members of the Invincibles' Committee, was arrested along with five Dublin artisans, and imprisoned as a suspect in connection with the crime; Mullett's *protégé*, Joseph Brady, being appointed a member of the committee in his place.

Mr Forster was very busy arresting and releasing suspects on the reports of magistrates and police. His arrest of Mullett enraged the Invincibles, who were now continually lying in wait for him as he moved to and fro. On the day of the Skipper's Alley murder he released Mr James Tuite, chairman of the Mullingar Town Commissioners, after nine months' imprisonment as a suspect. I got to know Mr Tuite very well, when he became a member of Parnell's parliamentary party in 1886. He was a

jeweller and watchmaker, a strong temperance advocate, and a most respectable man. On the night of
Tuite's release, the houses of two farmers at Feakle,
in county Limerick, named McNamara and Moroney,
who had paid their rents, were visited by moonlighters. McNamara was compelled to apologise on
his knees, while rifles were discharged over his head.
Moroney was deliberately shot in the knee, most
seriously wounded and disabled for life. Three days
after this, a caretaker on an evicted farm not far
away was shot in the head with five pellets, and
left for dead.

Immediately after these outrages Mr Forster visited
Limerick, went into county Clare with Mr Clifford
Lloyd, the special magistrate for these parts, and
actually addressed a meeting in the market square at
Tulla on March 1st, telling the people that his object
was to put down outrages and law-breaking for their
protection. He visited Moroney, the wounded farmer,
and gave him ten pounds. He also visited Constable
Wallis, who had been shot in an attack made on the
Resident Magistrate. On his way back to Dublin he
addressed a meeting from the windows of Hayes
Hotel at Tullamore—a district in which his fellow-
Quakers, the Goodbodys, had many prosperous
factories.

At the time of his visit Mrs Moore, one of the most
prominent lady Land Leaguers, was arrested near
Tullamore. She and Miss Hannah Reynolds and Miss
Nally were Anna Parnell's most prominent assistants,
and were urging people everywhere to obey the No
Rent Manifesto. Some years after this I lived for a
while in a lodging-house in Nelson Street, Dublin,
kept by a sister of Miss Nally, and saw a good deal of

her. She was perfectly sincere in her devotion to the Nationalist cause, and certainly did not appear to have feathered her nest with any of the thousands which were now being so lavishly disbursed by the Ladies' Land League.

On Forster's return to Dublin he arrested James O'Rourke, partner of Patrick Egan, as a suspect. This caused a great outcry, and a movement to obtain his release was instantly set on foot by the Nationalists, a petition being presented by Maurice Brooks, M.P., and signed by the leading members of the Dublin Chamber of Commerce, which resulted in his liberation.

Outrage and murder now prevailed in many parts of the country, though happily our district was almost free from serious crime or lawlessness. On Patrick's Day, March 17th, a boy named Gibbons, aged seventeen, son of one of Lord Ardilaun's gamekeepers, was killed on the highroad near Clonbur in county Galway, his head broken with large stones, and his mother, who was with him, was found wounded and insensible. Many persons who were present ran away on seeing the attack. Two nights afterwards a hairdresser's assistant, aged eighteen, was found dead with a bullet in his head in a lane off Queen Street in Dublin. This murder was not traced to the Fenians, but it shows how ready the young men were to slay each other. There were constant moonlight attacks, accompanied by wounding of farmers and others; men were continually found insensible on the roadside, and not a few attempts were made to blow up dwelling-houses with gunpowder.

On Monday, March 27th, the Invincibles arranged an elaborate scheme for the murder of Forster. They posted men at several points along the quays with orders to kill him on sight, Fitzharris's cab preceding the Chief Secretary's vehicle to give the signal ; but none of the "executioners" had the strength of nerve to make the attack, each giving a different excuse. Joseph Macmahon, a young vandriver living with his parents, was one of the appointed "executioners" that day, and next morning he said he felt too ill to go to work. Just before noon he and two other young Fenians, James Brennan, a shoemaker aged 22, and Thomas Martin, a compositor aged 21, went into the snuggery of a public-house in Dorset Street and were served with drink. A report of firearms was immediately heard, and Brennan dashed out into the street, leaving Macmahon shot dead through the heart in Martin's company. Brennan was pursued and arrested, and a six-chambered revolver with one barrel discharged was found on his person. Martin, who was likewise arrested, was found to be armed, and Macmahon also had a revolver on his person. On searching Martin's and Macmahon's houses the police found many rifles and revolvers, as well as a large supply of ammunition ; but despite this and many previous and subsequent clues they did not discover the Irish Invincible Society.

On the day after Macmahon's murder Mr Sexton in the House of Commons specifically asked that Parnell, Dillon, and O'Kelly should be let out on parole to vote in an impending division, but the request was refused.

At this stage Mr A. M. Sullivan, intending to practice at the English bar, and not feeling in sympathy with the new methods, retired from the representation of Meath, and the Nationalists of Ireland's richest pastoral county horrified Mr Forster

by electing as their member without opposition Mr
Michael Davitt, the father of the Land League, then
a convict in Portland prison. This endorsement of
Land Leagueism called public attention to Davitt's
imprisonment, but Mr Forster had no intention of
releasing him, and the Law Officers declared the
election invalid, whereupon the Nationalists elected
Mr Edward Sheil, a grandson of Richard Lalor Sheil,
the leading orator of the Repeal movement.

Three days after the slaying of Joseph Macmahon,
Mr A. E. Herbert, J.P., owner of a small estate in
Kerry and also a land agent, was shot dead while
walking home from Castleisland petty sessions. Mr
Herbert had been protected by the police, but the
protection was withdrawn at his own suggestion. He
always carried a loaded revolver, and let it be known
that he would " sell his life dear " if he were attacked.
The sub-inspector of constabulary, having some doubts
as to the wisdom of letting Mr Herbert go home
alone, was following him at a considerable distance in
the rear, and came upon his body while it was still
warm. That night twenty armed constables, patrolling the premises of the murdered landlord at Killien-
hierna, found eleven of his lambs dead on the lawn,
having been killed with pikes. The Government
offered a reward of £2000 for information leading to
the discovery of the murderers.

Mary Power O'Connor, of the Ladies' Land League,
sister of Mr T. P. O'Connor, M.P., was charged at
Athlone petty sessions with inciting tenants in county
Westmeath to pay no rent, and was committed to jail
on April 1st on her refusing to give bail for her future
good conduct. On the following day, Palm Sunday,
Mr W. Barlow Smythe, of Barbavilla House, county

Westmeath, was returning from church in a carriage with two ladies—his sister-in-law, Mrs Smythe, and Lady Harriet Monck—when three men with blackened faces openly fired at him, missing him but shooting Mrs Smythe dead. Mr Smythe was engaged in a quarrel with his tenants, and his life had been threatened. He was much criticised at the time for allowing the ladies to share his risk, but he probably never expected attack on a high holiday like Palm Sunday. On the same day in Limerick an attempt was made to blow up a police barrack with a bomb, which happily was discovered before it exploded.

Just at this time Mr T. M. Healy, M.P., replying to a vote of confidence from his constituents at Wexford, was reported by 'The Times' to have written : "I look upon the English in Ireland as a gang of brigands, whose rule has degraded and whose exactions have impoverished our country, and the captain of the gang is Mr W. E. Forster."

During the week following Palm Sunday the Invincibles attempted to take Forster's life on four evenings, but all the plans miscarried. On Spy Wednesday two "executioners" went on the platform at Westland Row from which the English mail train started, and looking into the compartment reserved for the Chief Secretary found only two ladies, whom they took for his wife and daughter. Had Forster been there Carey says he would have been killed that night, but, as on other occasions, he had gone to Kingstown by an early train, and dined at a yacht club before going on board the mail boat.

The accounts of the Ladies' Land League, published this Easter week when the Invincibles made so many efforts "to make history," show that during the previous seven days £4536 had been received, of which £1285 was reported as being spent on evicted tenants and £690 on the support of suspects.

Two days after the effort to kill Forster a man whom I knew very well was arrested for treasonable practices—John W. Sullivan, a book auctioneer of D'Olier Street, from whom I bought hundreds of books. He was deep in the secrets of the Fenians and, from certain hints he often gave in conversation, seemed to know everything that was going on. Like most secret society men he was silent, passionate, and proud. It was no uncommon thing to see his rooms filled with Loyalist book-lovers, including Fellows of Trinity and other well-known Dubliners.

On Good Friday a letter from Patrick Egan in Paris to Patrick Ford in America, acknowledging the receipt of £20,000 for Land League purposes, was published, in which Egan said : " All advices from Ireland are of the most encouraging character."

The discussion of the new rules of debate in the House of Commons excited keen interest in Dublin, and popular indignation was aroused against the city members, Maurice Brooks and Dr Lyons, for having voted in favour of the rule empowering a majority of the House to apply the closure whenever it thought fit. On Easter Sunday, April 9th, a meeting was held in the Phœnix Park, close to the Viceregal Lodge, to denounce the Dublin members for their action. Mr T. D. Sullivan, M.P., presided, and amongst those on the outskirts of the crowd who heard him speak was Earl Cowper, who, oblivious of the Invincibles, was exercising his right as a free citizen to attend a public meeting. He alone of all present knew the surprise which the next day had in store for Nationalist Ireland.

The effect produced on Mr Gladstone's mind by the nine murders mentioned in this chapter, of which six were agrarian and three non-agrarian, as well as by other murders and many other outrages besides those specified, was speedily made manifest. Realising that the imprisonment of the suspects did not diminish crime, the Prime Minister began to make preparations for retreat from the resolute position taken up six months before by the arrest of Parnell.

CHAPTER XIX.

MRS O'SHEA INTERVENES.

On Easter Monday, April 10th, Parnell was released on parole from Kilmainham, and secretly left Dublin by the morning steamer. Mr T. D. Sullivan, who had an appointment with him at 11 A.M., only heard of the release when he called at the jail, and Parnell was already at Holyhead. The news, as it reached us, was that he had been released absolutely, and beaming faces were seen on all sides, and loud laughter was heard wherever people congregated. There was much disappointment when we learned that he was only out on parole for fourteen days to attend the funeral of a nephew, son of his sister, Mrs Thomson, who died—of all places in the world—in Paris, where the Land League treasurer, Mr Egan, now lived in company with other exiled revolutionaries, including "Father Murphy," who had so often crossed and recrossed to Ireland to arrange "the removal" of the tyrants Cowper and Forster.

What happened now was as follows, though the public had no suspicion of it at the time. An intermediary to negotiate Parnell's release had been found in the person of Captain O'Shea—or it would be more accurate to say Mrs O'Shea. Captain O'Shea was a Dublin man by birth, educated at the English

Catholic college at Oscott and Trinity College, Dublin, and had been an officer in the 18th Hussars. His wife was a Miss Wood, a beautiful and highly intellectual woman of good English family, who had fallen in love with Mr Parnell, unsuspected by the world and least of all by Nationalist Ireland. Mrs O'Shea, troubled at Parnell's long imprisonment, wrote to Mr Gladstone reminding him that she was the niece of his former Lord Chancellor, Lord Hatherley, and asking the Prime Minister to call on her. Mr Gladstone, to obtain a visit from whom many a society hostess would have sacrificed a year's income, eagerly accepted Mrs O'Shea's invitation. She undoubtedly acquired influence over him, and told him that " a great change had come over Parnell with reference to the Liberal party." " She assured me," says Gladstone, " that Parnell desired friendly relations with us ! " Gladstone, on his part, told Mrs O'Shea that he had " no objection to friendly relations with Parnell, and wished to meet him in a fair spirit." Gladstone's communications to her were always oral, his notes being only bare acknowledgments of her letters ; but the two remained in constant touch until the defeat of the Home Rule Bill in 1886.

Parnell, now on his way to London, was met at Willesden Junction by Justin McCarthy and Frank Byrne, secretary of the Land League of Great Britain, in the London office of which the surgical knives procured by Sheridan for the Invincibles had lain concealed for some time. He left the train at Willesden and drove into London in order to avoid a number of London Irish who, having heard of his release, were waiting for him at Euston. After consultation with Mr McCarthy, Byrne, and some others,

he went on to O'Shea's place at Eltham in south-east
London, O'Shea being now reconciled to Parnell's
friendship with his wife. Next day he gave the
O'Sheas a message for Mr Gladstone, in which, amongst
other things, he said that "the Tories had adopted
peasant proprietary," thus beginning the policy, which
afterwards proved so successful, of playing off one
English party against the other. He crossed to Paris
that night.

On the next day Forster wrote dolefully to Gladstone : "My six special magistrates all bring me
very bad reports." Lord Cowper said afterwards of
this time : "The police led us quite astray. They
said they knew all the people who got up the
outrages, and that, if the Habeas Corpus Act were
suspended, they could arrest them. Of course we
found that the police were quite mistaken." This
was the natural consequence of having an English
Lord-Lieutenant and Chief Secretary who had no
first-hand knowledge of Ireland. "You can't resist
the demand of the Minister who is responsible for
Ireland," said John Bright at this time, excusing
the Cabinet for having passed the Coercion Act.
Assuredly not, if you are as ignorant of Ireland as
the Minister himself ! Conservatives in parliament
were calling for the abandonment of coercion and
denouncing the detention of the suspects as "repug-
nant to the spirit of the constitution," notably Mr
Gorst and Sir John Hay ; while Mr W. H. Smith
asked for the introduction of a Land Purchase Bill.
Under these circumstances Mr Gladstone had a
receptive mind for Parnell's statement that the
Tories were willing to establish peasant proprietary.

O'Shea wrote to Gladstone on April 13th, the day

Forster's dispiriting report came to hand, and also wrote to Mr Chamberlain, putting former conversations into writing, and suggesting to the Government to pass a Bill stopping evictions for arrears of rent, but not asking for Parnell's release. Mr Gladstone replied on the 15th, thanking O'Shea for " the length and freedom of his letter." " I am very sensible of the spirit in which you write," he added, " but I think you assumed the existence of a spirit on my part with which you can sympathise." The same day Chamberlain replied to O'Shea saying that he was " really very much obliged," but pointing out that " if the Liberal Party are to show greater consideration for Irish opinion, the Irish Party must pay some attention to public opinion in England." The proposition was that, if the Government would prevent evictions for arrears of rent, Parnell would stop outrages immediately on his release from jail.

The negotiations were now on a business footing ; but Forster, resenting Chamberlain's interference, described them as " an underhand proceeding from which no good could come." Meantime Parnell was ostensibly remonstrating with Egan, who, as the holder of the money, was alleged to control the men who were committing murder and outrage at home. Mr Parnell was thus officially admitting that he was leader of the secret and illegal side of the revolutionary movement, and the Government were admittedly making use of his influence as leader to gain political advantage for themselves. He had agreed to make no speeches and hold no meetings while on parole ; and, having said what he had to say to his henchmen of the extreme physical force party in Paris—urging them to do no more murder in Ireland, as Mr Gladstone fondly hoped—he returned to the O'Sheas on April 22nd, and learned from them that, "as the result of the negotiations, the suspects might be permanently released." He had a long interview on the 23rd with Justin McCarthy, who was in personal touch with Mr Chamberlain, then left for Dublin secretly, and, on April 24th, returned to Kilmainham jail. Next day he wrote a long letter to Justin McCarthy, requesting him to show it to Chamberlain at the earliest opportunity. "If the Government propose a satisfactory settlement of the arrears difficulty," he wrote, "we would make it known that the No Rent Manifesto was withdrawn, and advise them to settle with their landlords. We should also then be in a much better position to put a stop to the outrages which are unhappily so prevalent."

While Parnell was on parole on April 13th, the naked corpse of a quay porter, named Michael Short, who had been missing for over a fortnight, was found in the Liffey with the legs tied together. Four days afterwards Richard Roache, a bailiff employed by the Property Defence Association, was murdered at Kilteely in county Limerick, his body being riddled with bullets. On the same day, April 17th, a police hut at Golden, in Tipperary, was blown up with gunpowder while the constables were out on duty. Mr William O'Brien, editor of 'United Ireland,' was released from prison on that day, and Parnell's paper was allowed to be printed and sold without restriction — a substantial earnest of the greater results about to follow from the O'Shea negotiations. A few days afterwards a score of labourers who had gone to work on farms from which tenants had been

EDMUND DWYER GRAY.

"As a newspaper owner Gray was in advance of his time, especially in throwing himself with equal energy into the business and literary sides of his paper, advertising it in novel ways, and getting it into the country towns hours before other Dublin papers."—PAGE 283.

evicted near Strokestown were attacked by the farmers of the district, and a fierce fight ensued which was stopped by the police, who arrested a dozen of the combatants. Wherever the farms were many and small, the farmers were able to keep down the labourers by physical force.

On Sunday, April 23rd, one Patrick McCormack had a dispute with Thomas Brady about a piece of bog-land, shot Brady dead at their native place near Longford, and, after shooting him, jumped on the body. A week afterwards, at Kingwilliamstown in county Cork, John O'Keefe, recently evicted from a small farm by his brother, was cruelly murdered. I cite these to show that it required no wirepullers to organise a murder, but that the bad passions aroused by the land hunger caused the lives of tenants as well as landlords to be held of little account.

Miss Hannah Reynolds was arrested at Parsonstown on April 25th for inciting tenants to pay no rent; and on the same day the Ladies' Land League, at its usual weekly meeting, acknowledged the receipt of £5464 during the preceding week, of which £1482 was spent on evicted tenants and £529 on the support of suspects.

Mr Parnell wrote to Captain O'Shea on April 28th : " If the arrears question be settled upon the lines indicated by us, I have every confidence—a confidence shared by my colleagues—that the exertions which we should be able to make strenuously and unremit-tingly would be efficient in stopping outrages and intimidation of all kinds. The accomplishment of the programme I have sketched out would, in my judgment, be recognised by the country as a practical settlement of the land question, and would, I feel sure, enable us to co-operate cordially for the future

with the Liberal Party in following Liberal principles,
and the Government at the end of the session would,
from the state of the country, feel themselves
thoroughly justified in dispensing with further
coercive measures." This was Parnell's endorsement of Mrs O'Shea's assurance to Gladstone about
his altered disposition to the Liberals.

On the day this letter was written, Mr Gladstone
wrote to Lord Cowper: "Parnell and his friends
are ready to abandon 'No Rent' formally, and to
declare war against outrage energetically, intimidation included, if and when the Government announce
a satisfactory plan for dealing with arrears." Lord
Cowper promptly resigned, and it was announced *instanter* that Earl Spencer was appointed in his place.
On the day following Parnell's momentous offer of
alliance with the Liberals, Captain O'Shea was in
Kilmainham jail with him from 11 A.M. till 5 P.M.
Next day, April 30th, he took the letter to Forster's
house in Eccleston Square, telling Forster that he
hoped it was a satisfactory exposition of "the union
with the Liberal Party," and adding: "What is
gained is that the conspiracy which has been used
to get up boycotting and outrages will now be used
to put them down and there will be union with
the Liberal Party." O'Shea further told Forster
that Parnell hoped to make use of P. J. Sheridan,
alias "Father Murphy," whom Forster described as
"a released suspect against whom we had issued a
fresh warrant, and who, under disguises, had hitherto
eluded the police, coming backwards and forwards
from Egan to the outrage-mongers in the West."
Forster's answer to O'Shea was: "I can do no more
at present than tell others what you have told me."

Forster sent O'Shea's letter to Gladstone, with the comment that he "expected little from these negotiations." Gladstone, on the contrary, went into ecstasies over the letter. "This is a *hors d'œuvre* we had no right to expect," he said; "on the whole, Parnell's letter is, I think, the most extraordinary I ever read. I cannot help feeling indebted to O'Shea." He ought to have written "Mrs O'Shea"! A Cabinet Council was held to act on the *hors d'œuvre*, and it was decided to release Parnell, Dillon, and O'Kelly *instanter*. Lord Cowper, still at his post, wrote: "The proposed release of the M.P.'s so took me by surprise that I have hardly been able to form a deliberate opinion on it. Nothing but a series of formidable objections has yet occurred to me." Gladstone pressed him to sign the order for the release of Parnell and the others, assuring him that, as he had resigned, his so doing "would be merely ministerial and without political responsibility."

On May 2nd, the fourth day after Parnell's offer of alliance with the Liberals, the most important date, so far, in the history of the revolution, Irish Nationalists were delighted by the news that the Government had released Parnell, Dillon, and O'Kelly from Kilmainham jail, and had promised that they "would closely examine into the nature of the charges under which hundreds of suspects were still under custody." Mr Gladstone thus threw over Mr Forster, who resigned the Chief Secretaryship and was not provided with a new post, but was lucky to get away from Ireland without falling a victim to the countless schemes for his murder. Lord Frederick Cavendish, younger brother of Lord Hartington, became Chief Secretary. The abortive No Rent

Manifesto was formally withdrawn. And, on the next day, Sir William Harcourt announced that Michael Davitt was about to be released from Portland prison. The Government also announced its intention of substituting a new Crimes Bill for the existing Coercion Act, and, in the universal joy, this was taken to mean that coercion was to be dropped.

Never was Parnell less kingly than in the manner of his egress from Kilmainham. He went in a hero; he stole out like a man in disgrace. He and Dillon and O'Kelly left the jail at 10.45 P.M. in a cab, and it is said he would have gone to Avondale that night by goods train if one had been available. Failing that, he went to Kingstown, and, returning secretly to Dublin next morning, spent the day there without showing himself in public. The same evening he left by the night boat for London, being accompanied, it is said, by Mr Dillon and Mr O'Kelly. Did he know that something dreadful was about to happen? Or was this hurry to get out of Ireland simply the result of shame at his surrender to Gladstone, and fear lest that surrender might be discovered and disapproved by the people? He was honest, at least, in not openly triumphing. His faithful followers in Dublin got no leading as to what to do; for their Chief knew, and his lieutenants suspected, how the release had been obtained, and feared to give the word for any scheme of national rejoicing. Parnell felt that he was safest for the present in the House of Commons and near Mrs O'Shea, the only person from whom he had no secrets in regard to the Kilmainham Treaty.

There was much rejoicing all over the country; bands parading the streets, tar-barrels being lit, and jubilant speeches made. The Nationalist papers were full of political *Te Deums*. Mr T. D. Sullivan wrote a poem, after Lord Byron, the first lines of which were :—

"Sound the loud timbrel o'er Ireland's blue sea,
  The Land League has triumphed, the Suspects are Free!"

The release of the suspects was generally regarded in Ireland as a surrender by Gladstone to Parnell, whereas it meant rather a surrender by Parnell to Gladstone. As Mr T. M. Healy characterised it afterwards, it was "one of the most sagacious arrangements that ever enabled a hard-pressed general to secure terms for his forces." In the national jubilation Mrs O'Shea's name was never mentioned, though of her it might be said as truly as of Dido, *dux femina facti!*

In the House of Commons, on May 3rd, Mr Forster explained his policy and his resignation. He said he had arrested Mr Parnell in default of a promise of good behaviour, and by doing so had defeated the Land League, and compelled its leaders "to take shelter behind the ladies, or fly to Paris for safety." Urging the Government "not to buy obedience or make any blackmail arrangements," he condemned Mr Gladstone's new policy and took credit for having determined on resigning "rather than present the disgraceful spectacle of a Minister carrying out a policy he had been compelled to swallow against his will." He evidently little knew at that moment the sinister associations of the Land League in Paris, and had no prevision of the crimes which were so soon to follow. But he had known all about the Kilmainham Treaty, which he distrusted from the first. "A surrender is bad," he said, "but a compromise is worse. I think we may remember what a Tudor king said to a great Irishman : 'If all Ireland cannot govern the Earl of Kildare, then let the Earl of Kildare govern all Ireland.' In like manner if all England cannot govern the member for Cork, then let us acknowledge that he is the greatest power in all Ireland to-day."

In the debates which ensued the particulars of the means adopted for procuring the liberation of Mr Parnell were made public. O'Shea declared he had many interviews with Parnell at Kilmainham with the knowledge of Mr Forster, claimed that he had got the withdrawal of the No Rent Manifesto, but denied it was the price of Parnell's release. The promise of "union" and "cordial co-operation" with the Liberals was given, the release of Mr Parnell took place after it was given, and the No Rent Manifesto was withdrawn. It was not necessary that either side should admit that its performance was a *quid pro quo* for that of the other.

Mr Parnell read for the House the formal letter he had given O'Shea to hand to Forster, but omitted the sentence in which he said that the settlement of the arrears question would enable him " to co-operate cordially for the future with the Liberal party in following Liberal principles." Forster called attention to the omission and Parnell stood corrected, explaining that he was reading, not from the original letter but from a copy supplied to him by Captain O'Shea ! He admitted he had suggested that Sheridan should be permitted to return to Ireland—an indefensible proposition—and that Davitt should be released, which was quite reasonable and absolutely necessary to cover Parnell's retreat.

CHAPTER XX.

THE GREATEST OF ALL THE MURDERS.

THE Kilmainham Treaty was detestable to the Invincibles and their paymasters, because an alliance with the Liberals would mean the total loss of Parnell to the revolutionary movement. They therefore resolved that the treaty should not be kept, and this gave them a new and more urgent motive than ever for "making history." On Wednesday, May 3rd, while Parnell was still in Dublin, they arranged their last and nineteenth attempt to "remove" Forster, not knowing that he had left Ireland six days before. When they ascertained that he had gone, they resolved to take the life of "his chief prompter," Mr Thomas Henry Burke, the permanent Under Secretary. According to Carey, "Number One" was now in Dublin and ordered this step to be taken.

In Ireland, as in all unhappy countries, there is a great deal of "government"; and the Under Secretary does most of the actual work of signing documents. Thomas Henry Burke was regarded as a singularly capable official, and, having been in his post for thirteen years, the longest time for which it was ever held by an individual, had become something of an autocrat. He was a Catholic, being the grandnephew of Cardinal Wiseman on his mother's side; and, relying overmuch on his connection with the Church, was more unbending to the Nationalists than a Protestant would have been. It was not long before this that a well-known parish priest, Father O'Dwyer of Enniskerry, near Bray, came into the office of a Protestant friend of mine, manager of the largest Catholic printing-house in Dublin, and blurted out that he had just come down from the Castle after an interview with "that tyrant Burke." Father O'Dwyer was a fine - looking man, and greatly respected. I dined with him at Enniskerry more than once in company with priests, and he was the soul of hospitality. He now told my friend that two fellow - Tipperarymen had been sentenced to death by Judge Lawson for murder, and, having been asked to intercede for them, he had called at Lawson's house in Bray. The servant told him that the judge was out, but O'Dwyer saw him through a curtain in the front sitting-room, and naturally went away very angry. Judge Lawson was at this time the most outstanding of the Irish judges, and was selected to try the most dangerous cases. He was a man of much erudition, a conscientious Protestant, and a writer of church hymns, being always caricatured in 'United Ireland's' cartoons with a hymn - book in his hand.

Father O'Dwyer appealed to the Catholic Under Secretary, pledging his word as a priest that the young men were innocent; but Mr Burke said the law must take its course, for which O'Dwyer called him "a worse tyrant than Forster." It must not be inferred from this that Burke was independent of ecclesiastical influence, for, in refusing O'Dwyer's request, he was fortified by the knowledge that

Cardinal McCabe and the majority of the bishops were against the Land League. He was a regular attendant at the Dominican church in Dominick Street, where he delighted in the rousing sermons of his namesake and fellow-Galwegian, Father Tom Burke, the last of the Irish orators, who was, however, no relative of the Under Secretary's.

On Thursday, May 4th, Earl Cowper with his household left Dublin in state, and was presented with a farewell address by Lord Mayor Dawson, M.P., and the Corporation, in which regret was expressed at the Government's coercion policy, and a clear distinction drawn between Lord Cowper's "individual conduct and his official position." In this act of policy we may see the hand of Parnell and the result of the Kilmainham Treaty. The Nationalist outsiders in the streets cheered the departing Viceroy, while at the same moment in various parts of the country effigies of his Chief Secretary were being burned with groans and execration.

On Friday, May 5th, when Parnell was safe in London and Earl Cowper had gone, James Fitzharris drove Councillor Carey to the Phœnix Park in his cab at 10.30 A.M., and there met several "executioners at command of the Invincibles," as well as Number One himself. Daniel Curley, Joe Brady, Tim Kelly, Pat Delaney, Thomas Caffrey, and many others were present, and their scheme was to slay Mr Burke on his way from the Under Secretary's Lodge to his office at the Castle. When they had waited a long time —and it passes comprehension how they can have escaped the notice of the police—Joe Brady had the audacity to go up to Mr Burke's gate-lodge and ask the woman if the Under Secretary was at home; and, on being told that he had gone into town, the gang returned to Dublin. The same evening twenty Invincibles met at Kingsbridge, visiting the Royal Oak public-house and looking round the entrance to the Park, but the Under Secretary escaped them.

That night, after considering the matter for three days, the Dublin Land Leaguers organised a torch-light procession to celebrate Parnell's liberation, and there was a great deal of rowdyism in the streets. The same day in Ballina, county Mayo, the police foolishly fired on a crowd who were celebrating the release of Parnell and shot seven people, one of whom, a little boy, died of his wounds.

On Saturday morning, May 6th, Earl Spencer, accompanied by Lord Frederick Cavendish, the new Chief Secretary, arrived in Kingstown Harbour to make his state entry into Dublin, which was gaily decorated with flags and full of good-humoured people waiting to welcome him. At 9.30 A.M., while the Viceroy was still at Kingstown, Michael Kavanagh yoked his brown mare and drove his outside-car to Joe Brady's house in North Anne Street. Brady mounted the car, which then moved farther down the street and picked up Thomas Caffrey and Patrick Delaney. Crossing the Liffey, they drove up Parliament Street, and at 10 A.M. halted at Andrew Wrenn's public-house in Dame Street, opposite the main entrance to Lower Castle Yard, where a number of Invincibles congregated. James Fitzharris's cab was waiting hard by in Parliament Street, near the corner of Essex Street. There was little work done in Dublin that day, and while idlers of all kinds were loitering about to see the viceregal procession, which was expected between twelve and one o'clock, Kavanagh drove Tim Kelly more than once to Kelly's house in Thomas Street, returning again to Wrenn's.

Councillor Carey was very busy. Having served out knives to Joe Brady, he was showing himself to various respectable people. He called at the City Hall, which stands almost in the Castle. He went to his former employers, Michael Meade & Son, and had a long talk with the principal. He appeared in the street with his children, like a loyal citizen out to see the display.

The new Viceroy arrived at Westland Row shortly after noon, and, in accordance with the Kilmainham Treaty, was received by Lord Mayor Dawson, M.P., several members of the corporation (not including Councillor Carey), and the corporate officials, who laid the keys of Dublin at his feet! The procession was then formed and wended its way to the Castle between lines of troops and cheering crowds. The Invincibles saw it pass through Dame Street, Kavanagh having backed his mare and car into Sycamore Alley, near Wrenn's, when the street was closed to traffic. At 1 P.M. they heard the rockets sent up from the Castle as a signal to the artillery at the Magazine in the Phœnix Park that the Viceroy had taken the oath; and soon afterwards the guns began to boom down the Liffey with the west wind.

While Earl Spencer was taking lunch at the Castle with Lord Frederick Cavendish, Mr Burke, and other officials, Mr Parnell was waiting outside Portland jail to be the first to greet Michael Davitt on his release. It is said that Mr Dillon and Mr O'Kelly were with him, the three having travelled down to Weymouth from London that morning. He had special knowledge of the hour Davitt was to be liberated, 2 P.M., and he was eager to have the first word with the Father of the Land League, lest Davitt might disapprove of the surrender involved in the Kilmainham Treaty and "upset Parnell's apple-cart." It might have gone badly with Parnell if Davitt had got into Fenian hands and heard the Fenian version of Mrs O'Shea's diplomacy before seeing Parnell. Hence the Uncrowned King's unwonted deference to Michael Davitt, in whose company he returned to London that evening! As they travelled up to London, Parnell "denounced the Ladies' Land League, which," he said, "had taken the country out of his hands, and should be suppressed." He was fresh from the company of Mrs O'Shea, whom the lady Land Leaguers were then denouncing in secret as "cowardly Kitty" for her share in the Kilmainham Treaty. Mrs O'Shea would lead her lover towards Gladstone and along the peaceful path of union with the Liberals. His sister Anna and her friends would force him to embark on the stormy sea of revolution.

At 3 P.M. Joseph Smith, a bricklayer who did jobs in the Castle, and had been sworn in on the penknife by Carey himself, came out of the Castle Yard, having got his week's pay, and met Councillor Carey, who invited him and other Invincibles to dine at Fleming's in South George's Street—a cheap, unlicensed eating-house whose owner lived in affluence in Dalkey.

After dinner, Joe Brady, Tim Kelly, Thomas Caffrey, and Patrick Delaney drove to the Phœnix Park on Kavanagh's car. At ten minutes to five Carey, Smith, and Joseph Hanlon followed them in Fitzharris's cab. The car pulled up on the Main Road above the Gough Monument, the four passengers strolled off towards the Viceregal Lodge, and Kavanagh put the nosebag on his mare to give her a feed. The cab stopped in the same locality in a by-road which leads to the Nine Acres and a side entrance of the Viceregal Lodge. Its passengers too dispersed, Carey strolling to the Nine Acres, on the right of the Main Road, to watch a polo match ; Hanlon going to the left of the Main Road to see a cricket match ; Smith taking a seat on a bench facing the Main Road to look out for Mr Burke, with whose appearance he only was acquainted. Other Invincibles were already in the Park, or found their way thither afterwards by tram and afoot. Daniel Curley bought a bottle of whisky at William Burke's in Lower Mount Street at 6 P.M. and proved it at his trial to establish an *alibi*.

Every one who has visited Dublin knows the three official lodges in the Phœnix Park, midway on the straight Main Road between the Dublin Gate and the Castleknock Gate. The Viceregal, the largest of the three, is nearest to Dublin ; beyond it, and separated from it by a cross-road, is the Under Secretary's ; both being on the right side of the Main Road as you go from Dublin. The Chief Secretary's is on the left side of the Main Road, facing the Under Secretary's. At the cross-roads, between the lodges, is the Phœnix Monument, the most central landmark in the Park. Each lodge stands in spacious private grounds, separated from the public park on every side by a deep-sunken fence, between which and the Main Road is a wide margin of open park. The Gough Monument is near the Dublin Gate of the Park at a point about one-fifth of the distance between the Dublin Gate and the Phœnix Monument.

At six o'clock Lord Spencer on horseback, accompanied by an *aide-de-camp* and a groom, left the

Castle for the Viceregal Lodge, and, on entering the Park, went for a ride to enjoy the bracing air and renew his acquaintance with the Liffey valley and the Dublin Mountains. It was nearly seven o'clock when he found himself in the Nine Acres looking at the polo match, little knowing that Councillor James Carey was one of his fellow-spectators. It occurred to him to ride out to the Main Road and enter the Viceregal Lodge by the chief entrance opposite the Phœnix Monument, but he changed his mind and rode in by the back entrance in the Nine Acres. This he always regretted afterwards, thinking it probable that, if he had gone out to the Main Road, the impending tragedy might have been prevented. At that time the Nine Acres were screened off from the Main Road by a double row of magnificent elms—nearly two hundred feet high and planted in the viceroyalty of Lord Chesterfield, long before the Union—which were all blown down in the great gale of January 1903.

At half-past six Lord Frederick Cavendish, having refused Lord Spencer's offer of a carriage, left the Castle on foot to walk to the Viceregal Lodge, where he was to dine. Sometime afterwards Mr Burke also left for the Phœnix Park, taking an outside-car on the way and catching up the Chief Secretary at the Gough Monument. On seeing Lord Frederick, Mr Burke dismissed the car and joined his new chief on the footpath on the left-hand side of the Main Road farthest from the Viceregal Lodge; and they had not taken many steps together when Smith descried them.

Carey, meantime, showed little inclination to be present at the impending "execution," which he seems to have been devoutly hoping might not take place. But at a little after seven o'clock Dan Curley came and ordered him to "hurry up" and go to Smith, while he himself hastened up the Main Road to where Brady and the others were. Smith's startling message for Carey was : "Here they come! Mr Burke is the tall gentleman in grey!" Kavanagh was "white and shivering" as he took the nosebag off his mare. Smith, in the same condition, mounted the car with Carey, one at each side, Kavanagh in the dickey in front. They drove off slowly until they reached the group of Invincibles who were scattered about on both sides of the Main Road near the Viceregal Lodge, passing on the way two uniformed men of the Royal Irish Constabulary seated on the bench next to that on which Smith had been on the watch. There were a number of people about on every side and cars driving to and from Dublin. Carey and Smith held up white handkerchiefs, which was the prearranged signal that Mr Burke was coming, and Kavanagh heard Smith say: "It's the big man in grey!" Nobody knew Mr Burke's companion.

The car stopped and Carey and Smith got off. Kavanagh stayed in the driver's seat and stood by. Curley, Brady, Kelly, Delaney, Caffrey, Fagan, and Hanlon came around Carey, who pointed out the two men walking up the road and still many hundreds of yards away, telling them that Mr Burke was the tall man in the grey suit. Carey then asked Brady what was to be done with Smith, and the answer was : "Let him go to hell out of this!" Whereupon Smith went off across the Park towards Island Bridge. "What am I to do?" was Carey's next question. "You may go," said Brady. And, as Carey went off in Smith's track, his last words were: "Mind the gentleman in the grey suit." Carey, as a member of the Corporation, was in a sense Brady's employer, but the master gladly took his man's order to depart. Seven Invincibles were then left, and Carey says that Curley was "in command of the operation," but Brady was "the executioner."

Meantime the Secretaries were walking "arm in arm" towards their doom in animated conversation. The brilliant reception of the new viceroy, unmarred by one discordant note, coupled with the promised alliance between the Uncrowned King and the Liberal Party, made the outlook bright in the extreme. Around them the Park was alive with people pleasantly employed, and, when two draper's assistants, named Foley and Maguire, rode past them on tricycles, going in the same direction, the Secretaries noticed the machines, which were then a novelty, and the riders distinctly heard their comments. They passed the bench with the two Royal Irish Constabulary men, who had no notion of their identity; and they were fast approaching the Viceregal Lodge when they met the seven Invincibles.

Carey was some distance off on the grass, and he could not resist the temptation to stop and observe what was happening. He saw Curley, Fagan, and Delaney walking abreast down the Main Road towards Dublin. Four yards behind them came the "executioners," Joe Brady and Tim Kelly, walking together; and at about the same distance in the rear came Caffrey and Hanlon.

The Secretaries walked to meet the men as if oblivious of their approach. The front rank divided, and the unsuspecting Secretaries found themselves between the ranks and face to face with Brady and Kelly. Just then a car passed with a single passenger and driven by a man who bade Kavanagh good-day. Brady and Kelly were disconcerted at this and let the Secretaries pass them. Carey, looking on, felt certain that another "failure" had taken place. But when the car had driven by, Brady and Kelly turned about suddenly, and the Secretaries were surrounded on the instant. Carey saw Brady raise his arm and strike Mr Burke several times until the Under Secretary fell.

Lord Frederick Cavendish struck Brady with his umbrella and called him a ruffian, whereupon Brady, having killed Mr Burke in the most savage and thorough fashion, sprang at the Chief Secretary, followed him out into the road and stabbed him until he lay dead. A servant girl on the opposite footpath, going to visit a servant at the Chief Secretary's Lodge, saw the murder and the flash of the knife, and in terror turned back to Dublin. A boy of sixteen on the Viceregal Lodge side also saw the murder. But, most amazing fact of all, a young English lieutenant of the Royal Dragoon Guards was standing with his dogs on the very footpath where it took place about a hundred yards higher up and saw it. Behind him was "a labourer," to whom the officer, turning round, said : "This is a bad business." To which the man, who was probably an Invincible, replied : "It is a bad business." This officer, whose name I refrain from giving, had his dogs with him, having just walked across from the Magazine ; and he explained afterwards to the coroner's jury that one of the dogs was an invalid, presumably as an excuse for his having done nothing to stop the assassins.

Carey, seeing Joe Brady wipe his knife in the grass and climb on Kavanagh's car, which was already on the move, walked off towards the swing-gate at Island Bridge; and, looking at his watch with a view to an *alibi*, saw that it was 7.17 P.M. The draper's assistants were at the Phœnix Monument resting, when Kavanagh's car swept past them "with a buzzing sound" and sped down the cross-road leading to the Chapelizod Gate in the valley of the Liffey. The dragoon officer looked round for the labourer, and, not seeing him, sauntered towards the prostrate bodies of the Secretaries, passed them by without trying if they were dead, and walked down towards the Dublin Gate. He met a Royal Engineer in uniform, and, walking on together, they met the Royal Irish Constabularymen on the bench, whom they told that two men had been killed up the road. The Constabularymen replied that "it was no business of theirs," as the Park was in the jurisdiction of the Metropolitan Police. The lieutenant of dragoons went on, "every one he told the story to paid no attention," and before he reached the police station at the Dublin Gate one of the draper's assistants on his tricycle had passed him and given the alarm.

These assistants acted very well. The passing of the car had not aroused their suspicions, and they were cycling down the Main Road homewards when they came on the bodies. They at once dismounted and ascertained that the victims were dead. Then one agreed to remain with the bodies while the other cycled to the police station.

Meantime Lord Spencer had arrived at the Viceregal Lodge, and his account is: "Shortly after reaching the lodge I heard a shriek which I shall never forget. I seem to hear it now; it is always in my ears. The shriek was repeated again and again. I got up to look out. I saw a man rushing along. He got over the sunk fence and dashed up to the lodge, shouting : ' Mr Burke and Lord Frederick Cavendish are killed.' There was great confusion, and immediately I rushed out ; but someone of the household stopped me, saying that it might be a ruse to get me out and advising me to wait and make inquiries."

Colonel Foster, Master of the Horse, and Colonel Caulfield—who afterwards became Viscount Charlemont, and from whom, when on a visit with him many years after at Dungannon, I heard his account of this fatal day—bravely went out into the park and were the first to come upon the draper's assistant keeping guard over the bodies.

"Who are the poor men, I wonder?" said the assistant.

"This is Mr Burke, the Under Secretary," replied Colonel Caulfield, "and this is Lord Frederick Cavendish."

The Royal Irish Constabularymen also came up, and afterwards the Dublin police appeared on the scene and removed the bodies to Stevens's Hospital at Kingsbridge.

All the gates of the Park were now ordered to be locked, but Kavanagh had long ago passed out and was by this across the Liffey and on his way to Inchicore. Fitzharris's cab, to which Curley, Fagan, and Hanlon had walked, had also passed quietly out with these Invincibles under the very nose of the police. Carey and Smith went into town by tram ; and Carey instantly made himself conspicuous at Clery's public-house in Grafton Street. James Clery, who was a very intelligent and well-to-do young man and no Nationalist, never forgot Carey's talk with him that evening, and I often heard him tell how Carey had bored him, for Clery took little interest in anything but Sunday Closing Bills, horse racing, speculation, and cards.

Fitzharris put up his cab and his passengers dispersed ; but Kavanagh was out for a long drive. Having crossed the Liffey at Chapelizod, he turned to the left up the steep wooded hill leading to Inchicore ; and, keeping outside the city, went by a circuitous route to Terenure, or Roundtown. There he followed the quiet road along the Dodder until he came to Palmerston Park, which is diametrically opposite to the site of the murders, with all Dublin lying between. Then he returned into the city by Ranelagh Road, and halted at Thomas Davy's public-house in Upper Leeson Street. Davy was one of the most respectable, and least Nationalist, publicans in Dublin at the time, and, curious to say, an intimate friend of Clery's. There Kavanagh was paid off, receiving a sovereign from Joe Brady. The four public-houses which the Invincibles visited this day —Andrew Wrenn's, William Burke's, James Clery's, and Thomas Davy's—were owned by well-to-do men absolutely unconnected not merely with the Fenians but with the Land League. The Invincibles studiously avoided the public-houses of their own friends.

Brady and his confederates then strolled into town, and Brady actually went round to the newspaper offices and dropped a card into the letter-box of each, informing the editors that Mr Burke and his companion " had been executed by order of the Irish Invincibles." Brady revelled in the thought that he "had made history," and had meant to pin the cards on the bodies of his victims but had not time to do so. He had been one of the first to join the Invincibles, had been at every meeting and at every "execution." Nobody suspected the young stone-cutter, with his broad, full, good - humoured, fat Irish face, his loud and pleasant laugh, and his "excellent character" as an employee of the Corporation. He had not been at his work on this or the previous day, but he relied on Councillor Carey to defend him if asked for an explanation.

At nine o'clock that evening Councillor Carey was walking in Holles Street, which runs from Denzille Street, where he lived, to Merrion Square, when he met Dan Curley and got a detailed description of "the removal of the tyrants." An hour later Carey and his wife, taking the air in Denzille Street, met Joe Brady, who, as the two strolled along, gave fuller particulars of the history that had been made that day. Brady said that when the Secretaries got in amongst the Invincibles Burke was telling Cavendish of attempts made on Forster's life. He also told Carey that he would not have killed the Chief Secretary if Cavendish had not called him a ruffian. After this the Careys went home to their six young children, and Joe Brady went across the city to his father's house unchallenged and unsuspected, though all Dublin was in a state of panic as the news of the murder began to spread. The opera at the Gaiety Theatre was cut short; other places of amusement closed early; the troops were kept under arms in barracks; and the streets were deserted long before the usual hour.

Thus happened what may well be called one of the

most daring political assassinations in modern history; having regard to the number of the conspirators present and engaged in it; the time it was committed; the great authority of the victims; the vast force of soldiers and police at their command; and, above all, the place where the deed was done—within sight of the three official lodges in an enclosed park, patrolled by rangers and police, with a uniformed keeper at every gate, containing a Constabulary depôt, two Metropolitan Police stations, a magazine with a military garrison, a barrack of the Royal Engineers, and with people and vehicles freely moving about, yet with no crowd or covert of any kind to hide the perpetrators.

The scene of this terrible assassination is marked by no monument; but at the spot where the bodies were found there are two holes caused by tourists taking away handfuls of earth as *souvenirs*. There are poor men who live by guiding pedestrians thither, and for thirty years jarveys driving visitors round the Park have pulled up to breathe their horses while their fares have been examining the site of a tragedy which will never be forgotten.

CHAPTER XXI.

THE GREAT MURDER DESTROYS THE KILMAINHAM TREATY.

NEXT morning, Sunday editions of the Dublin papers were published—an unprecedented occurrence. While Dubliners were talking in awestruck whispers of the unheard-of crime which had given their city such unenviable notoriety, the Invincibles moved about as if it did not concern them. They must have smiled at the circular issued by the detective department announcing that two men, "stout-built with fair whiskers and dressed like sailors or fishermen," were wanted for the Phœnix Park murders; and at the further statement that the Liffey was to be dragged for a horse and car alleged to have been thrown over the quay at high water soon after the murders! The Invincibles, including Number One himself, met at M'Caffrey's house in Peter Street that Sunday, and received an official account of the "execution" from Dan Curley and Joe Brady Number One ordered the knives to be destroyed Joe Brady gave Michael Kavanagh two pounds more for his services, the brown mare was sent out to grass, and the outside-car was repainted. James Carey gave Smith two five-pound notes for his help in identifying Mr Burke. In his information, Carey swears he had no more to do with the Society after that day. While directing its operations, the pious casuist said he "had only been playing at soldiers" and "had never hurt the hair of a man's head in his life." "I would have had no compassion for Forster," he swore, "I would not like to see him going to heaven. I would not like to meet him there." Neither did he feel for Mr Burke, who was "Forster's chief prompter." He attended a meeting of the Home Manufactures Association on Tuesday, May 9th, and actually seconded a resolution condemning the Phœnix Park murders!

In London that Sunday morning, Parnell read of the murders in 'The Observer,' and went forthwith to Davitt at the Westminster Palace Hotel. His conduct this day was the reverse of heroic. In an ordinary man it would have been called cowardice. "How can I carry on a public agitation," he cried to Davitt, "if I am stabbed in the back in this way?" The secret and unconstitutional side of the movement had washed out the Kilmainham Treaty with English and Irish blood. Parnell was apparently stunned. The castle in the air which he and Mrs O'Shea had been building was destroyed past hope of reconstruction. All the accounts of eye-witnesses show that he was reduced to a state of terror, of which nobody had deemed him capable. He went from Davitt to Justin McCarthy, and the two called on Sir Charles Dilke, then regarded as a friend by the Nationalists. "I never saw a man so cut up in my life," says Dilke. "He was pale, careworn, and altogether unstrung." Parnell and McCarthy then went to Mr Chamberlain, who had been a prime mover in the Kilmainham Treaty, and Parnell offered to resign—a course from which Chamberlain dissuaded him. Parnell wrote to Gladstone that day asking whether he ought to retire from public life, and the answer was that his retirement "would do harm rather than good." Mrs O'Shea wrote to Mr Gladstone inviting him to call on her again, and he did so—getting from this "beautiful, weeping and passionate as well as brilliantly able woman," as Mr F. H. O'Donnell calls her, a complete justification of her lover.

Parnell, Davitt, and Dillon hastily issued a manifesto, in which they said : "We feel that no act has ever been perpetrated in our country, during the existing struggle for social and political rights of the past fifty years, that has so stained the name of hospitable Ireland as this cowardly and unprovoked assassination of a friendly stranger, and that until the murderers of Lord Frederick Cavendish and Mr Burke are brought to justice that stain will sully our country's name." While there need be no doubt as to the genuineness of this expression of regret, it must be remembered that this was the only murder specifically condemned. Mr Parnell, as the chief talker, had been encouraging the slayers ever since his visit to America. He had stood by them when they slew landlords and bailiffs and landgrabbers, and one feels at liberty to say that it is doubtful whether he would have condemned this political murder if it had not been committed immediately after the Kilmainham Treaty in which the slayers had no hand.

The extraordinary step was taken of summoning a Cabinet Council in London that Sunday, and Mr Forster telegraphed to Mr Gladstone bravely offering to resume his post as Chief Secretary, but his offer was rightly declined. The general impression in England and Ireland was that Cavendish had been assassinated in pursuance of the anti-English policy, and that Burke's death was unpremeditated; for nobody knew of Councillor James Carey and the Irish Invincibles.

I shall never forget the feeling of sorrow and desperation in our district on that fatal Sunday; but there were some, it must be admitted, who felt no sympathy for the victims or shame at the crime, because, as they said, it made for national independence. They only spoke in whispers, however, and the general verdict was that the murders were the work of an enemy. No formal public meeting or resolution was needed, as hatred of the crime was in every heart. But the Cork Land Leaguers came together and resolved : " That this meeting, spontaneously assembled, hastens to express the feeling of indignation and sorrow with which it has heard of the murder of Lord Frederick Cavendish and Mr T. H. Burke ; to denounce it as a crime that calls to Heaven for vengeance ; to repudiate its authors, whoever they may be, with disgust and abhorrence, as men with whom the Irish nation has no community of feeling ; and to convey our condolence with the families of the murdered."

The unprecedented reward of £10,000 was offered by the Government for the discovery of the murderers. When Charles Kickham was asked if the Fenians had done the deed, his answer was : " If it was committed by Fenians, they were Fenians corrupted by the Land League ! " Parliament met on May 8th, and after the leaders of all parties had expressed horror,

condemnation, and sympathy, both Houses adjourned
without transacting any business. The question on
all lips was : What of the cordial co-operation of the
Parnellites and the Liberals ? Parnell came through
the ordeal successfully. His words were simple,
deliberate, apparently straightforward, and uttered
with the dispassionate earnestness so characteristic
of him. He expressed his "most unqualified detestation of the crime," and said it had been committed
"by men who detested the cause with which he had
been associated, and devised it as the deadliest blow
at his party and the new policy of the Government."
It would have been nearer the truth to say "by men
who detested the arrangements made for his release,
and devised it as the deadliest blow to his new policy
of union with the Liberals."

A man intimately connected with the secret side
of the revolutionary movement told me that the
murder of Burke and Cavendish was beneficial
because it dealt a death-blow to the alliance between
Parnell and Gladstone. The physical force men were
displeased with Parnell for having promised, in order
to obtain his release, "to co-operate cordially for the
future with the Liberal party in following Liberal
principles." Had he kept that promise, his movement
would have ended like Isaac Butt's and his party
would have become a mere tail of the Liberal party.
Those who decided on a murder of the first magnitude immediately after the Kilmainham Treaty
wanted to save Parnell from being caught in the
net of English politics. They wanted the revolution
to go on with Parnell in it on the lines he had laid
down when starting in New York. The Invincibles
called his denunciation of the murders "an infamous

and hypocritical falsehood" and himself "the chief of Ireland's cowards."

It was announced that Mr George Otto Trevelyan, nephew of Lord Macaulay, had accepted the Chief Secretaryship; and Mr Burke was succeeded by Robert Hamilton, who was known as a Home Ruler from the moment of his arrival in Dublin, a shrewd Scotsman who had no notion of taking up Mr Burke's burden of hate. Thus we had given to us a half-Scotch Chief Secretary and a Scotch Under Secretary, as if there were no Irishman fitted to serve his country at her hour of need. Hamilton's Home Rule proclivities were a common topic of gossip in Dublin. Dick Adams, a humorous barrister who had been on the staff of 'The Freeman,' used to come into the Reporters' Room and tell how he had just met his friend George Fottrell, who was constantly in Hamilton's company, and, as Adams jestingly said, had the Government of Ireland in his hands. This Mr Fottrell, a clever Dublin solicitor, was the first secretary to the Land Commission, and had written a pamphlet, with the official seal of the Commission on the title-page, urging farmers to buy their farms under the new Land Act. The publication was resented by the landlord party and Mr Fottrell resigned, but his friends in the Government afterwards gave him the clerkship of the Crown and Peace for Dublin.

Lord Frederick Cavendish was buried at Chatsworth, on May 11th, three hundred Members of Parliament following the Duke of Devonshire and Mr Gladstone in a great procession, the number of people at the obsequies being estimated at 30,000. The House of Commons specially postponed its hour of meeting until 9 P.M.; and, when the sitting began, Sir William Harcourt introduced the new Crimes Bill which was to be substituted for Forster's Coercion Act. He truly said the Phœnix Park assassination was not an isolated crime, but a link in a chain of crime which the new Bill was intended to stamp out. It is probable that the Bill would not have been introduced, and assuredly would have been much less drastic, if the Phœnix Park tragedy had not taken place. As Mr Chamberlain said many years after: "The Kilmainham compact would have been faithfully kept and a great change made in the affairs of Ireland, but the Phœnix Park murders came and made a difference." There was no opposition from the Irish Party that night, though the powers taken under the Bill were in many respects greater than those in Forster's Act, Parnell being too astute to exasperate English public opinion at such a moment. The time had not yet come to dispel the illusory prospect of "cordial co-operation" with the Government by means of which he had secured his liberty.

The Government took power to appoint special commissions of judges of the High Court to try agrarian murders and other serious offences without juries: and to appoint two Resident (or stipendiary) Magistrates, as a special court, to dispose summarily of less serious cases. Forster's Act had given power of imprisonment without any form of trial whatever. This Bill provided a special form of trial in which neither juries nor independent justices of the peace were to have any part. To the Nationalist mind such a form of trial was a fraud and a mockery, because the Castle could always arrange for conviction beforehand, and the last state of the revolutionaries would be worse than the first. This Bill would give a Chief Secretary power to hang as well as to imprison. Another feature of the Bill was that it gave the executive unreserved powers of searching premises, arresting persons, holding secret sworn inquiries, and examining witnesses in private without formulating any definite charge against individuals, so as to secure the conviction of criminals. The Nationalists denounced this as re-establishing courts of Star-Chamber; but, true as all this might be, Parnell had perforce to keep silence for the present, as it was too soon to violate the Kilmainham Treaty.

Mr Gladstone, mindful of his obligations under that unprecedented compact, brought in, on May 15th, the Arrears of Rent Bill on the lines of a Parnellite Bill introduced by Mr Redmond. It applied only to farms valued at under £30. Where a tenant had paid his rent for the year preceding November 1881, his antecedent arrears, if exceeding two years' rent, were to be cancelled by a payment of two years' rent of which the Government would pay one if the tenant paid the other — the necessary money coming out of the Irish Church surplus fund. The second reading was carried by a large majority and it became law, but it proved of comparatively little importance, for the distressed tenants could not pay the large proportion of arrears demanded by the Act. Captain O'Shea had put the arrears question forward to mask his real object in opening negotiations for Parnell's release; and, while Gladstone may have believed that the measure would prove the universal panacea promised by Parnell, the Irish members must have known better. As the Marquis of Waterford said, "it could not possibly reach the broken tenants."

The Kilmainham Treaty was put to the test on
May 18th, when the Parnellites openly objected to
the Crimes Bill. Renewing the opposition next day,
Parnell, still retaining a friendly and grateful manner
towards Gladstone, said he believed in the good intentions of the Prime Minister and the Chief Secretary,
but complained that they asked for too much power.
He said that "for years they had been struggling
with the Prime Minister and had found him a strong
man"—an insinuating compliment—but "they regretted now to find him once more forsaking the paths
of justice and conciliation and following the well-
beaten track of force and coercion." When the bells
rang for the division on the second reading, the Bill
passed by a majority of 383 to 45, the minority being
composed of 36 Parnellites and 9 Radicals. On Derby
Day, May 24th, the House sat discussing the Crimes
Bill—the first time it had transacted business on that
day for thirty-six years. Mr Dillon declared that
"boycotting, like Lynch law, was an unwilling
measure forced upon the people because the Government would not give them protection." Mr Trevelyan
justified the system of trial without jury under the
Crimes Bill by citing the fact that thirty agrarian
murders had been committed recently with impunity
under the existing jury system.

A few days after this the physical force party gave
a finishing blow to all hope of co-operation between
the Nationalists and Liberals by perpetrating one of
the most dramatic murders of the whole agitation.
Mr Walter Bourke of Rahassan, county Galway, and
his escort, Corporal Wallace of the Dragoon Guards,
were shot dead near Gort through a loopholed wall on
June 8th; and so impressed was the Government by

the daring character of the crime that it instantly offered a reward of £2000 for information leading to a conviction—the slaying of the soldier in uniform seeming to alarm the Cabinet more than the death of half-a-dozen land agents.

After this, Parnell's spirits seemed to revive; and the opposition to the Crimes Bill, instead of being lessened by this daring murder, only grew apace. Many Radicals objected to the abolition of trial by jury, even in Ireland, and a particularly embittered attack was made upon Mr John Bright for being a party to such a measure. Mr Bright, defending himself, said : " We must protect ourselves from American criminals of the deepest dye." Whereupon Mr Healy called Mr Bright a " renegade." Mr Sexton complained of the enforcement of an old statute of Edward III. against the Ladies' Land League ; but Trevelyan replied that the custom of imprisoning persons in default of giving bail was not exclusively used against political offenders or members of the Ladies' Land League. Mr Sexton then elicited that the number of suspects arrested was 917, and as 23 of these had been arrested twice, the total number of arrests was 940. Up to June 26th, 755 suspects had been released, leaving 162 still in jail. The revival of such bitter memories proved that henceforth it was to be war to the knife again, as if there had been no release of prisoners and no Phœnix Park assassinations.

The fight against the Crimes Bill waxed hot in committee, the " curfew clause," authorising the arrest of suspicious people found out of their houses between sunset and sunrise, and the clause empowering the police to make night searches in private houses being especially resented, but the Conservatives invariably supported the Government. The obstruction reached its climax on June 30th, when Mr Parnell, still maintaining his friendly tone, began with a broad compliment to Mr Trevelyan on his behaviour during the short time he had been Chief Secretary, but went on to say that within twelve months after the Crimes Bill had passed he would be as bad as his predecessor Forster. Discerning the iron hand inside the velvet glove, Mr Trevelyan replied that "at least in one respect his rule had not been a failure, it had prevented Mr Parnell and his friends from governing Ireland." This taunt of Trevelyan's rang the death-knell of the "cordial co-operation" promised to secure Mr Parnell's release.

The opposition then became so fierce that the chairman, Dr Playfair, named Messrs Biggar, Callan, Commins, Dillon, Healy, Leamy, McCarthy, Marum, Metge, T. P. O'Connor, F. O'Donnell, Parnell, R. Power, J. Redmond, Sexton, and T. D. Sullivan to the House for "systematic obstruction." They were suspended, and, being ordered to withdraw, left in a body. The obstruction still continued. Messrs Byrne, Corbet, Gray, Lalor, Leahy, A. O'Connor, O'Kelly, O'Sullivan, and Sheil were named, and their suspension carried by 123 to 7. Two other Nationalists, Macfarlane and McCoan, retired, leaving in the House only The O'Gorman Mahon and Mr J. A. Blake. Progress was then reported, a great number of Nationalist amendments were struck off the paper, and after thirty hours continuous sitting the House adjourned.

The obstruction was resumed on July 3rd, and next day Mr Gladstone moved that the Crimes Bill be proceeded with until finished. Mr Justin McCarthy thereupon read the following resolution adopted by the Parnellites : " That inasmuch as the Irish Parliamentary Party have been expelled from the House of Commons under threats of physical force during the consideration of a measure affecting vitally the rights and liberties of Ireland, and as the Government during the enforced absence of the Irish members from the House pressed forward material parts of the measure in committee, thus depriving the representatives of the Irish people of the right to discuss and to vote upon coercive proposals for Ireland ; we, therefore, hereby resolve to take no further part in the proceedings in committee on the Crimes Bill, and we cast upon the Government the sole responsibility for a Bill which has been urged through the House of Commons by a course of violence and subterfuge, and which, when passed into law, will be devoid of moral force and will be no constitutional Act of Parliament." Mr McCarthy and his friends then left the House.

The war in Ireland, which had never ceased, made the war at Westminster necessary if Mr Parnell was to retain his position as " Leader of the Irish Race at Home and Abroad." Almost every day brought news of some daring crime to justify the passing of the Crimes Bill. New courage seemed to have been infused into the assassins by the successful murder of the Secretaries and the escape of the murderers. On June 29th, Peter and Paul's Day, a Catholic holiday of obligation, Mr J. H. Blake, agent to the Marquis of Clanricarde, and his steward, Mr Keane, were shot dead near Loughrea. And, on the same day, Mr John McCausland of Belfast, while driving on a car, was attacked by a man with a scythe and killed, his servant being severely wounded.

The Parnellites having withdrawn from the House, Mr Gladstone said, on July 7th, that he had promised Mr Parnell not to press the clause giving the police a general power to make night searches in private houses, and proposed that the police be forbidden to search any house except where they had reason to think that a meeting of a secret society was being held. The Conservatives opposed this and the division almost resulted in the defeat of the Government, the numbers being 207 to 194, Mr Parnell and his colleagues sitting in the gallery as auditors. The same night the Bill passed its third reading, the only votes against it being those of five English Radicals. It became law on the 12th of July, and was to continue in force until the same day in 1885, at which time certain events were destined to happen no less unforeseen than the Phœnix Park assassinations.

Parnell, speaking some days later, contended that the Arrears Act, for which he had offered to ally himself with the Liberals, was a failure, pointing out that only £200,000 of the £2,000,000 which was expected to be spent under it had been applied for—the implied inference being that its failure released him from his obligations under the Kilmainham Treaty. The insolvent tenants who "kept a firm grip of their homesteads" would not have been benefited by anything less than a complete remission of debt, and Mr Parnell must have known this from the first. But the astute leader of the revolution was not likely to suggest a measure of real pacification. The main Land Act was working faster than he liked, in less than a year 11,364 cases having been settled by agreement and ratified by the courts, and rents had been fixed by the courts in 11,552 cases, making a total of 22,916 cases settled. Numbers of other cases were arranged without the cognisance of the courts. My father made such a friendly arrangement with the Longfield estate. Lord Midleton appealed against the fair rents fixed by the court in the cases of three tenants, and a public meeting was held, at which the senior curate, Father Lynch, presided, to denounce him for thus exercising his legal right! The total number of applications to the Land Courts was now 79,455, so that they had more business than they could keep pace with.

The new Crimes Act invested the Resident Magistrates with such important criminal jurisdiction that no picture of the times would be complete without some reference to the manner of man popularly known as an R.M. The post was usually given in the past to poor relations of rich landlords or members of Parliament, the minority of the R.M.'s who were Catholics being mostly recommended by the hierarchy. No examination was necessary, nor any definite qualification. Many were retired military or constabulary officers, others briefless barristers, others nondescripts. Their salary was about £600 a-year and their duty to adjudicate at petty sessions within their district and keep the unpaid magistrates informed as to the Government's views. Men of the old type, like Mr Dennehy, were unsuited for the new work, and they were superseded by men of more bellicose character. Of the "six special magistrates" referred to by Mr Forster, the most widely known was Mr Clifford Lloyd, who issued to the constabulary at this time a circular telling them that if a constable "should accidentally commit an error in shooting any person on suspicion of being about to commit a murder," the production of the circular would relieve the constable of all responsibility. A copy of this got into the possession of the Parnellites, and they raised such an outcry against it that it had to be withdrawn.

Other well-known Resident Magistrates at this time were Captain Plunkett, at Cork, and Captain McLeod, who had charge of our district and always carried fire-arms, a striking contrast to Mr Dennehy. They all felt that they carried their lives in their hands, though none were ever killed, so far as I can remember. One of them, Major Traill, in a letter to the papers, thus described the precautions he took to protect himself. He always had a guard of two policemen, one carrying a Winchester rifle with 12 lb. of ammunition ready and 15 lb. extra in his pocket, the other carrying a breech-loading gun with buckshot and eight extra rounds. He himself carried a loaded revolver and six spare rounds; his groom a revolver and five spare rounds. Never during the twenty-four hours was a revolver out of his reach. His wife had a revolver too and " knew how to use it." In fine, wrote Major Traill, " The man who attempts my life and lives to be tried by a jury is entitled to their merciful con-sideration as a brave man ! "

All hope of discovering the murderers of Burke and Cavendish seemed to be abandoned, as the Royal Irish Constabulary became transformed into soldiers rather than police under this *régime*. The news that a man had given himself up at a Venezuelan port as one of the murderers reminded us of the tragedy, but on his being brought to Ireland his confession was found to be false, and the opinion of the Nationalists was that he was in league with the police. Councillor Carey and his Invincibles were apparently safe in Dublin pursuing their usual avocations.

After the Phœnix Park murders, Parnell partially broke with Egan and the other exiles in Paris and with men like Brennan in Ireland, falling more than ever under the influence of Mrs O'Shea, yet powerless to effect a union between his party and the Liberals. When Davitt asked him for £500 for the Ladies' Land League to enable it to pay its debts, he only gave it on condition that he was to be asked for no more funds for that purpose, and the League was starved out of existence. He rejected Davitt's advice to make land nationalisation a plank in the parliamentary programme, and henceforward there was no cordiality between him and the Father of the Land League. He seemed weary of the Land Agitation with its accompaniment of outrage and murder, and resolved to make Home Rule the sole plank in his platform, as if with the vain hope of raising his revolutionary movement to the plane of respectability in which it stood in Butt's time, without decreasing its efficiency.

CHAPTER XXII.

THE first result of the Crimes Act and the increased
authority it gave the R.M.'s was one on which
Nationalists had not counted. The Royal Irish Constabulary—the custodians of law and order, without
whom it was thought the peace could not be preserved
for a single day—went out on strike because of the
non-distribution of £180,000 voted to them by Parliament for extra duties. Meetings of mutinous constables were held at Limerick, Cork, Waterford, and
elsewhere in the first week of August; and, though
the mutiny was suspended on receipt of a promise
that the Government would look into their grievance,
it broke out again and continued for a month. The
police, being all Irishmen, had the sympathy of the
public in their stand against the Government, and
even habitual law-breakers felt bound not to take
advantage of them in such a crisis. There was, therefore, no remarkable increase of lawlessness.

Dublin was not affected, the Metropolitan Police
being a separate force, and this was especially fortu-
nate, as great numbers of country people came to the
city for the opening of the Irish National Exhibition

on August 15th. On the same day Lord Mayor Dawson unveiled the elaborate monument to O'Connell in Sackville Street, the work of the famous Irish sculptor, Foley. Mr Parnell was present, and the great demonstration passed off with orderliness and good humour. The splendid new bridge which the statue faces, one of the best of its kind in the world, was named O'Connell Bridge. It had been previously called after Lord Carlisle, who was Lord-Lieutenant during 1858-64, which is noteworthy as showing how the Repeal movement had left the Dublin Corporation's reverence for the Castle unchanged.

The next day was signalised by two notable events. The Corporation conferred the freedom of the city on Messrs Parnell and Dillon; and Mr E. D. Gray, proprietor of 'The Freeman' and High Sheriff for Dublin that year, was committed to prison by Judge Lawson for contempt of court. Mr Gray had published a letter from Mr William O'Brien, editor of 'United Ireland,' in which Mr O'Brien said that the jury in the case of Francis Hynes, a young man sentenced to death by Judge Lawson, had been riotously intoxicated at the Imperial Hotel on the night before their verdict. Mr William O'Brien had been a 'Freeman' reporter before he became editor of 'United Ireland,' his most remarkable work being a series of letters on the quarrel between landlord and tenants on the Kingston estate in the Galtee Mountain district, near Mitchelstown, in county Cork, the region where what may be called the first blood of the Land Agitation was shed by the murder of Mr Bridge.

Mr William O'Brien then lived at the Imperial Hotel, which had always been a notable *rendezvous* of Nationalists. All Ireland heard about his "modest bedroom" there, and his property, consisting of two trunks, which he freely placed at the disposal of those who sued him for libel, if they succeeded in getting a verdict against him. The proprietor, Mr Charles Lawler, was a bachelor and a man of means, being a director of the Dublin Alliance Gas Company and a very typical middle-class Dublin Catholic. The smoke-room was on the ground floor off the hall, and the hall porter had liberty from the police to admit newspaper-men and their friends at all hours of the night. Many well-known Nationalists, who were not newspaper-men, also had the *entrée*, and the police had never been known to summon the proprietor for breach of the licensing laws.

Every night after eleven and up to three in the morning, one was sure to meet here several members of 'The Freeman' staff, and Nationalist M.P.'s or organisers passing through or staying in town. Here the most sensational stories were told, and the events of " to-morrow " discussed in the small hours of the morning over tobacco and whisky-and-water. Mr E. H. Ennis, then a leader-writer on 'The Freeman,' who afterwards became successively private secretary to Lord Chancellor Walker, Registrar in Chancery, and Assistant Under Secretary for Ireland, was the only man I remember who invariably drank tea on such occasions. The old Imperial Hotel has been swallowed up by Clery's large drapery establishment, and though a part of Clery's is still known as the Imperial Hotel, it bears no relationship to the house kept by Charles Lawler.

Another house which had liberty to entertain press-men after hours was the Ship Hotel in Lower Abbey Street, opposite ' United Ireland ' offices, its proprietor, Stephen Cunningham, being also a bachelor. In the Ship of an afternoon the best-known Dublin National-

ists were then to be found discussing the latest political crisis and local scandals—members of Parliament,
corporators, wire-pullers, gossips, and pressmen, saying
what they had left unsaid in Parliament, on the platform, in the City Hall, or in the papers. Those who
were not initiated were looked upon as intruders, and
made to feel themselves *de trop*.

'The Freeman' commented adversely on the conduct of the jury at the Imperial Hotel, where they
were kept under lock and key by the police during
Hynes's trial; Judge Lawson ordered Gray to appear
before him, and, with characteristic courage and
severity, fined him £500 and sentenced him to three
months' imprisonment, at the end of which Gray was
to give his own bail of £5000 and two sureties of
£2500 each, or go to jail for another three months.
As the High Sheriff could not be asked to take
himself to prison, Gray's intimate friend, Dr Whyte,
the city coroner, executed the judge's order. A
public subscription was started by Mr Parnell, and
Gray's fine instantly paid. The Judge kept him six
weeks in Kilmainham, during which he was allowed
to edit his paper and live in specially furnished
apartments, Mrs Gray taking lodgings opposite the
prison and spending the day with him, while his
friends were allowed to visit him freely. I often
heard his *levées* in Kilmainham jail humorously
described in the office of 'The Freeman's Journal.'

Mr Gray was fast becoming a rich man, for, thanks
to his versatile change from "West Britonism" to
Parnellism, 'The Freeman' was now read in every
corner of Ireland, as no other paper had ever been
read before, and its advertising revenue was proportionately large. He filled its columns with *verbatim*

reports of the speeches of the Chief and his lieutenants, paid Mr T. P. O'Connor a generous stipend
for his racy descriptions of what occurred "in the
House," acquired a capital London office in the Strand
(which the paper still possesses), and kept two
excellent men in it to compose the "London Correspondence," which was read eagerly all over Ireland.
The oppression of the farmers, the tyranny of the
landlords, and the stupidity or malice of the English
Government were the everlasting themes, by harping
on which Mr Gray made his paper the visible brain
of Catholic Ireland, and amassed a large fortune for
himself. His constant fear was that 'United Ireland'
might be converted into a daily paper. A. M. Sullivan once had hopes of starting 'The Nation' as a
daily paper; but Gray completely outwitted him, and
the Sullivans never succeeded in capturing the profitable part of Nationalist journalism.

As a newspaper owner Gray was in advance of his
time, especially in throwing himself with equal energy
into the business and literary sides of his paper,
advertising it in novel ways, and getting it into the
country towns hours before other Dublin papers. He
was not an orator, and rarely appeared at a public
meeting even at the head office of the League. The
Dublin Corporation afforded him a local platform, and
he reserved his best energy for 'The Freeman.' A
few years after this, when he retired from the Corporation, he had forgotten the ward for which he sat,
and issued a valedictory address to the burgesses of
another ward. His voice was weak and ineffective,
and he had no taste for speaking. He never aspired
to political leadership, setting his heart rather on a
monopoly of the journalistic profits of the revolution-

ary movement, with its larger personal liberty, content
to be the *vates sacer*, and leaving to Mr Parnell the
more glorious but less profitable *rôle* of Agamemnon,
King of Men.

While the public were eagerly discussing Mr Gray's
arrest, and the festivities connected with the Exhibition were in full swing in Dublin, a murder of unprecedented heinousness, or, as it would be more accurate
to call it, a massacre, was committed at Maamtrasna
in Joyce's Country, in county Galway, where a number
of disguised men entered the house of a family named
Joyce at dead of night, on August 17th, and slaughtered
the inmates as they slept—father, mother, two sons,
and a daughter. One little boy, severely wounded
and left for dead, escaped with his life. This was
the most atrocious crime committed by the agrarian,
as the Phœnix Park murders were the worst done by
the non-agrarian section of the secret wing of Parnell's
revolutionary movement; and, coming directly after
the opening of the National Exhibition, seemed almost
as much the outcome of a perverse fate. It arose out
of the murder of Lord Ardilaun's bailiffs, the Huddys,
whose slayers suspected that this family knew their
secret, and determined to put the whole of them
to death. Happily they were tracked, the horror
excited being so great that the neighbours gave
evidence against them, and out of this crime the
murderers of the Huddys were also discovered.

On the same day a Kilkenny farmer, who had
broken "the unwritten law," was dragged from his
bed at night and callously shot. Just at that time
there was a colossal funeral procession in Dublin, at
which the Nationalists turned out in their thousands,
for the interment of Charles Kickham, the member

of the supreme council of the Irish Republican Brotherhood who had distrusted Parnell from the first. This demonstration, following close upon the Maamtrasna murders, and organised entirely by Dublin Fenians, showed how curiously mixed in the Irish nature are sympathy for the dead and inhumanity towards the living. Needless to say, all the Invincibles who were at large took part in this display of Fenian power.

Before the horror caused by these crimes had subsided the Dublin Metropolitan Police came out on strike, and as the Constabulary were still out, there was great alarm amongst the law-abiding Dubliners. Two hundred and thirty-four constables were first dismissed for attending meetings of protest against their ill-treatment by the authorities. Six hundred then resigned on September 1st, others followed suit, and only twenty-five inspectors were left at their posts. A curious situation then arose in Dublin. Earl Spencer, as Lord - Lieutenant, issued a proclamation for the enrolment of special constables. At the same time Lord Mayor Dawson issued a counter - proclamation inviting citizens to enroll as special constables under his authority. This was the most revolutionary step yet taken—the representative of the people setting himself up in opposition to the representative of the Crown. The response to both proclamations showed that Dublin would not suffer from the want of special constables. It must have afforded Councillor Carey and his Invincibles much amusement to see the two sets of amateur policemen patrolling the streets wearing different badges, and there were not a few hostile encounters between the rival custodians of order. Rioting took place in Sackville Street, which the military suppressed; but many days did not pass before the Royal Irish Constabulary surrendered, and then the Dublin Police returned to duty.

Just as the strike was being settled, the agrarian slayers shot one Thomas Quin dead on September 5th, as he was driving on the highroad near Edenderry, in King's County. But a few days later they got their first exemplary check under the new Crimes Act, when Thomas Hynes was executed at Limerick for the murder of a herd named Doloughty, being the first man tried by a special commission of judges without a jury. On the 2nd of October two men were arrested in Ulster for treason-felony, the charge being that they were members of a secret society called the Irish Patriotic Brotherhood, having for its object the "removal" of landlords, agents, Government officials, and loyal people. The Invincibles were still walking the streets of Dublin as free men, swaggering in the public-houses and, as afterwards appeared, giving too loose a rein to their tongues. The discovery of this Irish Patriotic Brotherhood made them uneasy, for it was a local edition of their own society.

News from America, too, helped to spur them into action. Pat Ford of 'The Irish World,' disgusted with Parnell and Mrs O'Shea, closed his Land League fund, which had amounted to £68,000. "Since the day of the Kilmainham Treaty," he complained, "the agitation had been doing nothing but going backward. Reaction has set in. The Parliamentary party have it all their own way." The Land League was still in existence in America. Nor did 'The Irish World's' condemnation end its career, though it seems to have stimulated Mr Parnell to give an account of his stewardship; for, on October 13th, the balance-sheet of the Irish National Land League, suppressed a year before, was published, and is in every way a document worthy of note.

RECEIPTS.		EXPENDITURE.	
Relief of Distress fund .	£59,178	Relief of Distress, 1879-	
Land League fund .	30,825	1880	£50,000
Defence fund . .	6,563	State trials . . .	15,000
do. (per 'Freeman')	14,514	General expenses of	
Received by Mr Egan in		Land League (includ-	
Paris up to date .	129,907	ing Ladies' Land	
Investments . . .	2,583	League) . . .	148,000
Profit on sale of U.S.			
Bonds . . .	1,250		£213,000
		Balance in Mr Egan's	
		hands . . .	31,820
Total .	£244,820	Total .	£244,820

Thus we see that the large sum of £148,000 had been disbursed as "general expenses," undefined, in two years, an amount larger than the Secret Service Fund of the British Government, while Mr Egan in Paris still remained well supplied with cash. As the Land League had only been two years in existence, money had poured into its coffers at the rate of £330 per day—a wonderful record, considering that the revolution was in its infancy, and the subscribers mainly poor people at home and in America, for the well-to-do had not yet begun to subscribe.

Since the suppression of the Land League the people had been slipping away from the control of the leaders, the industrious fixing their thoughts on work, the idlers on fresh schemes of revenge. Now that the Kilmainham Treaty had fallen to the ground, it was imperative that money should be got for the support of the members and the attainment of the ultimate

object for which Mr Parnell had " taken off his coat."
Nothing could have come from an alliance with the
Liberals except a scramble for office, and that was not
to be thought of. Under these circumstances Mr
Parnell felt himself free to launch a new league, and
with this end in view presided over a conference at
the Antient Concert Rooms, Dublin, on October 17th,
at which the Irish National League was founded.

The I.N.L. more than supplied the place of the
I.N.L.L., its programme, as set forth by Mr Parnell
that day, comprising " national self-government,
land reform, local self-government, extension of the
parliamentary and municipal franchise, development
and encouragement of the labour and industrial
resources of Ireland." In founding it he aimed at
bringing professional men, traders, artisans, and
labourers into the revolutionary movement, convinced
that the reductions of rent by the land courts would
constantly tend to make the farmers indifferent. In
order to make good the loss of American subscriptions
he sent John Redmond to Australia now to collect
money amongst the Irish there, and afterwards sent
William Redmond to join his brother.

Immediately after the foundation of the National
League dissensions appeared within Mr Parnell's
party. Mr Davitt favoured state ownership of the
land, while Mr Parnell did not go farther than peasant
proprietary. The two men were utterly dissimilar,
Mr Parnell being an aristocrat and Mr Davitt a self-
educated peasant, while each was equally proud and
self-sufficient. Mr Davitt had only one arm, as I have
explained, which made him very irritable and sensitive. They had not seen much of each other before
this, Mr Davitt carrying on the agitation in

LORD MAYOR DAWSON.

"It was in Dawson's years of office, 1882 and 1883, that the Mansion House came under genuine popular control, . . . and Mr Dawson, as the first democratic Lord Mayor, did not underrate his own importance."—PAGE 223.

Connaught and afterwards going to Portland jail; Mr Parnell directing a parliamentary movement at Westminster and moving in an entirely different sphere before he went to Kilmainham. Since their release in May the two men were meeting and clashing, Mr Davitt being held up to veneration, especially in the west, as "The Father of the Land League," and his claim to popularity put into constant rivalry with that of the "Leader of the Irish Race at Home and Abroad."

At this juncture Mr Dillon, never very reliable, announced his intention of resigning his seat on the plea of ill-health, but on Archbishop Croke's advice he reconsidered his decision. He "wanted the land agitation kept at fever heat" instead of being slacked off in favour of Home Rule. But Parnell was now such a power with the mass of the people in Ireland, who knew and cared nothing for the intrigues of the wire-pullers, that he could ignore Davitt and Dillon. He had found his legs again after the Phœnix Park murders, largely owing to the kindness of Gladstone, Chamberlain, and the Englishmen whom he had been so mercilessly denouncing. The Shawites in his party had lost all power. Parnell had become "an institution" rather than an individual, and Catholic Ireland believed in him as a political Pope who could not err. Nothing but his autocracy could have held the revolutionary movement together now, overawing the ambitions of half a dozen would-be leaders, utilising their distinctive energies for the common cause, and still combining, as he had so candidly avowed in America, its constitutional and illegal activities.

Just at the foundation of the National League I came to live in Dublin, my intention being to enter

King's Inns and become a barrister. Knowing that my father had suffered financially by his connection with the Land League, I decided to work my own way to the Bar by means of tuition and journalism, and returned a cheque for fifty pounds which he sent me to pay the entrance fee and stamp duty at King's Inns. My lodgings were in Nelson Street at the north side, just off Eccles Street, where Cardinal Cullen and Isaac Butt used to live not many years before. I began at once to attend law lectures at 9 A.M. in Trinity College, as they cost nothing, and amongst the non-university students then or soon afterwards attending were Mr Timothy Healy, M.P., and Mr Timothy Harrington, who had just come to Dublin as one of the secretaries of the National League. This was essentially a day of great expectations amongst Irish Catholics, the success of the revolutionary movement making all hearts beat high with hope, and a career in Parliament or at the Bar was one of the most popular and apparently feasible objects of a young man's ambition.

The capital of Ireland then presented a strange spectacle. A number of soldier pensioners were imported into the city from England to do duty as plain-clothes constables. They were all arrayed in ready-made clothes of the same kind—black overcoat, dark trousers, bowler hat, and white neckerchief. They were always in couples, and everybody knew them as well as the uniformed police. In Grafton Street, Westmoreland Street, and Sackville Street, by day and night one would meet perhaps a dozen pairs of "marines," as they were called, walking at a leisurely pace between Stephen's Green and the Rotunda. The display of police in the streets then was such as one could not find anywhere else in the British Isles. In the main road of the Phœnix Park there were now many foot police permanently stationed ; two pairs of mounted constables with loaded rifles also patrolled the road along which the Secretaries had walked on the 6th of May ; splendid regiments of infantry and cavalry were always on the move to or from the many Dublin barracks, so that Councillor Carey, Dan Curley, and Joe Brady must often have had their heads turned with vanity at the thought of the vast expense to which they had put the British Government. The door was fast locked now that the steed had been stolen, the situation recalling Dean Swift's verses on the building of the magazine in the Phœnix Park in his time :—

> " Behold a proof of Irish sense !
> Here Irish wit is seen !
> When nothing's left that's worth defence,
> They build a Magazine ! "

Lord Spencer never stirred abroad without being surrounded by a large escort of cavalry, the officer riding by him with a drawn sword. When Lady Spencer went shopping she was similarly escorted. She was exceedingly popular, not only for her good looks and charming manners, but for her pluck as a horsewoman and her devotion to hunting, being a constant follower of the Ward staghounds and the Meath and Kildare foxhounds. Lord Spencer did not hunt, and was frequently accompanied in his drives by the Countess or some other female friend. A highly-connected lady, next whom I sat at a dinner party in the west end several years after, told me how Lady Spencer had often asked her to go out with Lord Spencer as a protection. But happily there was no such misadventure as that which befell Mrs Smythe of Westmeath.

In various parts of the country commissioners were sitting to investigate claims for compensation by the relatives of murdered men and women. Large rewards were advertised at all the police stations for information leading to the detection of murderers ; whenever such posters were stuck up elsewhere they were instantly torn down. On the first of November nine men accused of the Maamtrasna murders were brought to trial at Dublin before Lord Justice Barry and a jury. In the first week of that month Baron Fitzgerald resigned his seat on the bench as a protest against the provisions of the Crimes Act empowering the Government to call upon judges to try cases without juries.

The Invincibles, fearing that their own arrest and trial were imminent, began to lay plans for the intimidation of judges and jurors. On Saturday, November 11th — Saturday was the Invincibles' favourite day,—Patrick Delaney, one of the four who had driven off on Kavanagh's car after the murder of the Secretaries, went forth as "executioner at command of the Invincibles" to remove Judge Lawson. On that day, which was then the beginning of Michaelmas term, a fresh proclamation was issued offering £15,000 for the discovery of the Phœnix Park murderers, £5000 to any accomplice not one of the four occupants of the car, and £1000 for private information. Judge Lawson left his house in Merrion Square at 5 P.M. to walk across the city to King's Inns and dine with the Benchers, accompanied by his son and guarded by two detectives and two 'marines." The marines, who walked on the opposite side of the street, saw Pat Delaney moving along with them and watching the judge. One of them named Macdonnell, a retired Hussar, most sensibly accosted Delaney, saying, " I suppose you know who I am." The Invincible, apparently thinking that Macdonnell was a spy set on him by the society, replied in the affirmative, and crossed the street making straight for the judge. Macdonnell followed, and seeing Delaney about to draw something from his breast-pocket seized him, whereupon the detectives rushed forward and the Invincible was overpowered. On being searched Delaney was found to have a seven-chambered revolver fully charged in his breast-pocket. Judge Lawson took shelter for a while in the Kildare Street Club, and then kept his engagement with the Benchers. When he entered the Queen's Bench on Monday morning the members of the Bar, who were present in great force, cheered him loudly.

Councillor Carey was apparently one of the busiest and most lawfully employed citizens of Dublin at this time, unremitting in his attention to civic business, exemplary in his devotion to his religious duties, and prospering in his trade, having just secured a contract from the South Dublin Guardians, a body largely composed of Unionists and Protestants, to build them a mortuary chapel. But the arrest of Pat Delaney alarmed the Invincibles. They knew that, as one of the four, he could not secure a pardon by turning informer. Nevertheless anything might happen in jail, and they feared lest the police should terrify him into making a confession. The police always seem to have suspected Carey, and it seems almost inexplicable that they did not break up the Invincibles before the murder of the Secretaries. Superintendent Mallon saw Carey every day, for the detective office is next door to the City Hall, and Carey was more than once arrested and released.

On Saturday, November 25th, five Maamtrasna prisoners who pleaded guilty were removed from Dublin to Galway jail. On that night there were several Invincibles and other Fenians in Gilligan's public-house in Middle Abbey Street, and six detectives were waiting outside keeping watch on them. When the public-house closed the Fenians came out, and one of them actually went up to the senior detective and said : "You are training these young men to watch us. I will give them my photograph if you like." This Fenian was right, for three of the constables were young men who were being trained for secret society work. The Invincibles crossed the street, and the detectives followed them. All were apparently armed, and one of them, Christopher Dowling, a gasfitter, produced a revolver. Sergeant Cox then ordered his men to arrest Dowling, whereupon the gasfitter instantly fired and shot the sergeant dead. Eastwood, another of the detectives, then fired at and wounded Dowling, who was overpowered. Another Invincible, Thomas Devine, a housepainter, fired his revolver at Eastwood but missed him. There were some civilian spectators—including myself and other students who were attracted from Sackville Street by the shots,—but they feared to come within range of the guns. Some uniformed constables then arrived, and a sergeant of the King's Rifles bravely drew his sword and went to the aid of the police. Cabs were procured, and Cox and Dowling were taken to Jarvis Street hospital close by, the first to the mortuary, the second to the accident ward. Thirty uniformed constables remained on guard at the hospital for the night to prevent any attempt at rescuing Dowling.

Thomas Devine was arrested on the charge of trying to kill Eastwood, and four other Fenians, including Joseph Poole, a tailor, whom the police took to be the leader of the gang. These were a different set of men from the Phœnix Park "executioners." Poole said at the police court that "if the men were loitering about for any purpose it was for injuring him. Devine and he were not on good terms." This was confirmed afterwards by the confession of a Fenian who turned informer, and said the men at Gilligan's that night were "a vigilance committee," whose duty it was to see that the "executioners" carried out the orders given them. Poole was under suspicion, and the committee's object was to terrify and, probably, kill him that night.

On the day of this encounter Michael Davitt spoke at Navan, where Bishop Nulty's carriage was sent to convey him from the station to the place of meeting, and said : " We should make Irish landlordism support the people who are starving. I propose that, in case Mr Gladstone does not apply the surplus of the arrears estimate to save the people, no rent should be paid from this November till next May. Archbishop Hughes declared in 1848 that a man in danger of death by hunger would be justified before God in seizing upon the bread on the sacrificial altar. How much more justifiable then for our people to seize upon what landlordism steals from them and their children every year !"

On the next evening but one, the Phœnix Park "executioners" were ordered out on a mission in which they were more successful, using the knife and the outside-car which had proved so effective in "making history." The command this time was to slay a Dublin Protestant shopkeeper named Field, foreman of the jury who tried a youth named Walsh, who was executed for the murder of Constable Cavanagh at Letterfrack in county Galway—a crime for the discovery of whose perpetrators a reward of £5000 was offered. Mr Field kept a large stationery shop in Westmoreland Street close to the Bank of Ireland, and was as inoffensive a type of Dublin citizen as could be imagined. In striking him down the Invincibles were not making war against distinguished individuals or privileged classes, but against the average men who constitute the framework of civilised society. But there was a reason for his "removal." Under the Crimes Act the Government were trying cases like the Maamtrasna and other murders not in the locality where they occurred, except in the north-east, when the trials were held in Belfast, by special juries in Dublin. Mr Field's "removal" was intended to terrify the Protestant Dublin jurors who were bringing in verdicts of guilty in such cases. But it was especially meant to intimidate the jurors at the impending Dublin Commission at which Pat Delaney was expected to be tried, as well as the slayers of Lord Ardilaun's bailiffs, the Huddys, and probably the slayer of Sergeant Cox. Having failed in their attempt on a judge, they resolved to make an example of a prominent juryman.

Accordingly Michael Kavanagh, with his repainted outside-car and his brown mare (back from grass), drove Joe Brady and Thomas Caffrey to the corner of Hardwicke Street and North Frederick Street, under the shadow of St George's Church, where Joseph Hanlon and Timothy Kelly were awaiting them. The slayers alighted, and Kavanagh remained in his seat ready to whisk them away as before when the deed was done. Mr Field lived in Frederick Street, a few doors from the corner of Hardwicke Street, and he was watched as he came home by way of Sackville Street and Rutland Square. Just as he had passed Hardwicke Street and was looking for his latch-key to open his door, Brady plunged a surgical knife into his body and stabbed him as mercilessly as the Secretaries, leaving the body apparently dead on the footpath. A score of people were looking on, but, so smitten with terror were they, that they made no effort to stop the murderers. Brady and Kelly ran round the corner and Kavanagh drove them off on his outside-car, Hanlon and Caffrey escaping on foot into one of the many back lanes in the neighbourhood and getting away in the dark, no bystander daring to pursue.

Marvellous to relate, the victim was not dead. The knives were so sharp, and gave so clean a wound, that they had glanced aside and did not reach the heart, but his brief life afterwards was a lingering death. His daughters tried to carry on the business, but they were remorselessly boycotted, even their fellow-Protestants avoiding the shop for fear of their own lives.

Next day the Privy Council issued a proclamation putting Dublin under the curfew clause of the Crimes Act, but assuring law-abiding citizens that their liberty of action would not be interfered with. There was now a regular reign of terror in the city. The theatres and places of amusement were deserted, for people feared to be out at night. The escape of the

Phœnix Park murderers caused the police to be dis-trusted. And now the slaying of Sergeant Cox and the attack on Mr Field brought the danger closer than ever to the average citizen. On the day after the attempted "removal" of Mr Field, a process-server named Mellon was attacked by young men in Gardiner Street, cruelly stabbed, and left for dead.

When Judge William O'Brien opened the Com-mission for the trial of prisoners at Green Street on December 4th, he was accompanied by Lord Mayor Dawson and Mr Dwyer Gray, the city High Sheriff. Mr Gray remained seated when all in court rose to hear the Queen's commission read, but, on being called to order by the Clerk of the Peace, he rose to his feet. The judge, in his charge to the Grand Jury, lamented the prevalence of crime in the city and the insecurity of life and property. Lord Mayor Dawson heard him in silence, but, at the end of the address, drove in state to the City Hall, where the Corporation was in session, and delivered a counter-charge, in which he reminded Judge O'Brien that when he was seeking to be elected for Ennis in opposition to Lysaght Finigan a few years before, he said the real cure for the evils of Ireland was the restoration of their own parliament in College Green.

Pat Higgins and Michael Flynn were found guilty of the murder of the Huddys. Flynn said from the dock, after being sentenced to death, "I am sure Ireland will not see my poor wife and children starv-ing when I am gone. My old father and mother, now nearly eighty years of age, I hope will also be provided for by Ireland. I am brought up here for slaughter. I am as innocent as the babe unborn. I am as glad to go to my God as to my home and family." The

Ladies' Land League had been giving money to him and other men imprisoned for all the chief agrarian murders. Funds were also liberally subscribed for the defence of Dowling, who shot Sergeant Cox. Five Maamtrasna prisoners (including Myles Joyce) were executed at Galway on Friday, December 15th; and, on the next night in Dublin, the police and marines raided seventeen public-houses and searched no less than 600 persons found in them for arms and treasonable documents, in the hope of finding some clue to the perpetrators of the Phœnix Park murders.

Sergeant Danvers of the Rifles, who had aided the police in the Middle Abbey Street affray, was presented with a testimonial by the loyalist members of the Bar and the students of Trinity College; while the Government publicly commended him and gave him a meagre grant of five pounds.

Mr Joseph Biggar, M.P., had no such sympathy for those who helped the Executive in punishing criminals. Speaking at Waterford at this time he called Earl Spencer "that bloodthirsty English peer" who, as "the representative of English Whiggery," had "turned off the jury every man who professed the Catholic faith." He declared that Walsh, on whose jury Field acted as foreman, and Myles Joyce, one of the Maamtrasna prisoners, were both innocent of the crimes for which they had been hanged.

In Christmas week two men, named Poff and Barrett, were found guilty by a Cork jury of shooting a farmer named Brown dead in broad daylight on his own farm near Castleisland in Kerry—now one of the most lawless centres in Ireland; and Poff, after being sentenced to death, cried out: "This will not stop the work at Castleisland!" Patrick Egan was in Dublin in Christmas week, and had several interviews with William O'Brien, editor of 'United Ireland,' who was now leading the attack on Lord Spencer for the execution of the men found guilty of various murders—the Nationalist contention apparently being either that the criminals were patriots and should not be punished, or that the crimes were committed by undiscovered persons whose names the Nationalists knew but would not disclose.

During 1882 there were 26 murders in Ireland—one a fortnight—and 58 attempted murders, that is more than one a week. The number of people evicted from their homesteads—men, women, and children—was 26,836, as compared with 17,341 in 1881 and 10,457 in 1880. Mr Parnell's promise to Mr Gladstone "to declare against outrage energetically" was now utterly lost sight of; and, instead of condemnation of crime, the Nationalist leaders were exerting all their powers of vituperation to bring down public odium on judges and juries who brought home the responsibility for crime to any specific individual. Their exasperation with the officers of the law was doubtless due to grave fears aroused in their minds by secret inquiries now being held in Dublin Castle under the Crimes Act, from which, if any of the accused should turn informers, no man could foresee what consequences might flow.

CHAPTER XXIII.

DISCOVERY OF THE INVINCIBLES. PARNELL ON HIS
DEFENCE. JAMES CAREY CONSIDERED.

As 1882 had closed, so 1883 opened with bloodshed.
On the second day of the year three emergency men,
occupying evicted land, were attacked at Uppercross,
Tipperary, and in self-defence killed one of their
assailants and wounded others. There was now a
regular profession of Emergency Men, under the
direction of the Landlords' Property Defence Association, who, like the strike-breakers in the United
States, were sent to till boycotted farms and protect
property in all parts of Ireland. The police were
largely employed in protecting emergency men and
boycotted persons, and it was a common sight to
see armed and uniformed constables escorting a farmer
as he ploughed or reaped in his own field, or guarding
him as he travelled on the public road.

The emergency men used to bring their own provisions and frequently their own huts to live in, and
were usually able to shoe their own horses and do
everything else they required, so as to be independent
of the boycotters. The police, too, had huts—even
yet a quantity of these huts may be seen stored in
the Constabulary Depôt in the Phœnix Park—as well
as their own provisions, horses, cars, and craftsmen.
I have often seen in districts, where the buildings

on the evicted farms had been destroyed, not only an
emergency man's hut and a constabulary hut, but also
Land League huts, fixed in some waste spot by the
roadside near at hand, in which the evicted tenants
and their families lived supported by Land League
funds, too poor to avail themselves of the Arrears Act,
and waiting for the day when the revolution would
restore them to their farms in which their ancestors
had lived from time immemorial, and apart from which
their home-bred wits could not see how life was possible.   On some estates, where there were wholesale
evictions, villages of huts of all kinds were to be seen,
and, while the population of the district was thus almost doubled, the fields at each side of the road were
a forest of weeds ; for the emergency men often did
no more than occupy the farms for the landlord so as
to keep the old tenants out.   All these symptoms of
revolution were visible in some part of almost every
Irish county at this time, except in the north-east,
where business went on with unchecked industry and
prosperity.

During the last weeks of 1882, while the Fenian
Land Leaguers were terrifying all Ireland, a secret
inquiry was being held in Dublin Castle by Mr John
Adye Curran, a police magistrate, under the provisions
of the Crimes Act, at which witnesses were examined
on oath, though no definite charge was made against
individuals.   After a prolonged investigation, the
Dublin police raided several houses and made seventeen arrests, including Councillor Carey and the
Invincibles already named, in connection with the
attempts on Mr Forster's life and the Phœnix Park
murders.   This was the first fruit of those clauses of
the Crimes Act which Mr Parnell had so bitterly

opposed. The arrested men and Patrick Delaney, who was already in prison for the attempted murder of Judge Lawson, were at once charged with a conspiracy to kill members of the Dublin police, Government officials and others ; and, having been brought before the police magistrates on January 13th, were remanded without bail. Two days later three others were arrested on the same charge ; and there was intense, but suppressed, excitement in Nationalist circles. Mr Killen, the barrister who helped Davitt and Brennan to start the Land Agitation in Connaught, defended Joe Brady and Patrick Delaney.

The whole energy of the Parnellites now seemed concentrated on defending men accused of murder and in attacking not merely the Executive, but the judges and juries who condemned them. The official organ of Mr Parnell, ' United Ireland,' was circulating freely since the Kilmainham Treaty, and now definitely charged Lord Spencer with the murder of Francis Hynes, already mentioned, as well as of Myles Joyce, one of the men hanged for the Maamtrasna massacre ; and Mr William O'Brien, its editor, was brought before the magistrate two days after the Invincibles, and committed to take his trial for seditious libel. At that moment he was seeking election for the borough of Mallow, his native town, as Mr Parnell's nominee ; the former member, Mr Johnson, Attorney-General, having just been appointed a judge, and the Government candidate being Mr John Naish, the new Solicitor-General, who was a Catholic. There were only some 250 voters, and before the Ballot Act it was estimated that £10 a head for something over half of them would secure election. But Mallow now proved unpurchaseable, the issue its electors were asked to decide being whether or not Lord Spencer and the Castle lawyers were guilty of murder in executing Poff and Barrett, the two men already mentioned, for slaying the farmer named Brown near Castle-island. Mr O'Brien maintained that the condemned men's innocence was proved by documents brought to light after they were hanged, and by denouncing the executions as "judicial murders" so influenced his fellow-townsmen that they elected him by a majority of two to one over the Castle lawyer.

After a week's adjournment, when the twenty Fenians were brought before the magistrate again, Robert Farrell, a labourer, turned informer, and told how the long series of plans to kill Forster had failed owing to some bungle in the prearranged signal or the hour of Forster's arrival having been miscalculated. He was not himself an Invincible, though he had been engaged in one of the plots to murder the ex-Chief Secretary, and he told what he had heard from Joseph Hanlon of the attempt to kill Mr Field. It is worthy of note that on this day, January 20th, when Farrell became Queen's evidence, a diabolical dynamite outrage was perpetrated at Glasgow, to which I shall refer again.

After a week's remand, further evidence was given on January 27th against Joseph Brady, Timothy Kelly, John Dwyer, Joseph Hanlon, and Michael Kavanagh the car-driver, in connection with the attack on Mr Field, and it was announced that another of the prisoners, a tailor named Lamie, brother-in-law of Joseph Poole, had turned informer. He told how "vigilance committees" had been formed to see that the orders of the directory were carried out, explaining that the fight in Middle Abbey Street, when Sergeant Cox was killed, had resulted in breaking up one of these committees which apparently meant to assassinate Poole. Dr Webb, a distinguished ex-Fellow of Trinity, and Mr Richard Adams, a Cork man, now joined Mr Killen in defending all the prisoners.

There was a further week's adjournment, and, on February 3rd, the first mention was made of the Phœnix Park tragedy, the prisoners being charged with the murder of the Secretaries. The police produced knives found in Carey's house, and called doctors to prove that they were the knives used by surgeons for amputations, and that the wounds of Lord Frederick Cavendish and Mr Burke were such as would have been inflicted by those instruments. Witnesses swore to seeing one or other of the Invincibles in the Phœnix Park on the 6th of May. A chairmaker and his wife from the Strawberry Beds, on the north bank of the Liffey between the park and Lucan, saw O'Brien and Joseph Brady. Another witness identified Brady and Caffrey. There were at least nine Invincibles seen prowling about the park during the afternoon before the murder. A park-ranger identified Joe Brady as having driven out of Chapelizod gate in the evening on an outside-car when he and his fellow-murderers were flying after the crime.

After a further week's remand, Michael Kavanagh, the car-driver, turned informer on February 10th. He told how he had driven Brady, Kelly, Caffrey, and Patrick Delaney to the Phœnix Park on May 6th ; how they had met James Carey ; and how he had driven off with the murderers "across the Fifteen Acres," through Chapelizod and Inchicore, and back to the city by way of Terenure, Palmerston Park, and Leeson Street ; also how on the night of the attack on Mr

Field, he had driven Brady and Caffrey to the scene, waited on his car while the attack was being made, and drove Brady and Kelly away.

When, after another week's remand, the prisoners were again brought up on February 17th, Councillor James Carey came forward as an informer. The behaviour of Carey so far was typical of Dubliners of his kind. He dressed loudly, bore a swaggering mien, evincing contempt for the warders and police, and actually assaulting the Governor of Kilmainham. When he came to court, he lounged out of the prison van smoking a cigar, and kept a haughty distance from his fellow-prisoners to emphasise his higher rank in life. Having maintained his audacity at five appearances in court, he broke down when the car-driver turned informer and resolved to escape the hangman. He told how the Invincible Society had been formed, and how he had lured other men into it. He had plotted many murders, including the attack on Mr Field; had arranged the details of the Phœnix Park assassination; had chosen the knives; was present in the park and had given the signal for the deed. He insisted that Daniel Curley was chairman of the society; and that there was a supreme authority whom Carey never knew and who was always spoken of as "Number One." He told how he had met Frank Byrne and P. J. Sheridan, after the Invincible Society was formed, and discussed operations with them; and how "Number One" gave orders, after the attempts on Forster had failed, to "remove" Mr Burke. The impression left by Carey's confession was that he was a subordinate or colleague rather than a leader. He underrated his importance in the conspiracy to lessen his guilt, making large reservations we may be sure, and only telling enough to convict those already in custody, thereby hoping to win the gratitude of those whom he refrained from implicating. Thomas Brennan, secretary to the Land League, who used to attend the Fenian meetings in Carey's house before the formation of the Invincibles, was now safe in America. So was Sheridan, the Land League organiser, who had been in communication with Carey after the formation of the Invincibles. Frank Byrne was said to be on the Riviera "reporting Mr Gladstone's movements for the Press." James O'Connor, who had acted as chairman of the Fenian meetings at Carey's house before the Invincibles came into being, was still assistant-editor of 'United Ireland.' After Carey's evidence, all the prisoners were returned for trial to the County Dublin Commission, and for the intervening seven weeks the world anxiously awaited the result. Meanwhile, Joseph Biggar, M.P., was prosecuted for his denunciation of Dublin jurors, and compelled to give bail for future good behaviour. Soon afterwards Michael Davitt, Timothy Healy, M.P., and Joseph Quinn were prosecuted for similar speeches, and called on to find bail or go to prison for six months. They refused to give bail and went to prison, Mr Davitt, perhaps, as an ex-Fenian, finding it safer to be under lock and key while such blood-curdling revelations were being made by his fellow-Fenians. He had been disposed to differ with Mr Parnell upon the question of land nationalisation and the policy of the National League; but, after he came out of jail this time, he was never again even thought of as a possible rival to the Chief and lapsed into a secondary position.

When Parliament met on February 15th, Mr John Gorst, who had been denouncing coercion at the time

of the Kilmainham Treaty, asked the House to declare "that the recent change in the Government's
Irish policy be maintained, and that secret societies
continue to engage the energetic vigilance of the Government," pointing out the connection of Mr Parnell
with the Invincibles through P. J. Sheridan, his
fellow - traverser, who had been incriminated by
Carey's evidence. Mr William O'Brien defended
the Parnellites in a maiden speech, and justified
himself against the accusation that he had supported Carey's election to the Dublin Corporation
by saying he had not known why Carey had been
arrested as a suspect. It is possible that, in 1881,
Mr O'Brien knew nothing of the Invincibles; but
his assistant, Mr James O'Connor, can hardly have
been so ignorant.

Mr Forster challenged Mr Parnell, "as the avowed
leader and chief of an organisation which promoted
outrage and incited to murder," to give an open
disclaimer to his connection with the crimes recently
committed, quoting incitements to crime from speeches
of Brennan, Sheridan, Boyton, Redpath, and other
early Land Leaguers, and from 'United Ireland,' of
which Mr Parnell was the chief proprietor. He was
specifically charging Parnell with conniving at outrage and murder, but had only uttered the word
"conniving," when Parnell cried out "It's a lie!"
Mr O'Kelly repeated Parnell's observation three times
in defiance of the Speaker. No notice was taken of
Parnell, but O'Kelly was suspended. Mr Forster then
finished his speech, declaring that "the cruelty and
wickedness of this agitation had been unveiled, un-
masked, and exposed" by the Invincible disclosures.

The House expected Parnell to rise immediately

and answer Forster. But the Chief rarely did what was expected of him, and it was Mr T. P. O'Connor who spoke for the party. Next day the English Press, Liberal as well as Conservative, with a few exceptions, said Parnell had been proved guilty of "conniving at outrage." There was, however, no new evidence against him, for he had admitted in the Kilmainham negotiations that Sheridan was an outrage-monger; and, the Government having then condoned his connection with Sheridan, he did not feel called upon now to make an apology because Carey had implicated Sheridan. He maintained his mental balance at a time when the future looked very black—for, if Carey had only betrayed his insensate dupes, and, in hope of living, had reserved his connection with higher politicians, who could tell what further revelations might be made? The debate would have closed apparently without his intervention, if Lord Hartington had not informed the House that he had heard that the member for Cork wished to move the adjournment so that he might speak on the following day.

After this sportsmanlike hint from the brother of Lord Frederick Cavendish, Mr Parnell moved the adjournment, and, on February 23rd, rose to speak in a House labouring under intense excitement. The love of members for a sensation is proverbial, but calmer minds also breathlessly awaited Mr Parnell's words. The shrewdest observer of public affairs of his day, and the best politician of the century, King Edward VII., then Prince of Wales, came into the gallery with a number of notable people to take personal observations. But the Chief's reply gave their curiosity small gratification. He was not penitent or broken down, as he was after the murders. He knew that there was no evidence to make him legally responsible for Irish crime; and, having discovered that his moral responsibility did not lessen his power over the Irish people, his only answer now was to hurl defiance at his accusers. "The utmost I desire to do," he said, "is to make my position clear to the Irish people at home and abroad. . . . Why was Forster deposed and a 'prentice, though a very willing hand, put in his position? It would be better to have the Crimes Act administered by the seasoned politician now in disgrace and retirement. Call him back to his post. Send him to help Lord Spencer in the congenial work of the gallows in Ireland. Send him to look after the secret inquiries in Dublin Castle. Send him to distribute the taxes which an unfortunate peasantry have to pay for crimes not committed by themselves. . . . The time will come when this House and the people of this country will admit that they have been led astray as to the right mode of governing a noble, a brave, a generous, and an impulsive people, and they will reject their present leaders who are conducting them into the terrible courses into which the Government appears determined to lead Ireland."

On the day after this debate, Mr Parnell got a welcome proof that he had not appealed in vain to the judgment of the Irish people. Mr H. J. Gill, a wealthy Catholic publisher, having retired from the representation of Westmeath in a panic caused by the Invincible revelations, the Parnellite candidate, Mr Timothy Harrington, then a prisoner in Mullingar jail for an illegal speech, was elected in his stead, though an entire stranger in the constituency. This success was followed by two failures. In county Dublin a few days after, Colonel King-Harman, who had become a Conservative, was returned by a large majority over Mr Parnell's unattractive nominee, Mr Edward McMahon. On the same day in Portarlington, the Conservative, Mr Brewster, received 70 votes as against 57 polled for the Parnellite, Mr Thomas Mayne, a Dublin shopkeeper and member of the Corporation.

Parnell now led a life of "seclusion and mystery," being more than ever with Mrs O'Shea, hiding himself from his followers, and even living under assumed names—"Mr Fox" being one of his *aliases*. Meanwhile, he and his colleagues pursued their usual policy in Parliament, as if undisturbed by the Invincible revelations. Lord Mayor Dawson introduced a Borough Franchise Bill on March 7th. A week later, the Chief introduced a Bill to amend the Land Act, which Mr Gladstone firmly refused to support, on the grounds that the Land Courts were settling cases at the rate of 2350 a month; and the Bill was rejected by 250 to 63. Mr John Barry—one of the few well-to-do Parnellites, owner of a linoleum factory at Kirkcaldy—introduced a County Government Bill, proposing to substitute elected representatives of the ratepayers instead of the Grand Juries.

While the parliamentary revolutionists were thus playing their parts, the Irish Patriotic Brotherhood, the arrest of two of whose members I have recorded, had its secrets exposed in a trial before Judge Lawson at Belfast Assizes on March 28th. It was an assassination society on the lines of the Invincibles, but less ambitious; and its headquarters were in a Catholic district of rural Ulster. Twelve of its members were now found guilty of treason-felony, the principal witness against them being an informer named Patrick Duffy; and Lawson sentenced ten of them to ten years' penal servitude, one to seven years, and one to five years. No murder had been traced to them; but, if they had been allowed to develop, they would doubtless have taken many lives.

When the trial of the Invincibles was close at hand, Mr John Dillon resigned his seat for county Tipperary, on the plea that he was ordered to Colorado by his doctor. I do not remember to have heard it said that he had anything to fear from the disclosures of James Carey; but he left his leader's side at a time of great peril and responsibility. Mr Parnell sent Mr Thomas Mayne down to Tipperary, and, according to the Nationalist papers, there were to be two other candidates—Mr Bagwell, a landlord, and Mr Moore, a Catholic Liberal—but neither could get the requisite number of nominators, and Mayne was returned unopposed. This was another proof that Mr Parnell had not lost the approval of the people through his connection with Sheridan and Frank Byrne, and, through them, with Carey.

A new phase of the revolutionary movement, which promised to be more horrible even than the murder scheme of the Invincibles, came to light on March 29th, the day after the conviction of the members of the Patriotic Brotherhood, when two Irishmen, Deasy and Flanagan, were arrested at Liverpool for having dynamite in their possession with felonious intent, a flask of liquid explosive having been found in

Deasy's luggage on his arrival by steamer from Cork. A horrible dynamite plot to lay a large part of London in ruins was frustrated six days later by the arrest of a gang of conspirators, of whom the chief were Whitehead, Dalton, Dr Gallagher, and his brother Bernard Gallagher, who were found in possession of vast quantities of the most dangerous explosives known to science. These alarming disclosures, made just before the trial of the Invincibles, created such consternation in England that Sir William Harcourt, the Home Secretary, introduced, on April 9th, a special Crimes Bill for the dynamitards known as the Explosives Bill, which was rushed through all its stages that day in the Commons and in the Lords, and became the law of the land next day—Mr Parnell absenting himself from the House and writing to Justin McCarthy from an unknown address advising the party to give no opposition. He was determined to stand clear of the dynamitards; but, like the Invincibles, they were as integral a part of the revolutionary movement as the parliamentary party.

The trials of the Invincibles began on April 10th at Green Street before Judge William O'Brien, the Midleton man who had been defeated by Lysaght Finigan at the Ennis election in 1879. He was no relative of the editor of 'United Ireland.' He had been connected with the 'Cork Examiner,' and, in his earlier years at the Bar, had won the friendship of Edward Sullivan (a Midleton College man), who was now Master of the Rolls and soon to be Lord Chancellor of Ireland, and to whom O'Brien is said to have owed his promotion. Peter Carey, brother of James, now turned informer, and also Smith, who had identified

Mr Burke. The trials lasted a long time, the chief prisoners being arraigned separately, the others in a batch. No individual or society could be found to provide funds for their legal defence, and the Crown appointed Dr Webb and Richard Adams to defend them. They were utterly deserted by those who had lured them on. Joe Brady, Daniel Curley, and Michael Fagan were found guilty and ordered to be hanged. In Timothy Kelly's case the jury twice disagreed, but at the third trial he was found guilty and sentenced to death. Thomas Caffrey and Patrick Delaney pleaded guilty and were condemned to die, but Delaney's sentence was commuted to penal servitude for life. Mullet and Fitzharris, commonly known as "Skin the Goat," got penal servitude for life; the others were let off with lesser sentences.

Brady's sweetheart, Annie Maher, did her best to prove an *alibi* for him, swearing that he was in company with her at the time of the murder and until ten o'clock that night. His hearty laugh at all the jokes during the trial and his good-humoured appearance won general sympathy for him, and his last words leaving the dock after sentence were : "Thank you, Dr Webb ! Thank you, Mr Adams !" Curley also tried to prove an *alibi* and protested that he was innocent, but he said he was proud of being an Invincible and would give away no secrets. His last words as he left the dock were, "God save Ireland !" An immense crowd gathered outside the jail the morning of Joe Brady's execution, and a large force of soldiers and police were present. When the black flag appeared there was a howl of anguish at the martyr's death, and Brady is spoken well of amongst the Dublin working classes to this day. His mother's last words to him are said to have been : "Joe, if you know anything, don't tell it ; bring your secret to the grave !" Similar scenes were enacted outside the jail when Curley, Kelly, Fagan, and Caffrey were hanged. And all Ireland drew a breath of relief when even this partial justice had been done ; for, as Judge O'Brien had said : "The terrible thing about this conspiracy was that they were all respectable men who were indicted."

A young man whom I used to know very well at this time, Frederick Allan, who was employed in ' The Freeman' office, was a great admirer, and, I think, a member of the Irish Republican Brotherhood. He was one of the most honourable, pure-minded, and enthusiastic young men I ever knew, and was afterwards private secretary to Lord Mayor Pile, who officially received Queen Victoria, against the wish of the Corporation, when she visited Dublin in 1900. Mr Allan, writing in 'The Irish Independent' many years after the Invincible trials, said the conspiracy was not worked by genuine Fenians, but " by those who had repudiated the straightforward principles of revolution, and who preferred to look solely to the constitutional struggle for the solution of the Irish difficulty."

These were, in fact, the men behind and above Carey, and on whom he did not inform. " The majority of the men that were hanged," wrote Mr Allan, "and of the men who still are in jail, were seduced from the principles of the I.R.B. by the grossest misrepresentations. Those who started and worked the Invincible conspiracy were not members of the I.R.B. ; on the contrary, they were working on entirely different courses. But they sought for tools amongst the men of the I.R.B. . . . The disgrace of the Invincible Society lay in the gross treachery of its leaders towards the I.R.B. They sneaked into its ranks in Dublin and turned many of its best men from their work by playing upon their loyalty. Then, when the blow was struck, some of them went round the country besmirching the Fenian organisation and endeavouring to throw the entire responsibility for their own work upon it." Of the rank and file of the Invincibles he says : "They were animated by the highest ideas. I knew many of them personally, and shall always remember them as men imbued with strong and enthusiastic patriotism, willing to sacrifice themselves to benefit their country."

There was nothing disclosed to establish any personal collusion between Parnell and the Invincibles, beyond his connection with Sheridan and with Frank Byrne, who had met him when on parole and had the knives used by the assassins under his custody at the offices of the Land League in London before they were brought to Dublin by a woman believed to be Byrne's wife. As an offset against these damning facts, there was the evidence of a diary kept by one of the Invincibles and seized by the police, in which were found entries expressing the writer's contempt for Parnell and constitutional agitators. I feel bound to say for the Midleton branch of the Land League that, though there were some ex-Fenians in it, they had no power to change its constitutional policy, and many of the ex-Fenians refused to join it on that account. Its members made no attacks on men's lives, nor committed any bad outrages beyond such boycotting and other incidents of warfare as we ourselves suffered, and, perhaps, some indefensible maimings of cattle many miles away.

Mr Forster's policy was now shown to have been no

check on crime of the worst kind. The respectable men in jail served no useful purpose as hostages for the good behaviour of the deluded men whom Carey gathered around him, or for the misguided peasants in Connaught who were committing such heinous murders. If it be true that the worst outbreak of crime followed the release of the suspects after the Kilmainham Treaty, it was not the work of the men who were then liberated.

After the trials, Carey remained in Kilmainham jail, for he would have been slain instantly if he had appeared in the streets. If he escaped lynching, it would have been because it was impossible, but he would assuredly have been shot by some of the undiscovered Invincibles. For, as the Fenians remained after the rising, so the Invincibles remained after the conviction of the slayers of Burke and Cavendish. The public indignation against Carey was unbounded, informers being hated in Ireland, as in all countries since the days of the sycophants in ancient Greece. The "constitutional" Nationalists vented such unbounded rage upon his head that many people mistook their hatred of the informer for hatred of the crimes done by the Invincibles. Carey's behaviour now was that of one who had been worsted but not disgraced, and unable to perceive that he had proved himself unworthy of the name of man. He wrote from jail to the Corporation, saying he hoped to take his rightful place soon again at its meetings,—the letters being written as a mask to conceal the plans of the Government for his preservation. Loathing him, it was but natural that they should wish to send him out of the country and to be rid of their responsibility for his safe-keeping.

It is necessary to consider Carey's career dispassionately if we would understand the Irish revolution.
My opinion is that he was actuated by patriotic
motives and personal vanity rather than by lust
of murder. Disbelieving in parliamentary agitation,
he thought that by killing Cowper, Forster, or Burke,
he would help to procure the independence of Ireland
and reap a great reward. Son of an unlettered bricklayer, himself a bricklayer, he joined the Fenians at
sixteen and became exposed to all the dangers inherent
in secret societies which make the slaying of human
beings, whether in open warfare or in secret, a part of
their programme. The young man who joins such a
society, however patriotic his ideals, never knows to
what lengths he may be driven. He ceases to regard
the taking of human life as a crime, if only he believes
it will advance the cause.

None of the respectable Dubliners who came into
contact with Carey suspected that he was an embryo
Marat or Danton; yet it was in this obscure man
and his friends that the Irish revolution had its
closest affinity to the French revolution. His history
reveals a side of Irish character too often forgotten by
Britishers, namely, the overweening ambition of the
Gael. He was not a genuine Fenian. The Fenians
whom I knew would be incapable of doing a disreput-
able action for profit. They hated the idea of assassination, but were ready to risk their lives and kill
soldiers and policemen in fair fight in the hope of
freeing Ireland from English domination. Carey's
particular society, though composed of ex-Fenians,
departed from the true Fenian programme as it was
understood in Cork in 1867. He recruited his tools
amongst the Dublin lower classes, a mixed breed

impervious to the higher emotions of the Celt. He deemed himself in alliance with Parnell, though not acknowledged and probably quite unknown to the Chief; for his unnamed patrons were "providing large funds and promising him thousands," which he concluded "must be Land League money." The man who afterwards claimed to be "Number One" wrote: "There was no physical force party. There was a wing of the Irish Party more active than the others."

Apart from his connection with the Invincibles, Carey was a man of excellent character who by sobriety and industry had worked himself up from the position of a journeyman to that of a master. After his death the Invincibles called him "a thoroughly brave man and a practical Nationalist, until he was weakened in prison." His stolidity, cunning, selfishness, pluck, and ambition were in their way typical of his breeding, which was that of a born Dubliner of the labouring class. He was as essentially a leader of the revolution as Davitt or Parnell, being of the same age as they and aiming at the Irish Republic dreamed of by Tone and Emmet. He had been a trusted employee of the most respected firm of Catholic contractors in Dublin, whose principal, Joseph Meade, soon after this became an active worker on the constitutional side of the revolutionary movement, being elected Lord Mayor of Dublin, honorary LL.D. of Trinity College and Privy Councillor, and sticking devotedly to Parnell after the weaker spirits had deserted. Carey was bent on making money and getting on. He farmed out a number of tenement houses from Messrs Meade & Son, and by rackrenting the tenants made a profit for himself. He was in fact doing the very thing in Dublin for which landlord middlemen were being murdered in the country districts.

When he entered the Corporation he declared that he did so "solely for the good of the working men of the city," and in this again he may have really meant what he said, knowing what the working men wanted, because he had been one of them. It is said that when Mr Dawson was selected for a second year of office, in July 1882, it was suggested that Carey should be elected as a working-man Lord Mayor, but the revolution had not gone far enough for that in Dublin. He was a regular communicant and sodality leader in the Cardinal's parish at Westland Row, and his religious activity has led people to say that his parochial clergy must have known of his crimes. It does not follow, for it is likely that he confessed to a strange priest who did not know him—a liberty allowed to Catholics in Dublin—or, being a casuist, like too many Catholics, did not consider what he had done to be a crime and therefore did not mention it in confession.

CHAPTER XXIV.

TESTIMONIAL TO PARNELL. THE ECCLESIASTICS INTER-
VENE. THE DYNAMITARDS. THE END OF JAMES
CAREY.

WHILE the Invincibles were being tried an Irish
Convention was held at Philadelphia on April 25th,
at which Patrick Egan, ex-treasurer of the Land
League, was present, and Frank Byrne and his
wife were given seats on the platform. Egan had
crossed over from Paris to the United States, where
he was well received, and destined afterwards to
attain the high rank of an American ambassador.
Parnell was asked to attend, but was afraid to face
the American revolutionaries, even though the
Kilmainham Treaty was dead and buried. Having
climbed to power by the Fenians he was now disposed to spurn the ladder, confident of his hold on
the public outside the secret societies. He cabled to
the convention expressing a hope that "their platform
might be so framed as to enable him to continue to
accept help from America." He was now in a position
to patronise those who had patronised him three years
before. His message was not without effect, and the
National League of America was started; but Patrick
Ford, of 'The Irish World,' from whom Parnell had
received so much money, and other Irish-Americans,
openly continued to advocate the use of dynamite
in the war against England.

Immediately after the trials in May the Irish National League arrested the attention of the country by announcing that a mortgage on Mr Parnell's estate had been foreclosed, and that he had filed a petition for the sale of the property. 'The Freeman' called on the Irish people not to allow Avondale to be sold, and opened a subscription list to raise the £14,000 necessary to stave off the catastrophe.

The name of Charles Stewart Parnell was now a household word, a spell to conjure with, and none of the orators, great or small, made a speech without bringing in those three magic words, which sounded so well and always evoked a storm of applause. Once when a Midleton Land Leaguer was trying to induce me to make a speech, "for the credit of Midleton" as he put it, he said : " You can give them any sort of nonsense you like, and if you only say ' Charles Stewart Parnell' half a dozen times here and there everything else will be drowned with the cheering ! "

The Parnell testimonial was the first (but by no means the last) pecuniary appeal made for a Nationalist member, and, the people being unused to giving except for ecclesiastical purposes, the project hung fire for a time. Cardinal McCabe and the majority of the bishops resented this new claim on the laity's generosity, but Archbishop Croke not only subscribed but privately sent a whip to the priests of his rich diocese to do likewise. The bishops wished to discourage the testimonial, but impressed by the extraordinary popularity of Mr Parnell feared to do so. It was therefore from Rome that the condemnation of the " national tribute " came in the form of a letter from the Propaganda. Assuming that the Irish hierarchy hoped to find in Mr Parnell's difficulty an opportunity to cripple the leader of a revolutionary movement so largely independent of ecclesiastical control, it is also but right to say that the flood of crime justified them as ministers of religion in endeavouring to alienate the people from the apostles of what must have seemed to them a gospel of terrorism and outrage.

I was then often in company with priests, and more than once heard those well acquainted with ecclesiastical policy declare that the Propaganda would not have dared to interfere in such an essentially local question except on the inspiration of the Irish hierarchy.

Instead of stopping the testimonial the Vatican letter evoked an unanimous outburst of protest from the Nationalists, and clearly proved the independence of the movement from clerical control. Archbishop Croke was summoned to Rome to be reprimanded, it was stated, for his support of the Nationalists, but on such matters it is always wisest to find out what were the true interests of the papal system at the time. Judged by that test Archbishop Croke was the best friend the ecclesiastical order then had in Ireland, for he was saving the revolutionary movement from getting into permanent opposition to the Church and preventing political independence from developing into religious independence. The officials at the Vatican may be assumed to have perceived this, and instead of being reprimanded it is more likely that Dr Croke was commended. The Irish bishops left themselves an open retreat in case the letter did not succeed, because they could always transfer the blame to the Roman officials.

Mr Davitt and Mr Healy, then in Richmond prison,

wrote to support the testimonial, Mr Healy, whether he intended it or not, doing much to save the hierarchy by denouncing the action of the Propaganda as the result of " an English conspiracy at the Vatican." This cry was taken up by the Nationalists, and it was against Mr Gladstone and Lord Spencer, and not the papacy, that popular indignation spent itself. The grounds for suspecting " an English conspiracy" were apparently substantiated by the presence in Rome of Mr George Errington, M.P., one of the Shawite Home Rulers, on a mission which resembled that of Captain O'Shea in the Kilmainham Treaty, Errington being an unofficial ambassador receiving Government money and acting as intermediary between the British Cabinet and the Vatican, as O'Shea had done between the Cabinet and Parnell. All through this year the ballad-singers at the fairs and markets used to sing how the English Government "had sent that scoundrel Errington on a mission out to Rome." But though the Propaganda's letter was ignored and actually helped the Parnell testimonial, the ecclesiastical order in Ireland suffered no loss, pecuniary or otherwise, for when the testimonial became a success the priests said they had disapproved of the letter and put all the blame upon Errington.

While the " national tribute " to the leader of the revolution was thus progressing, the trial of the dynamitards arrested in London took place on June 14th before three judges and a jury at the Law Courts. The judges held that the prisoners had entered upon a campaign for " levying war against England to bring about the independence of Ireland by blowing up public buildings," and sentenced Dr Gallagher, the brain of the movement; Whitehead, the manufacturer of the dynamite, who held an immense store of deadly explosives; and Wilson and Curtin, their assistants, to penal servitude for life. Like the Invincibles and the Irish Patriotic Brotherhood their conviction was obtained by the evidence of one of themselves, an ex-Fenian named Lynch. Dr Gallagher was a man of a superior class perhaps to Carey, but in his efforts in the same cause he was equally dead to human pity, being prepared to injure or kill thousands of innocent people. The dynamitards' plan of campaign was evidently devised before the arrest of Carey and his accomplices, when the audacity of all the slayers was fomented by the supposed escape of the Invincibles. Two months later, on August 8th, five Irishmen were tried at Liverpool for conspiracy to blow up public buildings, four being found guilty and sentenced to penal servitude for life. At the end of the year, on December 21st, ten men were tried for the dynamite outrage in Glasgow, which took place the day Farrell turned informer, five being sentenced to penal servitude for life and five to seven years.

Michael Davitt, Timothy Healy, and Joseph Quinn were released from Richmond prison on June 11th, and, early in July, when a vacancy was announced in county Monaghan, Mr Parnell determined to carry the war into Ulster, and went down himself, taking Mr Healy, his private secretary, along with him as his candidate. They confined their speeches to the land question, pointing out what they had gained by the Land Act — laying special stress on the "Healy clause"—and promising greater victories over land-lordism in the future. There were two other candidates, John Monroe, a well-known Conservative barrister who afterwards became land judge, and Mr Pringle, a Liberal. The altogether unexpected result was that Healy got 2376 votes, Monroe 2011, and Pringle 274, the victory being a landmark in the revolutionary movement, because it was the first seat captured in Ulster and sounded the death-knell of Irish Liberalism.

Mr Healy, being already member for the borough of Wexford, Mr Parnell gave that seat to William Redmond, younger brother of John Redmond, thereby adding a youthful and devoted colleague to the strength of his party. If the Monaghan election was a victory over Protestant Conservatives this Wexford election was a triumph over the Catholic Whigs, for Mr Redmond's defeated opponent was The O'Connor Don, a lineal descendant of the High Kings of Ireland, a Catholic and a *persona grata* to the hierarchy.

Besides getting Mr Harrington, Mr William O'Brien, Mr Mayne, Mr William Redmond, and Mr Healy elected, Mr Parnell secured the return of Mr Small for county Wexford instead of a retired Parnellite, Garrett Byrne. He also returned Mr Edward MacMahon for Limerick city, instead of Mr O'Shaughnessy, the Shawite, who accepted a Government post ; and got in Nicholas Lynch for Sligo instead of another Shawite, Denis O'Conor. Lynch's return on August 18th was a victory over the last Connaught stronghold of loyalty to the British connection, Colonel O'Hara, the Conservative, receiving 983 votes as against 1545 polled for the Parnellite. Whenever a Home Rule seat became vacant it was filled by a Parnellite, thus increasing Parnell's power and reducing the " Moderates " to insignificance. Parnell's custom now was to send his candidate down to be elected by voters claiming no voice in the selection of their representatives. In making his choice he did not look for oratorical ability—he had enough of that and to spare—but rather for men able to support themselves in London, who would never open their lips in the House, but would be always present to vote as he directed, like safety matches, as Mr Healy put it afterwards, which only lit when struck on the box. He aimed at keeping the ability of his party directly under his thumb. Of the members elected this year, Mr William O'Brien and Mr Harrington owed him everything; Mr Healy was his paid employee; Mr William Redmond was a youth whose devotion might be trusted; Messrs Lynch, Mayne, McMahon, and Small were men whose sole duty it was to obey, and not to think or speak.

He was bombarded with personal appeals from aspirants and their friends, to whom he never replied, for he rarely answered a letter, and there was a regular waiting list of men deemed eligible for Parliament. He would select a man on the nomination of one of his chief lieutenants, such as Mr Sexton, Mr T. P. O'Connor, Mr O'Brien, or Mr Healy, and never put forward a friend of his own. Captain O'Shea was the only case I remember in which he had a personal interest in a candidate.

After the Monaghan election the Ulster Orangemen began to hold meetings in imitation of the Land League, but they lacked the Catholic genius for agitation, and, as the Nationalists used to hold rival meetings, both demonstrations were often suppressed by the Government. Lord Rossmore, who lived in Monaghan, led the Orangemen in defying and denouncing the Government, and when the Lord-

Lieutenant removed him from the commission of the peace there was a great uproar amongst the Loyalists, and both sides in Ireland became equally hostile to the Liberal Government. " The so-called Government of England," said Lord Rossmore, " stopped loyal men from assembling to uphold their institutions, and had sent down a handful of soldiers whom we could eat up in a second or two if we thought fit."

When I went home for my holidays I found an Industrial Exhibition in full swing in Cork, having been opened on July 4th with great *éclat* by the Earl of Bandon—for, unlike the Dublin Exhibition, its organisers were not exclusively Nationalists. Mr Parnell, as member for Cork, attended the banquet with Mr Shaw and Colonel Colthurst, and laid aside his *rôle* as dictator for the nonce. The Sovereign was toasted after the old loyal fashion, whereas at Land League and National League banquets the loyal toasts were never given now—" Ireland a Nation " taking the place of " the Queen," and the name of Charles Stewart Parnell, when he was present, always coupled with it.

I found the young men everywhere ceasing to respect those whom their fathers used to look upon as superiors. Many of them thought it possible they might become members of parliament, and the fancy raised them in their own esteem ; for Parnell's new members, who were now so famous, were all sprung from the common people, the ablest of them having received their education entirely in the National Schools or from the Christian Brothers and learning politics through the newspapers. Farmers ceased to touch their hats to landlords and agents, a practice which before the Land League was as customary as the capping of university dons by the undergraduates. Now the farmer seen saluting a landlord or agent was ridiculed and even pelted with stones and sods, and his life made miserable.

The established order of things having been thus upset, the young democrats were convinced that some eloquent Parnellite member had only to introduce a Bill to change anything in earth or heaven. It was considered high treason to speak of "our" fleet or "our" army, the proper expression being the "English" fleet or "English" army. Once I got into trouble for saying that "we" had done something in India. I was corrected and gravely informed that the "English" not "we" had done it. I used to hear ladies at a certain patriotic house in Dublin say the young Nationalists were so busy with projects of reform that they had no time to shave, and one could know them by their beards. Mr Parnell was again wearing a beard, as were Mr Dillon, Mr Sexton, Mr Healy, Mr O'Brien, Mr Davitt, Lord Mayor Dawson, Mr Gray, and many of the other leaders.

While the land was rising and heaving with republicanism, Parnell maintained his position largely by his aloofness and mystery, for which, however, there were two reasons. First, his determination not to implicate himself with the Fenians; and secondly, his *liaison* with Mrs O'Shea, who used to come down to the House and take him away in her brougham, while Captain O'Shea would be searching for him in the lobbies to the amusement of those who were in the secret. This entanglement with Mrs O'Shea delighted Mr Gladstone, who felt deeply "indebted" to the fair sinner as long as she was not found out. But, even if there were no *liaison*, Parnell would not have tolerated familiarity from his lieutenants, whom he always kept at a distance while remaining on excellent official terms and wielding great influence over them. At one of his first banquets in Cork I saw many of the Cork Land Leaguers make very free with him after dinner, calling him Charlie and laying hands on him, slapping him on the back and pulling him about as they would have done to a popular idol of their own rank. He bore it with gravity and self-restraint, and, without openly resenting it, brought them to their senses by the iciness of his demeanour, and he was never again so treated.

It would be wrong to suppose that the discussion of politics and crime entirely engrossed the attention of Irish people at this time. There were circles in which one might have lived, even in Dublin during the reign of terror in 1882-83, without hearing much of those things, the Dubliners behaving with characteristic Irish good humour. Dr Shaw, a witty Fellow of Trinity, whose lectures on metaphysics I was attending, filled his hour one day with a caustic analysis of what he conceived to be the workings of Joe Brady's mind. A medical friend of his had examined Brady's head, and decided that the Invincible's brain was incapable of compassion or remorse. Dr Shaw told us of a highly cultured friend of his who would not have killed a fly, yet whose brain seemed as impervious as Brady's. This friend had been lamenting for years that he had never visited the Vale of Glendalough, an omission which he regarded as a disgrace to an Irishman. Shaw's comment always was, " Why don't you go and see it ? " After many years he burst into Shaw's rooms, exclaiming, " Oh, George, I was at Glendalough yesterday ! " Shaw congratulated him and asked how he liked the seven churches, but he said he had not noticed them. Neither had he seen Saint Kevin's bed, nor the lake, nor Lugduff, nor the Round Tower. "Then what did you see?" asked Shaw. "I don't remember anything in particular," was the reply, "but it is a nice place, and they have capital beer at the hotel!"

There were the usual parties and social festivities in Dublin, while the revolutionary movement was being pushed forward with such an accompaniment of crime. Dublin at this time presented the same outer shell of prosperity and loyalty to the stranger's eye as I have described in Midleton and Cork. A walk through Dame Street, Grafton Street, Sackville Street, Henry Street, Mary Street, and South George's Street showed that nine-tenths of the substantial shops and offices were owned by Protestants loyal to the British connection. A visit to the banks and insurance companies told the same tale. In the Chamber of Commerce and Stock Exchange not only all the most important personages but a large majority of the ordinary members were Protestant loyalists.

Behind this screen of solid prosperity and attention to business lived the great mass of the Catholics in the back streets, the small shopkeeper, contractor, or clerk struggling to maintain a house, the artisans and labourers swarming in thousands in tenement houses —all Nationalists and in favour of the Revolution, not merely for sentimental reasons but because they thought a government controlled by their kinsmen and co-religionists could not fail to improve their state.

In the great clubs, like the Kildare Street and the University, landlords, lawyers, civil servants, and politicians, standing on deep-piled carpets or reclining in luxurious arm-chairs, continued to discuss the problem of "governing" Ireland, whilst almost as completely out of touch with the people to be "governed" as with the Germans or Americans, centring all their hopes and fears on the results of the English elections. The return of the Conservatives meant a share of the political loaves and fishes of the United Kingdom and unlimited power in Ireland; whereas if the Liberals came in, only a small professional minority would benefit, and there was sure to be a further transfer of power from the clubmen to the unclubbable outsiders in the back streets.

Dublin has, perhaps, the largest staff of civil servants in the world for a city of its size; but, though all these were against Parnell and his revolutionary movement, they were forbidden to take part in politics or even in municipal affairs. Most of them, feeling that the existing system was doomed, took as their motto : "Eat, drink, and be merry, for to-morrow we die," their best energies going into amusements and social festivity. From the Lord-Lieutenant, the Chief Secretary, and the Judges, down to the junior clerks, they felt they were earning their livings by "governing" the country, and that Mr Parnell and his new men were indicting them on a charge of incompetence and trying to oust them. Parnell wanted to become governor of Ireland, and, if he succeeded, would install his own men in the best positions. The revolutionary movement was, therefore, from their point of view, a struggle between Parnell and themselves for the lucrative work of governing Ireland; the majority supporting Parnell;

the minority and the British Government supporting the civil servants.

There were constant rumours between June and July that Carey had left the country, but the reporters could discover nothing, though it was circumstantially stated once that he had gone as a prison warder in a crown colony. All doubts were at length set at rest on the 29th of July by a telegram from South Africa announcing that James Carey had been shot dead that day on board the liner *Melrose Castle*. He had been secretly conveyed from Kilmainham to England. The Invincibles were watching him and his wife and family. When Mrs Carey and the children crossed to England, they were followed by young Patrick O'Donnell, a Donegal man whom Carey did not know. When they boarded the liner, *Kinfauns Castle*, bound for Cape Town, O'Donnell took his passage in that ship. At Dartmouth the ship was stopped, and Carey came aboard under the name of Power and joined his family. O'Donnell bided his time and became friendly with "Power" on the voyage. "Power" was violent in his denunciations of England, and, when he went ashore at Cape Town, had an altercation with a Scotch fellow-passenger in a restaurant. "The English are too base to live," said Carey, "I want Ireland for the Irish." "You'd kill each other like the Kilkenny cats," said the Scotchman. O'Donnell was hoping to slay Carey on land and escape afterwards. I heard this categorically from one of the Parnellite members afterwards; and also that, if O'Donnell had performed his task, elaborate arrangements were made for his protection. His face and hands were to be blackened and he was to go up country with a mob of Kaffirs, who were ready waiting, having been sent down by a famous South African politician whose name I shall not mention any more than that of the Irish member who told me.

Carey and his family changed from the *Kinfauns* to the *Melrose Castle* bound for Natal, and O'Donnell paid the difference in the fare to follow him. When they had covered about a third of the voyage to Natal, O'Donnell found himself quite alone with Carey on the deck at four in the afternoon, and, imagining that Carey recognised him, drew his revolver and shot Carey in the throat. Carey shouted : " Maggie, I'm shot ! " and staggered towards his wife's cabin. O'Donnell shot him twice in the back, and was seized in the act by the passengers and put in irons. O'Donnell was in many respects a hero, and it is to be lamented on sentimental grounds that the British Government should have found it necessary to bring him back to England to be tried for the slaying of a man of whom the world was well rid. The Invincibles lamented what they called the " taking off " of Carey as a " melancholy duty," " a sad necessity." The meaning of which is that those above him in the society, whom he had not betrayed, felt bound to kill him for their own security. Whatever may be thought of Carey and those who provided him with funds to run the Invincible Society, it is incontestable that the murder of the Secretaries made the Home Rule agitation a reality, by showing the world that what seemed till then an agrarian quarrel was in fact a political revolution.

CHAPTER XXV.

THE Home Manufacture movement, started by the
National Exhibition of 1882, was warmly taken up
and became part of the propaganda of the National
League. Everything Irish was now lauded to the
skies. To be an Irishman was deemed the greatest
possible honour, and whatever Ireland produced was
held to be better of its kind than what came from
any other country. A great number of articles, such
as matches, candles, soap, starch, mustard, tobacco,
tweeds, flannels, linen, hosiery, boots, ropes, and
agricultural instruments, which had hitherto been
bought without inquiry as to where they had been
made, were now rejected unless they were of Irish
manufacture. British firms, doing an immemorial
business with Ireland, found themselves checkmated,
for the apostles of Home Manufacture took no account
of the fact that Great Britain purchased almost all
Ireland's produce which was not consumed at home.
A relative of ours who had a remunerative agency
for a great Scotch woollen house, and used to employ
several commercial travellers, bitterly lamented the

change, Irishman and Nationalist though he was. Where formerly he used to send his man to take periodical orders as a matter of course, he had now to go in person to beg for custom, and was well satisfied if he got half the old order. Struggling woollen mills became prosperous—this was notably the case with a little mill near Midleton,—new mills were started in many places, several in Cork and one at Castlemartyr in our district. A famous agricultural implement factory was developed at Wexford. Miscellaneous industries sprang up in almost every county. Young men took to wearing Irish-made collars, shirts, socks, hosiery, and poplin ties. Girls insisted on Irish material for their dresses.

Along with this movement there arose a desire to revive the Irish language. When I was a child, one heard almost as much Irish as English on a fair or market day in Midleton. Nevertheless, Irish had almost entirely died out amongst the young people educated at the National and Christian Brothers' and Nuns' schools, and was only spoken by the elder people, and not by all of them, in our district. In the west it was more generally spoken, but it was rapidly becoming a dead language—the boys and girls who could read and write in English priding themselves on not understanding Irish, and being ashamed to hear their parents speak it in the presence of strangers. When they said of a man that "he had no English," they spoke pityingly as if he were blind or deaf. This contempt for the old language really came from America, where the Irish emigrants found, like all other foreigners, that the Americans would not tolerate any language but English. The old people said admiringly of any one

CAPTAIN O'SHEA.

"An intermediary to negotiate Parnell's release had been found in the person of Captain O'Shea — or it would be more accurate to say Mrs O'Shea."— PAGE 236.

who spoke English fluently that he was "very Englified." My father spoke Irish, but he freely interlarded his conversation with English words which he often had to explain by signs, or he turned English words into original Irish thus : bank would be rendered *bawnka*, stock exchange would become *shtocha shanja*, and so he would invent an Irish pronunciation for the English word. Father Fitzpatrick at first Mass every Sunday preached a short sermon in Irish for the old people before giving his principal address in English. At Land League meetings I have often heard a speech delivered in Irish for the purpose of confounding the police note-takers, and those who understood it felt greatly elated. I think it was from this beginning that the revival of Irish now took its rise.

The dislike of English, as the result of Mr Parnell's clear and logical utterances, caused the young men to chafe at being beholden to the Saxon for their everyday speech, but it was some years later that the study of the grammar and text-books was taken up and Irish placed in the *curriculum* of the schools as the result of the agitation got up by the Gaelic League. Trinity had always encouraged the study of Irish by giving a sizarship for Irish alone—a valuable prize, meaning, as it did, free commons and the remission of all fees,—but the Catholic hierarchy gave it no encouragement, and not one in a hundred of the younger priests from Maynooth could speak their mother tongue. In this doubtless the bishops, as the sole directors of education, were influenced by the experience of Irish emigrants in America where so many Irish-born priests were settled. The agricultural editor of 'The Weekly

Freeman' in my time, a man of fifty, having succeeded in passing the entrance examination, got an Irish sizarship and lived in Trinity College. He was mercilessly chaffed in 'The Freeman' office when he spoke Irish for our amusement, and MacWeeny, the chief reporter, invariably addressed him as "Manure"! There was little respect for Irish in 'The Freeman' office then, Mr Gray's ideal being to make his paper as like the prosperous London daily journals of that time as possible.

The Labourers' Act, passed in 1883 by the exertions of the Parnellites, was an important by-product of the revolution. It empowered Boards of Guardians to acquire land compulsorily, erect cottages with half an acre of ground attached to each, and let them to agricultural labourers at suitable rents. When this Act was passed, the labourers, thinking they could choose the best land in their neighbour-hood, became very restive, but they behaved well on the whole, feeling for the first time that they had some inheritance in their native soil. The Nation-alist lawyers were much concerned about this statute, for it was not an uncommon thing for a solicitor to get a thousand pounds in costs for a single building scheme of moderate dimensions.

Our labourers expressed no anxiety for new cottages and half acres. The old thatched cottages were rent-free, and we were bound to keep them in repair, whereas if they got the new cottages they would have to pay at least a shilling a-week in rent to the Guardians. Looking on the rent as a charge for the land exclusively, they said no half acre was worth fifty-two shillings a-year, which was more than five pounds an acre. At present they got quarter of an acre of potatoes tilled and manured as part of their wages along with the grass of a sheep or two, and they did not see clearly what use they could make of an additional half acre. The new cottages which, nevertheless, were soon erected all over Ireland were a vast improvement on the old, having three rooms, attics, yards and out-offices, and being stone-walled and slate-roofed. They not only raised the labourers' standard of comfort and increased their self-respect, but they made the occupants independent of the farmers.

During the summer of 1883, the competition between the London and North - Western Railway Company and the Dublin Steam-packet Company for the carriage of the mails between Holyhead and Dublin excited much controversy,—the Nationalist members being unanimous for the Dublin Company which held the contract, and whose splendid mail boats, using Kingstown as their port, were an object of absorbing interest to all Dubliners who used Kingstown Pier as a fashionable rendezvous. Mr Gladstone favoured the North - Western Company, being a personal friend of Lord Richard Grosvenor and other directors. But he gave way, and, at the end of the session, the contract with the Dublin Company was renewed. Mr Edmund Dwyer Gray was the leader of this agitation, and it may be pardonable to relate how I made his acquaintance just at this time.

On returning to Dublin from my holidays in September, I determined to try and get a post on the Press, and, at my request, my father got me an introduction to Lord Mayor Dawson from a fellow-suspect with whom he had spent several months in

Limerick jail—a man who is now and has long been a Nationalist member of Parliament. At that time one Nationalist felt at liberty to ask another for a favour as a matter of course, and it was expected to be granted, if possible, as soon as asked. I shall never forget my first visit to the Mansion House— my own timidity and the Lord Mayor's friendly pomposity. "You want to get on the Press?" said the Lord Mayor; "that's right, my boy, I wish you every success. Dwyer Gray is the man to do it. Do you know him? No. Well then, I'll write a letter to him and see what comes of it. Youth and energy are what we require in the national ranks.

He gave me an open letter to the proprietor of 'The Freeman,' which was then as omnipotent in Ireland as ever newspaper was in any country. I found Mr Gray in his study at Pembroke House, Upper Mount Street, and Mrs Gray with him. She was a most uncommon woman, and had a mesmeric influence over her husband which he occasionally broke away from for a change. She had been a Miss Chisholm, daughter of Mrs Caroline Chisholm, whose labours to improve the treatment of the Irish emigrants on board ship had won for her the title of "The Emigrant's Friend." The day I saw her for the first time she had a large mass of bright yellow hair and looked dazzling and distinguished. I learned afterwards she wore a wig. She and Mr Gray seemed a picture of domestic bliss, and they were both exceedingly kind to me. "He wants to get on the Press, my dear," said Gray in his squeaky voice, "he is a friend of the Lord Mayor's." "Just the kind of young man to be encouraged, my dear," she replied,

smiling—" I am sure you can find a place for him."
They kept me with them for some time, asking me
to join them at tea, and at parting Mr Gray said :
" Go down to ' The Freeman ' office to-morrow and
the manager will give you a billet."

The manager of ' The Freeman,' who was drawing
the largest salary ever paid in an Irish newspaper
office, was a Scotsman called Gillies. The manager
of ' The Irish Times,' James Carlyle, was also a Scotsman. And the two, with another Scotsman who
managed a line of steamers, used to play golf in red
coats in the Fifteen Acres in the Phœnix Park, a
piece of ground about a hundred acres in extent and
as level as a croquet lawn, without bunkers, tees,
putting-greens, or any of the essentials of a modern
golf-course. At that time golf was unheard of in
Dublin, and the couple of men in red coats aimlessly
driving a little white ball were regarded as harmless
lunatics.

I entered Mr Gray's employment next day as sub-
editor of ' The Irish Fireside,' a paper which the editor,
James Murphy, a prolific writer of patriotic serials
many of which were published as novels, hoped to
develop into an Irish ' Tit-Bits'—for Mr George
Newnes had started his first lucrative venture a few
years before. The Frederick Allan already mentioned was manager of this paper. I only remained
a short time on ' The Fireside ' when I joined the reporting staff of ' The Freeman,' having special charge
of the Kingstown and Bray district.

While at home I found that the boycott of Lord
Midleton's fair had been proceeding in a way typical
of the revolt against landlord rule going on all over
Ireland in one shape or another. Lord Midleton at

length determined to bring a suit in chancery for an injunction and damages against six of the principal shopkeepers and farmers, whom he charged with having conspired to deprive him of his tolls and rights under his charter. My father was named as one of the six defendants, so that he suffered not merely at the hands of the Land League by being boycotted and having his house stormed, and at the hands of the Government by being imprisoned, but also at the hands of a landlord with whom he had no personal quarrel whatever.

This costly lawsuit was tried before Vice-Chancellor Chatterton without a jury. Chatterton was a county Cork man, and, when Attorney-General for Ireland, had created the post of Vice-Chancellor which he himself was the first to fill—and also the last, for it was abolished after he had held it for over forty years. He was a staunch Tory partisan of the old school—a man of no brilliancy, but enormous determination. He always refused to have a jury, and, if a party to a suit asked for one, his answer was : " Go elsewhere. I won't sit with a jury ! " The result of the case was therefore a foregone conclusion, as Chatterton would be sure to decide in favour of Lord Midleton and his charter, whereas, if there were a jury, there might have been a disagreement or an acquittal. My father and his co-defendants had to come to Dublin and undergo the mortification of losing their case and having to pay heavy costs. They might have appealed against Chatterton's decision, but they felt it would only mean more money for the lawyers and another victory for Lord Midleton.

Once the injunction was granted, it would have been contempt of court for the defendants or others to obstruct the entry of cattle into the fair green, or to keep them on the street for sale; for the Vice-Chancellor had decided that Lord Midleton, by his ancient charter, had the right to régulate the conduct of the fair. As the Nationalists did not see their way to being imprisoned indefinitely, the farmers were permitted to drive their cattle into the fair green again. For a while many people sent their cattle to other fairs, but Midleton was such a central position that they did not long continue that policy, and Lord Midleton recovered his tolls. A branch of the National League having been started in the town, it was decided that the six defendants should not pay Lord Midleton the costs of the action; but when one of them, a grocer, had a hogshead of whisky worth £100 seized before his window, they joined in a bill and raised the money to pay Lord Midleton and their own solicitor. Afterwards the branch made a series of collections to indemnify them, but the bill had to be renewed several times.

In striking contrast to the career of Vice-Chancellor Chatterton was that of Lord Chancellor Law, who died unexpectedly on September 10th, after he had held his position less than two years. Mr Gladstone could not make up his mind apparently as to Law's successor, and the office was put into commission for three months, when the Attorney-General, Mr John Naish, was passed over, contrary to precedent, and the post given to Sir Edward Sullivan, Master of the Rolls, a Midleton College man. Mr Law had been an Ulster Liberal member — a class against whom the Nationalists were now waging a war of extinction. The Loyalists resented this invasion of Ulster, and hearing that Lord Mayor Dawson was coming from Dublin to deliver an address on the franchise in the Derry Guildhall on November 1st, a Catholic holiday of obligation known as All Saints' Day, the Orangemen took possession of the building to prevent the address—in the same way as the Belfast men recently had arranged to take possession of their hall to keep out Mr Winston Churchill,—and in the rioting two persons were shot.

In the south, however disposed the people might be to support Mr Parnell against the bishops in selecting members of parliament, they had no toleration for free thought in religion. The Catholics of Wexford, for instance, who had just rejected The O'Conor Don in favour of Mr William Redmond, sacked a theatre on December 2nd in which evangelical services were being held by a colleague of Messrs Moody and Sankey. They assaulted ladies and attacked men going to the meeting, under the mistaken notion that such conduct was a legitimate protest against Protestant ascendancy. In the same quarter of Ireland next day, some five hundred farmers in the counties of Waterford and Kilkenny gave formal notice that they meant to stop hunting over their lands in the country hunted by the Marquis of Waterford, head of a family which had always been popular and respected—a proceeding which led to the stoppage of the Curraghmore Hunt. Both incidents were meant to forward the revolution.

Michael Davitt, the father of the Land League, now glowed as feebly as a rushlight eclipsed by the sun of the Leader of the Irish Race, and was devoting himself more to England, where he had spent his boyhood and early manhood. He addressed a large meeting at St James's Hall, Piccadilly, on October

30th, on "The Land for the People," and received a great ovation; but his adoption of Henry George's views, which Irish farmers naturally regarded as impracticable, caused him to lose his influence at home, and he did not succeed in arousing any enthusiasm for land nationalisation in England.

While Davitt was thus waning, Parnell was climbing near the zenith of his power. The "national tribute" was presented to him on December 11th, at a great banquet in the Rotunda, Dublin, the unexpected amount of the presentation being £38,000, which, as it had taken somewhat over six months to collect, represented an inflow of subscriptions at the rate of nearly £1500 a-week, while the total was almost three times the sum originally named. The success of the Parnell testimonial was the first great triumph of the National League, in addition to being the substantial expression of the Catholic people's gratitude to the leader who had led them so far on the road of revolution in so short a time.

I heard it from one who was close by him, that Parnell did not say "Thank you" when the cheque was handed to him. In his speech after the presentation, he traced the success of the revolutionary movement from the foundation of the Land League, saying there must be no more coercion and no more emigration. Parnell's wondrous gift of plain speaking and habit of disclosing his policy were most disconcerting to English politicians, who found it hard to believe that he meant what he said. In his speech to-night he uttered his plain words with that deliberation of manner so characteristic of him, pausing in the middle of his sentences as though thinking of what he was going to say. He spoke so slowly that all could follow him with ease, and his features bore such a stamp of thoughtful sincerity and earnestness that every word carried conviction to the hearer. I had often heard him before ; but this night at the Rotunda, at the zenith of his power, though with the greatest triumphs of his career still before him, he stood out from the whole company, a strange and superior being, apparently above all the weaknesses of the mere mortals by whom he was surrounded, yet subject to the most primitive of human frailties which was to prove his destruction. To-night he seemed something of the superman, as I had noticed him once before at a banquet in Cork. Eight years afterwards I was to see him once again at the Rotunda. It was just before he died—but I must not anticipate the course of events.

His forecast of the future is worth quoting. Standing in the midst of his admirers, and having in his pocket a cheque for more money than he had ever hoped to possess, fortune smiling on him all round after a period of trial and difficulty such as few political leaders have survived, he uttered these words, which I now seem to hear as distinctly as on the night of the banquet : " Beyond the shadow of a doubt, it will be for the Irish people in England —separated, isolated as they are—and for your independent Irish members to determine at the next general election whether a Tory or a Liberal ministry shall rule England. It is a great force and a great power. If we cannot rule ourselves, we can at least cause them to be ruled as we choose. This force has already gained for Ireland inclusion in the coming Franchise Bill. We have reason to be proud, hopeful, and energetic, determined that this generation shall not pass away until it has bequeathed to those who come after them the great birthright of national independence and prosperity."

Like others of his prophecies, this was almost literally fulfilled. The Representation of the People Bill, then being prepared by the Cabinet, was to give him so large a parliamentary party that he was bound to be arbiter of the situation at Westminster. Those who feared him consoled themselves with the hope that his party would break up before he had the opportunity of using it effectively. The 'Pall Mall Gazette,' then an exponent of advanced Liberalism under Mr John Morley and Mr W. T. Stead, said: "His claim cannot be fully recognised until he gives proof that he can hold together a party which never before has been held together for any length of time." This, too, was Mr Gladstone's hope, and he did not yield until Parnell had shown he could hold his party together, and use it indifferently against Liberals and Conservatives. Thus the revolution was going forward and still to advance, war being actively waged against the Liberal Government, and the Uncrowned King grown too big a man for Mr Trevelyan to arrest. Indeed, Parnell seemed determined never to bring himself within the meshes of the criminal law again, leaving it to his lieutenants to speak those fiery words which were the passport to the prison.

While wealth, power, and praise were thus the meed of the leader of the Irish race, the fallen soldiers of the illegal army corps of his revolutionary force were sinking to their dooms in outer darkness. Patrick O'Donnell, the slayer of Carey, was found guilty of murder by a London jury at the Old Bailey on December 1st, sentenced to death by Judge Denman, and hanged at Newgate on December 17th, despite a strong effort made in the United States and at home to obtain his reprieve. He was not deserted at his trial, like the Invincibles. Funds were provided for his defence by English counsel, and an American lawyer was sent over from the States. The brave man did not divulge the name of any accomplice, and though loudly protesting against the sentence passed upon him, died on the scaffold with his secret unrevealed. His last words to the priest were : " I am quite ready to meet my death. I have done my duty." A month after his execution, Mass was celebrated for the repose of his soul in his native village in Donegal, over 10,000 people assembling in and around the chapel. After Mass an empty coffin was carried in procession and solemnly interred in his family grave—a collection being made for the erection of a monument. For the rest of his life Judge Denman was protected by detectives, even when sitting on the bench. Judge William O'Brien, who tried the Invincibles, was similarly protected, his detectives being as well known as himself in Dublin; but the Corkonian did not lose the sly twinkle in his eye, or seem at all depressed by his danger.

Another soldier of the secret side of the revolutionary movement was hanged in Dublin on the day after O'Donnell's execution. This was Joseph Poole, whom the vigilance committee meant to assassinate in Middle Abbey Street, when Sergeant Cox was slain. He was convicted of murdering in the streets of Dublin James Kenny, a fellow-Fenian, who was suspected of being an informer; and Poole died, like O'Donnell, without giving any information to the authorities. For this he is still regarded as a hero by the lower classes in

Dublin. While no public demonstration has been held to commemorate the memory of the slayers of the Secretaries, though they too have their friends, thousands of labourers and mechanics celebrated the memory of " Joe Poole," because, in pursuance of his oath, he killed the supected informer, and though he himself had been marked down for death, did not prove unfaithful.

CHAPTER XXVI.

MR CHARLES DAWSON, M.P., was succeeded at the
Mansion House on the first of January 1884 by
Alderman William Meagher, owner of a prosperous
public - house near the North Wall, one of many
Tipperary men engaged in that trade in Dublin.
Meagher had that peculiar grandeur of manner,
typical of his county, which gives the impression
of great geniality and friendliness, but is usually a
mask covering a hard and politic temperament—
Tipperary men being always shrewd and often parsi-
monious under a reckless and offhand manner, and
the only southern Irishmen who habitually use the
smile as an aid to business. The licensed trade
interest was so strong in the Corporation that, after
Mr Gray and Mr Dawson, it seized on the great
prize of the lord mayoralty almost as of right.
Meagher, however, was a good selection, and did
credit to the Nationalist party.

The toast of "The Queen" had not yet been
dropped at the Mansion House; but at theatres,
music halls, and other gatherings, when "God Save
the Queen" was played at the end of a performance,
the Nationalists used to hiss or sing "God Save

Ireland"; while the Loyalists would cheer or indulge in "Kentish fire," which consisted of triple stamping of the feet or triple clapping of the hands, and was interpreted by the Nationalists as meaning "Damn the Pope." At Meagher's inaugural banquet, her Majesty's health was drunk by the Loyalists, but several Nationalists turned their glasses upside down and did not drink it. There was no hostile demonstration, but, as 'United Ireland' put it, "one-third of the company retained their seats, including a number of priests."

The impending Franchise Bill was now a cause of great apprehension to the Loyalists, who were striving to get Ireland excluded. Feeling ran especially high in those Ulster counties with a Protestant-and-Catholic population which were now regarded as the key of the position; Mr Parnell believing that if Nationalists won seats in Tyrone, Donegal, Derry, Fermanagh, Armagh, and Down, as well as Monaghan, the Loyalists could no longer say that Ulster was against Home Rule. The opening of the year saw rival meetings of Nationalists and Orangemen. At Dromore, where William O'Brien and T. D. Sullivan spoke, an Orangeman was killed by the police. There were also meetings at Dungannon, Newry, and Derry, which, despite its Protestant history, actually contains a slight majority of Catholics.

Amidst all this excitement little or no attention was now being paid to business by the farmers in the Catholic provinces. The imports of meat from the colonies, the United States, and the Argentine, by causing a fall in the price of cattle, supplied one of the main economic reasons for the agitation—the importation of Australian mutton alone having risen from 400 carcasses in 1880 to 193,645 carcasses in 1883. But the farmers, instead of striking out new lines of industry, only became more eager for new laws. Hanging on the words of Parnell and his lieutenants as they did, it was impossible for them to avoid brooding on their grievances. When Parliament met on February 5th, Mr Parnell, bent only on consummating the revolution, complained that " the exercise of free speech was practically extinguished in Ireland," and expressed his approval of Lord Rossmore for his defiance of the Government. Mr Trevelyan retorted that crime had " sunk to a point not discreditable, rents being well paid, and the tone of public meetings mitigated." Nevertheless, the war was being fiercely waged, the number of individuals evicted in 1883—including farmers and their wives and children—being 17,855.

Mr Parnell's colleague for Cork, Mr John Daly, having retired at this time—broken by his neglect of business, and in that respect a type of a large class of victims to this revolutionary movement—the Chief put forward John Deasy, a young farmer from the vicinity, who was elected on February 23rd by a majority of two to one over Mr Goulding, the Liberal - Conservative. This was a signal proof of the revolution effected in parliamentary representation. John Daly belonged to the old school of Nationalist : John Deasy was a type of the new school created by Mr Parnell. A few years before it would have been deemed absurd for an obscure tenant farmer to aspire to be member for the city of Cork. But now the Catholic merchants submissively accepted such a man, because he was the nominee of Mr Parnell. Deasy himself was typical of the revolution in the modes of life and thought of the farmers. Whereas Deasy's father would have been afraid to wear his hat in the presence of his landlord, and knew nothing beyond the values of crops and stock, John Deasy considered himself superior to his landlord, dressed like one of the landed gentry, never handled a plough, and, after his election to Parliament, studied for the Bar and became a barrister, with a view to qualifying for a post under a Dublin government. I remember once when he was a student at King's Inns and told us he was about to deliver a lecture at some Mayo village, the present Lord Chancellor of Ireland, Mr Redmond Barry, deemed it a signal honour to be allowed to accompany him.

No less noteworthy and typical than John Deasy's case was the career of a Midleton man, arrested with two others in England on Patrick's Day, March 17th, on suspicion of being a dynamitard. Born and bred in a small cottage on the roadside, and afflicted from birth with curvature of the spine, he had gone to the Christian Brothers' school, then went to Cork as a shop assistant and became a commercial traveller. His mental and physical development well illustrated the revolution which education was accomplishing amongst the labourers. He was sober and well-living, and used to come to see his people in fine clothes, wearing a gold watch and chain and showy rings. His training led him to the conviction that extreme methods were justifiable to secure the independence of Ireland from England, and he was now a powerful political " boss." But, though he was for stronger measures than talk, he succeeded in satisfying the authorities that he was not connected with the dynamite conspiracy and was released.

On the day of this man's arrest, Parnell spoke at the Patrick's Day banquet in London and said : " I do not depend upon any English political party. I should advise you not to depend upon any such party. Some people desire to rely on the English democracy. I say, do not rely even upon the great English democracy, but rely upon yourselves, upon the devotion of the sea-divided Gael, whether it be under the Southern Cross or beyond the wide Atlantic. But, above all, rely upon the devotion and determination of our people on the old sod at home." This was a thrust at Davitt, whose idea now was to convert the English democracy. A month later, Parnell openly condemned Davitt's other policy of land nationalisation in a speech at Drogheda, and Davitt had become so powerless that he had not a platform in Ireland from which to reply.

The physical force men were now overshadowed by the parliamentary party, to whom the new Reform Bill opened such a vista of power. When Lord Hartington moved the second reading on March 24th, Mr Bright maintained that Ireland should retain her full 103 members, though she was then only entitled to 90 on the democratic basis of population. Mr Forster, approving the extension of the Bill to Ireland, and alleging that he was undaunted by the threat that Parnell would become "arbiter of the destinies of the country," held that the number of Irish members should be in proportion to population. His advice was not taken, and the second reading was carried, on April 7th, by 340 to 210. In committee, Mr Brodrick, son of Lord Midleton, proposed the exclusion of Ireland, the gist of the argument for which, as put in a single sentence by Mr

David Plunket, was that "the better educated, the more civilised, all those classes best able to form an opinion on political questions, would be practically disfranchised," because they would be outvoted by the ignorant and illiterate. Mr Gladstone's reply was that Loyalists need have no fear, because "no laws could be passed in Parliament under Irish influence adverse to the loyal minority in Ireland, except by the consent of the representatives of England and Scotland."

If Mr Gladstone foresaw that within two years he would be proposing to hand "the loyal minority" over to a Parnellite parliament in Dublin, he would hardly have said that no law affecting the loyal minority could be passed "except by the consent of the representatives of England and Scotland." His position now was this. He was secretly trying to use the Pope against Parnell by means of Errington and to keep Parnell quiescent by means of Mrs O'Shea, with whom the Cabinet were in constant touch. But both efforts were unsuccessful. The Fenians, Irish and American, neutralised the work of Mrs O'Shea and kept Parnell to his guns. The Irish bishops, being now the paymasters of the Vatican, would only take the Pope's advice when it was tendered on their own suggestion, and the laity were so enamoured of Parnell that the hierarchy had either to keep silent or follow the lead of Dr Croke. Although Parnell's activity, since he received the £38,000, had perceptibly decreased, he and his party in Parliament and the National League in Ireland continued to work openly against the Government; and the concession as to the number of Irish members— which Parnell had prophesied in 1883 as a victory even then won by "force"—was soon to give the revolutionists supreme political power in Ireland.

During the debate on the Franchise Bill, the illegal side of the revolutionary movement, as if to insure the inclusion of Ireland, committed a dynamite outrage in St James's Square, London, by which the Junior Carlton and other clubs were damaged; and on the same day, May 30th, there was an explosion at Scotland Yard which wrecked a public-house opposite the detectives' offices; while during the afternoon some boys discovered a black bag at the foot of Nelson's monument containing sixteen cakes of dynamite. Lord Granville, the Foreign Secretary, had addressed " a firm remonstrance " to the United States Government against the encouragement the dynamitards were receiving from America. But the American Government's rejoinder was : "So long as disturbances continue in Ireland, so long will an agitation hostile to England prevail amongst the Irish population abroad; and until contentment prevails amongst her Majesty's subjects in her own dominions, it is impossible to expect a state of peace amongst the Irish here."

During 1884, the weeding out of Liberals and Shawites from the Irish representation and their replacement by Parnellites continued. Mr Metge, who represented Meath, was replaced by Lord Mayor Meagher. J. A. Blake was succeeded in county Waterford by P. J. Power. Sir John Ennis (Liberal) made way for Justin Huntley McCarthy at Athlone, where the electors met at once and decided "to support any candidate recommended by Mr Parnell." Whenever a Parnellite fell out of the ranks his place was filled by another Parnellite—Lysaght Finigan in

Ennis being succeeded by Matthew Kenny, and John Daly in Cork by John Deasy.

But every other phase of the revolutionary movement was now completely overshadowed by the accusations made in 'United Ireland' by Mr William O'Brien and his solicitor, Mr Patrick Chance, who afterwards became a Parnellite member, against Government officials in Dublin, whom they specifically accused of infamous crimes. This crusade probably helped to secure the over-representation of Ireland, and was part of the vengeance with which Mr Parnell repaid the imputations against himself. Two of the officials were charged with unnatural sexual crimes. Both moved in high society and had control of numbers of youths : one, an Englishman, being Secretary to the Post Office, with authority over the postmen and telegraph messengers ; the other, an Irishman, being Detective Director of the Royal Irish Constabulary, with authority over the recruits and young constables. It came to the knowledge of Mr Chance that these men, along with others holding no official position, had formed a society for sensual indulgences more heinous from a moral standpoint than the Invincible Society, and unrelieved by any patriotic motive. The special Crown Solicitor, who had conducted the prosecutions of Francis Hynes, the Maamtrasna murderers and the Invincibles, was also denounced as a "blackguard," but on other grounds.

Mr William O'Brien gave notice in the House of Commons, on May 19th, that he would draw attention to "the charges of felonious practices" against the three officials named. Thereupon the Crown Solicitor served a writ on 'United Ireland' for £30,000 damages. Mr O'Brien's answer to the writ was thus given in 'United Ireland': "We have designated him [the Crown Solicitor] a forger, an adulterer, a swindler, a bankrupt, a defrauder of his own wife, a suborner of felonious affidavits. But there are depths of villainy at which he draws the line. He must not be bracketed with [the Detective Director and the Secretary of the Post Office]. We assure him his character in this respect is as stainless as his abhorrence of the crimes he has no mind to is edifying. This journal has never imputed the unmentionable abomination to him."

In the same paper was a cartoon of Lord Spencer and Mr Trevelyan, naked, flogging the Crown Solicitor, the Chief Detective and the Secretary, all naked, to force them to work a battering-ram against the door of 'United Ireland' office; or, as the cartoon put it, "goading the foulest scoundrels in the Castle service, under pain of losing their salaries, to assail 'United Ireland' with a legal battering-ram of £40,000 damages." It was admitted that the attack on the three officials was for the purpose of besmirching the Government. In regard to the Crown Solicitor, 'United Ireland' said: "The vile Government of Earl Spencer leaves us single-handed to rid the public service of the monster—nay, adopts him, self-convicted thief, fraud, bankrupt, brutal adulterer, wife-cheater and heartless debauchee, as the type and flower of a meritorious Castle official."

For this the Queen's Bench, consisting of Justices May, Lawson, and William O'Brien, fined Mr O'Brien £500. In a previous issue of the paper Judge Lawson had been thus referred to: "A decent scavenger or a half-sober coalheaver would exhibit less brutality in his calling than Mr James Anthony Lawson on the

Bench." The Detective Director had served a writ claiming £5000 damages, but failed to prosecute the action on the grounds of ill-health. 'United Ireland' moved to have the action dismissed, and wrote: "What is to be thought of Spencer and Trevelyan who, knowing the atrocious crimes of which he has been guilty, not only keep him on in their service but connive at his shamming to escape from justice?" The Detective Director then retired, and the Secretary to the Post Office served a writ on Mr O'Brien, claiming £5000 damages. Whereupon 'United Ireland' denounced the Lord-Lieutenant and Chief Secretary as "compounders of felony," who, "having failed to force [the Chief of Detectives] to tackle this journal in the law courts, now put forward as the Castle champion the wretched man who is to be the nominal plaintiff in this action. We are only at the beginning of our perquisition into the ways and morals of their stronghold."

Mr Arthur O'Connor, M.P. (now County Court Judge of Durham), moved for a committee of inquiry into the charges against the three officials, but Conservatives as well as Liberals resented the methods adopted by Mr Parnell's paper for discrediting the Government; and, after a debate in an empty house, the motion was defeated by 62 to 21. 'United Ireland,' commenting on the discussion, assured its readers that it had established "the full complicity of the Castle in the Detective Director's villainies." The action brought by the Secretary to the Post Office resulted in a verdict for Mr O'Brien, which was received with loud jubilation; and then the Government instituted a criminal prosecution against the Chief Detective, the Secretary to the Post Office, and others concerned in what was, perhaps, the worst public scandal known in Dublin in modern times.

The Crown Solicitor's actions against Mr O'Brien and 'United Ireland' were tried before Lord Justice Barry at the July assizes in Belfast, and the jury awarded £3050 damages against Mr O'Brien and £500 against the paper. The trial of the other two officials took place in Dublin in August before Baron Dowse, and resulted in the acquittal of the Secretary to the Post Office. The Chief Detective pleaded insanity and behaved like a madman in the dock. One of their associates, a suburban grocer, was found guilty and sentenced to twenty years' penal servitude ; others got lighter sentences. 'United Ireland' was dissatisfied with the result, and said : "The *bonâ-fides* of the Crown in these cases rests under a shocking suspicion."

There was, perhaps, more heart-searching in Dublin, because of these exposures, than in 1883 with its Invincible revelations. Then the criminals belonged to the lower classes and were all Catholics, now they belonged to a higher class of society and were mostly Protestants. Men of various trades and professions were implicated in the riot of infamy : a Protestant stockbroker who escaped from the country ; a young Protestant merchant who likewise fled. The stockbroker, after reading 'United Ireland,' asked his partner's advice. "If you are innocent," was the answer, "stand your ground ; if you are guilty, fly !" A well-connected young priest also disappeared and his place knew him no more.

Just when the trials were going on, a Nationalist convention was held at Boston, at which Mr Sexton and Mr William Redmond attended as a deputation from the Irish National League. Mr Patrick Egan was elected President of the National League of America and £1000 was voted to Mr William O'Brien " for his battle against Castle bestiality." There was also an indemnity fund started in ' United Ireland.' The exposures inflicted a damaging blow on the system of Castle government; quite wrongly, of course, for it was unjust to condemn the system for the misconduct of a few black sheep. It was really an attack in force by the Nationalists on the Civil Servants, whom they aimed at supplanting. But those Britishers who supported Home Rule were set thinking; the Nationalist antipathy and contempt for Dublin Castle were increased; Mr Trevelyan's resignation was hastened; it is said that Lord Spencer was converted to Home Rule; and one cannot help feeling that Mr Gladstone's mind was biassed in favour of the revolutionary movement.

Mr Parnell could not, and did not seek to, evade responsibility for this attack on the Liberal Government; and it helped to rehabilitate him with the Fenians and Invincibles whom he had offended. Some years afterwards, when passions had cooled down, Mr William O'Brien confessed his willingness " to black Lord Spencer's boots " if anything said or written at this time had given him pain. Earl Spencer was said to be one of the most upright viceroys who ever came to Dublin, and assuredly the Countess was one of the most charming Lady-Lieutenants. While writing this book, I happened to stay at a hotel kept by a man who was house-steward to Lord Spencer for many years at Althorp and during the whole term of this viceroyalty. I discussed Lord

Spencer's character with him, and the old servant's reiterated verdict was : " He was noble by name and noble by nature."

The campaign against immorality did not diminish ' United Ireland's ' antipathy to the landowners, and when a large meeting of landlords, mortgagees, and encumbrancers was held in Dublin early in the summer, Mr Parnell's paper described those attending it as " a number of public swindlers and convicted thieves who have been found guilty in the courts of the country of corporate and individual robbery." At this stage Mr O'Connor Power dissociated himself from the Parnellites and wrote a letter to his Mayo constituents in which he said : " For the pure Nationalism of a former day they have substituted a gross and debasing Socialism. I decline to share this new delirium." Meantime the Arrears Act of 1882, which Mr Parnell had condemned soon after its passage, was being used, and, by virtue of it up to the middle of 1884, the Government had paid £767,584 to landlords, while the amount of arrears compulsorily remitted was £1,760,823.

Despite the alarm prevalent amongst Ulster Protestants, the Twelfth of July celebrations there passed off peaceably ; but, in Cumberland, an Orange procession was attacked by Roman Catholics, one of whom was shot dead and others injured. Early in August the dynamitards were once more brought before public notice—three of them, John Daly, Egan, and McDonnell, being found guilty at Warwick assizes on August 3rd, the first getting penal servitude for life and the second for twenty years, while the third was released on bail. The next day three packages of nitro-glycerine with a fuse and cap attached were found in the letter-box of Nottingham post office. I remember meeting this John Daly with Irish members after the Nationalists had got him released from prison some years afterwards, and he seemed an impulsive, hysterical man. When he returned to his native city, Limerick, he was elected mayor for several years, as a testimony to the public sympathy for the secret side of the revolutionary movement, and an expression of opinion that extreme courses were justified in the war against England. Another striking display of admiration for the physical force men was given in Dublin on Sunday, September 14th, at the funeral of Denis Duggan, a prominent Fenian, when over 12,000 men marched in procession after the coffin as a message of defiance to a Government which had recently hanged and imprisoned so many Fenians.

In England the Liberal leaders could speak of nothing but the Franchise Bill and the scheme for redistributing the seats. The feeling of the Parnellites was that the Government were working to give them the mastery of the House of Commons; and, when on October 22nd Mr Trevelyan resigned the Chief Secretaryship, there was great jubilation over "the downfall of the nephew of Macaulay and biographer of Fox." Parliament met next day for a special autumn session, and the Parnellites began by attacking the judge and jury who had convicted the Maamtrasna murderers. Mr Timothy Harrington said " the officials in Ireland from the Crown Solicitor to Lord Spencer had, with the knowledge of the facts before their minds, endeavoured to hang ten innocent men upon evidence which they knew to be false!" Mr Trevelyan retorted that there was nothing to support this attack but the evidence of "a thrice-perjured man"; and Harrington's motion was rejected by 219 to 48, receiving no support except from the Parnellites.

Another step along the road of revolution was taken by the Dublin Corporation at its December meeting, when, on the motion of Sub-Sheriff Clancy, a well-known physical force man, it decided to rename several Dublin streets after Nationalist patriots. It was first proposed to change Sackville Street (named after Lionel Sackville, first Duke of Dorset, who was Lord - Lieutenant in 1731 and 1751) to O'Connell Street; but this was opposed by a majority of the residents, and Vice - Chancellor Chatterton promptly issued an injunction forbidding the Corporation to make the change under penalty of arrest for contempt of court. The Corporation, like the Midleton defendants, accepted Chatterton's decision, but resolved not to repaint the name on the tablets at the corners, with the result that Dublin's principal thoroughfare— the widest and straightest in the British Isles—had no official name for thirty years, being called O'Connell Street by the Nationalists and Sackville Street by the Loyalists and principal residents. A number of minor streets were renamed without opposition, and such names as Sarsfield, Brian Boru, Emmet, and Lord Edward made their appearance at street corners; but the idea of changing the names of the principal streets was dropped.

The titles of the Dublin streets illustrate the continuous loyalty of its Corporation to the English connection until the arrival of Mr Parnell, being almost a complete index to the Lord - Lieutenants. Clarence Street, for instance, recalls Lionel, Duke of

Clarence, son of Edward III. and Lord Deputy of
Ireland in 1361 ; George, Duke of Clarence, who
ruled at the Castle a hundred years after, as well as
later holders of the title. Talbot Street tells of Sir
John Talbot in 1414, and of Dick Talbot, Earl of
Tyrconnell, James II.'s Catholic viceroy. Ormond
Street, Quay, and Market tell of James, fourth Earl
of Ormond, in 1419 and again in 1443; of James,
first Marquis of Ormond, in 1644, during the Civil
War, and again, as first Duke, after the Restoration
for seventeen years ; and of James, second Duke, in
1703 and 1711. York Street tells of Richard, Duke
of York, in 1449 and 1459 ; of the son of Edward IV.
in 1499 ; and of a still greater Lord Deputy, Henry,
Duke of York, in 1494, afterwards Henry VIII. Lincoln
Place tells of the Earl of Lincoln in 1485, and a later
bearer of the title. Bedford Street recalls Jasper,
Duke of Bedford, in the same year, and John Russell,
fourth Duke, in 1753, after whom are called Russell
Street and Russell Place. Mountjoy Square, Place,
and Street recall Sir Charles Blount, Lord Mountjoy,
James I.'s viceroy, who stayed for thirty-seven years
till he was succeeded by Thomas Wentworth, Earl of
Stafford, after whom are called Thomas Street and
Wentworth Place. Berkeley Street recalls Lord
Berkeley of Stratton, in 1670; Capel Street is called
after Elizabeth's viceroy, Arthur Capel, Earl of Essex,
after whom Essex Bridge (facing Capel Street and re-
named Grattan Bridge) and Essex Quay were also
named. Clarendon Street reminds us of Henry Hyde,
Earl of Clarendon, father-in-law of James II., who was
deputy for a short time before his son-in-law appointed
Dick Talbot, and of a more recent viceroy of the name.
Herbert Street and Pembroke Street recall Thomas

Herbert, Earl of Pembroke, viceroy in Queen Anne's reign, and his successors.

The following streets are all called after eighteenth or nineteenth century viceroys : Bolton Street, after the Duke of Bolton, 1717 ; Grafton Street and Duke Street after Charles Fitz-Roy, Duke of Grafton, 1721 ; Sackville and Dorset Streets after Lionel Sackville, Duke of Dorset, in 1731 and 1751 ; Cavendish Row, after William Cavendish, Duke of Devonshire ; Stanhope and Harrington Streets, after William Stanhope, Earl of Harrington, in 1747 (many country Nationalists thought this street was called after Mr Timothy Harrington !) ; Montagu Street, after George Montagu, Earl of Halifax, in 1761 ; Northumberland Road, Percy and Northumberland Places, after the Earl and Duke of Northumberland ; Townshend Street, after the Marquis Townshend, in 1765 and 1767 ; Hartcourt Street, after the Earl of Hartcourt, in 1772 ; Buckingham Street, after the Earl and Marquis of that name ; Portland Row and Street, after the Duke of Portland, in 1782 ; Grenville and Temple Streets, after George Grenville, Earl Temple, in the same year ; Rutland Square and Street, after the Duke of Rutland, in 1784 ; Westmoreland Street, after the Earl of that name, in 1790 ; Fitzwilliam Square, Place, and Street, after Earl Fitzwilliam, the popular viceroy who retired before the Union ; Camden Street, after Earl Camden, who succeeded him.

There is no street called after Lord Cornwallis, in whose time the Union was carried. But after the Union the list continues all through the nineteenth century. Hardwicke Street recalls the Earl of Hardwicke, first Lord-Lieutenant after the Union. Lennox and Richmond Streets were called after Charles

Lennox, Duke of Richmond, in 1807 ; the Whitworth Hospital reminds the public of Earl Whitworth in 1813. The names of all these later viceroys are to be found in the streets also: Anglesey, Haddington, Bessborough, Heytesbury, Montgomery (Earl of Eglinton), Carlisle, Wodehouse, Spencer, and Abercorn. Thus before and after the Reformation, during the Civil War and after the Restoration, during the Great Rebellion, all through the penal laws of the eighteenth century, during the period of liberty synchronising with Grattan's Parliament, but not at the Union, the Corporation blazoned its loyalty to the English connection at its street corners. After the Union, despite the reform of the Corporation and the lord mayoralty of Daniel O'Connell, the process continued until Parnell's revolutionary movement put an end to the practice.

Mr Parnell, who more than filled the place of Viceroy in the public eye, was one day about this time my travelling companion from Dublin to Wicklow. I was sitting with a Wicklow reporter in a first-class smoking compartment at Hartcourt Street terminus. The hour for departure had arrived, the carriage doors were closed, the guard was waiting whistle in mouth, and there was nobody on the platform except a few people who had come to see their friends off; but the station-master would not start the train. I looked out to see the cause, and after a few moments Mr Parnell appeared on the platform as suddenly and mysteriously as if he had fallen from the sky. He was so erect that his feet hardly touched the ground, and it seemed as if he could fly away again at will. He struck one as very tall and spiritual-looking, full of fire and determination, a man who might break but would never bend. His lion-hued hair and beard were long and in need of trimming, under his left arm a topcoat, and in his right hand a large spade or shovel with a black bog-oak handle and gleaming silver blade. He glided towards our compartment smoking a cigarette and seeming so self-centred as to be unconscious of anybody's existence but his own, while those on the platform stared at him and curious heads were stuck out of the windows.

He was still so new to the people and so different in appearance from all previous leaders that the crowds always seemed hypnotised at the sight of him. He stepped into our compartment with the leisurely air of a man to whom time was no object, and, his luggage being placed in the van, the station-master bareheaded closed the door. This station-master, a Tipperary man called Ryan and a great Nationalist, took a personal pride in the fact that his terminus was used by the Leader of the Irish Race on the way to and from Avondale. Having seen Mr Parnell driving up he held the train for him, and he told me afterwards " he would not have done the same for any other man in Ireland."

I was much interested in the Uncrowned King, and noticed that the spade had been presented to him by the directors of a small railway in the west, for which ⬥he had just dug the first sod, thus performing a ceremony heretofore reserved for the Lord-Lieutenant. I did not dare try to draw him, as he seemed to regard my companion and myself as mere boys beneath his notice. He did not speak until we got to the bare coast between Greystones and Newcastle, where two sailing ships lay on the beach driven ashore by the gale of the preceding night. Standing up to look at them he said he thought one would become a total wreck, and wondered what they were and if any lives had been lost. I said I was going to inquire about them at Wicklow, and hoped he would find full information in the next day's 'Freeman.'

He turned his wonderfully piercing eyes upon me and seemed to make a note of the fact that I was connected with the 'Freeman,' but he said no more and retired into his corner with the previous day's 'Times' open before him like a screen. He was a man who could only be popular at a distance, his refined features and splendid appearance acting as a charm on the large crowds of people who were never to meet him at close quarters. His habit of isolation and his strange disappearances had a weird and fascinating influence over his colleagues, who felt in awe of a man who never made free with them and with whom they could never make free, and who, despite the secret in his life, could arouse the enthusiasm of followers and the fear of foes to a degree which the most eloquent of them could never hope to rival. One felt that he was every inch a leader, and could understand how he had joined the talkers and the slayers in one forward movement under his leadership.

The slayers had almost finished their work in Ireland. The Franchise Act, which became law in December 1884, trebled the number of Irish electors and concentrated all power in the parliamentarians. But in England the slayers still hoped for some results from dynamite, and on December 13th several of them put off in a boat from Rotherhithe, and rowing to London Bridge inserted a canister charged with a powerful explosive in a scaffolding erected before one of the buttresses. Then they rowed off, and soon afterwards a terrific explosion took place, the scaffolding being entirely blown away and several large blocks of stone hurled into the air. If they had been able to place the dynamite in the fabric itself London Bridge would have been blown up that evening. The Corporation was so alarmed that it offered a reward of £5000 for the discovery of the perpetrators, but at the suggestion of Sir William Harcourt the offer was withdrawn. Three days afterwards a case containing two hundredweight of dynamite was landed at Dover and seized by the authorities. Though Mr Parnell declined to have any connection with the dynamitards such incidents increased his power by keeping the revolutionary movement before the English public.

CHAPTER XXVII.

AT the Lord Mayor of Dublin's inaugural luncheon on New Year's Day, 1885, the toast of the Sovereign was received with hisses from the Nationalists, mingled with applause from the Loyalist minority—the incident, of which I was an eye-witness, being unprecedented at the Mansion House,—and the toast of the Lord-Lieutenant, which had always followed that of the royal family, was omitted from the card. When the toast of the Irish members was proposed, there were cries of "Hurrah for Charles Stewart Parnell!" but, when it was coupled with the names of Mr Maurice Brooks and Dr Lyons, the members for the city, who were both present, their names were received with groans and hisses and they were not allowed to speak. Then the Lord Mayor proposed the same toast coupled with the names of Messrs O'Kelly and Mayne, Parnellites, and it was received with thunders of applause.

Alderman John O'Connor, the Lord Mayor who assumed office that day, was a product of the revolution worth noticing. Like his predecessor, Alderman Meagher, he was a publican, and his occupancy of

the Mansion House illustrates incidentally the
dominant influence which the licensed trade now
wielded in Parnell's as compared with previous
Nationalist movements. Meagher was a presentable man, with good manners and uniform self-
restraint, not uncommon amongst Tipperary Catholics.
O'Connor was a Kildare man, born near the Meath
border, in "the country of the short grass," where the
farmers were mostly graziers and almost as inarticulate
as the cattle they buy and sell. I knew his brother,
a rich grazier, a massive, monumental, smileless man,
who would sit in company or play cards for a whole
evening without uttering a word. The Lord Mayor
often spoke and even smiled, but his speech was a
growl which only those who knew him understood.
He was rough, gruff, resolute and over-bearing, but
kind-hearted, and if you took him into your confidence
beforehand he would support you almost blindly in
any project; but if you took him by surprise he would
resist you with the obstinacy of a mule and the ferocity
of a tiger. He had come into Dublin from the rich
territory of the High Kings of Ireland at thirteen
years of age, to serve his time as an apprentice—or
"curate," as it is called in Dublin—inside a grocer's
counter. He always read with difficulty and his
writing was chiefly confined to signing his name—the
hieroglyphic signature of an honest man. Needless to
say he was a Catholic; and he never wittingly passed
a chapel without taking off his hat.

When he came to Dublin as a boy the grocers used
to sell groceries, but, as years went by and fashions
changed, their shops became public-houses for the sale
of drink. There was no business then in which a man
might get rich quicker in Dublin than the publican's.

The tied-house system did not prevail there, and the publicans, instead of being mere managers for the brewers as in England, were their own masters. When a young man had served his time and worked a few years as a foreman, he asked the bank for a loan to enable him to buy a public-house at one of the weekly sales. If his friends could raise a few hundred pounds for him, or if he himself had saved that amount, the bank would advance thousands on the security of a house.

O'Connor and many of his contemporaries acquired a number of public-houses ; for the then Recorder of Dublin, Sir Frederick Shaw, did not object to one man holding several licences. It was O'Connor and his fellow-traders who fought tooth and nail against the Sunday Closing Act of 1878, and regarded A. M. Sullivan and Mr T. W. Russell as their deadly enemies. When Mr Falkiner became recorder and refused to give one man more than one licence, O'Connor and his friends put forward young men to apply for the licences, employing them as managers with the option of acquiring the ownership if they could. If the house cost, say, £3000, the young man would be charged £4000 ; if the rent was, let us say, £50 a-year, the young man had to pay perhaps £70 ; if the interest charged by the bank was six per cent, the young man had to pay eight or nine. In this way O'Connor and his contemporaries became rich men. The Temperance Party in Dublin raised an outcry when he was appointed Lord Mayor, their objection being not against him personally, but against the selection of a publican two years in succession. Even 'The Freeman' protested, pointing out that the appointment would give the impression that the publicans ruled the Nationalist movement — which was to a great extent true in Dublin.

In the first week of January a convention was held at Thurles to select a member of Parliament for county Tipperary; and a Mr John O'Connor of Cork, no relation whatever of the Lord Mayor, was put forward by Mr Parnell. A local Nationalist named O'Ryan was also a candidate ; and, a vote of delegates being taken, he was selected. When this unexpected result was telegraphed to Mr Parnell, he directed the calling of a second convention, which he attended in person, ignoring the Town Commissioners of Cashel who declared that "they viewed with alarm the exercise in certain quarters of dictation" and warned the dictators that "they did not yet know the spirit of Tipperary." Mr Parnell, on arriving at Thurles, met Archbishop Croke and Mr O'Ryan, and an arrangement was made that O'Ryan was to withdraw.

Archbishop Croke was a man to whom it would be unnatural to go against the people. Some months before this he was staying at the International Hotel, Bray, and certain local Nationalists decided to present him with an address. I told him their intention, and he fixed an hour for their reception. About twenty of them came, the affair being organised by a Tipperary man who owned a public-house in Kingstown ; and it was at once affecting and amusing to see them scrambling on their knees before the Archbishop in the drawing-room of the International, eagerly seizing his hand and passing it from one to the other to kiss, like a lot of pups caressing a kennelman.

There was a twinkle in Croke's eye as he said : " I hope there are no informers here. Who knows but I may be excommunicated for daring to give a blessing in another man's diocese?" We were in the diocese of Cardinal McCabe, whose opposition to the Nationalists was unconquerable. Indeed the members of the deputation were largely actuated by an unchristian desire to pique the Cardinal in thus displaying their admiration for Dr Croke. The address, hurriedly written on a sheet of foolscap, was couched in the vein of fulsome flattery then so popular ; and Croke's reply was that he was "unchanged and unchangeable," the phrase in which he invariably described his own position. I was going home between eleven and twelve with the chief reporter, when he asked if I had put in "applause" and "hear, hear" at intervals in the Archbishop's reply. I said I had not ; and he sent me back to the office to do so, saying it would read insipidly without such a garnishing. As we were in the last tram I had to walk back, and I shall never forget the face of the editor, J. B. Gallagher, when I told him MacWeeny's orders. He was reading the proof and snapped out : "I'll do no such thing. If they applauded in the drawing-room of the International Hotel it was very vulgar and improper, and I will not put it in."

At Thurles Mr Parnell defended himself from the charge of dictation, saying that the National League, which he represented, claimed only the right " to consult and advise Irish constituencies on the choice of their representatives." He promised O'Ryan another seat, but the promise was never kept. O'Connor having been selected unanimously, Mr Parnell made a speech which was mainly devoted to the land question. He said " the pretended fair rents of the Land Courts would have to give way to real fair rents before half the fifteen years expired ; for bankruptcy would swallow up the tenant farmers long before that if they were compelled to pay the rents at present fixed." He addressed himself especially to the labourers, as if to remind the farmers that he could coerce them from below, claiming credit for the Labourers' Act, which was on right lines, but would have been better if his advice had been taken by the Government.

Parnell spoke in Cork on January 21st, and, foreseeing that an offer of Home Rule by English statesmen was not far off, he prepared the people for the acceptance of something less than the full national demand : " We cannot ask for less than the restitution of Grattan's Parliament, with its important privileges and wide, far-reaching constitution. We cannot *under the British constitution* ask for more. But no man has a right to fix the boundaries of a nation. No man has a right to say, *Thus far shalt thou go and no farther*. And we have never attempted to fix the *ne plus ultra* of Ireland's nationhood, and we never shall." He would take what he got and ask for more.

While Mr Parnell was successfully maintaining his dictatorship in Tipperary, and preparing the country for the temporary acceptance of something less than complete independence, the dynamitards were trying to terrorise the Government in London. A lady discovered a package of dynamite in the Parliament buildings on January 24th, and at once showed it to the policeman, who carried it into Westminster Hall, where it exploded, injuring him and doing great damage. Almost at the same moment an explosion occurred in the very chamber of the House of Commons, caused by an infernal machine which had been placed there, serious harm being done to the chamber and a second policeman severely injured. On the same day there was a dynamite explosion at the Tower of London, for which two men, Cunningham and Burton, were arrested ; and soon afterwards letters were received by the authorities threatening an attack by dynamite on the British Museum, the General Post Office, and Somerset House.

These outrages caused great alarm in England, but Mr Parnell, speaking in county Clare on January 26th, made no reference whatever to them. He was busy rousing the people on the land question, and denounced those who were " tempted by the Father of Evil " to take evicted farms. Referring to some local land-grabber, he said that he ought to repent and enable "the bulk of his fellow-countrymen to say there was more joy in Heaven over one lost sinner who repents than over ninety-nine just men who needed no repentance."

One of the most outspoken Irish-American advocates of criminal methods against England, O'Donovan Rossa of New York, an ex-Fenian who had been amnestied, was shot in the streets of New York on February 2nd by an Englishwoman named Dudley, the wound, though serious, not being mortal. Mrs Dudley had written to Rossa expressing a desire to learn his plans with a view to subscribing to his Fenian fund, and he made an appointment with her in the street. When he revealed his scheme she was so horrified by his indifference to human life and his readiness to kill innocent people in order to attain his ends that she dropped behind him and discharged a revolver at his back. She was arrested and brought to trial, but was acquitted on the grounds of insanity. It seemed insane in a person of English blood to take revenge on an Irishman who was plotting the wholesale slaughter of the English.

It was bruited about now that the Prince and Princess of Wales, afterwards Edward VII. and Queen Alexandra, were to pay a state visit to Ireland, and Rossa's paper, the ' United Irishman,' printed a letter from Dublin signed " Shaun O'Neill," offering a reward of ten thousand dollars " for the body of the Prince of Wales dead or alive." So intense was the feeling of insecurity caused by the dynamite outrages in England that one of the sentries at Woolwich powder magazine on February 8th bayonetted a comrade in uniform who was about to pass without taking notice of his challenge or giving the password. At the same time Colonel Williams, of Ottawa, patriotically offered the Government a regiment of Canadians six hundred strong for garrison duty in England.

At this moment an event occurred which was destined to give the Nationalists a vast increase of power. Cardinal McCabe, the most consistent and influential opponent of Parnell's revolutionary movement, died at Kingstown on February 10, at the age of sixty-nine. It was my duty to await his death at the house where he lay dying. While we were waiting the old reporter of 'The Irish Times,' Frank Sullivan, brother of a well-known Dublin priest, asked the doctors if they could oblige him by getting the dying Prince of the Church " to claim his crown in Heaven " before the last train left for Dublin. The worthy Cardinal did not pass away until long after that train had gone, and Sullivan and I drove together on an outside-car to the city with the news which was to excite so much speculation next morning. The obituary was ready printed in 'The Freeman' office, and when I announced the death J. B. Gallagher sent for the head printer and told him to put the paper in deep mourning. Then, addressing his favourite leader-writer, he said : " Write a column, Ennis, on the lines I told you." This was E. H. Ennis, who was appointed Assistant Under Secretary for Ireland twenty years after by the Campbell-Bannerman Government. McCabe died at an even more critical moment than Cullen. If Cullen, who lived to be seventy-five, had been only sixty-nine at the foundation of the Land League, and lived six years after, the history of the Irish revolution would have been different. And now, had McCabe's successor proved to be a man like Cullen, it is doubtful if we should have ever seen a British Government propose a Home Rule Bill. Cardinal McCabe's strength consisted in a mulish obstinacy and gruff outspokenness. He was a sensible and capable diocesan, but had no charm of manner, no gift of oratory. With an unattractive personal appearance and no dignity of presence he affected to despise popularity—which is a characteristic of Dubliners,— and in his tilting at the Nationalist movement had no positive success.

I met him several times. Once in Arklow, whither he went to bless the foundations of a new chapel-of-ease, I had an instance of his indifference to popularity. The parish priest, Father Dunphy, was a gigantic man, over six feet high and broad in proportion, whose two brothers, one parish priest of Aughrim and the other of Naul, were so like him that a stranger could hardly know the brothers apart. There was a reception in the parish priest's parlour before we set out for the site of the new chapel. The

Cardinal in scarlet sat by the window and the priests of the neighbourhood were gathered round, the elder priests seated and the curates standing in a group near the door very nervous. Some town commissioners and poor-law guardians, whom Father Dunphy thought fit to notice, were presented to the Cardinal, who, without making any remark, gave them his ring to kiss as they knelt before him, and they retired into a corner or left the room when they had made their obeisance, unless Father Dunphy ordered them to do otherwise.

I was presented as "the reporter from 'The Freeman' come down especially to record the doings of your Eminence." "I know this young man," said the Cardinal; "I wonder an innocent youth like him could belong to such a paper." Father Dunphy laughed so loudly that he shook the floor and all the movables in the room. I blushed, and, feeling nettled at the slight on 'The Freeman,' stammered out that it was "the best paper in Ireland and had the largest circulation." "It writes very bad Latin," said McCabe gruffly, "and you may tell the editor I said so."

A procession of cars was formed, Father Dunphy leading the way in a covered car with the Cardinal and his Secretary, Dr Tynan, with whom I was very intimate, while hundreds of people followed in vehicles of various kinds. After a pleasant spin we reached the site where the foundations had been dug, and found a large assemblage. The Cardinal went down into the trenches and carefully performed his rites. Then, instead of coming up to the ground level and getting into a car to address the people, he stood in a wide part of the trench and with his mouth in a line with the people's knees gave them a short exhortation which nobody heard. I could not catch his words, and was not at all surprised to hear afterwards that Father Dunphy wrote an indignant letter to the chief reporter complaining of the inadequate report of " the Cardinal's grand speech," which it appears was full of praise for Father Dunphy. He said it was especially wrong of me to have treated him so badly, as he had got " the most respectable people in the town to invite me to share a roast fowl, a leg of mutton, puddings and all *et cæteras!*" The dinner at the parish priest's, at which the Cardinal was present, was not deemed a function at which the presence of a reporter was advisable, and Father Dunphy, who was the soul of hospitality, handed me over to the richest parishioner. This I mention as giving a clue to Dr McCabe's character, and how little he valued the popularity which Dr Croke so highly prized.

Parliament met on February 19th, and on the same day there was a meeting of Irish dynamitards at Paris, which issued a formal notice to the British Government that, if the Crimes Act were renewed, they would have recourse to retaliatory measures. On the next day, there was a robbery of British Government despatches from the mail bags on board the White Star liner *Celtic*. Then and for many years the Nationalists had been procuring Government letters and telegrams through their friends who were clerks in the various offices. We had a leader-writer on ' The Freeman' who had been dismissed from the Chief Secretary's office on suspicion of giving information. This was deemed quite justifiable, as the Government lost no opportunity of spying on the Nationalists.

Three days afterwards, a congress of Fenians and

dynamitards was held at Paris, the result of which was that the French Government arrested James Stephens, Head Centre of the Irish Fenians, Eugene Davis, said to be the head of the dynamitards, and ten other Irish revolutionaries, and expelled them from France. I used to know this Eugene Davis slightly in Dublin. He was quiet, unassuming, and cultured in his manner and appearance; and was a member of the literary staff of the papers published by A. M. Sullivan. I state this as showing that the men connected with the dynamite movement were far from being deemed outlaws or pariahs by the National-ists. They were the same class of men as, and were in a real but unavowed alliance with, the so-called constitutionalists. The republican Government of France, liberal as its views were, could not regard the blowing-up of public buildings and the slaughtering of innocent people as part of a legitimate political pro-gramme; but the republican Government of America had no such scruples.

When, on February 24th, there was a motion to apply the closure for the first time under the new rules of the House of Commons, Mr William O'Brien being its first victim, the Conservatives evinced a disposition to support the editor of 'United Ireland' against the new Speaker (Mr Peel), who declared his surprise at their action and said that if the motion had not been carried he would have resigned. Mr O'Brien expressed his gratitude to the Conservatives, and, on the next day but one, the kind of alliance thus begun developed into a coalition of Conservatives and Parnellites which almost led to the defeat of the Ministry, whose majority sank to 14 on a formal vote of censure upon its Egyptian policy.

All the spring the Redistribution of Seats Act kept the politicians in Ireland busy "jerrymandering"—an American word then heard for the first time, and meaning a kind of doctoring, or "faking," of the boundaries of constituencies, of which one or two instances will suffice. A small district of Liverpool, called the Scotland division, was made a separate constituency, because it was chiefly inhabited by Irish, with the result that it has ever since returned a Nationalist member. South County Dublin was allowed to include the suburban township of Rathmines, which was and is mainly Unionist; and the Stephen's Green division of the city was allowed to include the Pembroke township, which is also largely Unionist. This was done in the hope that the "loyal minority" might retain some representation in the Irish capital. In Belfast, the West division was arranged so as to include all the Roman Catholic streets, with the result that one of the four Belfast members is now a Nationalist.

While all this, which was "not understanded of the people," was being arranged, a case was tried at the March assizes at Nenagh, which illustrated the primitive ideas prevalent in Ireland. A young man backed by a number of his friends armed with guns went by night to the home of a girl whom he wanted to marry, seized the young woman and carried her off forcibly to the house of another farmer fourteen miles away. She escaped the next day and made her way back; and her abductor, having been arrested, was now found guilty and sentenced to seven years' penal servitude. At the same time at Camlough, near Newry, a woman of the lower classes was killed almost precisely like Mrs Smythe of Barbavilla. As she was walking along the road with her husband, John Turley, he was set upon by a band of men. Mrs Turley threw herself in front of her husband, and, receiving a blow meant for him, was killed, while he was left for dead on the road.

As the time for the visit of the Prince and Princess of Wales approached, feeling began to run high in Dublin. When the Loyalists brought up the question at the Corporation on March 16th, it was decided by a majority of 41 to 17 that no official notice should be taken of the event. On the same day a meeting of dynamitards was held in New York, by which a manifesto was issued stating that " the Prince of Wales was an alien meriting death by all laws if he should set foot in Ireland." At the Patrick's Day banquet in London, Parnell said : " England will respect you in proportion as you respect yourselves. Englishmen will not give anything to Ireland out of justice or righteousness. They will concede your liberties when they must and no sooner." ' United Ireland ' had been soliciting representative opinions about the royal visit, and all those who responded to its invitation, including the Archbishop of Cashel, were unanimous in their disapproval. Mr Parnell wrote to say that the Prince " was not entitled to any recognition save from the garrison of officials and landowners and place-hunters who fatten upon the poverty and misfortunes of the country." He insinuated that the royal visit was an electioneering dodge of Mr Gladstone's.

The disturbing effect of all this on Lord Mayor O'Connor's mind was so great that he declared passionately a few days before the royal visit, at a meeting in the Phœnix Park, that when the Prince

WILLIAM O'BRIEN.

" Every other phase of the revolutionary movement was now completely over-shadowed by the accusations made in 'United Ireland' against Government officials in Dublin. . . . This crusade probably helped to secure the over-representation of Ireland, and was part of the vengeance with which Parnell repaid the imputations against himself."—PAGE 357.

of Wales landed he would haul down the Mansion House flag. This evoked a storm of protest from the Loyalists, and the Trinity College undergraduates raided the Mansion House garden that night and carried off the flag, so that the Lord Mayor might not have the pleasure of hauling it down as he had boasted, which set all Dublin laughing and greatly embarrassed O'Connor.

I was sent across the Channel to meet the Prince and Princess on April 7th, and during the afternoon went on board the *Osborne* in Holyhead harbour. Having seen the arrival of the royal party by night and their safe departure for the royal yacht, I sent a telegram to 'The Freeman' and spent the time from about midnight until the departure of the mail-boat, at 3 A.M., at the priest's house along with a Midleton man who was then captain of one of the North-Western steamers.

The priest was a very jolly soul and, as a true-born Irishman, was delighted to meet a compatriot. He said he would stay up in my honour, and suggested that to pass the time we should play penny nap. He said the offertory on the preceding Easter Day had been mostly copper, which he had not had time to turn into silver, and "to save us the trouble of looking for change," as he said, he laid the coppers in a heap on a cloth on the table, at one side of him, and at the same time threw a loose pile of cut tobacco at the other side, telling us to fill our pipes as we required. The heap of coppers amounted to several hundred coins, and at 2 A.M. I had won it all, the priest dolefully asking me to change sixpences and shillings for him. As the moments flew by and the hour of my departure to catch the mail-boat drew near he became frantic with excitement, but could not win back his pile. "Oh, my Easter offering!" he cried; "what'll I do if I lose it, and only one Easter Sunday in the year?" At a quarter-past two the luck changed, in half an hour he had won back the whole heap of coppers, and I ran off into the darkness to catch the mail-boat which had already blown her first whistle.

When I landed at Kingstown at six o'clock in the morning I found my telegram in double-leaded type several columns long in 'The Freeman' handed to me by Davy Stephens—the *Osborne* with the royal party on board being then snug in Kingstown harbour, and a large fleet of warships in the bay. Most of the houses on the front were decorated, and the Prince and Princess got a cordial reception when they landed later in the day. The exit from Westland Row station, where they arrived in Dublin, is narrow and awkward, and I was standing close to the carriage as they came out into the street, the Princess looking pale and nervous, but, as usual, very beautiful. The carriage horses were restive, one of the leaders rearing and almost falling on the slippery stone pavements which made driving in Dublin so risky. The Prince, who was looking pleasant and at his ease, grew pale when the carriage stopped and a steady disagreeable hiss made itself heard through the cheering. The Loyalists took off their hats and cheered, but the Nationalists pressed theirs tightly on their heads and booed.

The streets presented a gay appearance with Venetian masts and bunting on the side-walks, innumerable flags in the windows, and a close double line of soldiers all the way to the Castle; but the hissing set one's teeth on edge and was painful to hear. Lord Mayor O'Connor's friends said he lost a baronetcy by not receiving the Prince, and it is not improbable. But duplicity was not in his character, and he would sooner have cut off his right hand than join in a tribute of respect to any representative of English Government.

That evening there were splendid illuminations in College Green, Grafton Street, Dame Street, and elsewhere; but the Nationalists broke many of the windows, and the crashing of the glass caused a panic in the dense crowds, many women fainting. For this reason and at the request of the authorities the illuminations were not renewed next night. The Prince performed many public functions in Dublin, being well received by the people on the whole, notably laying the foundation-stone of the Science and Art Museum and National Library; and the Princess took a degree at the Royal University — an institution which made a university training possible to Irish women for the first time.

They left Dublin for a tour in the south on April 13th, and *en route* Mr William O'Brien, Mr Deasy, and other Nationalists organised a hostile demonstration at Mallow; but, just before the train was due, the authorities had the platform cleared, and on its arrival the Prince was loyally greeted. Two days later there was a hostile demonstration at Cork which nearly developed into a serious riot, the tall figure of John O'Connor, the newly elected Parnellite member for Tipperary, being prominent in the crowd; but the hissing and groaning exhausted the energies of the Corkonians and nothing worse was attempted. The Prince and Princess of Wales returned to Dublin and thence proceeded to Belfast, where, on April 23rd, they received a wondrous welcome unmarred by one discordant note. This royal visit was the only positive or statesmanlike step taken to stop the Away from England movement since the foundation of the Land League and the beginning of the revolution. And no British soldier ever more surely risked his life in going into battle than the royal couple risked theirs in thus bravely doing what they believed to be their duty.

CHAPTER XXVIII.

PARNELL TURNS GLADSTONE OUT OF OFFICE. A
NATIONALIST BECOMES ARCHBISHOP OF DUBLIN.
PARNELL SECRETLY MEETS THE LORD-LIEUTENANT.

ON the day after the royal visitors had left Ireland by
the Larne steamer an appointment was announced
which, doubtless, Lord Spencer hoped would do something to allay Nationalist antipathy to himself. Mr
John Naish, the Attorney-General, who had been
previously passed over, was appointed Lord Chancellor
in place of Sir Edward Sullivan who had just died—
being the second Roman Catholic to hold the office
since the Reformation. His brother, a stockbroker,
was married to Edmund Dwyer Gray's sister. As a
politician Naish was a failure, but as a lawyer he was
highly respected.

During the Whitsuntide recess Sir Charles Dilke
came to Dublin to study the progress of the Irish
revolution, and try to decide how far the Liberals
ought to go in conceding Parnell's demands. I met
him at Holyhead and came across with him, endeavouring to sound him on the views of the
Cabinet. I did not feel down-hearted at my failure
to draw him, as Mr Gray himself, who entertained
him at Pembroke House, did not succeed in obtaining
any illumination. The Nationalists then regarded

Dilke as a true friend, but he soon fell under a cloud and was never able to serve them. The universal cry of the Liberal leaders now was for a majority large enough to make them independent of Conservatives and Parnellites combined. Mr Trevelyan asked for the return of at least 380 Liberals, saying that it would be better thus to give the party which had passed the Franchise Act a clear majority than to return 290 Conservatives and 80 Parnellites to rule the House of Commons. This was an open thrust at the Conservatives for their recent joint action with the Parnellites.

Meantime there was keen speculation as to whom the parish priests of the archdiocese of Dublin would select as successor to Cardinal McCabe. Mr Gladstone wanted the appointment of Dr Moran, Archbishop of Sydney and nephew of Cardinal Cullen, and Errington was urging Leo XIII. to that effect. The most outstanding personality in the diocese was Dr Donnelly, the assistant bishop, and it was said that overtures were made to the Vatican for his appointment, not only by private individuals but by the Government. Donnelly was an ecclesiastic of the Whig school, and in favour of the British connection. He had the management of considerable wealth, as sole guardian of the children of his brother-in-law, Patrick Boland, a rich Dublin baker who left a fortune of half a million, which gave Dr Donnelly much influence in Dublin and at Rome. The result of the first communications with the Vatican was that the Dublin parish priests almost unanimously declared they would not have either Moran or Donnelly. Amongst themselves they said they would not have "another master like McCabe," who had been a strict disciplinarian, objecting to their keeping saddle-horses or attending political meetings, and otherwise restricting their freedom. They now acted towards Leo XIII. just as the Fellows of Trinity had acted towards Mr Gladstone to prevent the appointment of Dr Ingram.

The most popular candidate was Dr William J. Walsh, President of Maynooth College. When I say popular, I do not mean that the public liked him. That would have been impossible, for they did not know him. But the parish priests knew and liked him. He was known to be a Nationalist, and as the parish priests were unwilling to continue in opposition to their parishioners on the great political issue, it was understood that Walsh would be elected by a large majority, but it was hardly expected that the Vatican would ratify his election. Three names have to be submitted to Rome, *dignissimus*, *dignior*, and *dignus*, in the order of the number of votes from the parish priests of the diocese, who are the electors; and the Pope may appoint any of the three, or even an outsider. After the parish priests had elected Dr Walsh as *dignissimus* by an overwhelming majority, and while Rome was considering whether it would appoint him, the Government still continued to press for Moran, and an inspired announcement appeared in the newspapers that Moran had been appointed. Upon this Errington wrote to Lord Granville, the Foreign Secretary: "The premature report about Dr Moran will cause increased pressure to be put on the Pope, and create many fresh difficulties. The matter must therefore be most carefully watched, so that the strong pressure I can still command may be used at the right moment."

The Dublin Corporation took a further step away from England by designing a new city flag, which was hoisted on May 25th and consisted of a gold harp on a green ground, with three white castles on a blue ground in one corner; whereas the immemorial flag of Dublin used to be simply three white castles on a blue ground. On the first night after the new flag was hoisted at the Mansion House, the Trinity undergraduates scaled the wall and stole it, to the great amusement of the Dubliners and the chagrin of Lord Mayor O'Connor.

So far the public had no reason for suspecting that either English party was likely to propose the establishment of a Dublin parliament. It was Mr Chamberlain, at Birmingham on June 3rd, who gave the first indication that self-government might possibly be conceded by the Liberals. He said that Mr Gladstone had disestablished an alien Church and reformed the land laws, but there remained a question as important, and that was to give, in Mr Gladstone's own words, " the widest possible self-government for Ireland consistent with the maintenance of the integrity of the empire." To find a " safe means between separation and excessive centralisation," said Mr Chamberlain, " that is the problem, and I do not believe it will be impossible to find a solution." At that time Mr Chamberlain was cultivating the friendship of Mr Healy, as if with the intention of getting into touch with Parnell in that way, as Mr Gladstone kept in touch with the Irish leader through Mrs O'Shea. He asked Healy to dine one evening, and Healy asked Parnell's permission, but the Chief " angrily said No." Mr Chamberlain afterwards suggested the establishment of four elective provincial councils with legislative powers, subject to the control of the British Parliament, as the limit to which self-government might be conceded without breaking the Union. This was received by the Nationalists with contempt, mingled with rejoicing. Provincial councils would not satisfy the revolutionary movement, but it was a great point gained to have the leading Liberals beginning to make offers in the direction of Home Rule.

It was well known in Dublin that Mr Parnell was only waiting for a chance of turning out Mr Gladstone, being anxious to bring the new Franchise Act into play, weed out the rest of the Shawites, and capture many Ulster seats. His opportunity came unexpectedly on June 8th, two days before the date the Government had fixed for introducing a Bill to renew the Crimes Act. The Conservatives, acting as usual with the brewers, strenuously contested a proposed increase of the beer duty, and, a division being taken, thirty-nine Parnellites joined with them and defeated the Government. Parnell liked the Tories as a party (being on speaking terms with Lord Randolph Churchill), because he felt that they could pass a Home Rule Bill through the House of Lords; but he had no affinity with Lord Salisbury. It was not at first expected that the Cabinet would resign, as their defeat was due to the temporary absence of many of their supporters; but Mr Gladstone, for tactical reasons, tendered his resignation and left office without renewing the Crimes Act. When it was announced that he had refused an earldom, he rose considerably in the esteem of the Nationalists, who just then had a boundless contempt for all titles, except those held by ecclesiastics. Amongst the honours he distributed was a baronetcy for Mr George

Errington, but he conferred no distinction on Captain or Mrs O'Shea, to whom he had been so much "indebted."

Lord Salisbury became Prime Minister on June 24th, with the Earl of Carnarvon as Lord-Lieutenant and Sir William Hart Dyke as Chief Secretary. Earl Spencer made his official exit from Dublin on June 26th, amidst hisses from the Nationalist crowds in the streets and merited applause from the Loyalists, looking, as usual, the personification of dignity and disinterestedness. The close of Mr Gladstone's second Irish *régime* brought to an end five most eventful years, in which the revolutionary movement grew from infancy to manhood, and spread from a small section of secret society men to the entire Catholic population, headed, as we shall see, by the Archbishop of Dublin.

By a notable coincidence the day of Lord Spencer's departure witnessed another event, which was a no less striking landmark in the history of the Irish revolution. After the long delay of over four months since the death of Cardinal McCabe, the Pope announced his ratification of Dr William J. Walsh's election, and appointed him Archbishop of Dublin. The parish priests had convinced the Vatican that they would not accept any other diocesan ; and Leo, never having been a temporal sovereign, and having none of Pius IX.'s autocratic ideas, did not dare to pass over their nominee. But the Roman officials resented the stand made by the Dublin priests, and Dr Walsh has always been cold-shouldered at the Apostolic See. One of Archbishop Walsh's electors, Canon Daniel, was a constant visitor to ' The Freeman ' office at this time, and often wrote a leading article ; but he never gave any ecclesiastical tips in his leaders, whereas his conversation was most enlightening. A Church of Ireland clergyman, named Carroll, used also to write leaders, being a member of the staff—the last relic of the day when 'The Freeman' was under Protestant ownership. He used to amuse us with stories of his brethren : how some commuted, others compounded, and others "commuted, compounded, and cut" after disestablishment—that is to say, got all the ready money they could from the Church Commissioners and left the country. In justice it must be said that those who acted thus were only a small minority—the great majority taking a lump sum in lieu of their life stipends and putting it into a common fund, which was invested so as to produce a yearly revenue for distribution amongst the whole body of the clergy in perpetuity.

Dr Walsh's appointment caused much rejoicing. A short time afterwards I was travelling to Cork with a priest of the Passionist Order, and, while the train was stopped at Kildare, Dr Kavanagh, the parish priest of the place and one of the electors of Dr Walsh, came to the carriage window. My companion spoke of the new Archbishop's appointment. "Magnificent!" exclaimed Dr Kavanagh, "it is just the keystone of the arch of the Nationalist movement. We are now knit together, and no opposition can break us down." This was precisely what all Catholics felt. Dr Kavanagh, one of the most outspoken and prepossessing of the Nationalist priests, was then building a beautiful church at Kildare. Not long afterwards, he was celebrating his first Mass in it when the supports of a large statue gave way, and the block of marble falling right down on him, killed him instantly at the altar. The Christian Brothers in our town told their pupils that his death was a judgment on him for having urged the local Brothers to discontinue the practice of keeping statues in their schools, because it disqualified them for the Government grant. Henceforth we had an Archbishop of Dublin as nationalist as the Archbishop of Cashel. As the death of Cullen had facilitated the birth of the revolution, so now the coming of Archbishop Walsh hastened the completion of its triumph over Mr Gladstone.

A few days after Dr Walsh's appointment, I was present in the Privy Council chamber when Lord Carnarvon and Sir William Hart Dyke were privately sworn-in. Lord Carnarvon, in his place in the House of Lords on July 6th, declared that crime had so decreased in Ireland that the Crimes Act was no longer needed, and the Conservative Government did not intend to renew the measure which had procured the conviction of the Invincibles. The famous statute expired on July 12th, with the immediate result that agrarian outrages, which during the first half of 1885 numbered 373, rose in the second half to 543, and the number of people boycotted increased threefold.

The repeal of this hated Crimes Act, having long been the leading plank in the revolutionary programme and openly demanded by the dynamitards and Fenians, caused great jubilation amongst the Parnellites, and was attributed to Tory gratitude for the turning out of Mr Gladstone. But, though Lord Carnarvon said he was " fully prepared to trust the people of Ireland," the Nationalist Lord Mayor and Corporation did not take any notice of him next day when he made his state entry into Dublin. I asked Lord Mayor

O'Connor if he meant to haul down the second new flag, but he looked very black as he replied: "If it wasn't for them young chums of yours in Trinity College, I would have publicly announced my intention of doing so!"

A week after the new viceroy's arrival, on July 14th, the public were astounded by the news that the Munster Bank, our only southern banking institution, with its head - office in Cork, had stopped payment. This completed the political ruin of Mr William Shaw, who was its chairman; but the immediate cause of the failure was ascribed to the managing director, a Scotsman called Farquharson, who absconded leaving personal defalcations amounting to £70,000. There was great panic and distress not only in the south but in Dublin amongst the shareholders and depositors who were largely Catholic; and a deputation of shareholders at once waited on Lord Carnarvon to ask for State help; but his reply was that the Government could not come to the aid of a commercial concern in active operation. The greatest loss fell on the shareholders, as they were liable for an unpaid call on their shares, and I knew several who were severely hit by having to pay this call in order that the depositors might be paid in full. The failure of the Munster Bank, by increasing discontent in the south, enhanced Parnell's power and gave a fresh stimulus to the revolution.

Three days after the failure Mr Parnell, in the House of Commons, charged Lord Spencer's Government with miscarriage of justice in connection with the Maamtrasna prisoners and asked for a committee of inquiry. Sir Michael Hicks-Beach, Chancellor of the Exchequer, so far from supporting Lord Spencer, astonished the House by saying that, if a memorial were presented to the Government, he would inquire personally into the subject. This extraordinary concession to Parnell was regarded as disloyalty, and alarmed not only the Liberals but all the Conservatives who had property in Ireland. When Parnell offered to withdraw his motion for an inquiry, in consequence of Hicks-Beach's promise, Mr Brodrick and other Conservatives opposed his doing so, insisting that the motion should be rejected by the House, so that it might be on record that there was nothing to question in Lord Spencer's administration of the criminal law. The motion was then negatived without a division.

On the same day in the House of Lords, Lord Ashbourne (Edward Gibson), the new Irish Lord Chancellor, introduced a Land Bill by which the Government took powers to advance £5,000,000 for land purchase in Ireland — thus verifying Parnell's message to Gladstone through Captain O'Shea that the Tories had been converted to peasant proprietary. It is said by those who ought to know that the introduction of this and the dropping of the Crimes Act were part of a pact between Parnell and the Conservatives. Where a landlord was willing to sell and his tenants to buy, the Commissioners appointed by this Bill (one of whom was Mr John George MacCarthy) were empowered to advance the whole price agreed upon, each tenant to repay his share by an annuity calculated at four per cent for forty-nine years. Lord Spencer made three objections to the measure : first, that it would be bad policy to put the State in the position of a landlord in Ireland ; second, that it would throw a burden on the tax-payers of the United Kingdom ; and third, that it put a premium on unthrift amongst the tenants to advance the whole of the purchase money. But the Bill became law with the consent of the Liberals and proved a notable success.

Lord Spencer was entertained at a banquet in Westminster Palace Hotel, on July 24th, by some two hundred peers and members of Parliament as a mark of approval of his Irish administration. Lord Hartington was in the chair, and Mr Bright, who was the chief speaker, denounced "the disloyalty to the Crown and hostility to Great Britain of those who, pretending to represent Ireland, had assailed Lord Spencer and Irish judges with an insolence never before equalled." This indicated a radical change from Bright's view of Irish Nationalists five years before when Mr John Dillon's father organised a banquet to him in Dublin. The doings of the past five years had altered many friendly Englishmen's views about Irish politics. When Mr Philip Callan, in the House of Commons a few days afterwards, moved that Bright's speech constituted a breach of privilege for which he should be called to account, the motion was defeated by 154 to 23, nobody voting for it but the Parnellites.

Just at this time one of the most extraordinary political occurrences in the modern history of Ireland took place in London, of which the public were long kept in ignorance, but which must be narrated here in its due order, so that the events which followed may be properly understood. The Earl of Carnarvon, the Viceroy, followed up his friendly assurances in the House of Lords by a step which of all others was the most unexpected and unprecedented. He commissioned Mr Howard Vincent, M.P., who had just retired from the post of Director of Criminal Investigations, to ask Justin McCarthy whether Parnell would be willing to have a secret talk with the Lord-Lieutenant on Irish affairs. Parnell's reply to McCarthy was: "I will see Carnarvon at his own house if he wishes to see me. There must be no mystery." Justin McCarthy called on Lord Carnarvon at his London residence with this message, and the Lord-Lieutenant asked him for suggestions as to the government of Ireland. McCarthy's advice was, first of all, to go about without a military escort and show that he trusted the people. Lord Carnarvon said he had already decided to do so. McCarthy then asked if Lord Carnarvon was in favour of Home Rule; and the Lord-Lieutenant replied that he was, and further suggested that the meeting between Mr Parnell and himself should take place at the house of Lord Carnarvon's sister in Grosvenor Square, which was then unoccupied. To this Mr Parnell assented, and there the interview took place between the Lord-Lieutenant and the Leader of the Irish Race. It is characteristic of Parnell's closeness and his relations with his followers that he did not tell Justin McCarthy what passed at this unprecedented meeting. That the interview should have taken place was so extraordinary that the actual views interchanged seem of secondary importance; and these we may gather from the versions given by Lord Carnarvon and Mr Parnell a year afterwards.

The Nationalist leader said the Lord-Lieutenant distinctly offered him that, in the event of the Conservative party obtaining a majority at the general election then pending, it would submit to Parliament not only a plan for "the complete autonomy of Ireland with power to protect Irish industries," but also for a large scheme of land purchase. Mr Parnell said that Lord Carnarvon personally declared in favour of Home Rule, and gave him to understand that, while he could not pledge his Government, he was most anxious to see the question settled to the satisfaction of Ireland and the Irish party. Lord Carnarvon, on his part, denied that "he had conveyed the intention of the Conservative Government to offer a statutory parliament to Ireland with power to protect Irish industries," but admitted he had agreed, through the medium of a Conservative politician, to meet first some leading Parnellites and afterwards Mr Parnell. His object had been entirely personal—namely, "to acquire information with regard to the feelings of the country and the views and opinions of Mr Parnell himself," and he had distinctly stipulated before the interview, first, that he was not acting for the Cabinet; second, that there was to be "no agreement however shadowy" between him and Mr Parnell; and, third, that as the Queen's servant, he was not prepared to "hear or utter a word inconsistent with the Union."

On the contrary, Mr Parnell said : "Lord Carnarvon did not lay down any condition whatever as a preliminary to his entering into conversation with me. I left him believing that I was in complete harmony with him regarding the main outlines of a settlement conferring a legislature upon Ireland. In conversing with him I dealt with the Lord-Lieutenant of Ireland who was responsible for the government of the country. I could not suppose that he would fail to impress the views which he had disclosed to me upon the cabinet, and I have reason to believe that he did so impress them, and that they were strongly shared by more than one important member of the body and strongly opposed by none." Considering that Lord Carnarvon was both viceroy and cabinet minister, as well as being an eminent English statesman, Mr Parnell was amply justified in assuming that so important a man would not have taken this unprecedented step behind the backs of his colleagues in the Cabinet. The interview was the greatest triumph of Parnell's career so far, the most convincing testimony to the success of his double-barrelled revolutionary movement.

In meeting the Irish leader face to face in private conference, Lord Carnarvon set a precedent worthy of imitation; for the bane of Ireland has been the constant enmity between the popular leaders for the time being and the actual governors of the country. Dublin politicians said the interview was devised by Parnell's friend, Randolph Churchill, and Robert Hamilton, the Home Rule Under Secretary. But, whoever originated the project, it cannot be denied that the interview, given under such peculiar circumstances, constituted a telling victory for Parnell, and must have justified, to his mind, all the excesses of his revolutionary movement. It gave him a signal advantage in his future negotiations with the Liberals, and undoubtedly played an important part in transforming Home Rule from "a chimera" into "a burning question."

PART IV

TRIUMPH AND DEFEAT OF PARNELL

CHAPTER XXIX.

PARNELL DECLARES FOR PROTECTION AGAINST ENG-
LAND. PERSONAL REMINISCENCES. LICENSED
TRADE INFLUENCE. GLADSTONE BEGINS TO GIVE
WAY.

PARLIAMENT being prorogued on August 14th, members issued their addresses to the new constituencies—
those who had hitherto sat for a whole county or city
having now to seek election for a division of their
former seat, the rule being "one constituency, one
member." The county Cork was divided into seven
constituencies, our district being known as East Cork;
but Cork city remained a double-member constituency,
being one of the exceptions. The general trend of
Liberal oratory was against Home Rule, Mr Forster
objecting even to Chamberlain's elective councils as
"Home Rule in disguise."

But this was of little moment, for it left Parnell un-
dismayed and buoyant in the conviction that the
Conservatives who had kept faith with him about
Land Purchase and the Crimes Act were also prepared
to satisfy Nationalist aspirations by establishing a
parliament in College Green. Elated by this extraordinary triumph, it now seemed to Mr Parnell that
the time was ripe for formally making Home Rule,
to obtain which he had "taken off his coat," the

only plank in his platform. Accordingly, in a speech at Arklow on August 21st, where he entertained the Corporation of Dublin to dinner, he sketched what the future of Ireland would be when it was separated from England, and openly declared in favour of the protection of Irish manufactures by high duties against English competitors. This speech, over-candid and premature as it then seemed to many, was perfectly true to type, for Parnell, like Bismarck, despising eloquence and mystification, always relied on plain speaking on great occasions to confound the English party leaders.

His auditors were not recondite politicians, but they had implicit confidence in their leader, and, being all city men, they heard his prophecy with delight, especially as the home manufacture movement was being so warmly taken up all over the country. Mr Parnell, whose place at Avondale was not many miles from Arklow, had a personal motive in entertaining the Dublin Corporation. He was the owner of granite quarries in the neighbourhood, and actually induced the Corporation to purchase all their dressed stone for the Dublin streets from him, instead of getting it from North Wales and foreign countries as heretofore. This was a large order, almost all the chief thoroughfares in the Irish capital being laid down with granite, and his success in this undertaking, as well as his recent interview with the Lord-Lieutenant, made him outspoken that day on the policy of protection against English and foreign manufacture.

He never considered English susceptibilities, and would never condescend to make the way of concession easy for Liberals or Conservatives. His dislike of the English habit of compromise was well known, and extended even to the English smile. I never saw him smile in public, and he scorned the man who used any facial tricks to help him in carrying a point. When he was at the hour of his direst need his warning to those who deserted him was : " Beware of the Saxon smile ! " But I must not anticipate, as this will be considered in its due order.

Three days after this Arklow speech, being entertained at dinner in Dublin by his Parliamentary Party, he calmly reviewed the events of the previous five years, and, relying on his interview with Lord Carnarvon, which a few of those present knew had taken place, he proclaimed amidst the cheers of his friends that the future work of the Nationalist Party would be " to obtain the restoration of legislative independence to Ireland." This was the specific announcement that Home Rule was to be thenceforth the sole objective of the revolutionary movement. He spoke as if the victory was already won : " It is not now a question of self-government for Ireland ; it is only a question of how much of the self-government they will be able to cheat us out of. You are therefore entitled to say that so far you have done well, almost miraculously well. I hope that in the new (British) Parliament it may not be necessary to devote our attention to subsidiary measures, and that it may be possible for us to have a programme and a platform with only one plank—and that National Independence."

If one were not aware of his recent interview with the Viceroy, this speech would seem quite out of keeping with his calculating temperament. Not a few of his followers, who were not in the secret, said he was counting his chickens before they were hatched. I heard one declare that the Chief was going to die, which the Irish say when a person does something very unusual. "We have a great work before us," Parnell went on, "both in the English House of Commons *for a while* and in the Irish Chamber; *for I hope it will be a single chamber* and that we shall not have a House of Lords." He felt that he could play his *rôle* of dictator or benevolent tyrant more successfully in a single chamber where all things would be under his own eye.

The behaviour of the Conservative leaders tended to confirm Parnell's certainty of Home Rule. Lord Salisbury was silent or vague. Lord Randolph Churchill, then Secretary for India, whom Parnell believed to be a Home Ruler, was known to be the instigator of what Irish Conservatives indignantly branded as "the Maamtrasna policy" of discarding the Crimes Act and impeaching Lord Spencer for executing justice upon the perpetrators of that massacre.

The English newspapers of both parties condemned Parnell for his "single-plank" speech. Lord Hartington candidly told what he thought of the audacious new policy, and if he had remained leader of the Liberals the Home Rule Bill of 1886 would never have seen the light. At Waterfoot on August 29th he said: "Mr Parnell has for once made a mistake in so openly advocating his demands. I do not believe he will be able to maintain such absolute, such despotic power over the people of Ireland that they will consent to forego the prosecution of all the other objects they have at heart by following him in an impossible and impracticable undertaking. But if it should be so, if he should return to Parliament his 80 or 90 members pledged to obey his behest, still I am convinced he will not have accomplished the object which he has in view. . . . The time will come after these inconveniences have been endured for a time when all minor parliamentary differences amongst the parties in Great Britain will be obliterated, and means will be found by which a practically united parliamentary representation—a practically united country—will impose a firm and decided veto upon proposals which are in their opinion so fatal and so mischievous."

Mr Parnell was entertained at a banquet by Lord Mayor O'Connor on September 1st, and replying to the toast of " Ireland a Nation "—for the Sovereign's health was not drunk—gave this characteristic answer to Lord Hartington : " I believe that if it be sought to make it impossible for our country to obtain the right to administer her own affairs, we shall make all other things impossible for those who strive to bring that about. If they (the Liberals) have not succeeded in squelching us during the last five years they are not likely to do so during the next five years. . . . They must brace themselves up to do one or other of two things—to grant to Ireland the complete right to rule herself, or to take away from us the share, the sham share, in the English constitutional system which was extended to us at the Union, and govern us as a Crown colony without any parliamentary representation." Knowing that Lord Hartington was heir to large Irish estates, and that the animus of the farmers against the landlords was the best means of exciting people to violence, he added significantly : " It will be for Irish landlordism to show of what stuff it is made during the coming winter, and if it attempts to exact its full pound of flesh I am confident it will be left with very little flesh to be exacted in the future."

Two days after this threat Lord Randolph Churchill, speaking at Sheffield, made no reference to the Irish question, no reply to Parnell, though he represented the responsible Government of the day to a greater extent than any other man except Lord Salisbury. Mr Chamberlain, on the contrary, spoke out plainly on September 8th : " This new programme of Mr Parnell involves a great extension of anything we have hitherto understood by Home Rule. . . . If these are the terms on which Mr Parnell's support is to be obtained I will not enter into the compact. . . . Mr Parnell demands a parliament equivalent to the State legislature in America. If this claim were conceded we might abandon all hope of maintaining a United Kingdom, and should establish within thirty miles of our shore a new foreign country animated from outside with unfriendly intentions towards ourselves. I hold we are bound to take every step in our power to avert so great a calamity."

Difference of opinion was appearing in the Liberal ranks, while the Conservatives were standing by and trimming their sails. Mr John Morley, in London on September 16th, said that Ireland " could no longer be governed by landlords or priests." " While separation might not much weaken England it would dishonour her," but he would utilise the desire of Ireland to govern her own affairs and would not repudiate Home Rule as it existed in Canada. The same day Mr David Plunket said that Mr Parnell's daring demand was the result of the surrender of Lord Hartington and the Whigs to Mr Chamberlain and the Radicals on the question of the Irish Franchise. If the secret interview had not taken place perhaps this would have been strictly accurate ; for if Ireland had been excluded from the Bill, or even if Forster's advice had been taken and the number of Irish members fixed on the basis of population, Parnell would not have been master of the House of Commons after the then impending general election.

Mr Gladstone's Mid-Lothian address on September 18th, though studiously vague as compared with the plain talk of Lord Hartington and Mr Chamberlain, was calculated to raise Irish hopes high. "The two sister kingdoms," he said, "will make yet another effort to complete a reconciling work which has already done so much to redeem the past, and which, when completed, will yet more redound to the honour of our legislation and our race." Nor was Lord Salisbury less oracular at Newport on October 7th, though he said that "to maintain the integrity of the Empire must undoubtedly be our first policy in regard to Ireland." That vague expression, "the integrity of the Empire," was just then more in fashion than the more explicit and relevant phrase, "the integrity of the United Kingdom." Each side in Ireland interpreted the Newport oracle to suit itself, and to the Nationalist mind "the integrity of the Empire" seemed quite compatible with Mr Parnell's demand. An "empire" which included so many home-ruled countries could also include a home-ruled Ireland. Imperial federation, said Lord Salisbury, "is one of the questions of the future. But, with respect to Ireland, I have never seen any plan or suggestion which gives me at present the slightest ground for anticipating that in that direction we shall find any solution of the problem." In Ireland this was held to show an open mind and a readiness to negotiate.

In October I was appointed to a position which

gave me a deeper insight into the working of the Nationalist movement than I had yet obtained; and, as the manner in which it came about illustrates an important phase of Irish life at this stage of the revolutionary movement, I hope I may be forgiven for relating it. One Sunday afternoon towards the end of August, I was walking on the Esplanade at Bray, which is perhaps of all watering-places on the East Coast the most frequented by priests. It was very crowded, and, happening to meet a priest whom I knew, we walked up and down together. After a while we met a group of opulent-looking and expensively dressed men, wearing silk hats, frock-coats, white silk ties with diamond pins, and diamond rings on their hands. They all knew the priest, who addressed one of them as Alderman and another as Councillor. The Alderman, who was staying with his family in a house on the Esplanade, just opposite where we met, invited us all in and opened a couple of bottles of champagne for our refreshment. This lavish expenditure took me by surprise, but the rest of the company seemed to see nothing unusual in it.

The priest had introduced me as a member of ' The Freeman' staff, and one of those present, a young man who was neither an alderman nor a councillor, but who wore more diamonds than any of them, said that he knew of a good post with very little work attached to it which would just suit me. This was the James Cleary in whose house Carey "made himself conspicuous" on the evening of the murder of the Secretaries. The salary he mentioned was treble what I was then receiving, and would be increased; the office hours were only from eleven to three with a whole holiday on Saturday; and there was an assistant - secretary to do the rough work. The priest at once decided that I ought to apply for this easy berth. I had been keeping my terms at Trinity College since I came to Dublin, and had taken my Bachelor of Arts degree at midsummer this year. But the work on the Press made it impossible for me to read for honours, and I also began to see after nearly two years' experience that it would not enable me to get to the Bar. Such a post as this, therefore, seemed just what I wanted, and I said I would gladly become a candidate.

The others were then taken into consultation. They looked me over, as dealers look at a colt for sale, and agreed that my youth was the only objection that could be made; but they pledged themselves there and then to secure my election, though they had never laid eyes on me before. The post was the secretaryship to the Irish Wine and Spirit Trade organisation, a body supported by the subscriptions of brewers, distillers, wine merchants, and retail licence-holders, or publicans, but governed by a committee of forty retailers, two of whom were ex-Lord Mayor Meagher and Lord Mayor O'Connor, and locally known as the Grocers' and Vintners' Association. I had heard of the society, but had no clear conception of what it meant or who were its members. This, however, seemed to be quite unnecessary, and, after the election, in which I won by a large majority over a host of candidates, I had to be introduced to over thirty of the forty members of the committee which elected me.

In this position my work was chiefly parliamentary, and I soon got to know the mysteries of blocking and talking-out bills, coaching and canvassing members, or

"lobbying" as it is called—in short, I was pulling
some of the strings which work the parliamentary
show behind the scenes. I also heard both sides of
the Irish question and preserved my impartiality, for
nearly all the brewers, distillers, and merchants who
subscribed to the funds were Unionists, while the
bulk of the retail members were Nationalists. We
worked in alliance with the English trade, and, as the
Conservatives were the friends of the English brewers
and retailers, I got to know a good deal of the inner
working of the Conservative Party, while I got the
Nationalist members, with a section of whom I was
exceedingly intimate, to do all our Irish work in the
House of Commons.

One of the first facts which came to my knowledge
as secretary was that the committee had been large
subscribers, through themselves and their friends, to
the fund got up for the widow and children of Mr
A. M. Sullivan, then recently deceased, who had been
all his life the most active enemy to their trade in the
interests of temperance. And during my first weeks
of office the committee were engaged in an active
canvass all over the city, trying to get people to
subscribe for shares in the new Munster and Leinster
Bank, so as to save something for the old shareholders and keep the large staff of officials from
unemployment. So much I am free to state without
any breach of confidence, and as explaining my own
position in regard to the revolutionary movement in
Ireland and the Nationalist members in particular;
but there is much connected with all this period of
my life which does not come within the purview of
this book, in which nothing personal should be related
unless it illustrates the general state of the country.

Soon after my appointment I had a striking illustration of the change Cardinal McCabe's death had made in the politics of the Catholic ecclesiastics. The Lord Mayor came into my office one day and said in high glee : " Do you know what ? The Archbishop is actually coming to dine with me at the Mansion House—a thing that didn't happen since Cardinal Cullen dined there when Peter Paul McSwiney was Lord Mayor ! It will not be a large dinner party, only about fifty or so, and I want you to come." Alderman O'Connor considered that Archbishop Walsh conferred a high honour on him, for Cardinal McCabe would never accept an invitation to the Mansion House. Dr Walsh, in doing so, officially proclaimed his departure from the policy of his predecessor in the only way open to him, for he never attended meetings of the National League.

The dinner was given in the Oak Room, not in the Round Room where the large banquets are held, and the guests were the Aldermen and Councillors, leading vintners, Catholic merchants, and Dublin parish priests. There were not more than half-a-dozen ladies present, including the Lady Mayoress and Miss O'Connor, then one of the loveliest girls in Ireland. After dinner, at which it is no exaggeration to say that the champagne flowed like water, the company went into the drawing-room and, instead of mixing about promiscuously and freely entering into conversation, sat round by the wall, leaving a great vacant space in the centre of the room. All were silent or spoke in subdued whispers because of the presence of the Archbishop, though the talk had been loud enough at the dinner-table.

The Archbishop, very short of stature and by no

means handsome in features, was dressed in a purple
soutane and wore his large gold cross and chain. We
were all very curious about his personal appearance,
for scarcely anybody present except the priests had
seen him before, as he had spent his life in seclusion
at Maynooth. He sat in the best chair, which for the
occasion became a kind of throne, in the central position by the wall. On his right sat Mr James J.
O'Kelly, M.P., and on his left some lady whose name
I forget. Mr O'Kelly was famous because of his imprisonment in Kilmainham with Mr Parnell, and the
company kept harping (in whispers) on the proof
positive thus given them that the Church had come
over to the National League. There were not a few
ex-Fenians present — one of whom, Sub - Sheriff
Clancy, could not suppress his delight at seeing, as
he put it, "a freebooter, like himself, sitting jig be
jowl with an anointed Archbishop of our Holy
Mother the Church." Mr O'Kelly, before becoming a
Parnellite member, had gone to Cuba as a war correspondent and joined the Cuban rebels. He had also
fought in the French army in the Franco-Prussian
War, and done a number of things which endeared
him to his Nationalist fellow-countrymen. The Irish
Fenian, recollecting the condemnation of himself and
his fellow-rebels by Cardinal Cullen, regarded this
visible hobnobbing of Cullen's successor with another
rebel as a welcome vindication of Fenianism. This
unconvivial party in the drawing-room was enlivened
by a young curate's singing of Mr Alfred Graves's
'Father O'Flynn,' then a novelty and sung wherever
Nationalists met, as well as by some operatic airs and
pieces—after which Dr Walsh departed and the flood-
gates of talk were opened, card-tables being pro-

duced and congenial occupation found until the small hours.

The vintners of Dublin, so many of whom met the Archbishop that night, had undoubtedly greater political influence than any other trade in the city. All through the year there were weekly auctions of licensed houses, giving a great deal of business to banks and lawyers, and there were exciting scenes at the licensing sessions which were held eight times a-year, four times at Green Street for the city, and four times at Kilmainham for the county, which included the important suburbs of Rathmines, Rathgar, Sandymount, Blackrock, Kingstown, and Dalkey. At Green Street the Recorder sat alone, but at Kilmainham he sat with the county magistrates, who used to attend in such numbers that there was not room for them on the bench, and they had to be accommodated in the jurors' gallery. Occasionally I have seen them not only overcrowding bench and gallery but also sitting with the Clerk of the Peace under the Recorder and standing in the passages, the greatest crowd being in October when new licences were granted and all licences granted at other sessions confirmed.

At Green Street the court used to be crowded to suffocation, and the most eminent men at the Bar used to appear. The Vintners' Society used to be professionally represented by Richard, commonly called Dick, Adams, who afterwards became a county court judge, or by Mr Macinerney, now a Dublin police magistrate. The Temperance Society used to be represented by its secretary, Mr T. W. Russell, who afterwards became Unionist member for South Tyrone and was appointed parliamentary secretary to the Local Government Board by Lord Salisbury, and is now (1912) Liberal member for North Tyrone and Vice-President of the Irish Board of Agriculture. Russell was the most active and tireless opponent the Dublin licensed trade ever had. His society used to be represented nominally by a solicitor named Tobias; but Russell used to take the conduct of the business out of his hands and make impassioned speeches in court, though he had no legal status whatever. The angry encounters between Mr Russell and the counsel for the applicants for licences were such as English practitioners would scarcely deem possible in a court of justice. Mr Russell used to get, or appear to get, into a white heat of temper; and all through the licensing sessions none of the professional advocates, working for large fees, ever did as hard work as he did for his society.

I once said to Dick Adams, who was a recognised wit and chartered libertine in the matter of repartee, that he ought not to allow Russell to interfere so much, as it was illegal—the only persons who had the right to speak being the applicant or his legal representative, and a resident in the parish for which the licence was demanded—but Adams's answer was: "Whisht, man! Russell is our best friend. But for him, none of us would be wanted here!" Russell used to procure a parishioner as a rule to oppose the grant of a licence to which he objected. But sometimes this parishioner would not turn up and Russell would insist on making speeches notwithstanding. Recorder Falkiner's method of conducting business was very irregular, there being no fixed rules and the proceedings in court often becoming farcical; but, through all the topsy-turvy, Mr T. W. Russell used

to ride the whirlwind and direct the storm, Falkiner
sympathising with him and giving him great latitude.
The active members of the Temperance party were all
Protestants. Their society was non-sectarian and
had a few Catholic members, while an exceptionally
liberal Catholic bishop would sometimes attend their
annual meeting, but in the main it represented a
philanthropic effort on the part of the Protestant
minority in Dublin to save the city from the evils of
excessive drinking. Mr Russell, of course, had a
salary as secretary, but surely there never was a man
who did more heart-whole and energetic work for his
employers.

Lawyers like Peter O'Brien, now Lord Chief-
Justice; John Atkinson, now a Law Lord; The
Macdermot, who was to be Irish Solicitor-General in
Mr Gladstone's first Home Rule Government; Dr
Webb, one of the most brilliant scholars of Trinity
College, and afterwards county judge of Donegal;
and Mr Thomas O'Shaughnessey, now Recorder of
Dublin, were frequent pleaders in these licensing
courts. Dr Webb, who defended the Invincibles,
used to get into a towering rage at Russell's interference. One day he said he deemed it an indignity,
as a member of an honourable profession, to come into
a court where an unprofessional person like Russell
got such latitude. Falkiner, who was afraid of Webb,
squirmed under the attack, while Russell sat silent.
"See what you've brought on us all!" said the
Recorder plaintively to Russell, as, after hours of
argument, he refused Webb's application.

Edward Carson also used to appear, and I was so
struck by his ability that I expressed surprise to
Richard Adams that the Unionist Government did

not make him Solicitor-General. "Are you mad?" said Adams; "how could a man that is not a Q.C. be Solicitor-General? He must crawl before he can walk; such posts are not got without biting somebody's hind leg." To bite a man's hind leg meant to become a parasite to some influential person. Adams thought Carson at that time entirely beneath himself. I considered him the ablest of all the young men at the Dublin Bar. Mr J. H. M. Campbell, who afterwards became Attorney-General for Ireland, and may hold that office once again, was also a frequent pleader at licensing sessions.

Confusing as the procedure was at Green Street, it was even worse at Kilmainham, for the barristers had to address a bench scattered over two sides of the court-house and high up in the gallery. It was most amusing (but not for the applicants) to see the Recorder counting the uplifted hands when a poll was being taken. Very often Mr T. W. Russell, or the counsel for the applicant, or Mr Adams for the vintners, would object to the numbers as given by the Recorder, and often a second or third poll had to be taken. Some magistrates who had been canvassed and had promised to vote for an applicant would first hold up their hands for, and then, when they found they were in a minority, hold their hands up against. Moreover, Falkiner had a habit of not seeing hands held up in opposition to his own views. He used to say that to give a man a new licence in Dublin was like making him a present of from two to five thousand pounds—he might have added that it was also tantamount to making him a political boss in his ward or district,—and he would compel such a man to buy up the licence of a struggling publican in some decadent quarter, or give a couple of hundred pounds to some poor widow or orphans on his list. These licensing sessions were more intimately connected with the revolutionary movement than the public or many of those engaged at them ever supposed.

The war against landlords who evicted their tenants and land-grabbers who took vacant farms was being waged as fiercely as ever, and, when I went home for my holidays, I found that, though there was peace on the Midleton and Longfield properties, there was war on the Ponsonby estate not far away. The cattle-dealers of Cork were as enthusiastic for the National League as they had been for the Land League, and were threatening to boycott the Cork Steam-packet Company for carrying cattle belonging to members of the landlords' Property Defence Association. A special meeting of the company, called on October 10th to consider the question, decided by a majority of 11,909 to 707 shares to carry all cattle indiscriminately. A Nationalist meeting, held immediately afterwards, then resolved to boycott the company; and, as there were a number of cattle waiting to be exported, a special train was chartered by which they were sent to Waterford and shipped thence to England.

At the end of October, Justin McCarthy met Lord Carnarvon by arrangement at dinner in London, and the Lord-Lieutenant showed him a copy of the ' New York Herald ' containing an interview with Parnell, in which the Irish leader said he expected a larger measure of self-government from Mr Gladstone than from the Conservatives. While Parnell was in direct touch with the Conservatives, being friendly with

Churchill and having interviewed Carnarvon, his only knowledge of Mr Gladstone's views came through Mrs O'Shea, who was fast convincing him that the Liberal Codlin, and not the Tory Short, was his real friend. "If this interview be true," said Lord Carnarvon, "there is no use in our going on." Justin McCarthy could not give any answer, as he had not seen the interview and as usual heard nothing from Parnell.

"Why do you not give guarantees that legislative independence will not be used to bring about separation?" asked the correspondent of the American paper, who was not improbably Mr T. P. Gill, the present secretary of the Irish Board of Agriculture.

"I refuse," replied Parnell, remembering his *ne plus ultra* speech at Cork, "because I have none of any value to give. I can only argue by analogy of what has happened in other states placed in similar circumstances to England and Ireland, but cannot guarantee absolutely what will happen if our claims are conceded."

I visited Belfast in connection with my new post early in November, and heard Lord Hartington on Guy Fawkes' day deliver one of his straightforward speeches against yielding to Mr Parnell. He had come to save the Liberal Party in Ulster from extinction in the general election now at hand—a forlorn hope, for henceforth there was to be no room for Laodiceans in Irish politics. "He that is not with me is against me" was to be the law and the prophets for the future. Lord Hartington appealed to Ulster, as his colleagues were appealing everywhere, to elect a powerful Liberal Party which would outnumber Conservatives and Parnellites together.

Four days afterwards, Mr Gladstone travelled from Hawarden to Mid-Lothian and said: "Whatever demands may be made on the part of Ireland, if they are to be entertained, must be subject to the condition that the unity of the empire shall be preserved"—a reiteration almost of Lord Salisbury's words at Newport. He called for a large Liberal majority: "It will be a vital danger to the country if, when the demand of Ireland for large powers of self-government is to be dealt with, there is not in Parliament a party totally independent of the Irish vote." This utterance gave great satisfaction to the Nationalists, for Mr Gladstone not only did not reject Parnell's claim, but showed a willingness to make it the subject of negotiation. The view taken of his speech was that he would try to make self-government, such as Mr Parnell wanted, consonant with the unity of the empire—a vague phrase which nobody understood—though not, of course, with the unity of the three kingdoms.

CHAPTER XXX.

PARNELL, ever on the alert, grasped at the opportunity
given by the Liberal leader. He was then in Liverpool helping Captain O'Shea, who was standing as a
Liberal Home Ruler for the new Exchange division,
and Mr T. P. O'Connor standing as a Nationalist for
the Scotland division. The outside public did not as
yet suspect Parnell's intimacy with Mrs O'Shea,
though it had now existed over four years,—nor is
this the place to dwell on it, beyond saying it explained many of his mysterious disappearances, and
placed him, like every man who has a secret in his
life, at a great disadvantage. Speaking on November
10th, Parnell declared Mr Gladstone's statement of
the previous day to be "the most important pro-
nouncement on the Irish national question ever
delivered by an English statesman"—an expression
of opinion which must have been most grateful to
Mrs O'Shea. He went on to compliment the ex-
Premier on "approaching the subject of Irish autonomy with that breadth of statesmanship for which he
was renowned," and urged Mr Gladstone to formulate
a constitution for Ireland "subject to the conditions

and limitations he had stipulated for retaining the supremacy of the Crown and the maintenance of the unity of the Empire—*which no man could do better.*"

In the verbal duels between Gladstone and Parnell, each regarded the other as the fish and himself as the skilful angler.   Gladstone was fishing for Parnell through Mrs O'Shea.   Parnell was fishing for Gladstone with the same attractive bait.   It is hard to decide whether the result showed that Parnell was hooked by Gladstone or Gladstone by Parnell.   The Irish leader's weapons were terrorism and flattery, and flattery was the fly he now threw out with signal success.   "If your claim can be made consistent with the unity of the empire," said Gladstone.   "You are the genius to make it so," replied Parnell.   Terrorism and flattery often went hand in hand, whether by accident or design, in Parnell's dealings with Gladstone.   Four days after the Liverpool speech, for instance, one of the bloodiest frays connected with the land agitation took place near Castleisland, when a party of Moonlighters attacked the house of Mr John Curtin, a boycotted farmer who was making a plucky fight for his right to act as he thought best in his own interests.   The Curtins defended themselves; one Moonlighter was shot inside the house; two were found dead outside; while Mr Curtin himself was mortally wounded and died in a few hours.   Mr Parnell, of course, did not instigate this affray, but it served his purpose.

It is rarely indeed in Gladstone's career that one meets a flash of humour, but now he was evidently so gratified by Parnell's flattery that he became positively jocose.   Ignoring the Castleisland affray in his speech at West Calder, on November 17th, he referred jestingly to "the confidential communications made to him through the public press" by Parnell, and said he would now reply "through the same confidential channels"—an obvious invitation to Parnell to enter into confidential correspondence on the subject of Home Rule. As befitted "an old parliamentary hand," he did not give himself away, but went on to say—"Until Ireland has chosen her members there can be no authoritative representation to the country of Ireland's wishes, without knowledge of which any proposals would be made in the dark. The actual Government of the country has kept its own counsels on Ireland, probably because it does not wish to say anything that would alienate the Irish vote, and it is impossible for me to intervene when the responsible Government is silent."

Lord Salisbury and Lord Randolph Churchill were not prepared to show their hands until the result of the general election was known. It was during this election that Lord Randolph Churchill came to Dublin, met Colonel Saunderson by appointment, and told the Ulster leader privately that he meant to give Ireland Home Rule. I had this many years afterwards at Castle Saunderson from Colonel Saunderson, who was a straightforward, honest man, better able to cope with Parnell than any other politician of the time. He had represented his county as a Liberal when Gladstone was as staunch a Unionist as Disraeli; but at this election, valuing the maintenance of the Union above everything else, he stood as a Conservative and was elected for North Armagh. He told Churchill that neither he nor Protestant Ulster would agree to Home Rule, and probably saved

Churchill from openly committing himself to the Nationalists.

Mr Gladstone's answer displeased Parnell, inasmuch as it conveyed a hint that the Nationalist leader ought to approach the Conservatives. Whereupon Parnell, constitutionally unfitted for political flirtation, did so with a vengeance and in a way that Gladstone must have least expected. The general election was upon him and he must strike now or never. Quite certain of the result in Ireland, he advisedly exaggerated the power of the Irish voters in England, and answered Gladstone with a manifesto to the Irish electors in Great Britain ordering them to vote everywhere against the Liberals—always, of course, excepting Captain O'Shea. He aroused their passions by every device known to him. Though he was probably in favour of unsectarian education, he tried to win the support of the English Catholic hierarchy and priesthood by declaring for denominational education. In fact, now as ever, he believed that the end justified the means and any stick was good enough to beat the enemy.

" Vote against the men who coerced Ireland, deluged Egypt with blood, menace religious liberty in the schools and freedom of speech in Parliament, and promise to the country generally a repetition of the crimes and fallacies of the last Liberal Administration. . . . Ireland has been knocking at the English door long enough with kid gloves. I tell the English people to beware and be wise in time. Ireland will soon thrown off the kid gloves and she will knock with a mailed fist." Such was Parnell's answer to Gladstone; and, coming close upon the affray at Castleisland, it conjured up visions of dagger and dynamite in the minds of timid Gladstonians. Irrespective of what Gladstone said, it was Parnell's interest to cast the Irish vote in England for the Conservatives, because the Liberals were likely to win the majority of seats and his policy was to strengthen the weaker side, so that the two parties might be nearly equal and neither able to govern the country without his aid. Above all, he was as yet confident that Lord Carnarvon would be as good as his word.

In Ireland there were now being enacted scenes of electoral excitement and responsibility calculated to satisfy the most extreme revolutionist. The National League ordered a convention to be summoned in every constituency to select a parliamentary candidate—the delegates being chosen by the local branches, township boards, and Poor Law Guardians, and the priests being, as a rule, admitted *ex officio*. The delegates from the League branches always formed a majority of the convention, and the men from the Township and Poor Law Boards were also invariably Leaguers. The priests constituted only a small minority. Neither had they any collective power, each priest only commanding whatever personal influence he had earned by his prominence in the work of the League. Judged by every recognised standard, this represented a genuine revolution—the people meeting for the first time to select their candidates absolutely independent of landlord or priestly control; while all the hitherto privileged interests stood aside and held their breath, as it were, waiting to see what would happen.

But, though there was all the appearance of freedom, the conventions were not really free. It was Mr Parnell who convened and packed them; it was he who selected the chosen candidates. The list of aspirants for parliamentary honours was carefully gone through by him, and his decision was final. In nominating the future members, he did not put forward a single personal friend. Captain O'Shea had become so odious to Biggar and the others, who knew the Chief's relations with Mrs O'Shea and Mr Gladstone, that Parnell did not dare to nominate him in Ireland. He selected men—outsiders for the most part—who appeared to be impressed with a belief in his own superiority or semi-divinity, and who would obey him blindly. Men of original or independent views were brushed aside. It was a "machine"—to quote his own word—that Parnell wanted. Wherever there was a strong local desire for a particular candidate to whom Parnell had some objection, means were taken to induce the local man not to come forward at the convention, and, if he persisted in doing so, one of Parnell's chief lieutenants would attend and secure the election of the Chief's nominee by an overwhelming majority. Where there were rival claimants in a constituency, the Chief would send down a stranger, and "the Parnell hall-mark," as it was called, always proved irresistible.

When a candidate was selected by the convention, he was required to sign a pledge there and then that, if elected, he would "sit, act, and vote" with the Irish Party, and, if he failed to do so, that he would immediately resign his seat. This pledge bound him to sit with Parnell on the Opposition side of the House; prevented him from taking any individual action in Parliament unless it was approved by the party; compelled him to vote with the party whether he approved or not. The iron rigidity of this pledge will

be apparent when we compare it with the vague
wording of the honourable undertaking which used to
be given by the members of Butt's party : "Deeply
impressed with the importance of unity of action, we
engage to each other to obtain that unity by taking
counsel together, by making all reasonable concessions
to the opinions of each other, by avoiding as far as
possible isolated action, and by sustaining and supporting each other in the course that may be deemed
best to promote that grand object of self-government
which the nation has committed to our care."

Lord Mayor O'Connor was Mr Parnell's nominee
for South Kerry ; and, as his private secretary, Mr
Joseph Cox, was also a Parnellite candidate (for Captain O'Shea's constituency, county Clare), and could
give no attention to his work at the Mansion House,
the Lord Mayor asked me to accompany him on his
election tour. O'Connor had never set foot in Kerry
before, for I think he did not attend the convention,
but sent a letter enclosing a signed pledge, and Parnell selected him because he thought he would be a
docile follower, a free subscriber and a self-supporting
member. O'Connor was unanimously adopted, and
regarded his selection as the appropriate reward of
merit for having threatened to haul down the city flag
at the coming of the Prince of Wales and afterwards
making it a national emblem. He was the worst
public speaker I ever heard, but it was his vote and
not his talk that Parnell wanted. I had been asked
to stand for East Cork by Mr Harrington, the secretary
of the National League, though I was only twenty-
two years of age, but I declined for two reasons—I
did not approve of many of the methods adopted by
the Nationalists, and I should have been obliged to

give up my new post.   The Lord Mayor also brought
with him a Dublin Passionist priest, who made an
imposing figure and spoke well, and we made our
headquarters at Caherciveen, the chief town of the
constituency.

This is the district of Ireland in which Daniel
O'Connell was born, and where he maintained a proverbial Irish hospitality at his ancestral home, Derrynane Abbey.   And now — wonder of wonders — the
Liberator's grandson and heir, Daniel O'Connell of
Derrynane, was the man we went down to oppose
and keep out of Parliament in the name of Irish
Nationalism!   In one of our drives through this
beautiful land of mountains, lakes, waterfalls, fiords
and islands, we came to Derrynane.   Though it was
November the air was balmy as spring, and the rooks
were cawing as if they were already building their
nests in the trees about the abbey.   An old Kerry-
man of the clan Sullivan, who was with us, remembered when the Liberator lived at Derrynane.   "Sure,
it is not forty years ago," he said, "I remember it
better than yesterday.   He used to come down himself, when the courts in Dublin rose for the vacation,
or when he was not in Parliament, and the roads used
to be full of coaches bringing or taking away his
guests.   The house was always full, even when he was
not there, with people from all parts of Ireland and
from England as well.   He had plenty of money and
he spent it freely like a real Irish gentleman."   The
house stood as it was at the Liberator's death thirty-
eight years before, the beautiful scenery was still the
same, but the life had departed from Derrynane and
it was but a ghost of its old self—no longer the centre
of the political thought of Ireland.   There was now no

centre even remotely corresponding to what it had been. Avondale was usually closed up and presented the appearance of a haunted house fitfully occupied by uneasy spirits of the Parnell family, and its owner only unbent when in company with a lady whose illicit fascinations were already sapping his strength and preparing his downfall.

Wherever Lord Mayor O'Connor went, wearing his huge gold chain of office, he was received by cheering crowds who groaned and hissed at the name of Daniel O'Connell. Canon Brosnan, the parish priest of Caherciveen, was at that time building a parish church which he called the O'Connell Memorial Church—a structure entirely too ambitious and costly for the small community it was meant to serve. Invoking the magic name of O'Connell, he was begging all over the world for funds for its erection, and had already received many thousands of pounds, including subscriptions from Lord-Lieutenants, Chief Secretaries, and famous Liberal and Conservative statesmen, as well as from rich English merchants, not to mention the American and Australian Irish. He had at first great difficulty in supporting Lord Mayor O'Connor against the grandson of that Liberator whose name he was exploiting all over the world; but, some days before we left Dublin, I found him closeted with the Lord Mayor and going away soon afterwards with a cheque.

The present Daniel O'Connell was a man from whom no pecuniary support was to be expected, and Canon Brosnan, bowing to the wondrous power of Parnell's name, determined, after a brief hesitation, to support the Nationalist candidate, and gave a dinner at his house in our honour at which many of the

JOHN E. REDMOND.

"In order to make good the loss of American subscriptions, he sent John Redmond to Australia now to collect money amongst the Irish there."—PAGE 288.

parish priests of the constituency attended. He was not on cordial terms with some of those priests, and while dinner was in progress he rebuked one of them for speaking too disparagingly of Daniel O'Connell, the landlord's candidate, and too eulogistically of Mr Parnell. A hot argument ensued, in which the Parnellite priest said the host and his memorial church were "a pair of frauds." Canon Brosnan got up and seized the offender by the collar, ordering him not only to leave the dining-room there and then, but also not to set foot again in the parish of Caherciveen until he had done penance for his offence and got Canon Brosnan's written permission. The offending guest was a younger man than the host and raised his arm as if to strike, but withheld the blow. Though the other parish priests distrusted Canon Brosnan politically, regarding him as a trimmer, they sided with him now against his junior, who had to leave the room very angry and crestfallen; whereupon the dinner proceeded and the incident seemed to be forgotten. Returning to the hotel at a late hour, we found the expelled parish priest in the coffee-room. He told us he was not going home, but meant to stay for the night, and invited us to address a meeting in his parish, whither I went with him the next day. Our opponent, Mr Daniel O'Connell, was not able to hold any successful meetings, as wherever he appeared he was hooted down.

Valentia Island, the residence of Sir Maurice Fitzgerald, Knight of Kerry, is in the constituency; and its parish priest, Father Casey, an active supporter of ours, assured me that all the cable operators would vote for O'Connor. I drove with him over the island, visiting the schools and canvassing for the Lord Mayor, and drove in the same way with many other parish priests through their parishes. It was in this constituency that the Glenbeigh evictions were taking place on the property of the Marquis of Lansdowne, who then owned some 95,000 acres in Kerry, valued for rating purposes at some £9500 a-year, or two shillings an acre. Lord Lansdowne was at this time Governor-General of Canada, and the poor cotters, being unable to pay their rents, were being evicted by his agent. Harrowing descriptions of their poverty and the agent's cruelty were appearing in 'The Freeman' and 'United Ireland,' Lord Lansdowne being depicted as a monster of iniquity, whom Mr William O'Brien made a special expedition to Canada to denounce to the Canadians. But I must not anticipate events, as that will be dealt with in due order.

When the day of nomination came, we went early to the court-house, handed the sheriff our papers and cash, and then waited for our opponent to do likewise. It was just twelve o'clock—the legal limit—when a man arrived with a nomination paper for Daniel O'Connell very irregularly filled and to which we objected. But the sheriff overruled us and accepted the paper. Mr O'Connell did not appear, and no money was given to the sheriff, who waited for nearly an hour over the time, to which we also objected. Then he said he was satisfied that the money would be paid, and declared Lord Mayor O'Connor and Daniel O'Connell duly nominated, rejecting our application that O'Connor should be declared elected. A week of canvassing and meetings then ensued, in which the Glenbeigh evictions were freely used against our opponent, and the result, which had never been in doubt, was the election of Lord Mayor O'Connor by an overwhelming majority.

When we returned to Dublin after our triumph, a crowd of the Lord Mayor's friends met us at Kingsbridge, chiefly Dublin vintners and their employees. Our achievement was only a drop in the ocean of Nationalist victory which then overwhelmed Ireland from North Donegal to South Kerry, from East Wicklow to West Mayo, and there was hardly space in the papers to record the defeat of Daniel O'Connell. Nevertheless, O'Connor's friends proposed to take the horses from the mayoral carriage and draw it over the long distance from the station to the Mansion House. But it was a large landau and very weighty, and, as we had the heavy Mansion House coachman and footman on the box, not to speak of the Lord Mayor himself, whose proportions were herculean, discretion prevailed over valour. We accordingly drove along the quays followed by an increasing mob, and, having reached the Mansion House, the Lord Mayor stood at the top of the steps and gesticulated, inarticulately glorying in his triumph over the Liberator's grandson, and declaring that he hoped the Corporation's new flag would not want to be replaced before he would be representing South Kerry in a College Green parliament, with Charles Stewart Parnell as prime minister of Ireland.

The result of the general election entirely realised Parnell's ambition. The completed returns early in December showed that the number of Liberals (including 4 Independents) was 335; of Conservatives, 249; and of Irish Nationalists, one being elected for the Scotland division of Liverpool, 86. This great Parnellite party was called "the Eighty-six of '86," for it was in the year 1886 it began its operations. The truth of Parnell's prophecy, made when the national testimonial was presented to him, was now manifest : " Beyond the shadow of a doubt, it will be for the Irish people in England—separated, isolated as they are—and for your independent Irish members to determine at the next general election whether a Tory or a Liberal ministry shall rule England. If we cannot rule ourselves, we can at least cause them to be ruled as we choose." Now the Conservatives and Parnellites together numbered 335, or half the House. If the Liberals elected one of themselves as Speaker, it would leave them in a minority of one ; whereas, if the Parnellites joined with them, they would have a majority of 171.

Out of 103 members for Ireland, only 18 represented the Loyalist or Unionist interest. The historic city of Derry and the west division of Belfast were only held by the narrow margins of 28 and 37 votes, and were destined soon to fall to the Nationalists. The Irish Liberals were completely extinguished, and Nationalists were returned for most of the doubtful constituencies in Ulster. Mr William O'Brien was now member for South Tyrone, Mr Matthew Kenny for Mid-Tyrone, Mr W. J. Reynolds for East Tyrone, and Mr Timothy Healy for South Derry. The Ulster counties of Cavan, Monaghan, Fermanagh, and Donegal were completely captured by the Nationalists, as well as the southern divisions of Armagh and Down. County Antrim alone had remained intact with the Loyalists.

Not a single non - Parnellite member had been returned in Leinster, Munster, or Connaught, except the two members for Trinity College. The county

Dublin, always a Tory stronghold, was now represented by two Nationalists; the "jerrymandering"
in the south division being powerless to keep out
the Parnellite, Sir Thomas Esmonde—the Catholic
nephew of Henry Grattan—who got in by a considerable majority.   The four divisions of the city
were represented by Nationalists, the "jerrymandering" in Stephen's Green being of no avail for the
Conservative candidate, Sir Edward Cecil Guinness
(now Viscount Iveagh), head of the Dublin brewery,
who was defeated by Mr E. Dwyer Gray.   In 1880
the licensed trade organisation had worked heaven
and earth for Mr Philip Callan in county Louth.
Now it did not raise a finger to help him, and he
disappeared from public life, though he frequently
paid me a visit at my office after his defeat.   Five
years before he had beaten A. M. Sullivan, one
of the ablest Irish Nationalists, and defied the open
opposition of Parnell himself.   Now he was chased out
of his native county by a total stranger, whose only
recommendation was that he bore the hall-mark of
the Uncrowned King.   Mr Shaw and Colonel Colthurst disappeared from the electoral field in county
Cork.   Great   names   like   Mitchell   Henry,   The
O'Donoghue, and P. J. Smyth disappeared from
Irish politics.   The Blennerhassets of Kerry were
submerged in the *débâcle*.   George Errington's place
in Longford was taken by an unknown named
Connolly.   Count Arthur Moore and Frank Hugh
O'Donnell disappeared along with their constituencies
of Clonmel and Dungarvan.   John O'Connor Power,
the able and eloquent, was heard of no more.

The indifference to local feeling displayed in the
selection of Parnellite members may be illustrated by

a few examples. Jeremiah Jordan, an Enniskillen Methodist, was returned for Clare. Dr Joseph Kenny of Dublin and Edmond Leamy of Waterford were elected for South and North - East Cork respectively. Pat O'Hea, a Cork attorney, was consigned to one division of Donegal, and Arthur O'Connor of London to another. J. F. Small of Wexford was transferred to South Down. Patrick Chance, the legal adviser of 'United Ireland,' was selected for county Kilkenny. Timothy Harrington, a stranger from Kerry, was given a division of the city of Dublin; H. J. Gill, a Dublin publisher, was billeted on the city of Limerick; Peter Macdonald, a Dublin wine merchant, was bestowed upon Sligo. Daniel Crilly, an employee of T. D. Sullivan's, J. F. X. O'Brien, an ex-Fenian who lived in London, and John Deasy of Cork, were quartered upon county Mayo. Joseph Nolan of London and T. P. Gill of Tipperary were allotted to Louth. Sir Joseph McKenna, who had submitted to Parnell's autocracy, was ordered down to Monaghan. Westmeath was commanded to elect Donal Sullivan, a brother of T. D. Sullivan. J. J. Clancy, an employee of T. D. Sullivan, was elected for North county Dublin.

The members of "The Eighty-six of '86" were: William Abraham, John Barry, Joseph Biggar, Alexander Blaine (a revolutionary tailor), Garrett Byrne, Henry Campbell (Parnell's private secretary *vice* Mr Healy), James Carew, Patrick Chance, J. J. Clancy, Dr Commins, Thomas Condon, L. Connolly, M. Conway, Joseph Cox, W. J. Corbett, Daniel Crilly, John Deasy, John Dillon, Sir Thomas Grattan Esmonde, John Finucane, J. C. Flynn, P. J. Foley, Dr Fox, James Gilhooly, H. J. Gill (who had retired

in 1883), T. P. Gill (now secretary to the Irish
Board of Agriculture), Edmund Dwyer Gray, Edward
Harrington, Timothy Harrington, Matthew Harris,
Luke Hayden, Maurice Healy, T. M. Healy, John
Hooper, Jeremiah Jordan, Bernard Kelly, Dr Kenny
(one of the sincerest men in the party, who lost his
post as medical adviser to the Local Government
Board and to Maynooth College through his adherence
to the Land League and Parnell), Matthew Kenny,
R. Lalor, W. J. Lane, James Leahy, Edmund Leamy,
Justin McCarthy, Justin Huntly McCarthy, Peter
Macdonald, Sir Joseph McKenna, E. M. Marum,
T. Mayne, B. Molloy, William Murphy, Colonel
Nolan, Joseph Nolan, J. F. X. O'Brien, P. J. O'Brien,
William O'Brien, Arthur O'Connor, John O'Connor,
Lord Mayor O'Connor, T. P. O'Connor, J. E.
O'Doherty, Kevin Izod O'Doherty, T. O'Hanlon,
P. O'Hea, J. J. O'Kelly, C. S. Parnell, P. J. Power,
R. Power, J. D. Pyne, John Redmond, William
Redmond, W. J. Reynolds, Thomas Sexton, Jeremiah
Sheehan, David Sheehy, E. Sheil, J. F. Small, J. F.
Smithwick, John Stack, Donal Sullivan, T. D.
Sullivan, Dr Tanner, and James Tuite.

Four of those eighty-two members were elected
for two constituencies each : Arthur O'Connor (for
Queen's County and Donegal), T. P. O'Connor (for
Galway and the Scotland division of Liverpool),
E. D. Gray (for Carlow and Stephen's Green), and
T. M. Healy (for South Derry and Monaghan). And,
when each of these decided which constituency he
would sit for, the four additional members completed
the eighty-six. Mr Parnell, in striking contrast to
his action in 1880, only offered himself for re-election
in the city of Cork and did not stand elsewhere,

leaving all the hard fighting in Ulster and Dublin to his lieutenants. It is also worthy of note that, though the elections were carried through independently of priestly influence, "The Eighty-six of '86" made the Irish representation at Westminster more "Catholic" from a religious point of view than ever it had been before. Only five members— Abraham, Jordan, Parnell, Pyne, and Tanner — or less than one-seventeenth of the whole, were non-Catholics.

While Parnell was not a Catholic, his management of the Irish representation was essentially papal, he himself being the political pope from whose decision there was no appeal. He gave the semblance of liberty in packed conventions whose selected candidates were not the free choice of the delegates but his own nominees; and there was no freedom of action, or even of opinion, in his pledge-bound party. This was a *régime* to which his Catholic followers were accustomed and readily submitted—standing for union in politics as the papacy stood for union in religion. It abolished the free play of political thought of Butt's day, making a solitude in which Parnell reigned and calling it peace. No man, however great his personal merits, no vested interest, however important, could secure a seat in Parliament. Nationalists were encouraged, nay compelled, to subordinate individual to "public" interests. Attention to business was contemned; devotion to the "cause" openly praised—the objective of the "cause" being to transfer the government of Ireland to Parnell.

CHAPTER XXXI.

WHY HOME RULE BECAME A BURNING QUESTION.
PARNELL TURNS OUT THE CONSERVATIVE GOVERN-
MENT, QUELLS A MUTINY AT GALWAY, AND FORMS
A NEW ALLIANCE WITH GLADSTONE.

IT was now that Home Rule became "a burning
question" — not for justice or righteousness, not
because of any increasing desire of the Irish people
to obtain it or of the English people to grant it,
but because it was only by promising to concede it
that the Liberal Party, despite their majority in the
British constituencies, could acquire a sufficient
number of votes in the House of Commons to maintain themselves in office. If Home Rule should
become law and the Irish members cease to attend at
Westminster, the Liberals, as returned at the general
election, would possess an ample majority to maintain themselves in power for the full period allowed
by the Septennial Act. The Conservative leader,
being in a minority, could not, even if he would,
promise to satisfy the demand of the revolutionists,
and the question was: Would the Liberal leader pay
Parnell his price in order to obtain office for himself and his party?

The Conservatives at once informed Parnell, through
Justin McCarthy, that "there was no chance of their
touching Home Rule"; and, in reply to this intima-

tion, Parnell put on record this singularly false prophecy : " In shrinking from dealing with the question,
they are bringing about the destruction of their party
and are little regardful of the interests of the Irish
landowning class." Mr Gladstone lost no time in
causing it to be known privately that he was prepared
to grant a separate Irish parliament; though, when
an announcement appeared in the papers that he was
to propose a Home Rule Bill, he said it was published
" without his knowledge or authority." He met Mr
A. J. Balfour late in December at the Duke of Westminster's and told him, with a view to its trans-
mission, that " if Lord Salisbury wished to deal with
the Irish demand in a just and liberal spirit, no
obstacles would be thrown in his way by the
Liberals." Lord Salisbury declined a proposal which
its author must have known could not be accepted.
It did not occur to Mr Gladstone to take the patriotic
course foreshadowed by Lord Hartington and suggest
a temporary coalition of the two British political
parties to meet the unprecedented emergency and
save the union of the three kingdoms. Failing this,
there was nothing for Lord Salisbury but to leave to
Mr Gladstone the task of satisfying the master of
the powerful Irish party which the Liberals had
helped to create by their disproportionate treatment
of Ireland under the Franchise Act.

Nothing was done in Ireland to make surrender
easy for Mr Gladstone. On New Year's Day, 1886,
Mr T. D. Sullivan, M.P. for the new College Green
division, became Lord Mayor of Dublin, and began
his year of office not merely by refusing to toast the
Queen, but by refusing to have the hitherto customary
cavalry escort and military bands in his procession,
having the Dublin Trade Societies instead with their

thirty bands and the Irish National Foresters in their Robert Emmet costumes. Unlike his predecessor, Mr Sullivan was far from wealthy, his publications having been ousted from favour by 'The Freeman' and 'United Ireland'; and I used to hear it said with characteristic Irish generosity, and a fine disregard for the Loyalist ratepayers, that the author of "God Save Ireland," having lost so much in business, ought to get the £3000 a-year for at least three years "in order to give him time to make something out of it." T. D. Sullivan's new style of procession delighted the anti-Englanders and drew the artisans and urban labourers into the National League, to which they had been indifferent heretofore, complaining that all its benefits were for the farmers, while the city had lost considerably by the impoverishment of the landed gentry. Dubliners now began to hope that a College Green parliament would replenish the large vacant houses in Rutland and Mountjoy Squares and the adjoining streets, and make them once again the abode of people of wealth and fashion.

The first political surprise of the year was Lord Carnarvon's retirement from the Lord-Lieutenancy. The Conservative leaders declared unequivocally against Home Rule, and, borrowing a phrase of Mr Gladstone's, made "resistance to the dismemberment of the Empire" their battle-cry. They had lost, despite the Irish vote in England, and their hope was that Lord Hartington and his followers would secede from Mr Gladstone on Home Rule, and, joining the Conservatives, outnumber the Gladstonians and Parnellites.

The new Parliament met on January 12th, and, the swearing-in of the members being completed on the 21st, Queen Victoria opened the session in person. In the interval, a deputation of loyalist manufacturers, merchants, and traders from Dublin, Belfast, and Cork waited upon Lord Salisbury, the premier, to protest against any measure separating Ireland from Great Britain. The prospect of a Home Rule Bill was causing the greatest alarm in Belfast and the north-east, where the people regarded government by Parnell and the Fenians as the worst of all evils, involving the loss of commercial prosperity, legal rights and religious freedom, and equivalent to a sentence of slavery or exile. The same view was held by the scattered loyalists in Dublin and the rest of Ireland, except by a very small minority who were prepared to submit to the nationalist *régime* and even join the Roman Catholic Church whose hierarchy were now unanimously in favour of Parnell's platform. All the Nationalists were now looking forward to a Home Rule Bill with the same certainty as the farmers had expected a Land Bill five years before.

The speech from the throne was firm for the Union, and bore evidence of the strong hand of Queen Victoria in the following paragraph, which, unlike Parnell's prediction about the Conservatives, proved a true prophecy : " I have seen with deep sorrow the renewal, since I last addressed you, of the attempt to excite the people of Ireland to hostility against the legislative Union between that country and Great Britain. I am resolutely opposed to any disturbance of that fundamental law, and, in resisting it, I am convinced that I shall be heartily supported by my parliament and people." Mr Gladstone, speaking on the address in reply to the Queen's speech, said : " To maintain the supremacy of the Crown, the unity of the Empire, and the authority of Parliament necessary for the conservation of that unity, is the first duty of every representative of the people. Subject to this governing principle, every grant to portions of the Empire of enlarged powers for the management of their own affairs is, in my view, not a source of danger, but a means of averting it, and is in the nature of a new guarantee for increased cohesion, happiness, and strength."

Mr Parnell spoke at length, but without elucidating his demand. Cast off, and, as he thought, betrayed by the Conservatives—but with the consolation that he had used them to bring Mr Gladstone up to the scratch—he reverted to flattery of the Liberal leader, who, as he put it, "had spoken in a manner worthy of the traditions that attached to his name and power." He threw the responsibility of producing a definite scheme of Irish self-government upon Mr Gladstone, and said that, if they could come to a discussion, they would not find the details formidable. As compared with the land agitation, he described the Home Rule movement as "spontaneous." But, even if this were true, it lacked the earnestness and force of the agrarian movement of which it was no more than a thin aftermath, a dying echo. If the large share of the Land League money paid out to evicted tenants justified a belief that the land agitation was to some extent bounty-fed, assuredly none of the money subscribed to the National League was returned to the subscribers in the form of relief of distress, unless we include the Parnell and many other testimonials. Some of the relief in the Land League went to the rank and file, in the National League it all went to the leaders themselves.

Colonel Saunderson, having made his first speech as leader of the Irish Loyalists, was followed by Lord Randolph Churchill, who said from the treasury bench that "the state of things in Ireland would not justify the Government in discussing any extension of local government." On the day after the opening of parliament, the Prince of Wales (Edward VII.) and his sons paid a visit to the Duke of Westminster at Eaton Hall, and the royal party, instead of alighting at Chester, left the train at a small station outside, the explanation given being that the Government feared an outrage by Irish dynamitards. This the Nationalists took as an insulting notification that the Carnarvon "trusting" policy had been discarded—and without any justification.

Mr W. H. Smith, who had been appointed Chief Secretary, now went on a hurried trip to Dublin and was sworn-in, though no successor was appointed to Lord Carnarvon; and, as the result of Mr Smith's visit, Sir Michael Hicks-Beach announced, on January 26th, that the Government would immediately introduce a Bill to suppress the National League. The Irish Attorney-General, Mr Holmes, by way of justifying this proposal, stated that the number of League branches had increased from 592 in 1884 to 1200 in 1886. But as the growth of the League was well known six months before, when the Government refused to renew the Crimes Act, and Lord Carnarvon was discussing Home Rule with Mr Parnell, Mr Holmes's figures did not convince his hearers.

I was much in the House of Commons at this time, and used to sit under the clock, being almost as free of the place as if I were a member—thanks to the Nationalist members, who were radiant and revelling in their new strength. Listening to the comments of members of all parties, I gathered that no section of them believed in the sincerity of the Conservative policy; and there was a growing respect and even sympathy for Parnell, who now seemed to be following Mrs O'Shea's advice and ready to throw himself into the arms of Mr Gladstone almost unreservedly. The decision to suppress the National League sealed the fate of the Conservative Government, which Parnell resolved should not remain another instant in office. That evening an amendment to the address was moved by Mr Jesse Collings advising the provision of small holdings for English labourers—commonly spoken of as the "three acres and a cow" amendment. Nobody attached much importance to it, but Mr Parnell had a strong force of Nationalists in the House, and, when a division was taken, he went into the lobby with the Liberals and defeated the Ministry by a large majority—this being the second time in eight months that he had altered the Government of the United Kingdom.

Lord Salisbury resigned, and Mr Gladstone set to work to form a cabinet. As it was evident that he could only hold power by an alliance with Parnell, the chief Liberals who had declared against Home Rule — Lord Hartington, Mr Goschen, Sir Henry James, and Mr Bright — refused to join him, Sir Henry James declining the offer of the lord chancellorship, a unique example of disinterestedness. Mr Chamberlain and Mr Trevelyan took office, but, as was explained later, they did not expect Mr Gladstone to propose a separate parliament for Ireland. Mr John Morley was appointed Chief Secretary with a seat in the cabinet, the Earl of Aberdeen becoming

Lord-Lieutenant outside the cabinet. Lord Spencer also took office, being now a convert to Home Rule; and the other Ministers were Sir William Harcourt, Chancellor of the Exchequer; Mr Childers, Home Secretary; Lord Rosebery, Foreign Secretary; the Marquis of Ripon; Lord Granville; Mr Campbell-Bannerman; Mr Mundella; Mr Heneage; with Lord Herschell as Lord Chancellor, and Mr Charles Russell as Attorney-General.

Mr Chamberlain, seeking re-election in Birmingham, said "he would consent to no plan which would not sufficiently guarantee the continued supremacy of the Crown and the integrity of the Empire." These two almost meaningless phrases, "supremacy of the Crown" and "integrity of the Empire," were in the mouth of every public speaker at this time. The integrity of the United Kingdom was what was at stake, yet this was the one expression which the politicians systematically avoided. Mr Gladstone, seeking re-election in Mid-Lothian, said "his hope and purpose in taking office was to try some other method more safe and effectual, going nearer to the source and seat of the mischief, and offering more promise of stability than the method of separate and restrictive criminal legislation." He said he was confident, because he believed he was engaged in a work of peace. According to Mr Morley, their aim was "to build up such a social state that order would be based upon the affections of the people, to set up a system which should draw the sting even from the hostility of those who were opposing them across the Atlantic." The reception of the new Lord - Lieutenant by the Nationalists in the streets of Dublin was so warm that one might have supposed that Parnell himself was coming with a Home Rule Act in his pocket.

But Parnell was at this moment engaged in work of a less congenial character. The four members who had been elected for two seats each had made their choice, and Parnell had nominated Mr Patrick O'Brien, a Liverpool Irishman, for Monaghan, instead of Mr Healy; Mr J. A. Blake, who had been converted from Shawism to Parnellism, for Carlow, instead of Mr E. D. Gray; and Mr W. A. Macdonald, a blind man, for Queen's County, instead of Mr Arthur O'Connor. Mr T. P. O'Connor elected to sit for the Scotland division of Liverpool; and Parnell, being very friendly with him, asked if the Galway people desired to put forward any particular local man. O'Connor answered "No." "Then," said Parnell, "I will propose Captain O'Shea." Mr Barry O'Brien says that T. P. O'Connor had a candidate of his own to propose, but, such was his awe of Parnell, that he dared not do so, once the Chief had mentioned a man for the vacancy.

This terror of Parnell was what we should have expected; but T. P. O'Connor did worse. He went off post haste to Joseph Biggar, of whose hatred for O'Shea he was well aware, and told him with protestations of disapproval that Parnell was going to put O'Shea in for Galway. He also went to Mr Timothy Healy with the same message. He even crossed to Ireland with Biggar, meaning to go down to Galway with him and Healy and set up a local candidate publicly before Parnell should announce his selection of O'Shea. Such was their fear of the Uncrowned King that they preferred to do all this rather than face the ordeal of a private interview and

discussion with him.   But the Chief was beforehand
with them, and T. P. O'Connor, on reaching Dublin,
found an official announcement in 'The Freeman' that
Captain O'Shea was to be the new member for Galway.   Once again O'Connor's courage failed him, and
he stayed in Dublin, refusing to accompany Biggar
and Healy to Galway.

But the old Fenian and the ex-private secretary
went to the City of the Tribes and started a local
candidate named Lynch.   Biggar did not mince his
words.   Parnell was not hedged in by any divinity
for the Belfast bacon merchant, who told the people
of Galway that Mrs O'Shea was Parnell's mistress,
and asked them not to disgrace themselves by electing a cuckold to represent them in Parliament.   'The
Freeman,' fearing a libel action and the wrath of
Parnell, suppressed every reference to Mrs O'Shea in
its reports of the proceedings, so that the great bulk
of the Irish people did not know what was happening.
But all Ireland stood aghast—not merely Nationalist,
but Loyalist Ireland—at the spectacle of two of Parnell's men daring to dispute the Uncrowned King's
right to dispose of a Nationalist seat as he deemed
fit.   Those who knew of Parnell's relations with Mrs
O'Shea thought the downfall of the Dictator was
imminent.   But in this their hopes deceived them.
Parnell's personal power had never yet been really
tested, and it was now to emerge triumphant from
the severest possible ordeal, illustrating by contrast
the weakness of even his cleverest lieutenants.

Parnell hastened over to Dublin and commanded
T. P. O'Connor to accompany him to Galway; and
O'Connor did so without explaining to the Chief that
he had aroused Biggar and Healy, and had come to

Ireland expressly to prevent the election of O'Shea.
Parnell also took down to Galway with him Sexton,
James O'Kelly, and Henry Campbell, his new private
secretary. When they reached Galway, a mob received them with hisses and cries of disfavour, a dead
set being rightly made at T. P. O'Connor, who, we
are told, after being struck by one of the mob, was
protected by Parnell on the way to the hotel.

There Parnell met Biggar and Healy, whom he
faced as a king might have faced two rebellious subjects. He ignored his relations with Mrs O'Shea, and
acted precisely as if she were no more to him than
any other woman. "A rumour has been spread," he
said indignantly, "that if Captain O'Shea is withdrawn, I would retire from the party. I have no
intention of resigning my position. I would not resign
if the people of Galway were to kick me through the
streets to-day." Healy yielded *instanter*. But the
Supreme Councillor of the Irish Republican Brotherhood held out.

Parnell then went to the window and found all
Galway in the Square before him. His appearance
mesmerised the people who had come to hiss and
hoot, and they listened to him with such intense
silence as only a mob of Irish hero-worshippers can
give to its hero.

"I have a parliament for Ireland in the hollow of
my hand," said Parnell. "Destroy me and you take
away that parliament. Reject Captain O'Shea, destroy me, and there will arise a shout from all the
enemies of Ireland : ' Parnell is beaten. Ireland has
no longer a leader.' "

The battle was won. The people of Galway declared for Parnell. Biggar was forgotten. Lynch

had been already nominated; otherwise he would have withdrawn. On the next day but one, the poll was declared as follows: O'Shea 935, Lynch 65.

Biggar, the leader of this *émeute*, was far from being a man of puritanical morals, and, though he was unmarried, and, so far as the public knew, had no relationship with married women, he should hardly have thrown the first stone. Besides the moral objection to O'Shea, however, there was also the fear that he and his wife would weaken Parnell's nationalism and revive the alliance with the Liberals, which had been destroyed by the Phœnix Park murders. There was also jealousy lest O'Shea, in his *rôle* of go-between, should oust Parnell's chief lieutenants from their leader's confidence. We have seen how Mr Healy would have cultivated an intimacy with Mr Chamberlain, which might have developed into a relationship like that of Mrs O'Shea with Mr Gladstone but for Parnell's disapproval. It was also said that Mr Healy's head had been turned by his success in South Derry and by the election of so many Sullivanites—T. D. Sullivan, Donal Sullivan, J. J. Clancy, Daniel Crilly, Maurice Healy, and Mr Healy himself forming a kind of party within the party. But when it is said, in condemnation of Mr Healy's behaviour, that he would never have got into parliament but for Mr Parnell, and that of all the men in the party he owed most to his Chief, it must be remembered that, as the nephew of A. M. Sullivan and the son-in-law of T. D. Sullivan, he came of a stock who had been in the field before Parnell, and naturally shared the family's loss and disappointment caused by the supplanting of their publications and themselves in the affections of the Irish people.

Joseph Biggar was a peculiar character, being one of those cunning Belfast Catholics who are sharpened by the Protestant atmosphere in which they live. His affliction with curvature of the spine gave him cause to be sensitive and perhaps vindictive. I heard one of the titled English Whips unfeelingly and in a loud voice describe his appearance as he walked up the floor of the House one evening as that of "a wounded crow in a potato garden." He was in the House before Parnell and felt none of the hero-worship which younger members of the party now had for the Chief. Like most Belfast Catholics, he was clannish, averse to co-operation with Protestants, uncultured and in some ways impulsive. His action was not mutiny in the same degree as Healy's, and several Irish members told me afterwards that Biggar was sorry for what he had done at Galway.

The time had not yet come for overthrowing Parnell. I met Mr Timothy Harrington, M.P., one of the new members for Dublin, in Sackville Street the day the news of this Galway revolt was published, and asked him what was going to happen. His answer was that nobody minded Joe Biggar and that Healy would be brushed aside like a troublesome insect, even his own relatives in the party refusing to follow him. The general opinion, freely expressed by Nationalists, especially the young men, was that any man chosen by Parnell ought to be elected without question, irrespective of his morals ; and those who suspected the *liaison* said that the Irish people should judge their leader by his public not by his private life.

Thus for the second time the parliamentary dictator, by quelling opposition in his own ranks, secured the return of his nominee against a local candidate. In Tipperary his opponents had been the rank and file—with Archbishop Croke perhaps in the background—who genuinely wished the election of a local man against a stranger. In Galway the opposition was from two of his most trusted parliamentary colleagues. In both cases he triumphed by sheer strength of character; and, when he returned from Galway to London, he could have said as truthfully as Cæsar that "he came, he saw, he conquered." On the eve of a Home Rule Bill no testimony to his power could have been more timely. Biggar was forgiven. I was told that whenever Parnell gave him a word of open praise at the party meetings afterwards, the tears used to roll down Biggar's cheek while his large mouth would stretch to its full width in a North of Ireland smile. The general opinion was that Healy was never forgiven, and that Healy never quite forgave himself.

Two days after the Galway election, Lord Randolph Churchill said : "Let the Irish members bear this in mind, that, if by any manœuvre of theirs, a change of the government of the country is again effected and Lord Salisbury returned to power, Lord Salisbury's Government will be the only Government in Ireland." The next Conservative Viceroy, as far as Churchill could foresee, would not hold secret interviews with Mr Parnell—unless something then unexpected should occur in the meantime! Mr Gladstone obviously intended to repeal the Act of Union and effect the dissolution of the United Kingdom, under the impression that he was engaged in "a work of peace." "By Heaven, gentlemen," said Churchill with splendid audacity, "it is a policy of civil war, and imminent civil war. It is only Mr Gladstone— it is only the insanity which is engendered by a monstrous and unparalleled combination of verbosity and senility—it is only Mr Gladstone who would imagine for a moment that the Protestants of Ireland would yield obedience to the laws of a parliament in Dublin—a parliament of which Mr Parnell would be the chief speaker and Archbishop Walsh the chief priest!" 'The Times' asked pertinently: "Have we any guarantee that the Conservatives, after turning out Mr Gladstone's Cabinet, may not themselves come to an agreement with the Parnellites on a basis of Home Rule?"

Parliament reassembled on February 18th, and Mr Gladstone said that by the end of March he would give the House "an indication of his measure for dealing with the great question of the state of Ireland." The excitement in Dublin about Home Rule was now intense. The Nationalists trod the streets as if walking on air, and were busy everywhere distributing the patronage. Government officials wore a hang-dog air, and in some country districts even Clerks of Petty Sessions were boycotted so as to prepare them for the dismissal which awaited them under Home Rule. Once more the Mansion House and the Castle were on friendly terms. Lord and Lady Aberdeen now drove through the streets without the cavalry escort which had been indispensable to Lord Spencer, and were always cheered by the people. The Lord Mayor did not go to the Castle, but the Viceroy came to the Mansion House.

It was at a meeting in the Round Room to collect funds for the distress prevailing in the city. A number of brewers, distillers, and wine merchants attended and subscribed liberally. Lord Aberdeen was tumultuously applauded when he rose to address the meeting. Archbishop Walsh did not attend, but sent Bishop Donnelly to represent him. Lord Plunket, the Protestant Archbishop, was present. His wife was the only daughter of Sir Benjamin Lee Guinness, and sister of Sir Edward Guinness, the present head of the brewery. Archbishop Walsh refused every invitation to attend meetings at which Lord Plunket was likely to be present, because it was the rule to give precedence to the Protestant Archbishop, if he had been appointed before the Catholic Archbishop, and Dr Walsh would not give the *pas* to the Protestant dignitary. Dr Donnelly, the Assistant-Bishop, was a much more imposing figure on a platform than Dr Walsh, who required vestments to give him dignity.

A number of Protestant merchants were present, having come to see the new Viceroy and discover how the land lay in the storm already bursting upon them. I happened to be in the midst of a group, the best known of whom was old Sir John Barrington, twice Conservative Lord Mayor of Dublin—"Soapy Sir John" he was called because he was a soap-maker,— a merry old man, reminding one of the Cheeryble Brothers, a type then fast disappearing from Dublin life. Lord Plunket's speech was very badly received by these Protestants. His style was somewhat lachry-mose, and he did not seem at home on a platform with a Home Rule Viceroy, a Nationalist Lord Mayor, and a Catholic Bishop, even though the business in hand was the relief of distress, to which his brother-in-law was sure to subscribe handsomely. There were

cries of "Enough" and "Sit down" from the Protestants before he had finished—which I was amazed
to hear. But Dr Donnelly, on rising and finishing,
was vociferously applauded, and by none more loudly
than by the Protestants. He spoke with an air of
confidence which Lord Plunket lacked, and was besides
a venerable figure to look at. He seemed to know
his ground thoroughly and his speech made an excellent impression. While Plunket's demeanour was
that of a defeated man who felt overwhelmed by the
revolution, Donnelly seemed the personification of
victory. Outside in Dawson Street a large crowd
awaited Lord Aberdeen and sent him off with cheering
and waving of hats.

The tongues of the English Conservatives were now
unloosed, and their leaders spoke in favour of maintaining the Union with the fervour and ability of men
who believed what they were saying. Lord Salisbury
was never so brilliant. Speaking on February 17th,
he thus epitomised the revolution which had been
accomplished in Ireland : " By the Land Act of 1870,
the Land Act of 1881, and the Reform Act of 1884,
the power of the landed gentry of Ireland is absolutely
shattered, and Mr Gladstone now stands before the
formidable problem of a country deprived of the system
of government under which it has existed for many
generations, and absolutely without even a sketch of
a substitute by which the ordinary functions of law
and order can be maintained." As to the probable
completion of the revolution in the future he said : " Do
not let there be any mistake about this—once set up
a legislature at Dublin and that legislature will make
an independent nation. That legislature will have
the power of the purse. Has the power of the purse

ever failed to carry every other power with it? That legislature will have the power of enrolment of volunteers, of patriotic persons who will be entrusted with rifles, and, under the official approval of that legislature, any amount of executive force which it may choose to provide will be provided for the purpose of carrying out such further encroachments upon English supremacy as they may meditate. Of course, you may say that it is always possible for us to go to war with them. But you know very well that a remedy so extreme as that is never carried out."

He foretold that Mr Gladstone would propose to set up "a parliament at Dublin bristling with securities which would be of the precise value of any paper barricades that you might like to erect. In Ireland the majority which you are asked practically to place upon the throne of that country is descended from a long line of ancestors who have never ceased to hate and fight with England. In time of war you will have on your western side an island controlled, filled, possibly prepared and equipped, by a Government that hates you bitterly; a portion of your navy will be effaced in the task of masking this new enemy which you are now, in the gaiety of your heart, creating for yourselves." If the Loyalists of Ireland were to be "flung aside like a sucked orange," what would become of the English in India? He went on to illustrate the evil effects of partisan government by the surrender of Gladstone to Parnell, from which he drew the conclusion that "English partisanship is a quicksand on which no man can take his stand."

CHAPTER XXXII.

PARNELL AND HIS MEN AT ST STEPHEN'S. FORSTER
DIES WHEN PARNELL MEETS GLADSTONE.

In the months before the introduction of the Home
Rule Bill, "The Eighty-six of '86" were an object of
interest and amazement to politicians all over the
world. To those accustomed to the wealthy and cultured members of parliament of former days, the dress
and manners of many of Parnell's new men seemed
absurd if not abhorrent. They stared and gasped at
honest old John Finucane, the county Limerick farmer,
enjoying his clay pipe in a corner of the smoking-
room and looking up furtively as if expecting to be
ordered out to make way for some well-dressed and
self-confident Englishman — at Douglas Pyne, the
eccentric Protestant from Tallow, who, lacking the
modest self-depreciation of the Catholics, gesticulated
and shouted like a wild man of the woods—at Alexander Blaine, fresh from the tailor's bench—at James
Gilhooly from Bantry, a harmless Irish Sim Tappertit
—at James Francis Xavier O'Brien, the Fenian with
the blanched cheeks and ghostlike eyes who had never
lost the look of terror which came into his face when
he had been sentenced to be hanged, drawn, and
quartered — at W. A. Macdonald, the blind man,
whose wife used to conduct him to the door of the
chamber and there hand him over to the attendant to

be led to his seat—at Tom Condon, the fierce-looking butcher from Clonmel—at long John O'Connor from Cork, striding like a giraffe amongst the ordinary members—and at many other sights unprecedented at Westminster.

The discipline of the Eighty-six was perfect. They were in Parliament but not of it, a foreign body whose business at St Stephen's was to break up the Mother of Parliaments, working temporarily with a great British party on condition of being dismissed from the British Parliament and endowed with the government of Ireland. The green Parnellite recruits (shop-keepers, farmers, and nondescripts), who had never before been in Parliament or even in England, literally squatted at St Stephen's, coming down .early and never leaving until the attendants shouted " Who goes home." They were not allowed to pair or hold commerce with the members of either British party, and looked on themselves as mere sojourners in a foreign land, believing that the Home Rule Bill would pass and that they would be in the "old house at home" in College Green within a year. Their commonest topic of conversation with their friends from Ireland who came in large numbers to visit them in the precincts of the House was the distribution of patronage after Home Rule. This man was to be the Irish Chancellor of the Exchequer, another Speaker, another Home Secretary, another Minister of Agri-culture, another President of the Board of Trade, another Minister of Volunteers and Police, and so forth.

As the House of Lords was not then expected to throw out a Government Bill which had trium-phantly passed the House of Commons, they all felt floating on the full tide to victory, and it seemed only a question of months until the Bank of Ireland would get notice to quit its historic premises. " Parnell will drive the money-changers out of the temple" was a saying heard on all sides. Few of the English who looked with disdain on the uncouth new Parnellites realised how immeasurable was the Irish peasant's scorn for the obvious wealth and superior social status of his fellow-members from England and Scotland, how unbounded his delight at the triumphs scored by the Chief and his leading lieutenants over them in the House.

The remnants of Butt's party who had succumbed to Parnell were deferentially spoken of as "old members" and held themselves aloof from the recruits, except when on the green benches of the House. The pre-Parnellite and post-Parnellite sections did not drink, or dine, or converse together, or visit at each other's lodgings. The Chief himself, though in constant attendance, stood aloof from both sections, passing by his men in the corridors, or sitting near them in the smoke-room (where he occasionally went to drink a lemon-squash and smoke a cigarette while he read his letters) or on the terrace, without seeming to recognise them. A word from him to one of the rank and file was regarded as the highest honour and put the recipient into a state of jubilation. Such men as ex-Lord Mayor O'Connor rarely got a word from him, and when they did, the memory was treasured as a precious heritage. Parnell was now surrounded by so much mystery, and possessed such unprecedented power, that he was undoubtedly the most outstanding personage at Westminster. When he opened his mouth, he was accorded a more breath-

THE IRISH REVOLUTION

less attention than Mr Gladstone. He was always brief and sensible, and delighted in tearing off the masks and coverings in which many English speakers wrap up a subject for their own protection and the mystification of outsiders. Parnell held up the skeleton of a theme, as it were, to the House, and left it for Englishmen to re-incarnate the dry bones and re-envelop them in conventional costume.

He was most difficult of access, and rarely seen in company with any one except when sitting in the House. I saw Archbishop Croke in the lobby one night very anxious but unable to get an interview. The Secretary got the Archbishop a seat under the clock, where I was sitting. These seats are actually but not technically in the House itself, and are intended for secretaries and other persons who come to coach members on the occasion of special debates. The Archbishop seemed very restless, and recognising me, told me he wanted to see Mr Parnell and hoped he would not be kept long. More than one of the members for Tipperary came up deferentially and spoke to the Archbishop, sitting in front of the low partition which is only the same height as the back of a bench. Mr Parnell was in his accustomed place, a few yards from where we were sitting, reading letters and apparently oblivious of Dr Croke's presence, of which all the Irish members in the House were aware. The Secretary came over and assured the Archbishop that the Chief would see him at the first opportunity. After a long time, Mr Parnell got up and walked down the floor of the House, observed as usual by all the members on both sides. Just as he was passing without recognising the waiting dignitary, Dr Croke jumped up and climbed over the low partition with the object of stopping Parnell or of walking out of the House with him. The attendants, horrified at the sight of a stranger penetrating into the sacred enclosure, seized the Archbishop and made him climb back again. Mr Parnell passed on, and, when Dr Croke found himself in the lobby surrounded by an obsequious bevy of Tipperary members, the Chief had disappeared and nobody dared go in search of him.

Only the members of his " cabinet " presumed to approach him uninvited, or to speak to him without being spoken to, and then the conversation was brief and strictly confined to business. I never saw him in congenial talk with any one, even his leading lieutenants. Constant meetings of the party were being held at uncanny hours of the night, and I have more than once seen his secretary rush into the smoke-room at midnight and call his men together by name or pick them out with some such words as, " The Chief wants you," or " There's a meeting. You're wanted at once." The rank and file would then go off, leaving their guests to await their return. They usually came back soon, and, though I and others often asked them about the business on which they had been summoned so urgently, none of them ever revealed anything except that they had been to a party meeting. Occasionally, in an exceptionally candid mood, they said that some of "the others" had been in favour of a course with which Parnell did not agree, but that the Chief as usual had clearly convinced the party that he was right. They believed Parnell to be infallible and would not hear anybody in opposition to him.

The necessity for frequent meetings at this time was obvious. Mr Parnell and Mr Morley were conferring in the hope of coming to terms about the Home Rule Bill, and the Chief had to take his lieutenants into counsel. Moreover, as the Government was being kept in office by the Nationalist vote, the Parnellites often had to decide suddenly whether they should support it in some policy which seemed opposed to their principles. All the members obviously were not summoned to every meeting, and it was usually when the Chief wanted to carry a point that he sent for the recruits and outsiders. The pledge to " sit, act, and vote " with the party, and the further resolution binding the minority to accept the decision of the majority, made Parnell omnipotent, for he could always command an overwhelming majority when he put his foot down. The new members desired to know nothing further than the Chief's wishes in any contested question, for, as an Englishman well said about this time, Parnell had " that rare power which induces people to lay aside their own judgment altogether and to place implicit reliance in the guidance of another."

The wine and spirit trade sent a deputation to Parnell at this time to ask him not to countenance any penal or restrictive legislation on their business. He received them with alacrity, standing in the corridor off the outer lobby surrounded by the delegates, and with his private secretary, Mr Henry Campbell, M.P., now the Town Clerk of Dublin, at his side. I shall never forget the earnestness and dignity with which he made his reply. "I shall not vote for or support any such legislation," he said. " My belief and the belief of the Irish Party is that such social and domestic matters cannot be properly dealt with in the British Parliament, and should be left for settlement by a Dublin legislature under Home Rule." The vintners went off delighted, and, when Parnell's words were published in the Press, every licence-holder in Ireland became a Parnellite.

The great English politicians were now making Ireland the sole theme of their speeches. Randolph Churchill came to Belfast, where the Protestant majority were in terror at the probability of Home Rule, having no surety that the House of Lords, which had disestablished the Church and passed the Land Act, would reject a Home Rule Bill if it came up from the Commons with the large majority repre- sented by the union of Liberals and Parnellites. The certainty of Home Rule then felt in nationalist circles was naïvely expressed by Archbishop Walsh when he said of the coming of Mr Morley, whose atheistical views made the hierarchy somewhat nervous : "We may safely receive him with no unfriendly greeting. He is not coming to govern Ireland. He is coming to lend his help in the carrying out of the noble scheme of his great political leader as probably the last English Chief Secretary for Ireland." Lord Randolph Churchill, so far from creating a panic and fomenting disturbance in Belfast, only voiced the pre-existing sentiments of his audience when he said in the Ulster Hall, " Ulster will fight, and Ulster will be right," and paraphrased Byron's lines—

> " Wave, Ulster, all thy banners wave,
> And charge with all thy chivalry."

Lord Salisbury at the Crystal Palace, on March 3rd, said : " If you adopt Home Rule—that is to say, if you once relinquish your power in Ireland—you may depend upon it that, whatever else Ireland does, Ireland will not pay. You may advance millions upon millions, you may take the most sacred promises you please, but if you once relinquish the solid hold of power, you may write off these investments as if they had been subscribed to the maintenance of the Mexican Republic." Three weeks after this, on March 27th, the resignations of Mr Chamberlain and Mr Trevelyan were announced. Mr Gladstone in the meantime had submitted his proposals to the cabinet, and in Mr Chamberlain's opinion they were "tantamount to separation." I was in the House that evening, sitting under the clock, and heard them both speak from the Liberal back benches on some minor questions, when they were received with loud applause by the Conservatives, and derisive cries by the Nationalists near whom I was sitting. The hatred of Chamberlain in Parnellite circles was then intense. They did not resent Trevelyan's conduct so much, because he had always been their foe, and his personal influence was not so far-reaching; but they had looked on Chamberlain as their friend, like Dilke, and, when he passed them now in the lobby, their fists tingled to strike him.

The end of March came and went, and Mr Gladstone's promise to introduce the Home Rule Bill was not redeemed. It was known in the House that Mr Parnell was constantly meeting Mr John Morley, but it was understood that he did not actually meet Mr Gladstone until April 5th, when the Prime Minister and the Irish leader held a consultation in the Chief Secretary's room in the House of Commons. This meeting may be regarded as the supreme triumph of Parnell's career. Six years ago, when he had gone to America to bring the Irish-Americans into practical

British politics, no English statesman of repute would
have entered into serious consultation with him about
the government of Ireland, both sides then regarding
him as Cobden regarded Daniel O'Connell — with
whom the Free Trader said he would as soon think
of entering into partnership as with an Apache.
Even Parnell's respectable predecessor, Isaac Butt,
was not taken seriously by the English party leaders,
who esteemed him rather as a clever but somewhat
ridiculous Irishman, whom it was their duty to
humour and to hoodwink. Never had six years
brought about such a change in the position of an
Irish leader. The agitator whom Butt had renounced
had been acclaimed as the " Leader of the Irish Race "
—a title never before so authoritatively given to any
man, or carrying with it such influence over Irish
public opinion at both sides of the Atlantic, and such
absolute power over five-sixths of the parliamentary
representation of Ireland. Parnell, as the Americans
put it, " had made England listen," and had been
deemed worthy of a secret interview by a Conservative lord-lieutenant and of an open partnership by
a Liberal prime minister. And the question now
was not so much what the English leader was willing
to give, as what the Irish leader was willing to accept.

Almost at the instant that Gladstone was nominally discussing with Parnell the financial details of the
Home Rule Bill, but in reality taking the Irishman's
measure, W. E. Forster, the man who had fought
hardest to put down Parnell and prevent Home Rule,
was breathing his last. There was something ominous
in Forster's death on that 5th of April, when Gladstone and Parnell met as collaborators for the first
time to produce a Bill which, if passed, would make

the coercion of Ireland by England impossible. Four years before, no act of Irish government could be done save at Forster's command, and men were imprisoned or released at his nod without trial, though he had no personal knowledge of Irish affairs. To-day his death was not regarded by any party as a matter affecting in the slightest degree the fate of a Bill which was to abolish the Castle system and make the men whom he had imprisoned as suspects and *mauvais sujets* the legal governors of Ireland. There could be no more forcible proof of the absurdity of appointing non-Irishmen to positions of supreme authority in the government of Ireland under the Union than the rise and downfall of W. E. Forster. This practice, together with the maintenance of the lord-lieutenancy as an ostentatious reminder of separate nationhood, has been mainly to blame for the popular conviction that there was never a fixed principle in the British parliament's plan of Irish government— the arrival of new Englishmen or Scotsmen at the Castle giving fresh zest to every agitation.

CHAPTER XXXIII.

THE GREAT BATTLE IN PARLIAMENT AND ITS RESULT.

Mr Gladstone introduced his Home Rule Bill on April 8th, in a speech which was considered a great oratorical achievement at the time, especially by members of parliament, and was received by Nationalists all over Ireland in somewhat the same spirit as that in which the Israelites accepted the tables of the law from Moses on his descent from Mount Sinai. Something wonderful was happening which they did not understand, and of which they only had a dim and awesome glimmering. And yet to one reading the speech now it seems so much labour lost, and one marvels how it could have convinced any section of the House of Commons. Mr Gladstone said the Bill was only half of his scheme, and its complement, the Land Bill, would follow in a week. He proposed to set up what he called "a legislative body" in Dublin, and to exclude the Irish representatives from Westminster—thus ensuring for the Liberals, as he thought, a permanent majority in the British House of Commons. The Dublin "legislative body" was to consist of only one chamber, as Parnell had hoped; but in that chamber there were to be two "orders" with power of separate voting when desired; and each order could veto a measure brought

in by the other for three years or until the next
dissolution.   The first order was to consist of 28
representative peers and 75 others, 103 in all, elected
for ten years by electors with a rateable qualification
of not less than £25 ; and the members of the order
were to have a property qualification of not less than
£200 a-year, or a capital of £4000.   The second order
was to be composed of the existing 103 Irish members
with 101 members added, 204 in all, elected for five
years by a similar electorate.   Thus Irish tax-payers
were to subsidise an empire in the direction of which
they were to have no voice !   And Irish electors just
admitted to the British franchise were to be excluded
from the Irish franchise !

The office of lord-lieutenant was to be continued,
the holder changing with each British Government,
but was to be open to Roman Catholics.   The Royal
Irish Constabulary force was to remain under the British
parliament, but after a time was to come under the
control of the Dublin legislative body, which meantime
was to provide £1,000,000 yearly for its maintenance,
the British treasury contributing any additional sum
required.   Civil servants were to be at liberty
to claim their discharge on the terms usual on the
abolition of an office.   The customs and excise were
to continue under the control of the British parliament—Ireland paying a fixed contribution of one-
fifteenth of the sum needed for "imperial" charges.
And Mr Gladstone, with an almost childish fatuous-
ness (copied by Mr Asquith in 1912), prefigured an
ideal Irish budget showing a revenue of £8,350,000,
an expenditure of £7,946,000, and a surplus of
£404,000.   He claimed that Ireland had as much
right to Home Rule as the colonies.   They had been

saying to England for the past fifty years : "We do not want your good laws, we want our own." Ireland now was justified in saying the same, because the Irishman was more profoundly Irish than the Englishman was English, or the Scotchman Scotch ; and it did not follow that because his local patriotism was keen he was incapable of imperial patriotism.

It was an absurd, and, from a nationalist point of view, an inadequate Bill. As John Bright said : "If Mr Gladstone's great authority was withdrawn from it, I doubt if twenty persons outside the Irish party would support it." But Parnell and his followers supported it, not for its own sake, but because it was the first step towards the true nationalist goal of separation ; and, viewed in that light, as it was viewed in Ireland, it was like the first step of a child—a portentous event for the leaders of the revolution which had produced it. Parnell's words still held good : "We have never attempted to fix the *ne plus ultra* to the progress of Ireland's nationhood, and we never shall." If he accepted less than Grattan's parliament, he only did so as a beginning, and would not feel debarred from demanding more after he had secured this first instalment.

Mr Trevelyan, who made the chief speech against the Bill, said that the Liberal cabinet were all of one mind in supporting Lord Spencer's demand for a renewal of the Crimes Act, and nothing had happened since then to justify this colossal change of policy. Even if Mr Parnell had come back with 86 members, that was no justification. The laxity of the Nationalist leaders towards crime was the strongest argument against entrusting them with more power. Separation would be preferable to the

Bill. Then we should know where we were, whereas now we should come to the knowledge through a vista of bad blood. John Bright's opinion was: "I believe a united parliament can and will be more just to all classes in Ireland than any parliament that can meet in Dublin under the provisions of Mr Gladstone's Bill."

Mr Parnell's speech was as eagerly looked for as his speeches after the Phœnix Park murders and the Invincible trials. Now as then it consisted largely of a bitter personal attack, with Trevelyan as his butt, relieved by a plenteous administration of "blarney" to Mr Gladstone, who "had lent his voice on behalf of poor and helpless Ireland, his great mind and his extraordinary energy to the unravelling of this question and to the construction of this Bill." He candidly objected to the retention by the British parliament of the control of the customs and excise and the constabulary, but he would vote for the second reading and try to remove those objections in committee. He urged that one-twentieth should be Ireland's contribution to the "imperial" revenue. "I am convinced," he said, "that if our views are fairly met, the Bill will be cheerfully accepted by the Irish people as a solution of the long-standing dispute between the two countries, and that it will lead to the prosperity and peace of Ireland and the satisfaction of England." His acceptance of the measure was thoroughly understood in nationalist Ireland. He was ready to take any kind of a legislative body in Dublin to begin with—but only as a beginning to be developed into the separation and independence which were and are the aim of every Nationalist. This legislative offspring of the revolution might

totter at first, but it would walk and march like a
man and a soldier in due time.

Mr Chamberlain condemned the Bill as "a policy
which in his heart he believed to be injurious to the
best interests of Ireland and Great Britain." "The
Home Rule Bill," said Lord Hartington, who clearly
saw through Mr Parnell, "will be henceforth the
minimum of the Irish nationalist demand—the starting-point and vantage-ground for future proposals."
It would be regarded "as what a great minister has
proposed, not in response to any formulated demand
of the Irish representatives, but as what he himself
thinks a reasonable concession to justice to offer to
the Irish people. It will not restore Grattan's parliament, but a condition of things which Grattan
would have been the first to refuse. It is not local
self-government, but entire separation and an independent legislature which the Irish demand. The
Irish question and the government of Ireland have
too habitually been made the battle-ground of political
parties," he protested. "I believe that now at all
events the people of this country will require that
their representatives shall, in relation to Irish affairs,
agree to sink all minor differences and unite as one
man to hand down to our successors a great empire
compact and complete as we have inherited it from our
forefathers." If Lord Hartington had said "United
Kingdom" instead of "empire," it would have more
precisely described the issue at stake.

While the debate was proceeding, a funeral service
for Mr Forster was held in Westminster Abbey, at
which the members of both Houses attended in large
numbers. Some of the Parnellite members who did
not attend said of this function: "They are holding

a wake across the road over the body of Coercion;
while we are assisting at the birth of Ireland a
Nation." Mr Morley asserted that the Bill would
not disintegrate the empire, because parliament could
repeal it as soon as it was passed, and "if they
rejected Home Rule they would revive dynamite and
the dagger." The threat did not frighten Lord Hartington and the dissentient Liberals, who said that,
if Great Britain only held her position in Ireland by
the grace of assassins and outrage-mongers, the sooner
separation came the better. They would face the
duty of maintaining law and order in Ireland as
fearlessly in the future as in the past.

'The Times' now took up the battle for the
Union with a power greater than any individual,
however eminent, becoming, as it were, personified
and holding as distinctive a place in the fight as Lord
Hartington or Lord Salisbury. Hitherto it had been
mainly on the side of Mr Gladstone and the Liberal
party, and now, while it took its position in the
fighting line along with Conservatives and Liberals,
it was equally independent of both parties. "No
time is to be lost," it wrote on April 9th, "no pains
are to be spared in bringing before the popular mind
the consequences of this disastrous offer. The forces
of resistance are powerful; we hope and believe they
will triumph." It described the Bill as "a mass of
details resting on no solid foundation, which had the
same relation to practical politics as one of Jules
Verne's novels had to serious science." Three days
after this, four members of Mr Gladstone's Government announced their resignations—Earl Morley,
Commissioner of Works; Mr Heneage, Chancellor of
the Duchy of Lancaster; the Earl of Kenmare, Lord

Chamberlain; and the Earl of Cork, Master of the Horse. Lord Randolph Churchill, speaking that night, said he would vote against a policy " most unconstitutionally sprung upon an unwary House of Commons," and predicted the break-up of " The Eighty-six of '86," arguing that the written pledge demanded by Parnell from his followers showed that he did not trust them. In this Churchill was saying what he hoped rather than what he knew.

As it was deemed advisable to give the revolt in the Liberal party time to develop, the Bill was read a first time on April 13th without a division, and the Government fixed the second reading for May 6th, the anniversary of the Phœnix Park assassinations. Whether this date was selected inadvertently, or as a gentle reminder from Mr Morley that Home Rule was the alternative to the dagger, it is impossible to say; but, when the ominous coincidence was pointed out, it was changed.

A great meeting of Unionists was held next day at Her Majesty's Theatre, at which Earl Cowper, the Lord-Lieutenant of Land League days, presided and made an excellent speech. " My own experience has taught me," he said, " that for its own sake Home Rule is not really desired by anybody in Ireland. By many it is desired as a step to separation, by many as a step towards avoiding payment of rent. The priests are actuated by a wish to secure the supremacy of their religion; many of them, at all events, hoping to establish an intolerant hierarchy which will gradually squeeze every religion but their own out of the country." He forcibly reminded Mr Gladstone of his own words, when announcing the Coercion Bill, that " crime dogged the footsteps of the Land League."

Lord Hartington, who also spoke, said that if, as Mr Gladstone had said, "Ireland was to hold the field to the exclusion of every other political subject, they, as Liberals, were bound to take their part and to act with those, whoever they might be, with whose opinions on this greatest and most vital question they found themselves most closely in accord."

Mr Gladstone introduced his Land Bill on April 16th, which was by no means the less important part of his scheme, being in fact a bribe to the Irish landlords, and through them to the House of Lords, to assent to Home Rule as a condition precedent to having their properties bought by the British Government and so extricating themselves from an apparently hopeless position. The purchase was to be carried out by the new Dublin parliament on the basis of twenty years' rental; and, in order to effect it, he proposed to create £50,000,000 new three per cent consols, of which £10,000,000 was to be issued in the financial year 1887-8, and £20,000,000 in each of the two following years—a much faster rate of progress than we have been accustomed to in later Purchase Acts.

If Home Rule and Land Purchase were carried through, and the Irish members excluded from Westminster, he hoped to be still in power when this £50,000,000 had been exhausted and to be able to provide the further amount needed, which he estimated as more than as much again. We know now by experience that the amount required would have been nearly three times as much again. But all that Mr Gladstone said was that he would not now ask for "a sum founded on anything like the outside possibilities of the case." He gave more vital details

about Home Rule than he had given in his speech
on the Home Rule Bill. A great official, to be called
the Receiver General, was to be appointed under
British authority to receive not only all Irish rents
but all Irish revenues whatsoever. The rents and
revenues were to be levied by the Dublin parliament,
but they were to be received by this British official
who was not to be subject to the Dublin parliament.
Though Parnell was prepared to accept this arrangement under protest, it would never have been work-
able or tolerated by him when he attained power in
Dublin. To-night he candidly said it was "absurd,
unnecessary, and indicative of distrust."

Mr Gladstone's description of his scheme—which, in
the light of subsequent events, now seems so fan-
tastical and sanguine—was listened to by his devoted
followers with the utmost reverence and implicit faith.
"We are going to require that the money which has
been levied for the service of Ireland shall all con-
verge and run into a certain channel," he gravely told
the House. "We shall have the money, as it is sometimes said, between the body and the head, the head
being the Irish Government. The money must pass
through the channel of the neck, and the neck is the
Receiver General." The British Exchequer was to
receive £2,000,000 a-year interest on the £50,000,000
consols. As this was at the rate of four per cent and
the Exchequer was to pay only three, Mr Gladstone
expected to make half a million per annum on the
transaction. This £2,000,000 was to be a first charge
on the Irish revenue, and he actually said he anticipated that the authority to be appointed by the Irish
parliament to carry out the purchase of the land
"would show the greatest vigilance in collecting

rents, inasmuch as, until the first charge on the Irish rental was paid, the Irish Government could touch nothing!"

Mr Chamberlain said that Mr Gladstone's policy, as then fully disclosed, was worse than separation, "because it would set up an unstable and temporary form of government which would be a source of perpetual irritation and agitation until the full demands of the Nationalist party were conceded." It amounted to a proposal that "Great Britain should burden herself with an enormous addition to the national debt, and probably also an immediate increase of taxation, not in order to secure the closer and more effective union of the three kingdoms, but, on the contrary, to purchase the repeal of the union and the practical separation of Ireland from England and Scotland." "I would sooner go out of politics altogether," he continued, "than give my vote to pledge the capital of the country in order to modify the opposition of a small class of Irish land proprietors to a scheme which will infallibly lead to the separation of Ireland from England." The Bill was read a first time without a division, as the Unionists, Conservative and Liberal, were organising their forces for a battle on the second reading of the Home Rule Bill.

Lord Spencer, who stood firm for Mr Gladstone, speaking at Newcastle on April 22nd, said the Nationalist party was so powerful and the Loyalist party in Ireland so weak that law and order were maintained only by force, and the only remedy was to make the Nationalists responsible for law and order. "I can say without hesitation," he said, "that I have never heard or seen any evidence of complicity in crime against any of the Irish leaders. They may have employed for their own legitimate purposes men who had been employed in illegal acts. But I believe these men have an affection for and a real interest in the welfare of their country." That the Nationalists loved their country was in no doubt, but the question was whether their love for Ireland made them capable of securing her true welfare or implied any friendly interest in the welfare of the United Kingdom. A vigorous campaign was now waged all over England for and against Home Rule, Mr Gladstone telling the electors of Mid-Lothian that those who opposed it, or, as he called them, " the adverse host," consisted only of " class and dependants of class," whereas he had " the masses " with him.

The second reading of the Home Rule Bill was moved on May 10th by Mr Gladstone, who asserted that his attitude towards Home Rule always was (1) that it should be plainly demanded by a majority of the people; (2) that it should not be incompatible with " the unity of the empire." The first condition, he asserted, was fulfilled by the result of the general election; and the second—whatever it may mean— by Parnell's declaration that all he required was the power to manage Irish affairs in Ireland as given by this Bill. The Nationalist members adopted a suspiciously humble tone, Mr Dillon assuring the House that it was " a false allegation that this was not the Bill which the Irish people wanted, or that they would only take it as a means of getting more." Mr Mitchell Henry, formerly a leading Irish Home Ruler, but now an English Unionist member, explained his opposition to Home Rule by stating that " a great change had come over Ireland since Isaac Butt's death, and there was no such union of feeling at the present time between Catholics and Protestants as happily existed when Butt was leader." As already explained, Parnell's party was far more Catholic than Butt's, and the ecclesiastics were fast acquiring such a dominant voice in the revolutionary movement that Protestants were becoming convinced that the Government to be set up by the Home Rule Bill would be a Roman Catholic and not a national authority.7

Lord Salisbury, at St James's Hall on May 15th, discarding the hollow language of political diplomacy as an antiquated weapon for which an English statesman could find no further use against such a man as Parnell, said : " Whatever be the present disposition of the Irish members, their successors would repudiate the tribute. Ireland is two nations. There are races like the Hottentots and Hindoos incapable of self-government, and I refuse to place confidence in a people who have acquired the habit of using slugs and knives." He added that " the strong organisation of the Catholic Church in Ireland had fallen into bad hands," which Dublin took as a reference to Archbishop Walsh's appointment. His alternative policy was "that parliament should enable the Government of England to govern Ireland. Apply that recipe resolutely for twenty years, and then Ireland will be fit to accept any gifts in the way of local government you may wish to give her. What she wants is a Government that does not flinch, that does not vary, that she cannot hope to beat down by agitation at Westminster, that does not alter in its resolution or its temperature with party changes." This outspokenness was worthy of Parnell himself, and if the speaker were only as determined as Parnell to

ARCHBISHOP WALSH.

"The Archbishop was dressed in a purple soutane and wore his large gold cross and chain. We were all very curious about his personal appearance, for scarcely anybody present except the priests had seen him before. He sat in the best chair, which for the occasion became a kind of throne, in the central position by the wall."—PAGE 416.

practise what he preached, the "quicksand of English partisanship" might be transformed into firm ground on which the union of the three kingdoms could rest securely.

While the second reading of the Home Rule Bill was pending, Mr Morley, on May 20th, moved the second reading of the Arms Bill, which continued the provisions of the dropped Crimes Act for restricting the sale, importation, and carrying of arms, prohibiting their use without Government licence, and giving the police the right of searching private houses for arms in proclaimed districts. This showed a fatal want of confidence in the Nationalist majority on whom the Liberals were asking the House to bestow the control of a separate parliament and executive. Mr Parnell, perceiving this, said that, "while he had no desire to embarrass his friends, the Act had been unfairly used to disarm and annoy the Nationalist party," and he demanded that it "should now be enforced against Orangemen who were preparing to commit murder and outrage at the next general election"—from which it was inferred that he did not rely on the passage of Home Rule without another election. The second reading was carried by 303 to 89—the Conservatives voting with the Government, while some Radicals voted with the Nationalists in the minority—and the measure was hurriedly made law before the division on the Home Rule Bill.

Mr Gladstone now took a step which showed that he would gladly postpone Home Rule and remain in office for some time by the aid of the Parnellites. He called a meeting of Liberals at the Foreign Office on May 27th, and, in order to induce them to vote for the second reading of the Home Rule Bill, told n : (1) that Parliament could repeal it if it was found to work unsatisfactorily; (2) that he was open to argument on the question of keeping the Irish members at Westminster; (3) that, if the Bill passed its second reading, he would go no further with it that year, but would introduce a new bill next session and the whole question could be reconsidered in the interval. Mr Gladstone's first assurance suggested one of those strong remedies which, as Lord Salisbury said of going to war with the Irish after Home Rule, " could never be carried out."

In the ten days' interval between this and the division, some events were occurring in Ireland which betrayed the general nervousness then prevailing. There was a hand-to-hand fight in Dublin on May 30th between the Scots Guards and the civilians, in which many of the soldiers were injured. In the counties of Antrim, Down, Derry, and Tyrone they were melting lead for bullets—some of my friends of a later date being amongst those so engaged,—volunteers were being enrolled, drilling by night was taking place on the hillsides and in factories and large warehouses, and there was ample evidence of a determination to fight *pro aris et focis*. Rioting broke out in Belfast, on June 4th, between Harland and Wolff's men and some Catholic navvies, the shipwrights making the attack to avenge an assault by the Catholics on a Protestant workman. After a short fight the navvies were routed, one of them being drowned and others injured. In some Nationalist districts of Ulster the poor Catholics were casting lots amongst themselves for the property of the Protestants. Bank of Ireland and other stocks were falling in price; manufacturers were considering the transfer of their business to England; Protestants everywhere were in a state of depression, and the elation of the Catholics was unbounded.

At length June 7th arrived, the fatal day of the division on the second reading, when the forces of the Unionists would have to be disclosed and battle given to Gladstone and Parnell. In the closing hour of the debate, before the division, Mr Parnell struck a desperate blow in the hope of showing the dissentient Liberals that the defeat of Mr Gladstone would not necessarily secure them against Home Rule. Amid a painful silence, he told the House that the leaders of the Conservative Party had distinctly offered before the general election that, in the event of their obtaining a majority, they would submit not only a Bill for the complete autonomous government of Ireland, with power to protect Irish industries, but also for a scheme of land purchase on a much larger scale than that proposed by Mr Gladstone. It is but natural to suppose that Mr Gladstone had been made aware of this at his two-hours' personal interview with Mr Parnell on April 5th, and before that in the communications which passed between him and Mr Parnell through Mr Morley, and that the information had helped in changing Home Rule from "a chimera" into a "burning question."

Sir Michael Hicks-Beach sprang to his feet and categorically denied, for himself and his colleagues, that they had given Mr Parnell any reason to expect from the late Government "a statutory parliament with power to protect Irish industries." Mr Parnell asked if it was denied that "that intention was communicated to him" by one of Hicks-Beach's colleagues, "a Minister of the Crown." Sir Michael denied it, and appealed to Mr Parnell to name the person who made the communication. Mr Parnell replied sarcastically that "that was a safe appeal." He would give the name when Sir Michael's colleague had given his permission. When we remember that almost at the very moment that Lord Carnarvon was meeting Mr Parnell in secret, Sir Michael himself, as leader of the Conservative Government in the House of Commons, had offered to consider a Parnellite memorial impugning the conduct of Lord Spencer in regard to the Maamstrasna trials, we think Parnell might have been pardoned for thinking that Sir Michael was a party to Lord Carnarvon's proposition.

Parnell's blow, disconcerting as it was, lost much of its effect by the withholding of Lord Carnarvon's name; but, remorseless as Mr Parnell was, he never betrayed those who trusted him. He shot the bolt, but it did not alienate a single vote from the Unionist side. "I am convinced," said Parnell in conclusion, "that there are a sufficient number of wise and just members in this House to cause it to disregard appeals made to passion and to choose the better way of founding peace and goodwill among nations."

The division, feverishly awaited by so many millions of people, resulted as follows: For the second reading, 313, including 85 Parnellites; against, 343, including 93 Unionist Liberals. Majority against the Bill, 30. Captain O'Shea was the only member for an Irish constituency who did not vote. The Home Rule Bill was lost, and the union of the three kingdoms was saved for the present. Parliament had done its part, but a general election had still to decide if Queen Victoria was right in her conviction that the people would support the parliament.

On the day after the defeat of the Bill, Lord Carnarvon, in the House of Lords, gave his version of his secret interview with Parnell.   That day Parnell looked "ill and depressed" when he appeared in the House of Commons.   Mr Barry O'Brien says he urged Parnell to adopt Davitt's policy of educating the English democracy.   His reply was: "I admit that, *as Gladstone has joined us*, we must have a change of policy.   But we cannot persuade the English people. They will only do what we force them to do."   In that phrase, "the English will only do what we force them to do," and its corollary, "Gladstone has joined us," Parnell epitomised his achievements in the British parliament.   The greatest man in England had joined the Irish revolutionary movement, not as the result of persuasion but of force.

CHAPTER XXXIV.

THE BRITISH PEOPLE SUPPORT THE BRITISH PARLIAMENT.

THE way in which the defeat of the Home Rule Bill was taken by the general body of Nationalists in Ireland supplied the best criterion by which to judge the depth and reality of their desire for a native parliament and executive. In Dublin they laughed and made the best of it, taking it in the same spirit as they would have accepted the defeat of Ormonde, the famous Derby winner of that year. Wire-pullers and office-seekers who had played for large stakes felt sorely hit, but met with little sympathy from a public who, having staked nothing, rejoiced at having suffered no loss and drew a breath of relief at the end of the crisis. In the country districts there was not only no anger or indignation, but there was not even disappointment. Parnell's triumph over Gladstone had come so suddenly, the struggle for Home Rule had been so short-lived and so subordinate to the land agitation, that the people did not regard the parliamentary reverse in the light of a grievance. The farmers were so keen on getting reductions of rents in the land courts or otherwise, and the labourers so preoccupied by the prospect of new cottages with free half-acres of ground, that they did not feel as if they had lost anything by the defeat of Home Rule. There was no disturbance whatever in Dublin, and only in a few isolated quarters in the south were there any outbursts of ill-feeling, and those of no serious import. At Sligo there was a riot in which the houses of some Protestants were looted, but the Catholics alleged in self-justification that an outrage had been done to their bishop's palace.

In the north-east it was otherwise. There the anxiety had been intense, for the hard-working people felt that their lives and property were about to be placed at the disposal of their hereditary enemies, and that they were to lose their civil and religious freedom along with their birthright of British citizenship. Now their joy and relief were as great as if they had been reprieved from a sentence of death. Now it seemed as if the sun shone again after a prolonged eclipse, and the pent-up emotions of the workers found vent in violent displays against the Catholics, whose slaves they feared to have been if the Home Rule Bill had become law. At Lurgan on the day the figures were announced the houses of many Catholics were sacked. On the following day there were noisy and riotous demonstrations in Belfast, and the police, acting under instructions, fired on the crowd, killing five persons and wounding many others. In revenge for this unjustifiable homicide, the rioting was continued—being directed mainly against the police, who were called "Morley's Murderers," and only incidentally against the Catholics. There were disturbances at the same time in Coleraine and other Ulster towns. I was in Belfast during those riots. In the most disorderly quarters the shops were shut and nobody ventured in there. Business went on as usual in Royal Avenue and the leading streets, but walking or driving was dangerous in other sections of the town. Where, to the eye of a stranger, there seemed nothing unusual in the appearance of a thoroughfare, except its emptiness, a frenzied crowd would stampede round a corner to be suddenly followed by a fusilade of stones from a pursuing mob, or by a body of police or soldiers with fixed bayonets.

I was caught once or twice in rushes of this kind, and, but for a successful retreat into a lane, might not be now alive to recount my experiences. Once, in the Orange quarter, I saw the unique spectacle of a squadron of cavalry, which had come to the aid of the police, galloping into barracks in full retreat before a crowd, while stones, rivets, and small scrap-iron, known as Belfast *confetti*, hopped off the helmets and backs of the troopers and their horses. The barrack gates were held open wide as the squadron galloped in and then were closed fast, while the mob remained round a corner out of reach of rifle shots. These riots, of which so much has been said and written to the disparagement of Belfast, were undoubtedly continued from a desire of the working men to avenge the initial killing of some of their friends by the police rather than from political rancour, religious bigotry, or lust for plunder—the Orange craftsmen and labourers, who are the most hard-working men in the world all the year round, being most courageous, resolute and pugnacious, when roused to defend their rights. Those who charge them with illiberality and sectarian spite speak without knowledge, and forget the trials to which an industrious Protestant minority living in a country with an agitating Catholic majority are constantly subjected. Mr Gladstone was not disposed to make any allowance for the Belfast workers, and at once appointed a royal commission to investigate and report upon the origin and circumstances of the riots—one of the commissioners being Mr Richard Adams, who afterwards confided to Mr John Morley his private opinion of his fellow - commissioner, Mr Justice Day; but this must not be given until the proper time.

Mr Gladstone informed the House on June 10th that on his advice the Queen had authorised a dissolution of parliament, which would take place at the end of the month, and meantime the Liberal Government would hold office. On the same day, after the battle for Home Rule had been fought and lost, and it could no longer affect the issue, Lord Carnarvon made a statement in the House of Lords admitting and describing his secret interview with Mr Parnell, but denying that he had been acting for his Government. He added that, while he was favourable to a limited self-government and desired a settlement "satisfying real local requirements and, to some extent, national aspirations," he was not in favour of Mr Gladstone's Bill, "which settled nothing."

The general election began in July. This time Mr Parnell did not summon any conventions for the selection of candidates, fearing lest the claims of rival aspirants should provoke dissensions beyond even his power to control. All the sitting members stood again for the most part, with the notable exception of Captain O'Shea, whose place in parliament was to know him no more. Mr Parnell issued a manifesto to the Irish in England, calling on them to vote for the same Liberals whose "crimes and fallacies" he had denounced in such unmeasured terms only seven months before. He addressed a number of meetings in Great Britain, hoping to produce, if not a clear Gladstonian majority, at least an equalisation of the English parties which would give him the balance of power once again, and enable him to extort Home Rule from one side or other.

The Irish Unionists determined to make a strenuous fight, especially in Ulster, and Mr William O'Brien, editor of 'United Ireland,' found himself opposed by Mr T. W. Russell in South Tyrone, a constituency in which Russell, though a Scotsman by birth, had spent his earlier years as a hard-working youth. It was indirectly intimated to the vintners by Mr Lawler of the Imperial Hotel, in which O'Brien lived, that, as the contest would be very keen, Mr O'Brien would be glad of some assistance against an opponent who was, as the reader knows, an active antagonist of the licensed trade. Though most of the brewers and distillers who subscribed to the funds were Unionists, the application was acceded to; and I went to Tyrone, with a deputation from Dublin and Belfast, to induce the Protestant licence-holders to vote against their political convictions in the interest of their trade.

Mr O'Brien was a most energetic candidate, whose enthusiasm one could not help admiring. But from the first our mission was a forlorn hope, as no Protestant could be expected to vote for a Nationalist at a time of such intense political excitement. 'The Freeman' sent down a special reporter, and O'Brien's *verbatim* speeches were distributed broadcast in the constituency; but he got little aid from his leading colleagues, most of whom were trying to hold the doubtful seats they had won at the last election.

At this time the principal Nationalists—"Parnell's cabinet," as they were called—deemed it beneath their dignity to seek election for a seat unless it were hotly contested by the Unionists. Mr Sexton, for instance, was fighting in West Belfast, Mr Dillon in North Tyrone, Mr Healy in South Derry, and Mr Justin McCarthy in Derry city. Mr Matthew Kenny, who was not one of the "cabinet," but was a great friend of Mr Sexton's at that time, had no difficulty in getting elected for Mid-Tyrone, and, as we had our headquarters at the White Hart Hotel, Omagh, in his constituency, we saw a great deal of Mr Kenny.

It was a very hot July, and the pale-blue flowers of the flax were in bloom in the waving fields everywhere as we drove through the country canvassing. There was no disturbance of any kind, no excitement even, in any of the villages we visited—of which Clogher, Augher, Ballygawley, Aughnacloy, Fintona, Moy, and Caledon were the chief,—for there is no large town in South Tyrone. One could not avoid being impressed by the contrast in character between the Protestants of Tyrone and the Catholics of Kerry. Whether the Kerry Catholics were timid or defiant, their characters were on the surface, and they were always talkative, giving one the impression of being men who, if they ceased to be bad subjects, would be worse tyrants. The Tyrone Protestants were reserved, stubborn, and hard to diagnose, good listeners, but spare talkers, and rarely if ever gave expression to their real opinions. The majority of the licence-holders seemed to hold land or to have other businesses which made them partially independent of their drink trade; and they were therefore not so

THE IRISH REVOLUTION

keen on trade politics as their colleagues in the cities and large towns. The majority of them seemed to be Catholics, and therefore Nationalists — a fact typical of Ulster, and especially of Belfast, where, in making up the deputation for Tyrone, it was with the greatest difficulty we succeeded in getting one Protestant licence-holder. If the Sunday Closing Act had not been passed in 1878, and if Mr O'Brien and the Nationalists could have promised to prevent its passing, it is possible that the Protestant licence-holders might have turned the election ; but their feeling now was that, as they had lost their Sunday trade, Mr Russell could do them no more harm, and they would vote for him as the man to save them from Home Rule and Catholic domination.

Mr T. W. Russell got in by a majority of over ninety, and Mr William O'Brien lost the Ulster seat on the capture of which he had prided himself so much the previous year. He was not alone in his misfortune, for Mr Timothy Healy also lost South Derry ; but, to make up for this, Mr Justin McCarthy captured Derry city and Mr Sexton West Belfast—two sensational victories which produced a lasting impression in England. Many Nationalists expected that Healy would be kept out of parliament by Mr Parnell as a punishment for his mutiny at Galway, but after a while he got Mr McCarthy's old seat in Longford, while Mr O'Brien got North-east Cork.

When the completed returns showed that the new House of Commons was to contain 316 Conservatives and 78 Liberal Unionists, as against 191 Gladstonians and 85 Parnellites, thus giving the large majority of 118 in favour of the Union and against Home Rule, the disappointment of the Nationalist wire-pullers was extreme. But the result, which paralysed the politicians, was accepted by the general body of the Nationalist public without emotion; and now, if it were possible, they would have bent their distracted energies once more to the work of winning their daily bread and improving their condition. So far from there being any desire to renew the war with dagger and dynamite, there seemed to be rather a collapse of Parnell's revolutionary movement.

One scene still remained to be enacted in this national drama, which had begun seven years before with the first meeting of the Land League at Irishtown in county Mayo. Lord Aberdeen had to "go off" the stage which he had occupied for six months as the nominal ruler of Dublin Castle. Mr Morley might have slipped off unnoticed, but Lord Aberdeen had to make his exit in state; and he and his household left Dublin with all the customary honours—the gorgeous staff, strong escort of picked cavalry and imposing procession passing between lines of soldiers from the Castle to Westland Row, while military bands played at intervals along the route. The faces of the Loyalists beamed, for a load had been taken off their hearts, and smiles from the bay-window of the Kildare Street Club sped the departing Home Rule Viceroy on his way. But they loyally raised their hats none the less to the Queen's deputy as he rode by on horseback with Prince Edward of Saxe-Weimar, the then Commander of the Forces. The Trinity College students shouted frantically as the procession passed from College Green into Grafton Street, but their cries were cheers of joy; while the counter-cry from the street was a roar of encouragement to the departing viceroy. There were dense throngs of

Nationalists along the route, and the men took off their hats as they cheered, not from love to the outgoing Lord-Lieutenant but to show that defeat had not disheartened them. Their womenfolk waved their handkerchiefs and cried *Au Revoir*, or " You'll surely come back again to give us Home Rule ! " But, when the procession had passed, men and women dispersed and thought only to laugh over the matter.

Though the wire-pullers had been worsted at Westminster, the solid effects of the revolution in Ireland remained. The power of rent-fixing had been taken from the landlords, the divinity which had hedged them was no more, the process of converting the tenants into proprietors had begun. The farm-labourers had won the right to a good house and plot of land which the community could give them without the leave of the lords of the soil. Five-sixths of the parliamentary representation of Ireland had been "nationalised" and transformed into a machine for the confusion of the British parliament. The spirit of revolution was abroad in the land, and it seemed as if even the ecclesiastics would soon have to fight openly for their power over the awakened people. Many other fortresses too remained to be captured in the course of the revolution, but the story of how they were assailed and the result must be told in another volume.

Mr Parnell's party in parliament was as strong as before. But, as the large Unionist majority made it almost certain that the new Government, with Lord Salisbury as its prime minister, would hold office for the full period allowed by the Septennial Act, the outlook seemed full of gloom for the Nationalist leader and his colleagues—a weary march of seven years in the political wilderness during which the enthusiasm of the people would probably evaporate, and a scramble for office under the British Government as of old would make an end of the " Eighty-six of '86."

Like Milton's Satan, Parnell might truly have exclaimed :—

> "into what pit thou seest
> From what height fallen."

For some days the Nationalist henchmen were stunned. Parnell himself seemed shattered mentally and physically and leaned more than ever on Mrs O'Shea. But his lieutenants saw one bright ray of hope amidst the gloom. Lord Randolph Churchill had said that Lord Salisbury's Government was to be "the only Government" of Ireland. Lord Salisbury himself had promised twenty years of "resolute" government. This could only mean more coercion, and in the battle with coercion the revolutionary spirit might be kept alive and the Eighty-six, "in arms not worse, in foresight much advanced," might conquer Salisbury as they had conquered Gladstone.

PRINTED BY WILLIAM BLACKWOOD AND SONS.

A Catalogue

of

Messrs William Blackwood & Sons'

Publications

45 GEORGE STREET   37 PATERNOSTER ROW

EDINBURGH   LONDON, E.C.

GENERAL LITERATURE.

ACCOUNTANTS' MAGAZINE, THE. Monthly, except September and October. 6d. net.

ACTA SANCTORUM HIBERNIÆ; Ex Codice Salmanticensi. Nunc primum integre edita opera CAROLI DE SMEDT et JOSEPHI DE BACKER, e Soc. Jesu, Hagiographorum Bollandianorum; Auctore et Sumptus Largiente JOANNE PATRICIO MARCHIONE BOTHÆ. In One handsome 4to Volume, bound in half roxburghe, £2, 2s.; in paper cover, 31s. 6d.

ADAMSON, PROFESSOR.
THE DEVELOPMENT OF MODERN PHILOSOPHY. With other Lectures and Essays. By ROBERT ADAMSON, LL.D., late Professor of Logic in the University of Glasgow. Edited by Professor W. R. SORLEY, University of Cambridge. In 2 vols. demy 8vo, 18s. net.

THE DEVELOPMENT OF MODERN PHILOSOPHY. Edited by Professor W. R. SORLEY, University of Cambridge. Demy 8vo, 10s. 6d. net.

THE DEVELOPMENT OF GREEK PHILOSOPHY. Edited by Professor SORLEY and R. P. HARDIE, M.A. Demy 8vo, 10s. 6d. net.

A SHORT HISTORY OF LOGIC. Edited by Professor W. R. SORLEY, University of Cambridge. Crown 8vo, 5s. net.

FICHTE. (Philosophical Classics for English Readers.) Fcap. 8vo, 1s. net.

AIKMAN, DR C. M.
MANURES AND THE PRINCIPLES OF MANURING. By C. M. AIKMAN, D.Sc., F.R.S.E., &c., formerly Professor of Chemistry, Glasgow Veterinary College, and Examiner in Chemistry, University of Glasgow, &c. Second Impression. Crown 8vo, 6s. 6d.

FARMYARD MANURE: ITS NATURE, COMPOSITION, AND TREATMENT. Crown 8vo, 1s. 6d.

ALLEN, J. W.
THE PLACE OF HISTORY IN EDUCATION. By J. W. ALLEN. Crown 8vo, 5s. net.

ALMOND, HELY HUTCHINSON.
CHRIST THE PROTESTANT, AND OTHER SERMONS. By HELY HUTCHINSON ALMOND. Crown 8vo, 5s.

ANCIENT CLASSICS FOR ENGLISH READERS. Edited by Rev. W. LUCAS COLLINS, M.A. Price 1s. each net. *For List of Vols. see p. 32.*

ANDERSON, REV. GEORGE, B.D.
THE SCOTTISH PASTOR. A Manual of Pastoral Theology. By Rev. GEORGE ANDERSON, B.D., Minister of Renfrew, Lecturer on Pastoral Theology under the General Assembly of the Church of Scotland. Crown 8vo, 2s. 6d. net.

A PLAIN WOMAN.
POOR NELLIE. By A PLAIN WOMAN. Crown 8vo, 3s. 6d.

ARMYTAGE, A. J. GREEN-.
MAIDS OF HONOUR. By A. J. GREEN-ARMYTAGE. Crown 8vo, 5s.

ATKINSON, MABEL.
LOCAL GOVERNMENT IN SCOTLAND. By MABEL ATKINSON, M.A. Demy 8vo, 5s. net.

AYTOUN, PROFESSOR.
LAYS OF THE SCOTTISH CAVALIERS, AND OTHER POEMS. By W. EDMONDSTOUNE AYTOUN, D.C.L., Professor of Rhetoric and Belles-Lettres in the University of Edinburgh. New Edition. Fcap. 8vo, 3s. 6d. Cheap Edition. Cloth, 1s. 3d. Paper covers, 1s.

AN ILLUSTRATED EDITION OF THE LAYS OF THE SCOTTISH CAVALIERS. From designs by Sir NOEL PATON. Small 4to, 10s. 6d.

BAIRD, J. G. A.
THE PRIVATE LETTERS OF THE MARQUESS OF DALHOUSIE. Edited by J. G. A. BAIRD. Second Impression. With Portraits and Illustrations. Demy 8vo, 15s. net. Popular Edition. Demy 8vo, 6s. net.

BAIRD LECTURES.
(*See under* FLINT, MITCHELL, NICOL, and ROBERTSON.)

BANKS, D. C.
THE ETHICS OF WORK AND WEALTH. By D. C. BANKS. Crown 8vo, 5s. net.

BARBOUR, G. F., D.Phil.
A PHILOSOPHICAL STUDY OF CHRISTIAN ETHICS. By G. F. BARBOUR, D.Phil. Crown 8vo, 7s. 6d. net.

BARBOUR, R. W.
THOUGHTS FROM THE WRITINGS OF R. W. BARBOUR. Post 8vo, limp leather, 2s. 6d. net.

"BARFLEUR."
NAVAL POLICY. A PLEA FOR THE STUDY OF WAR. By "BARFLEUR." Demy 8vo, 2s. 6d. net.

BARRETT, C. R. B.
HISTORY OF THE 13th HUSSARS. By C. R. B. BARRETT. 2 vols. small 4to. Illustrated. 21s. net.

BARRINGTON, MICHAEL.
THE KING'S FOOL. By MICHAEL BARRINGTON. Crown 8vo, 6s.

THE REMINISCENCES OF SIR BARRINGTON BEAUMONT, BART. A Novel. Crown 8vo, 6s

BARTLETT, E. ASHMEAD-.
THE PASSING OF THE SHEREEFIAN EMPIRE. By E. ASHMEAD-BARTLETT. Illustrated. Demy 8vo, 15s. net.

BELLESHEIM, ALPHONS, D.D.
HISTORY OF THE CATHOLIC CHURCH OF SCOTLAND. From the Introduction of Christianity to the Present Day. By ALPHONS BELLESHEIM, D.D., Canon of Aix-la-Chapelle. Translated, with Notes and Additions, by Sir D. OSWALD HUNTER BLAIR, Bart., O.S.B., Monk of Fort Augustus. Cheap Edition. Complete in 4 vols. demy 8vo, with Maps. Price 21s. net.

BESANT, SIR WALTER.
RABELAIS. (Foreign Classics for English Readers.) By Sir WALTER BESANT. Fcap. 8vo, 1s. net.

BLACKBURN, DOUGLAS.
A BURGHER QUIXOTE. By DOUGLAS BLACKBURN, Author of 'Prinsloo of Prinsloosdorp.' Second Impression. With Frontispiece. Crown 8vo, 6s.

RICHARD HARTLEY : PROSPECTOR. Crown 8vo, 6s.

BLACKIE, JOHN STUART.
NOTES OF A LIFE. By JOHN STUART BLACKIE. Edited by his Nephew, A. STODART WALKER. Crown 8vo, 6s. net.

THE LETTERS OF JOHN STUART BLACKIE TO HIS WIFE. With a few earlier ones to his Parents. Selected and edited by his Nephew, A. STODART WALKER. Second Impression. Demy 8vo, 12s. 6d. net.

BLACKWOOD.
BLACKWOOD'S MAGAZINE. Monthly, 2s. 6d. Post free for one year, 30s.

ANNALS OF A PUBLISHING HOUSE. WILLIAM BLACKWOOD AND HIS SONS; THEIR MAGAZINE AND FRIENDS. By Mrs OLIPHANT. With Four Portraits. Third Edition. Demy 8vo. Vols. I. and II., £2, 2s. Large Paper Edition, £4, 4s. net.

ANNALS OF A PUBLISHING HOUSE. Vol. III. JOHN BLACKWOOD. By his Daughter, Mrs BLACKWOOD PORTER. With Two Portraits and View of Strathtyrum. Demy 8vo, 21s. Large Paper Edition, £2, 2s. net.

NEW EDUCATIONAL SERIES. *See separate Educational Catalogue.*

NEW UNIFORM SERIES OF NOVELS (*Copyright*).

Crown 8vo, cloth. Price 3s. 6d. each.

WENDERHOLME. By P. G. Hamerton.
THE STORY OF MARGRÉDEL. By D. Storrar Meldrum.
A SENSITIVE PLANT. By E. D. Gerard.
LADY LEE'S WIDOWHOOD. By General Sir E. B. Hamley.
KATIE STEWART, and other Stories. By Mrs Oliphant.
VALENTINE AND HIS BROTHER. By the Same.
SONS AND DAUGHTERS. By the Same.
MARMORNE. By P. G. Hamerton.
REATA. By E. D. Gerard.
BEGGAR MY NEIGHBOUR. By the Same.
THE WATERS OF HERCULES. By the Same.
FAIR TO SEE. By L. W. M. Lockhart.
MINE IS THINE. By the Same.
DOUBLES AND QUITS. By the Same.
PICCADILLY. By Laurence Oliphant. With Illustrations.
LADY BABY. By D. Gerard.
POOR NELLIE. By A Plain Woman.

BLACKWOOD—*contd.*
STANDARD NOVELS. Uniform in size and binding. Each complete in one Volume.

FLORIN SERIES. Illustrated Boards. Bound in Cloth, 2s. 6d.

THE CRUISE OF THE MIDGE. By the Same.
CYRIL THORNTON. By Capt. Hamilton.
THE PROVOST, &c. By John Galt.
SIR ANDREW WYLIE. By the Same.
REGINALD DALTON. By J. G. Lockhart.
PEN OWEN. By Dean Hook.
ADAM BLAIR. By J. G. Lockhart.
LADY LEE'S WIDOWHOOD. By General Sir E. B. Hamley.
THE PERPETUAL CURATE. By Mrs Oliphant.
JOHN : A Love Story. By the Same.

SHILLING SERIES, Illustrated Cover. Bound in Cloth, 1s. 6d.

THE RECTOR, and THE DOCTOR'S FAMILY. By Mrs Oliphant.
THE LIFE OF MANSIE WAUCH. By D. M. Moir.
PENINSULAR SCENES AND SKETCHES. By F. Hardman.
SIR FRIZZLE PUMPKIN, NIGHTS AT MESS, &c
VALERIUS : A Roman Story. By J. G. Lockhart.

BON GAULTIER'S BOOK OF BALLADS. Eighteenth Edition, with Autobiographical Introduction by Sir THEODORE MARTIN, K.C.B. With Illustrations by Doyle, Leech, and Crowquill. Small 4to, 5s. net.

BOWHILL, MAJOR J. H.
QUESTIONS AND ANSWERS IN THE THEORY AND PRACTICE OF MILITARY TOPOGRAPHY. By Major J. H. BOWHILL. Crown 8vo, 4s. 6d. net. Portfolio containing 34 working plans and diagrams, 3s. 6d. net.

BOWLINE, J., Skipper, and GREGORY, R. R. C.
YARNS FROM A CAPTAIN'S LOG. By J. BOWLINE, Skipper, and R. R. C. GREGORY. Crown 8vo, 6s.

BRACKENBURY, GENERAL SIR HENRY, G.C.B.
SOME MEMORIES OF MY SPARE TIME, 1856-1885. By General the Right Hon. Sir HENRY BRACKENBURY, G.C.B. With Portrait. Crown 8vo, 5s. net.

BREADALBANE, THE MARCHION-ESS OF.
THE HIGH TOPS OF BLACK MOUNT. By the MARCHIONESS OF BREADALBANE. Second Impression. With Illustrations from Photographs by Olive Mackenzie. Short demy, 6s. net.

BREBNER, ARTHUR.
PATCHES AND POMANDER. A Novel. By ARTHUR BREBNER. Crown 8vo, 6s.

BRIDGES, PHILIPPA.
THE GREEN WAVE OF DESTINY. By PHILIPPA BRIDGES. Crown 8vo, 6s.

BRODRIBB, W. J.
DEMOSTHENES. (Ancient Classics for English Readers.) By W. J. BRODRIBB. Fcap. 8vo, 1s. net.

BRUCE, MAJOR CLARENCE DAL-RYMPLE.
IN THE FOOTSTEPS OF MARCO POLO. Being the Account of a Journey Overland from Simla to Pekin. By Major CLARENCE DALRYMPLE BRUCE. With Illustrations. Demy 8vo, 21s. net.

BUCHAN, JOHN.
THE WATCHER BY THE THRESH-OLD, AND OTHER TALES. By JOHN BUCHAN. Second Impression. Crown 8vo, 6s.
A LODGE IN THE WILDERNESS. Second Impression. Short demy 8vo, 6s.
THE MOON ENDURETH : TALES AND FANCIES. Crown 8vo, 6s.
SOME EIGHTEENTH CENTURY BY-WAYS, AND OTHER ESSAYS. Demy 8vo, 7s. 6d. net.

BURTON, JOHN HILL, D.C.L.
THE HISTORY OF SCOTLAND. From Agricola's Invasion to the Extinction of the last Jacobite Insurrection. By JOHN HILL BURTON, D.C.L., Historiographer-Royal for Scotland. Cheaper Edition. In 8 vols. crown 8vo, 2s. 6d. net each.
THE BOOK-HUNTER. A New Edition, with specially designed Title-page and Cover by Joseph Brown. Printed on antique laid paper. Post 8vo, 3s. 6d.

BUTE, JOHN, MARQUESS OF.
THE ROMAN BREVIARY. Reformed by Order of the Holy Œcumenical Council of Trent ; Published by Order of Pope St Pius V. ; and revised by Clement VIII. and Urban VIII. ; together with the Offices since granted. Translated out of Latin into English by JOHN, MARQUESS OF BUTE, K.T. New Edition, Revised and Enlarged. In 4 vols. crown 8vo, 42s. net. In 1 vol. crown 4to, 63s. net.

BUTE, JOHN, MARQUESS OF—*contd.*
THE ALTUS OF ST COLUMBA. With a Prose Paraphrase and Notes. By JOHN, MARQUESS OF BUTE, K.T. In paper cover, 2s. 6d.

SERMONES, FRATRIS ADÆ, ORDINIS PRÆMONSTRATENSIS, &c. Twenty-eight Discourses of Adam Scotus of Whithorn, hitherto unpublished ; to which is added a Collection of Notes by the same, illustrative of the rule of St Augustine. Edited, at the desire of the late MARQUESS OF BUTE, K.T., LL.D., &c., by WALTER DE GRAY BIRCH, LL.D., F.S.A., of the British Museum, &c. Royal 8vo, 25s. net.

CATALOGUE OF A COLLECTION OF ORIGINAL MSS. formerly belonging to the Holy Office of the Inquisition in the Canary Islands. Prepared under the direction of the late MARQUESS OF BUTE, K.T., LL.D., by WALTER DE GRAY BIRCH, LL.D., F.S.A. 2 vols. royal 8vo, £3, 3s. net.

BUTE, MACPHAIL, and LONS-DALE.
THE ARMS OF THE ROYAL AND PARLIAMENTARY BURGHS OF SCOTLAND. By JOHN, MARQUESS OF BUTE, K.T., J. R. N. MACPHAIL, and H. W. LONSDALE. With 131 Engravings on wood, and 11 other Illustrations. Crown 4to, £2, 2s. net.

BUTE, STEVENSON, and LONS-DALE.
THE ARMS OF THE BARONIAL AND POLICE BURGHS OF SCOTLAND. By JOHN, MARQUESS OF BUTE, K.T., J. H. STEVENSON, and H. W. LONSDALE. With numerous Illustrations. Crown 4to, £2, 2s. net.

CAIRD, EDWARD, LL.D.
HEGEL. (Philosophical Classics for English Readers.) By EDWARD CAIRD, LL.D. Fcap. 8vo, 1s. net.

CAIRD, PRINCIPAL.
SPINOZA. (Philosophical Classics for English Readers.) By Principal CAIRD. Fcap. 8vo, 1s. net.

CALDWELL, PROFESSOR WILLIAM.
SCHOPENHAUER'S SYSTEM IN ITS PHILOSOPHICAL SIGNIFICANCE (THE SHAW FELLOWSHIP LECTURES, 1893). By Professor WILLIAM CALDWELL, D.Sc., M'Gill University, Montreal. Demy 8vo, 10s. 6d. net.

CALLWELL, COL. C. E., C.B.
THE EFFECT OF MARITIME COMMAND ON LAND CAMPAIGNS SINCE WATERLOO. By Col. C. E. CALLWELL, C.B. With Plans. Post 8vo, 6s. net.

TACTICS OF TO-DAY. Second Edition. Crown 8vo, 2s. 6d. net.

MILITARY OPERATIONS AND MARITIME PREPONDERANCE: THEIR RELATIONS AND INTERDEPENDENCE. Demy 8vo, 15s. net.

THE TACTICS OF HOME DEFENCE. Crown 8vo, 3s. 6d. net.

SERVICE YARNS AND REMINISCENCES. Crown 8vo, 6s.

CALLWELL, J. M.
OLD IRISH LIFE. By J. M. CALLWELL. Illustrated. Demy 8vo, 10s. net.

CANDLER, EDMUND.
THE MANTLE OF THE EAST. By EDMUND CANDLER. Illustrated. Crown 8vo, 6s. net.

THE GENERAL PLAN. Crown 8vo, 6s.

CAREY, WYMOND.
"No 101." Third Impression. By WYMOND CAREY. Crown 8vo, 6s.

CARLYLE, R. W., C.I.E., and A. J., M A.
A HISTORY OF MEDIÆVAL POLITICAL THEORY IN THE WEST. By R. W. CARLYLE, C.I.E., Balliol College, Oxford ; and A. J. CARLYLE, M.A., Chaplain and Lecturer (late Fellow) of University College, Oxford. In 3 vols. demy 8vo. Vol. I.—A History of Political Theory from the Roman Lawyers of the Second Century to the Political Writers of the Ninth. By A. J. CARLYLE. 15s. net. Vol. II.—Demy 8vo, 15s. net.

"CHASSEUR."
A STUDY OF THE RUSSO-JAPANESE WAR. By "CHASSEUR." Crown 8vo, 6s. net.

CHESNEY, SIR GEORGE, K.C.B.
THE DILEMMA. By General Sir GEORGE CHESNEY, K.C.B. A New Edition. Crown 8vo, 2s.

CHRISTIE, REV. GEORGE, B.D.
THE INFLUENCE OF LETTERS ON THE SCOTTISH REFORMATION. By Rev. GEORGE CHRISTIE, B.D. Crown 8vo, 6s. net.

CHURCH, REV. A.
OVID. (Ancient Classics for English Readers.) By Rev. A. CHURCH. Fcap. 8vo, 1s. net.

CHURCH, REV. A., and BRODRIBB, W. J.
PLINY. (Ancient Classics for English Readers.) By Rev. A. CHURCH and W. J. BRODRIBB. Fcap. 8vo, 1s. net.

CHURCH SERVICE SOCIETY.
A BOOK OF COMMON ORDER: BEING FORMS OF WORSHIP ISSUED BY THE CHURCH SERVICE SOCIETY. Seventh Edition, carefully revised. In 1 vol. crown 8vo, cloth, 3s. 6d.; French morocco, 5s. Also in 2 vols. crown 8vo, cloth, 4s.; French morocco, 6s. 6d.

DAILY OFFICES FOR MORNING AND EVENING PRAYER THROUGHOUT THE WEEK. Crown 8vo, 3s. 6d.

ORDER OF DIVINE SERVICE FOR CHILDREN. Issued by the Church Service Society. With Scottish Hymnal. Cloth, 3d.

CLIFFORD, SIR HUGH, K.C.M.G.
SALEH: A SEQUEL. By Sir HUGH CLIFFORD, K.C.M.G. Crown 8vo, 6s.

CLODD, EDWARD.
THOMAS HENRY HUXLEY. "Modern English Writers." By EDWARD CLODD. Crown 8vo, 2s. 6d.

CLOUSTON, J. STORER.
THE LUNATIC AT LARGE. By J. STORER CLOUSTON. Ninth Impression. Crown 8vo, 6s. Cheap Edition, 1s. net

COUNT BUNKER: Being a Sequel to 'The Lunatic at Large.' Third Impression. Crown 8vo, 6s.

THE ADVENTURES OF M. D'HARICOT. Third Impression. Crown 8vo, 6s. Cheap Edition, 6d.
OUR LADY'S INN. Crown 8vo, 6s.

GARMISCATH. Crown 8vo, 6s.

COLLINS, C. W.
SAINT SIMON. (Foreign Classics for English Readers.) By C. W. COLLINS. Fcap. 8vo, 1s. net.

SOPHOCLES. (Ancient Classics for English Readers.) Fcap. 8vo, 1s. net.

PLATO. (Ancient Classics for English Readers.) Fcap. 8vo, 1s. net.

COLLINS, W. E. W.
LEAVES FROM THE DIARY OF A COUNTRY CRICKETER. By W. E. W. COLLINS. Crown 8vo, 6s.

COLLINS, REV. W. LUCAS.
BUTLER. (Philosophical Classics for English Readers.) By Rev. W. L. COLLINS. Fcap. 8vo, 1s. net.

MONTAIGNE. (Foreign Classics for English Readers.) Fcap. 8vo, 1s. net.

LA FONTAINE, AND OTHER FRENCH FABULISTS. (Foreign Classics for English Readers.) Fcap. 8vo, 1s. net.

HOMER, ILIAD—HOMER, ODYSSEY—VIRGIL—CICERO—ARISTOPHANES—PLAUTUS AND TERENCE—LUCIAN—LIVY—THUCYDIDES. (Ancient Classics for English Readers.) Fcap. 8vo, 1s. net.

COMBE, MRS KENNETH.
CELIA KIRKHAM'S SON. By Mrs KENNETH COMBE. Second Impression. Crown 8vo, 6s.

SEEKERS ALL. Crown 8vo, 6s.

COMPTON-BURNETT, I.
DOLORES. By I. COMPTON-BURNETT. Crown 8vo, 6s.

CONRAD, JOSEPH.
LORD JIM: A TALE. By JOSEPH CONRAD. Fourth Impression. Crown 8vo, 6s.

YOUTH: A NARRATIVE. Third Impression. Crown 8vo, 6s.

COOPER, REV. PROFESSOR.
LITURGY OF 1637, COMMONLY CALLED LAUD'S LITURGY. Edited by the Rev. Professor COOPER, D.D., Glasgow. Crown 8vo, 7s. 6d. net.

COPLESTON, BISHOP.
ÆSCHYLUS. (Ancient Classics for English Readers.) By Bishop COPLESTON. Fcap. 8vo, 1s. net.

CORNFORD, L. COPE.
TROUBLED WATERS. By L. COPE CORNFORD. Crown 8vo, 6s.

COUNTY HISTORIES OF SCOTLAND. In demy 8vo volumes of about 350 pp. each. With Maps. Price 7s. 6d. net.

FIFE AND KINROSS. By ÆNEAS J. G. MACKAY, LL.D., Sheriff of these Counties.

COUNTY HISTORIES OF SCOT-LAND—*contd.*
DUMFRIES AND GALLOWAY. By Sir HERBERT MAXWELL, Bart., M.P. Second Edition.

MORAY AND NAIRN. By CHARLES RAMPINI, LL.D., Sheriff of Dumfries and Galloway.

INVERNESS. By J. CAMERON LEES, D.D.

ROXBURGH, SELKIRK, AND PEEBLES. By Sir GEORGE DOUGLAS, Bart.

ABERDEEN AND BANFF. By WILLIAM WATT, Editor of Aberdeen 'Daily Free Press.'

COUTTS, H. B. MONEY.
FAMOUS DUELS OF THE FLEET. By H. B. MONEY COUTTS. With Coloured Frontispiece and Illustrations by N. Wilkinson. Crown 8vo, 6s.

CRAIK, SIR HENRY, K.C.B., M.P.
A CENTURY OF SCOTTISH HISTORY. From the Days before the '45 to those within living Memory. By Sir HENRY CRAIK, K.C.B. With Portraits. Demy 8vo, 10s. 6d. net.

CRAWFORD, ALEXANDER.
KAPAK. By ALEXANDER CRAWFORD. Crown 8vo, 6s.

MONSIEUR CARNIFEX. Crown 8vo, 6s.

CRAWFORD, F. MARION.
SARACINESCA. By F. MARION CRAWFORD. Crown 8vo, 3s. 6d. Cheap Edition, 1s. net. People's Edition, 6d.

CROALL LECTURES.
(*See under* NICOL and ROBER

CROSS, J. W.
IMPRESSIONS OF DANTE AND OF THE NEW WORLD. By J. W. CROSS. Post 8vo, 6s.

THE RAKE'S PROGRESS IN FINANCE. Crown 8vo, 2s. net,

CUMMING, C. F. GORDON.
MEMORIES. By C. F. GORDON CUMMING. Demy 8vo. Illustrated, 20s. net.

AT HOME IN FIJI. Post 8vo, 6s.

A LADY'S CRUISE IN A FRENCH MAN-OF-WAR. Cheap Edition. 6s.

CUMMING, C. F. GORDON—*contd.*
FIRE-FOUNTAINS. Illustrated, 25s.

GRANITE CRAGS. Post 8vo. Illustrated. Cheap Edition. 6s.

WANDERINGS IN CHINA. Small post 8vo. Cheap Edition. 6s.

CURTIS, HARPER.
THE LORD DOLLAR (DON DINERO). By HARPER CURTIS. Crown 8vo, 6s.

CURTIS, MARGUERITE.
THE BIAS. By MARGUERITE CURTIS. Crown 8vo, 6s.

MARCIA: A TRANSCRIPT FROM LIFE. Crown 8vo, 6s.

OH! FOR AN ANGEL. Crown 8vo, 6s.

CUSTANCE, ADMIRAL SIR REGINALD N., K.C.B., K.C.M.G., C.V.O.
THE SHIP OF THE LINE IN BATTLE. By Admiral Sir REGINALD N. CUSTANCE, K.C.B., K.C.M.G., C.V.O. With Diagrams. Demy 8vo.

DAVIES, J.
HESIOD AND THEOGNIS. (Ancient Classics for English Readers.) By J. DAVIES. Fcap. 8vo, 1s. net.

CATULLUS, TIBULLUS, AND PROPERTIUS. (Ancient Classics for English Readers.) Fcap. 8vo, 1s. net.

DAVIS, JESSIE AINSWORTH.
"WHEN HALF-GODS GO." By JESSIE AINSWORTH DAVIS. Second Impression. Crown 8vo, 6s.

DE HAVEN, AUDREY.
THE SCARLET CLOAK. By AUDREY DE HAVEN. Crown 8vo, 6s.

DESCARTES.
THE METHOD, MEDITATIONS, AND PRINCIPLES OF PHILOSOPHY OF DESCARTES. Translated from the original French and Latin. With a new Introductory Essay, Historical and Critical, on the Cartesian Philosophy. By Professor VEITCH, LL.D. Fourteenth Edition. Crown 8vo, 6s. 6d.

"DIES IRAE." The Story of a Spirit in Prison. Second Edition. Crown 8vo, 1s. 6d. net. Paper cover, 1s. net.

DIVER, MAUD.
CAPTAIN DESMOND, V.C. By MAUD DIVER. Ninth Impression. Crown 8vo, 6s. Cheap Edition, 1s. net.

DIVER, MAUD—*contd.*
THE GREAT AMULET. Seventh Impression. Crown 8vo, 6s. Cheap Edition, 1s. net.

CANDLES IN THE WIND. Sixth Impression. Crown 8vo, 6s. Cheap Edition, 1s. net.

THE ENGLISHWOMAN IN INDIA. Crown 8vo, 5s. net.

DODDS and MACPHERSON.
THE LICENSING ACTS (SCOTLAND) CONSOLIDATION AND AMENDMENT ACT, 1903. Annotated by J. M. DODDS, C.B., of the Scottish Office; Joint-Editor of the 'Parish Council Guide for Scotland,' and EWAN MACPHERSON, Advocate, Legal Secretary to the Lord Advocate. In 1 vol. crown 8vo, 5s. net.

DONNE, W. B.
EURIPIDES. (Ancient Classics for English Readers.) By W. B. DONNE. Fcap. 8vo, 1s. net.

TACITUS. (Ancient Classics for English Readers.) Fcap. 8vo, 1s. net.

DOUGLAS, CHARLES, M.A., D.Sc.
THE ETHICS OF JOHN STUART MILL. By CHARLES DOUGLAS, M.A., D.Sc., late Lecturer in Moral Philosophy, and Assistant to the Professor of Moral Philosophy in the University of Edinburgh. Post 8vo, 6s. net.

JOHN STUART MILL: A STUDY OF HIS PHILOSOPHY. Crown 8vo, 4s. 6d. net.

DURAND, SIR H. MORTIMER.
A HOLIDAY IN SOUTH AFRICA. By the Right Hon. Sir H. M. DURAND, G.C.M.G., K.C.S.I., &c. Crown 8vo, 6s. net.

ECCOTT, W. J.
FORTUNE'S CASTAWAY. By W. J. ECCOTT. Crown 8vo, 6s.

HIS INDOLENCE OF ARRAS. Crown 8vo, 6s.

THE HEARTH OF HUTTON. Crown 8vo, 6s.

THE RED NEIGHBOUR. Crown 8vo, 6s. Cheap Edition, 1s. net.

THE BACKGROUND. Crown 8vo, 6s.

A DEMOISELLE OF FRANCE. Crown 8vo, 6s.

THE SECOND CITY. Crown 8vo, 6s.

ELIOT, GEORGE.
THE NEW POPULAR EDITION OF GEORGE ELIOT'S WORKS, with Photogravure Frontispiece to each Volume, from Drawings by William Hatherell, R.I., Edgar Bundy, R.I., Byam Shaw, R.I., A. A. Van Anrooy, Maurice Greiffenhagen, Claude A. Shepperson, R.I., E. J. Sullivan, and Max Cowper. Each Work complete in One Volume. Handsomely bound, gilt top. 3s. 6d. net. Ten Volumes in all.

ADAM BEDE.
SCENES OF CLERICAL LIFE.
THE MILL ON THE FLOSS.
FELIX HOLT, THE RADICAL.
MIDDLEMARCH.
SILAS MARNER; BROTHER JACOB; THE LIFTED VEIL.
ROMOLA.
DANIEL DERONDA.
THE SPANISH GYPSY; JUBAL.
ESSAYS; THEOPHRASTUS SUCH.

GEORGE ELIOT'S LIFE. With Portrait and other Illustrations. New Edition, in one volume. Crown 8vo, 7s. 6d.

LIFE AND WORKS OF GEORGE ELIOT (Warwick Edition). 14 volumes, cloth, limp, gilt top, 2s. net per volume; leather, limp, gilt top, 2s. 6d. net per volume; leather, gilt top, with bookmarker, 3s. net per volume.

ADAM BEDE. 826 pp.
THE MILL ON THE FLOSS. 828 pp.
FELIX HOLT, THE RADICAL. 718 pp.
ROMOLA. 900 pp.
SCENES OF CLERICAL LIFE. 624 pp.
SILAS MARNER; BROTHER JACOB; THE LIFTED VEIL. 560 pp.
MIDDLEMARCH. 2 vols. 664 and 630 pp.
DANIEL DERONDA. 2 vols. 616 and 636 pp.
THE SPANISH GYPSY; JUBAL.
ESSAYS; THEOPHRASTUS SUCH.
LIFE. 2 vols., 626 and 580 pp.

WORKS OF GEORGE ELIOT (Standard Edition). 21 volumes, crown 8vo. In buckram cloth, gilt top, 2s. 6d. per vol.; or in roxburghe binding, 3s. 6d. per vol.

ADAM BEDE. 2 vols.
THE MILL ON THE FLOSS. 2 vols.
FELIX HOLT, THE RADICAL. 2 vols.
ROMOLA. 2 vols.
SCENES OF CLERICAL LIFE. 2 vols.
MIDDLEMARCH. 3 vols.
DANIEL DERONDA. 3 vols.
SILAS MARNER. 1 vol.
JUBAL. 1 vol.
THE SPANISH GYPSY. 1 vol.
ESSAYS. 1 vol.
THEOPHRASTUS SUCH. 1 vol.

ELIOT, GEORGE—*contd.*
LIFE AND WORKS OF GEORGE ELIOT (Cabinet Edition). 24 volumes, crown 8vo, price £6. Also to be had handsomely bound in half and full calf. The Volumes are sold separately, bound in cloth, price 5s. each.

NOVELS BY GEORGE ELIOT. Popular copyright Edition. In new uniform binding, price 3s. 6d. each.
ADAM BEDE.
THE MILL ON THE FLOSS.
SCENES OF CLERICAL LIFE.
ROMOLA.
FELIX HOLT, THE RADICAL.
SILAS MARNER; THE LIFTED VEIL; BROTHER JACOB.
MIDDLEMARCH.
DANIEL DERONDA.

ESSAYS. New Edition. Crown 8vo, 5s.

IMPRESSIONS OF THEOPHRASTUS SUCH. New Edition. Crown 8vo, 5s.

THE SPANISH GYPSY. New Edition. Crown 8vo, 5s.

THE LEGEND OF JUBAL, AND OTHER POEMS, OLD AND NEW. New Edition. Crown 8vo, 5s.

SILAS MARNER. New Edition, with Illustrations by Reginald Birch. Crown 8vo, 1s. 6d. net. Cheap Edition, 2s. 6d.

SCENES OF CLERICAL LIFE. Cheap Edition, 3s. Illustrated Edition, with 20 Illustrations by H. R. Millar, crown 8vo, 2s. 6d.; plain cloth, 2s.; paper covers, 1s.

ADAM BEDE. New Edition, crown 8vo, paper cover, 1s.; crown 8vo, with Illustrations, cloth, 2s.

THE MILL ON THE FLOSS. New Edition, paper covers, 1s.; cloth, 2s.

WISE, WITTY, AND TENDER SAYINGS, IN PROSE AND VERSE. Selected from the Works of GEORGE ELIOT. New Edition. Fcap. 8vo, 3s. 6d.

ELLIS, BETH.
BLIND MOUTHS. Crown 8vo, 6s.

THE MOON OF BATH. Fourth Impression. Crown 8vo, 6s. Cheap Edition, 1s. net.

THE KING'S SPY. Second Impression. Crown 8vo, 6s.

A KING OF VAGABONDS. Cr'n 8vo, 6s.

ELTON, PROFESSOR.
THE AUGUSTAN AGES. By OLIVER ELTON, M.A., Professor of English Literature, University College, Liverpool. Crown 8vo, 5s. net.

EVERARD, H. S. C.
HISTORY OF THE ROYAL AND ANCIENT GOLF CLUB, ST ANDREWS. By H. S. C. EVERARD. With Eight Coloured Portraits. Crown 4to, 21s. net.

F.
STORIES OF THE ENGLISH. By F. With 50 Illustrations. Crown 8vo, 3s. 6d. net.

FERRIER, PROFESSOR.
PHILOSOPHICAL REMAINS. Crown 8vo, 14s.

FESTING, GABRIELLE.
WHEN KINGS RODE TO DELHI. By GABRIELLE FESTING. Illustrated, Demy 8vo, 7s. 6d. net.

FITZGERALD, JOHN GODWIN.
RUTH WERDRESS, FATHER O'HARALAN, AND SOME NEW CHRISTIANS. AN ANGLO-IRISH TALE. By JOHN GODWIN FITZGERALD. Crown 8vo, 6s.

FLINT, PROFESSOR,
PHILOSOPHY AS SCIENTIA SCIENTIARUM. A History of Classifications of the Sciences. By ROBERT FLINT, D.D., LL.D. 10s. 6d. net.
STUDIES ON THEOLOGICAL, BIBLICAL, AND OTHER SUBJECTS. 7s. 6d. net.
HISTORICAL PHILOSOPHY IN FRANCE AND FRENCH BELGIUM AND SWITZERLAND. 8vo, 21s.
THEISM. Twelfth Edition, Revised. Crown 8vo, 7s. 6d.
ANTI-THEISTIC THEORIES. Eighth Edition. Crown 8vo, 10s. 6d.
VICO. (Philosophical Classics for English Readers.) Fcap. 8vo, 1s. net.

FOREIGN CLASSICS FOR ENGLISH READERS. Edited by Mrs OLIPHANT. Price 1s. each net. *For List of Vols. see p. 32.*

FORREST, G. W., C.I.E.
HISTORY OF THE INDIAN MUTINY. By G. W. FORREST, C.I.E. Ex-Director of Records, Government of India. 2 vols. demy 8vo, 38s. net.
THE INDIAN MUTINY. Vol. III.— THE CENTRAL INDIA CAMPAIGN. With Plans and Illustrations. Demy 8vo, 20s. net.
LIFE OF FIELD-MARSHAL SIR NEVILLE B. CHAMBERLAIN, G.C.B., G.C.S.I. With two Photogravure Portraits. Demy 8vo, 18s. net.

FORSTER, E. M.
WHERE ANGELS FEAR TO TREAD. By E. M. FORSTER. Crown 8vo, 6s.
THE LONGEST JOURNEY. Second Impression. Crown 8vo, 6s.

FOULIS, HUGH.
THE VITAL SPARK. By HUGH FOULIS.
Illustrated. 1s. net.
IN HIGHLAND HARBOURS WITH
PARA HANDY. Crown 8vo, 1s. net.

FRANKLIN, MILES.
SOME EVERYDAY FOLK AND DAWN.
By MILES FRANKLIN. Crown 8vo, 6s.

**FRASER, PROFESSOR A. CAMP-
BELL.**
PHILOSOPHY OF THEISM. Being
the Gifford Lectures delivered before
the University of Edinburgh in 1894-
96. By ALEXANDER CAMPBELL FRASER,
D.C.L., Oxford; Emeritus Professor of
Logic and Metaphysics in the University
of Edinburgh. Second Edition, Revised.
Post 8vo, 6s. 6d. net.
BIOGRAPHIA PHILOSOPHICA. In 1
vol. demy 8vo, 6s. net.
BERKELEY. (Philosophical Classics for
English Readers.) Fcap. 8vo, 1s. net.
LOCKE. (Philosophical Classics for
English Readers.) Fcap. 8vo, 1s. net.

FRASER, DAVID.
THE MARCHES OF HINDUSTAN.
The Record of a Journey in Thibet,
Trans-Himalayan India, Chinese Tur-
kestan, Russian Turkestan, and Persia.
By DAVID FRASER. With Illustrations,
Maps, and Sketches. Demy 8vo, £1, 1s.
net.
THE SHORT CUT TO INDIA. The
Record of a Journey along the Route of
the Baghdad Railway. With 83 Illustra-
tions. Second Impression. Demy 8vo,
12s. 6d. net.
PERSIA AND TURKEY IN REVOLT.
With numerous Illustrations. Demy
8vo, 12s. 6d. net.

**FRENCH COOKERY FOR ENGLISH
HOMES.** Fourth Impression. Crown
8vo, cloth, 2s. 6d. French morocco, 3s.

FULTON, T. WEMYSS.
THE SOVEREIGNTY OF THE SEA.
An Historical Account of the Claims of
England to the Dominion of the British
Seas, and of the Evolution of the Ter-
ritorial Waters: with special reference
to the Rights of Fishing and the Naval
Salute. By T. WEMYSS FULTON,
Lecturer on the Scientific Study of
Fisheries Problems, The University,
Aberdeen. With Charts and Maps.
Demy 8vo, 25s. net.

FYFE, H. HAMILTON.
THE NEW SPIRIT IN EGYPT. By
H. HAMILTON FYFE. With Illustra-
tions. Crown 8vo, 5s. net.

GALT, JOHN.
THE PROVOST, &c. By JOHN GALT.
Illustrated boards, 2s.; cloth, 2s. 6d.
SIR ANDREW WYLIE. Illustrated
boards, 2s.; cloth, 2s. 6d.

**GENERAL ASSEMBLY OF THE
CHURCH OF SCOTLAND.**
SCOTTISH HYMNAL, WITH APPEN-
DIX INCORPORATED. Published for
use in Churches by Authority of the
General Assembly. 1. Large type, cloth,
red edges, 2s. 6d.; French morocco, 4s.
2. Bourgeois type, limp cloth, 1s.;
French morocco, 2s. 3. Nonpareil type,
cloth, red edges, 6d.; French morocco,
1s. 4d. 4. Paper covers, 3d. 5. Sun-
day-School Edition, paper covers, 1d.;
cloth, 2d. No. 1, bound with the Psalms
and Paraphrases, French morocco, 8s.
No. 2, bound with the Psalms and Paraphrases, cloth, 2s.; French morocco, 3s.
SERVICES OF PRAYER FOR SOCIAL
AND FAMILY WORSHIP. Prepared
by a Special Committee of the General
Assembly of the Church of Scotland.
New Edition, Revised and Enlarged.
Fcap. 8vo, 1s. 6d. net. French morocco,
3s. 6d. net.
PRAYERS FOR FAMILY WORSHIP.
A Selection of Four Weeks' Prayers.
New Edition. Authorised by the Gen-
eral Assembly of the Church of Scot-
land. Fcap. 8vo, 1s. net. French
morocco, 3s. net.
ONE HUNDRED PRAYERS. Prepared
by the Committee on Aids to Devotion.
16mo, cloth limp, 6d. net.
MORNING AND EVENING PRAYERS
FOR AFFIXING TO BIBLES. Pre-
pared by the Committee on Aids to
Devotion. 1d. for 6, or 1s. per 100.
PRAYERS FOR SOLDIERS. Prepared
by the Committee on Aids to Devotion.
Seventieth Thousand. 16mo, cloth limp,
2d. net.
PRAYERS FOR SAILORS AND
FISHER-FOLK. Prepared and Pub-
lished by Instruction of the General
Assembly of the Church of Scotland.
Fcap. 8vo, 1s. net.

GERARD, E. D.
REATA: WHAT'S IN A NAME. By
E. D. GERARD. Cheap Edition. Crown
8vo, 3s. 6d.
BEGGAR MY NEIGHBOUR. Cheap
Edition. Crown 8vo, 3s. 6d.
THE WATERS OF HERCULES.
Cheap Edition. Crown 8vo, 3s. 6d.
A SENSITIVE PLANT. Crown 8vo,
3s. 6d.

GERARD, E.
HONOUR'S GLASSY BUBBLE. By
E. GERARD. Crown 8vo, 6s.
A FOREIGNER. An Anglo-German
Study. Crown 8vo, 6s.

GERARD, DOROTHEA.
ONE YEAR. By DOROTHEA GERARD
(Madame Longard de Longgarde).
Crown 8vo, 6s.
THE IMPEDIMENT. Crown 8vo, 6s.

GERARD, DOROTHEA—*contd.*
A SPOTLESS REPUTATION. Third Edition. Crown 8vo, 6s.
THE WRONG MAN. Second Edition. Crown 8vo, 6s.
LADY BABY. Cheap Edition. Crown 8vo, 3s. 6d.
RECHA. Crown 8vo, 6s.
A FORGOTTEN SIN. Crown 8vo, 6s.

GERARD, REV. J.
STONYHURST LATIN GRAMMAR. By Rev. J. GERARD. Second Edition. Fcap. 8vo, 3s.

GIBBON, PERCEVAL.
SOULS IN BONDAGE. By PERCEVAL GIBBON. Crown 8vo, 6s.
THE VROUW GROBELAAR'S LEADING CASES. Crown 8vo, 6s.
SALVATOR. Crown 8vo, 6s.

GIFFORD LECTURES, EDINBURGH.
(*See under* FRASER and TIELE.)

GILL, RICHARD.
THE CHCL₃-PROBLEM. By RICHARD GILL. 2 vols. crown 8vo, 5s. net each.

GILLANDERS, A. T.
FOREST ENTOMOLOGY. By A. T. GILLANDERS, F.E.S. With 351 Illustrations. Second Edition, Revised. Crown 8vo, 15s. net.

GILLESPIE, REV. JOHN, LL.D.
THE HUMOURS OF SCOTTISH LIFE. By the Rev. JOHN GILLESPIE, LL.D. Crown 8vo, 3s. 6d. net.

GLASGOW BALLAD CLUB.
BALLADS AND POEMS. By MEMBERS OF THE GLASGOW BALLAD CLUB. Second Series. Crown 8vo, 7s. 6d. net. Third Series, 7s. 6d.

GLEIG, REV. G. R.
THE SUBALTERN. By Rev. G. R. GLEIG. Fcap. 8vo, 1s. net.

GOUDIE, GILBERT.
THE CELTIC AND SCANDINAVIAN ANTIQUITIES OF SCOTLAND. By GILBERT GOUDIE, F.S.A. Scot. Demy 8vo, 7s. 6d. net.

GRAHAM, HENRY GREY.
ROUSSEAU. (Foreign Classics for English Readers.) By HENRY GREY GRAHAM. Fcap. 8vo, 1s. net.

GRAHAM, J. EDWARD, K.C.
A MANUAL OF THE ACTS RELATING TO EDUCATION IN SCOTLAND. (Founded on that of the late Mr Craig Sellar.) By J. EDWARD GRAHAM, K.C., Advocate. New Edition. Demy 8vo, 25s. net.

GRAHAM, J. EDWARD.—*contd.*
MANUAL OF THE ELECTIONS (SCOT.) (CORRUPT AND ILLEGAL PRACTICES) ACT, 1890. With Analysis, Relative Act of Sederunt, Appendix containing the Corrupt Practices Acts of 1883 and 1885, and Copious Index. 8vo, 4s. 6d.
THE NEW EDUCATION (SCOTLAND) ACT. With Notes. Demy 8vo, 7s. 6d. net.

GRAHAM, E. MAXTONE, and PATERSON, E.
TRUE ROMANCES OF SCOTLAND. By E. MAXTONE GRAHAM and E. PATERSON. Illustrations. Second Impression. Crown 8vo, 5s. net.

GRAN, GERHARD.
JEAN JACQUES ROUSSEAU. By GERHARD GRAN. With three Portraits. Demy 8vo, 12s. 6d. net.

GRANT, SIR ALEX.
XENOPHON. (Ancient Classics for English Readers.) By Sir ALEX. GRANT. Fcap. 8vo, 1s. net.
ARISTOTLE. (Ancient Classics for English Readers.) Fcap. 8vo, 1s net.

GRANT, CAPTAIN M. H. ("LINESMAN.")
THE MAKERS OF BLACK BASALTES. By CAPTAIN M. H. GRANT ("LINESMAN"). Illustrating nearly 300 pieces. Demy 4to, 42s. net.

GREY, DULCIBELLA ETHEL.
POEMS. By DULCIBELLA ETHEL GREY. With a Prefatory Note by H. Cholmondeley Pennell. Demy 8vo. Vellum, 12s. 6d. net; half vellum, 7s. 6d. net.

GRIER, SYDNEY C.
HIS EXCELLENCY'S ENGLISH GOVERNESS. By SYDNEY C. GRIER. Third Impression. Crown 8vo, 6s.
AN UNCROWNED KING: A ROMANCE OF HIGH POLITICS. Third Impression. Crown 8vo, 6s.
PEACE WITH HONOUR. Third Impression. Crown 8vo, 6s.
A CROWNED QUEEN: THE ROMANCE OF A MINISTER OF STATE. Third Impression. Crown 8vo, 6s.
LIKE ANOTHER HELEN. Second Impression. Crown 8vo, 6s.
THE KINGS OF THE EAST: A ROMANCE OF THE NEAR FUTURE. Fourth Impression. Crown 8vo, 6s.
THE PRINCE OF THE CAPTIVITY. Second Impression. Crown 8vo, 6s.

GRIER, SYDNEY C.—contd.
THE GREAT PROCONSUL. The Memoirs of Mrs Hester Ward, formerly in the family of the Hon. Warren Hastings, Esq., late Governor-General of India. Crown 8vo, 6s.

THE HEIR. Crown 8vo, 6s.

THE POWER OF THE KEYS. With Illustrations by A. Pearce. Fourth Impression. Crown 8vo, 6s. Cheap Edition, 1s. net.

THE HERITAGE. Fourth Impression. Crown 8vo, 6s.

THE PATH TO HONOUR. Third Impression. Crown 8vo, 6s.

THE PRIZE. Crown 8vo, 6s.

THE KEEPERS OF THE GATE. With Illustrations by A. Pearce. Third Impression. Crown 8vo, 6s.

THE ADVANCED GUARD. Cheap Edition, 1s. net.

ONE CROWDED HOUR. With Cover Design and Coloured Frontispiece by A. Pearse. Crown 8vo, 6s.

A YOUNG MAN MARRIED. Illustrated Edition by A. Pearse. Crown 8vo, 6s.

THE LETTERS OF WARREN HASTINGS TO HIS WIFE. Demy 8vo, 6s. net.

GRIERSON, PROFESSOR H. J. C.
THE FIRST HALF OF THE SEVENTEENTH CENTURY. (Periods of European Literature.) By Professor H. J. C. Grierson. Crown 8vo, 5s. net.

GRIERSON, MAJOR-GENERAL SIR J. M., K.C.B., K.C.M.G.
RECORDS OF THE SCOTTISH VOLUNTEER FORCE, 1859-1908. By Major-General Sir J. M. Grierson, K.C.B., K.C.M.G. With 47 Coloured Plates. Crown 4to, 25s. net.

GROOT, J. MORGAN DE.
THE AFFAIR ON THE BRIDGE. By J. Morgan de Groot. Crown 8vo, 6s.

A LOTUS FLOWER. Crown 8vo, 6s.

EVEN IF. Crown 8vo, 6s.

JAN VAN DYCK. Crown 8vo, 6s.

THE BAR SINISTER. Crown 8vo, 6s.

HAMERTON, P. G.
WENDERHOLME. By P. G. Hamerton. Crown 8vo, 3s. 6d.

MARMORNE. Crown 8vo, 3s. 6d.

HAMILTON, CAPTAIN.
CYRIL THORNTON. By Captain Hamilton. Illustrated boards, 2s.; cloth, 2s. 6d.

HAMILTON, MARY, D.Litt.
GREEK SAINTS AND THEIR FESTIVALS. By Mary Hamilton, D.Litt. Crown 8vo, 5s. net.

HAMLEY, GENERAL SIR EDWARD BRUCE, K.C.B., K.C.M.G.
THE OPERATIONS OF WAR EXPLAINED AND ILLUSTRATED. By General Sir Edward Bruce Hamley, K.C.B., K.C.M.G.

A New Edition, brought up to the latest requirements. By Brigadier-General L. E. Kiggell, C.B. 4to, with Maps and Plans, 30s.

THOMAS CARLYLE: An Essay. Second Edition. Crown 8vo, 2s. 6d.

ON OUTPOSTS. Second Edition. 8vo, 2s.

LADY LEE'S WIDOWHOOD. Crown 8vo, 3s. 6d.; New Edition, crown 8vo, 2s.; cloth, 2s. 6d.

VOLTAIRE. (Foreign Classics for English Readers.) Fcap. 8vo, 1s. net.

HANNAY, DAVID.
THE LATER RENAISSANCE. "Periods of European Literature." By David Hannay. Crown 8vo, 5s. net.

SHIPS AND MEN. With Illustrations. Crown 8vo, 6s. net.

HARDEN, MAXIMILIAN.
WORD PORTRAITS: Character Sketches of Famous Men and Women. By Maximilian Harden. In a Translation from the German by Julius Gabe. Demy 8vo, 10s. 6d. net.

HARDMAN, F.
PENINSULAR SCENES AND SKETCHES. By F. Hardman. Illustrated cover, 1s.; cloth, 1s. 6d.

HARRADEN, BEATRICE.
SHIPS THAT PASS IN THE NIGHT. By Beatrice Harraden. Illustrated Edition. Crown 8vo, 3s. 6d. Velvet Calf Edition. Crown 8vo, 5s. net.

THE FOWLER. Illustrated Edition. Crown 8vo, 3s. 6d.

UNTOLD TALES OF THE PAST. With 40 Illustrations by H. R. Millar. Square crown 8vo, gilt top, 5s. net.

KATHARINE FRENSHAM. Crown 8vo, 6s.

HARTLEY, GILFRID W.
WILD SPORT WITH GUN, RIFLE, AND SALMON-ROD. By Gilfrid W. Hartley. With numerous Illustrations in photogravure and half-tone from drawings by G. E. Lodge and others. Demy 8vo, 6s. net.

WILD SPORT AND SOME STORIES. With Illustrations. Demy 8vo.

HASELL, E. J.
CALDERON. (Foreign Classics for English Readers.) By E. J. HASELL. Fcap. 8vo, 1s net.
TASSO. (Foreign Classics for English Readers.) Fcap. 8vo, 1s. net.

HASSALL, ARTHUR.
HISTORY OF BRITISH FOREIGN POLICY. By ARTHUR HASSALL. Demy 8vo, 7s. 6d. net.

HAY, BISHOP.
THE WORKS OF THE RIGHT REV. DR GEORGE HAY, Bishop of Edinburgh. Edited under the supervision of the Right Rev. Bishop STRAIN. With Memoir and Portrait of the Author. 5 vols. crown 8vo, 21s.

HAY, IAN.
"PIP." By IAN HAY. Fourth Impression. Crown 8vo, 6s. Cheap Edition, 1s. net.
"THE RIGHT STUFF." Some Episodes in the Career of a North Briton. Fifth Impression. Crown 8vo, 6s. Cheap Edition, 1s. net.
A MAN'S MAN. Third Impression. Crown 8vo, 6s. Cheap Edition, 1s. net.
A SAFETY MATCH. Third Impression. Crown 8vo, 6s.

HAYWARD, A., Q.C.
GOETHE. (Foreign Classics for English Readers.) By A. HAYWARD, Q.C. Fcap. 8vo, 1s. net.

HEATH, CHRISTOPHER.
PETER'S PROGRESS. By CHRISTOPHER HEATH. Crown 8vo, 6s.

HEMANS, MRS.
SELECT POEMS OF MRS HEMANS. Fcap., cloth, gilt edges, 3s.

HENDERSON, P. A. WRIGHT.
THE LIFE AND TIMES OF JOHN WILKINS, Warden of Wadham College, Oxford; Master of Trinity College, Cambridge; and Bishop of Chester. By P. A. WRIGHT HENDERSON. With Illustrations. Pott 4to, 5s. net.

HENDERSON, RICHARD.
THE YOUNG ESTATE MANAGER'S GUIDE. By RICHARD HENDERSON, Member (by Examination) of the Royal Agricultural Society of England, the Highland and Agricultural Society of Scotland, and the Surveyors' Institution. With an Introduction by Professor WRIGHT, Glasgow and West of Scotland Technical College. With Plans and Diagrams. Crown 8vo, 5s.

HENSON, H. HENSLEY, D.D.
THE RELATION OF THE CHURCH OF ENGLAND TO THE OTHER REFORMED CHURCHES (ROBERT LEE LECTURE, 1911). By Canon H. HENSLEY HENSON, D.D. Demy 8vo, 1s. net.

HERFORD, PROFESSOR.
BROWNING. "Modern English Writers." By C. H. HERFORD, Litt.D., Professor of English Literature, University of Manchester. 2s. 6d.

HERKLESS, PROFESSOR, and HANNAY, ROBERT KERR.
THE COLLEGE OF ST LEONARD'S. By JOHN HERKLESS, Professor of Ecclesiastical History in the University of St Andrews; and ROBERT KERR HANNAY, Lecturer in Ancient History in the University of St Andrews. Post 8vo, 7s. 6d. net.
THE ARCHBISHOPS OF ST ANDREWS. 3 vols. demy 8vo, each 7s. 6d. net.

HINTS ON HOCKEY. With Plans and Rules. New Edition. Fcap. 8vo, 1s.

HOBART-HAMPDEN, E.
THE PRICE OF EMPIRE. By E. HOBART-HAMPDEN. Crown 8vo, 6s.

HOLLAND, BERNARD, C.B.
VERSE. By BERNARD HOLLAND, C.B. Crown 8vo, 5s. net.

HOOK, DEAN.
PEN OWEN. By Dean HOOK. Illustrated boards, 2s.; cloth, 2s. 6d.

HOPE, JAMES F.
A HISTORY OF THE 1900 PARLIAMENT. By JAMES F. HOPE. In two volumes. Vol. I. Crown 8vo, 7s. 6d. net.

HUME, DAVID.
DIALOGUES CONCERNING NATURAL RELIGION. By DAVID HUME. Reprinted, with an Introduction by BRUCE M'EWEN, D.Phil. Crown 8vo, 3s. 6d. net.

HUME, E. DOUGLAS.
THE MULTIPLICITIES OF UNA. By E. DOUGLAS HUME. Crown 8vo, 6s.

HUNT, C. M. G.
A HANDY VOCABULARY: ENGLISH-AFRIKANDER, AFRIKANDER-ENGLISH. By C. M. G. HUNT. Small 8vo, 1s.

HUTCHINSON, HORACE G.
HINTS ON THE GAME OF GOLF. By HORACE G. HUTCHINSON. Twelfth Edition, Revised. Fcap. 8vo, cloth, 1s.

HUTTON, EDWARD.
ITALY AND THE ITALIANS. By EDWARD HUTTON. With Illustrations. Second Edition. Large crown 8vo, 6s.

INGLIS, JOHN.
GEORGE WENDERN GAVE A PARTY. By JOHN INGLIS. Second Impression. Crown 8vo, 6s.

INNES, A. TAYLOR, LL.D.
FREE CHURCH UNION CASE. Judgment of the House of Lords. With Introduction by A. TAYLOR INNES, LL.D. Demy 8vo, 1s. net.

INNES, A. TAYLOR, LL.D.—*contd.*
THE LAW OF CREEDS IN SCOT-
LAND. A Treatise on the Relations of
Churches in Scotland, Established and
not Established, to the Civil Law.
Demy 8vo, 10s. net.

INTELLIGENCE OFFICER.
ON THE HEELS OF DE WET. By
THE INTELLIGENCE OFFICER. Sixth
Impression. Crown 8vo, 6s.
THE YELLOW WAR. Crown 8vo, 6s.
A SUBALTERN OF HORSE. Second
Impression. Crown 8vo, 6s.

JAMES, ANDREW.
NINETY-EIGHT AND SIXTY YEARS
AFTER. By ANDREW JAMES. Crown
8vo, 3s. 6d.

JAMES, LIONEL.
SIDE-TRACKS AND BRIDLE-PATHS.
By LIONEL JAMES (Intelligence Officer).
Crown 8vo, 6s.

JAMES, LIEUT.-COL. WALTER H.
MODERN STRATEGY. By Lieut.-Col.
WALTER H. JAMES, P.S.C., late R.E.
With 6 Maps. Third Edition, thor-
oughly revised and brought up to date.
Royal 8vo, 16s. net.
THE CAMPAIGN OF 1815, CHIEFLY
IN FLANDERS. With Maps and
Plans. Demy 8vo, 16s. net.
THE PROGRESS OF TACTICS FROM
1740 TO THE PRESENT DAY.
Demy 8vo. [*In the press.*]

JOHNSTON.
ELEMENTS OF AGRICULTURAL
CHEMISTRY. An entirely New Edi-
tion from the Edition by Sir CHARLES
A. CAMERON, M.D. Revised and in
great part rewritten by C. M. AIKMAN,
M.A., D.Sc., F.R.S.E., F.I.C., Professor
of Chemistry, Glasgow Veterinary Col-
lege. 21st Edition. Crown 8vo, 6s. 6d.
CATECHISM OF AGRICULTURAL
CHEMISTRY. An entirely New Edi-
tion from the Edition by Sir CHARLES
A. CAMERON. Revised and enlarged by
C. M. AIKMAN, D.Sc., &c. 95th Thou-
sand. With numerous Illustrations.
Crown 8vo, 1s.

**JOHNSTON, CHRISTOPHER N.,
K.C., LL.D.**
AGRICULTURAL HOLDINGS (SCOT-
LAND) ACTS, 1883 to 1900; and the
GROUND GAME ACT, 1880. With
Notes, and Summary of Procedure, &c.
By CHRISTOPHER N. JOHNSTON, K.C.,
LL.D. Sixth Edition. Demy 8vo, 6s.
net.
MAJOR OWEN, AND OTHER TALES.
Crown 8vo, 6s.

JOKAI, MAURUS.
TIMAR'S TWO WORLDS. By MAURUS
JOKAI. Authorised Translation by Mrs
HEGAN KENNARD. Cheap Edition.
Crown 8vo, 6s.

JORDAN, HUMFREY.
MY LADY OF INTRIGUE. By HUM-
FREY JORDAN. Crown 8vo, 6s.
THE JOYOUS WAYFARER. Crown
8vo, 6s.

KENDIM, BEN.
EASTERN SONGS. By BEN KENDIM.
With Frontispiece in Colours by Lady
AILEEN WELLESLEY. Crown 8vo, 5s.
net.

KENNION, MAJOR R. L.
SPORT AND LIFE IN THE FURTHER
HIMALAYA. By MAJOR R. L. KEN-
NION. With Illustrations. Demy 8vo,
12s. 6d. net.
BY MOUNTAIN, LAKE, AND PLAIN.
Being Sketches of Sport in Eastern
Persia. With Coloured Frontispiece
and 75 Illustrations from Photographs
by the AUTHOR. Demy 8vo, 10s. 6d.
net.

KER, PROFESSOR W. P.
THE DARK AGES. "Periods of Euro-
pean Literature." By Professor W. P.
KER. In 1 vol. crown 8vo, 5s. net.

KERR, JOHN, LL.D.
MEMORIES: GRAVE AND GAY. By JOHN
KERR, LL.D. With Portrait and other
Illustrations. Cheaper Edition, En-
larged. Crown 8vo, 2s. 6d. net.
OTHER MEMORIES: OLD AND NEW.
Crown 8vo, 3s. 6d. net.

KINGLAKE, A. W.
HISTORY OF THE INVASION OF
THE CRIMEA. By A. W. KINGLAKE.
Complete in 9 vols. crown 8vo. Cheap
reissue at 3s. 6d. each.
—— Abridged Edition for Military
Students. Revised by Lieut.-Col. Sir
GEORGE SYDENHAM CLARKE, G.C.M.G.,
G.C.I.E. Demy 8vo, 15s. net.
—— Atlas to accompany above. Folio,
9s. net.
EOTHEN. Cheap Edition. With Por-
trait and Biographical Sketch of the
Author. Crown 8vo, 2s. 6d. net.

**KINGSBURGH, THE RIGHT HON.
LORD, K.C.B.**
FIFTY YEARS OF IT: THE EXPERI-
ENCES AND STRUGGLES OF A VOLUNTEER
OF 1859. By The Right Hon. LORD
KINGSBURGH, K.C.B. Demy 8vo, 10s.
6d. net.

KNEIPP, SEBASTIAN.
MY WATER-CURE. As Tested through
more than Thirty Years, and Described
for the Healing of Diseases and the Preservation of Health. By SEBASTIAN
KNEIPP. With a Portrait and other
Illustrations. Authorised English
Translation from the Thirtieth German
Edition, by A. de F. With an Appendix, containing the Latest Developments
of Pfarrer Kneipp's System, and a Preface by E. Gerard. Crown 8vo, 3s. 6d

KNIGHT, PROFESSOR.
HUME. (Philosophical Classics for English Readers.) By Professor KNIGHT. Fcap. 8vo, 1s. net.

LANG, ANDREW.
A HISTORY OF SCOTLAND FROM THE ROMAN OCCUPATION. By ANDREW LANG. Complete in Four Volumes. Demy 8vo, £3, 3s. net.
  Vol. I. With a Photogravure Frontispiece. 15s. net.
  Vol. II. With a Photogravure Frontispiece. 15s. net.
  Vol. III. With a Photogravure Frontispiece. 15s. net.
  Vol. IV. With a Photogravure Frontispiece. 20s. net.
TENNYSON. "Modern English Writers." Second Edition. Crown 8vo, 2s. 6d.
A SHORT HISTORY OF SCOTLAND. Crown 8vo, 5s. net.

LAPWORTH, PROFESSOR.
INTERMEDIATE TEXT-BOOK OF GEOLOGY. By CHARLES LAPWORTH, LL.D., Professor of Geology, University, Birmingham. 5s.

LAWSON, W. R.
BRITISH ECONOMICS. By W. R. LAWSON. Second Edition. Crown 8vo, 6s. net.
AMERICAN FINANCE. Second Edition. Crown 8vo, 6s. net.
JOHN BULL AND HIS SCHOOLS. Crown 8vo, 5s. net. New Edition, Paper Cover, 2s. net.
CANADA AND THE EMPIRE. Crown 8vo, 6s. net.
MODERN WARS AND WAR TAXES. A Manual of Military Finance. Crown 8vo, 6s. net.

LEATHAM, A. E.
SPORT IN FIVE CONTINENTS. By A. E. LEATHAM. With Illustrations. Demy 8vo.

LEHMANN, R. C.
CRUMBS OF PITY, AND OTHER VERSES; TO WHICH ARE ADDED SIX LIVES OF GREAT MEN. By R. C. LEHMANN, author of 'Anni Fugaces,' &c. Crown 8vo, 5s. net.
LIGHT AND SHADE: AND OTHER POEMS. Crown 8vo, 5s. net.

LEIGHTON, GERALD R., M.D.
THE LIFE-HISTORY OF BRITISH SERPENTS, AND THEIR LOCAL DISTRIBUTION IN THE BRITISH ISLES. By GERALD R. LEIGHTON, M.D. With 50 Illustrations. Crown 8vo, 5s. net.

LEISHMAN, VERY REV. T., D.D.
THE WESTMINSTER DIRECTORY. Edited, with an ntroduction and Notes, by the Very Rev. T. LEISHMAN, D.D. Crown 8vo, 4s. net.

LEWIS, ARTHUR.
THE PILGRIM. By ARTHUR LEWIS. Crown 8vo, 6s.

LINDSAY, REV. JAMES, D.D.
RECENT ADVANCES IN THEISTIC PHILOSOPHY OF RELIGION. By Rev. JAMES LINDSAY, M.A., D.D., B.Sc., F.R.S.E., F.G.S. Demy 8vo, 12s. 6d. net.
THE PROGRESSIVENESS OF MODERN CHRISTIAN THOUGHT. Crown 8vo, 6s.
ESSAYS, LITERARY AND PHILOSOPHICAL. Crown 8vo, 3s. 6d.
THE SIGNIFICANCE OF THE OLD TESTAMENT FOR MODERN THEOLOGY. Crown 8vo, 1s. net.
THE TEACHING FUNCTION OF THE MODERN PULPIT. Crown 8vo, 1s. net.
STUDIES IN EUROPEAN PHILOSOPHY. Demy 8vo, 10s. 6d. net.
THE FUNDAMENTAL PROBLEMS OF METAPHYSICS. Crown 8vo, 4s. net.
THE PSYCHOLOGY OF BELIEF. Crown 8vo, 2s. 6d. net.
NEW ESSAYS — LITERARY AND PHILOSOPHICAL. Crown 8vo, 6s. net.
LITERARY ESSAYS. Crown 8vo, 3s. 6d. net.

"LINESMAN."
THE MAKERS OF BLACK BASALTES. By "LINESMAN." With nearly 300 Illustrations. Demy 4to, 42s. net.

LITURGIES AND ORDERS OF DIVINE SERVICE (CHURCH SERVICE SOCIETY).
THE SECOND PRAYER BOOK OF KING EDWARD THE SIXTH (1552). With Historical Introduction and Notes by the Rev. H. J. WOTHERSPOON, M.A., of St Oswald's, Edinburgh; and THE LITURGY OF COMPROMISE. Used in the English Congregation at Frankfort. From an Unpublished MS. Edited by the Rev. G. W. SPROTT, D.D. 4s. net.
BOOK OF COMMON ORDER. Commonly called KNOX's LITURGY. Edited by Rev. G. W. SPROTT, D.D. 4s. 6d. net.
SCOTTISH LITURGIES OF THE REIGN OF JAMES VI. Edited by Rev. G. W. SPROTT, D.D. 4s. net.
LITURGY OF 1637. Commonly called LAUD's LITURGY. Edited by the Rev. Professor COOPER, D.D. 7s. 6d. net.
THE WESTMINSTER DIRECTORY. Edited by Very Rev. T. LEISHMAN, D.D. 4s. net.
EUCHOLOGION. A Book of Common Order: Being Forms of Prayer, and Administration of the Sacraments, and other Ordinances of the Church. Edited by the Rev. G. W. SPROTT, D.D. 4s. 6d. net

LOBBAN, J. H., M.A.
AN ANTHOLOGY OF ENGLISH VERSE FROM CHAUCER TO THE PRESENT DAY. By J. H. LOBBAN, M.A. Crown 8vo, gilt top, 5s.

THE SCHOOL ANTHOLOGY OF ENGLISH VERSE. Part I., Chaucer to Burns, cloth, 1s. net. Part II., Wordsworth to Newbolt, cloth, 1s. net. In One Volume complete, cloth, 2s. net.

LOCKHART, J. G.
REGINALD DALTON. By J. G. LOCKHART. Illustrated boards, 2s.; cloth, 2s. 6d.

ADAM BLAIR. Illustrated boards, 2s.; cloth, 2s. 6d.

VALERIUS: A ROMAN STORY. Illustrated cover, 1s.; cloth, 1s. 6d.

LOCKHART, LAURENCE W. M.
DOUBLES AND QUITS. By LAURENCE W. M. LOCKHART. Crown 8vo, 3s. 6d.

FAIR TO SEE. Crown 8vo, 3s. 6d.

MINE IS THINE. New Edition. Crown 8vo, 3s. 6d.

LUCAS, ST JOHN.
SAINTS, SINNERS, AND THE USUAL PEOPLE. By ST JOHN LUCAS. Second Impression. Crown 8vo, 6s.

LYNDEN-BELL, LIEUT.-COLONEL.
A PRIMER OF TACTICS, FORTIFICATION, TOPOGRAPHY, AND MILITARY LAW. By Lieut.-Colonel C. P. LYNDEN-BELL. With Diagrams. Crown 8vo, 3s. net.

MABIE, HAMILTON WRIGHT.
ESSAYS ON NATURE AND CULTURE. By HAMILTON WRIGHT MABIE. With Portrait. Fcap. 8vo, 3s. 6d.

BOOKS AND CULTURE. Fcap. 8vo, 3s. 6d.

McCARTHY, MICHAEL J. F.
THE NONCONFORMIST TREASON; OR, THE SALE OF THE EMERALD ISLE. By MICHAEL J. F. McCARTHY. Crown 8vo, 6s.

THE IRISH REVOLUTION. The Murdering Time, from the Land League to the first Home Rule Bill. Vol. I. With numerous Portraits. Demy 8vo, 10s. 6d. net.

MacCUNN, FLORENCE.
SIR WALTER SCOTT'S FRIENDS. By FLORENCE MacCUNN. With Portraits. Third Impression. Demy 8vo, 10s. net.

MACDONALD, NORMAN DORAN.
A MANUAL OF THE CRIMINAL LAW (SCOTLAND) PROCEDURE ACT, 1887. By NORMAN DORAN MACDONALD. Revised by the LORD JUSTICE-CLERK. 8vo, 10s. 6d.

MACDOUGALL, J. PATTEN, C.B., and J. M. DODD, C.B.
A MANUAL OF THE LOCAL GOVERNMENT (SCOTLAND) ACT, 1894. THE PARISH COUNCIL GUIDE FOR SCOTLAND. By J. PATTEN MACDOUGALL, C.B., and J. M. DODD, C.B. New and Revised Edition. [In preparation.

M'IVER, IVER.
AN IMPERIAL ADVENTURE. By IVER M'IVER. With Illustrations. Crown 8vo, 6s.

CAUGHT ON THE WING. Crown 8vo, 3s. 6d. net.

MACKAY, LYDIA MILLER.
THE RETURN OF THE EMIGRANT. By LYDIA MILLER MACKAY. Third Impression. Crown 8vo, 6s.

MACKENZIE, LORD.
STUDIES IN ROMAN LAW. With Comparative Views of the Laws of France, England, and Scotland. By LORD MACKENZIE, one of the Judges of the Court of Session in Scotland. Edited by JOHN KIRKPATRICK, M.A., LL.D., Advocate, Professor of History in the University of Edinburgh. 8vo, 21s.

MACKENZIE, W. A.
ROWTON HOUSE RHYMES. By W. A. MACKENZIE. Crown 8vo, 3s. net.

MACKINLAY, J. M.
INFLUENCE OF THE PRE-REFORMATION CHURCH ON SCOTTISH PLACE-NAMES. By J. M. MACKINLAY, F.S.A. (Scot.) Demy 8vo, 12s. 6d. net.

MACLEOD, OLIVE.
CHIEFS AND CITIES OF CENTRAL AFRICA. Across Lake Chad by way of British, French, and German Territories. By OLIVE MACLEOD. With 250 Illustrations and 3 Maps. Royal 8vo, 16s. net.

MACMUNN, MAJOR G. F. D.S.O., R.F.A.
PIKE AND CARRONADE. By Major G. F. MACMUNN, D.S.O., R.F.A. Crown 8vo, 6s.

MACNAMARA, RACHEL SWETE.
THE TRANCE. By RACHEL SWETE MACNAMARA. Second Impression. Crown 8vo, 6s.

THE SIBYL OF VENICE. Crown 8vo, 6s.

SEED OF FIRE. Crown 8vo, 6s.

SPINNERS IN SILENCE. Crown 8vo, 6s.

B

MACPHERSON, HECTOR.
BOOKS TO READ AND HOW TO READ THEM. By HECTOR MACPHERSON. Second Impression. Crown 8vo, 3s. 6d. net.
A CENTURY OF POLITICAL DEVELOPMENT. 3s. 6d. net.

MACPHERSON, HECTOR, Jun.
A CENTURY'S PROGRESS IN ASTRONOMY. By HECTOR MACPHERSON, jun. Short demy 8vo, 6s. net.
THROUGH THE DEPTHS OF SPACE: A PRIMER OF ASTRONOMY. Crown 8vo, 2s. net.

MACRAE, J. A.
FOR KIRK AND KING. By J. A. MACRAE. Crown 8vo, 3s. 6d.

MAHAFFY, PROFESSOR.
DESCARTES. (Philosophical Classics for English Readers.) By Professor MAHAFFY. Fcap. 8vo, 1s. net.

MAIR, REV. WILLIAM, D.D.
A DIGEST OF LAWS AND DECISIONS, Ecclesiastical and Civil, relating to the Constitution, Practice, and Affairs of the Church of Scotland. With Notes and Forms of Procedure. By the Rev. WILLIAM MAIR, D.D. Fourth Edition, Revised to date (1912). In 1 vol. crown 8vo, 12s. 6d. net.
SPEAKING; OR, FROM VOICE PRODUCTION TO THE PLATFORM AND PULPIT. Fourth Edition, Revised. Crown 8vo, 1s. 6d. net.

MALLOCK, W. H.
LUCRETIUS. (Ancient Classics for English Readers.) By W. H. MALLOCK. Fcap. 8vo, 1s. net.

MARSHMAN, JOHN CLARK, C.S.I.
HISTORY OF INDIA. From the Earliest Period to the Present Time. By JOHN CLARK MARSHMAN, C.S.I. Third and Cheaper Edition. Post 8vo, 6s.

MARTIN, SIR THEODORE, K.C.B.
HORACE. (Ancient Classics for English Readers.) By Sir THEODORE MARTIN, K.C.B. Fcap. 8vo, 1s. net.
POEMS OF GIACOMO LEOPARDI. Translated. Crown 8vo, 5s. net.
THE ÆNEID OF VIRGIL. Books I.-VI. Translated. Post 8vo, 7s. 6d.
GOETHE'S FAUST. Part I. Translated into English Verse. Second Edition, crown 8vo, 6s. Ninth Edition, fcap. 8vo, 3s. 6d.
GOETHE'S FAUST. Part II. Translated into English Verse. Second Edition, Revised. Fcap. 8vo, 6s.
POEMS AND BALLADS OF HEINRICH HEINE. Done into English Verse. Third Edition. Small crown 8vo, 5s.

MARTIN, SIR THEODORE—*contd.*
THE SONG OF THE BELL, AND OTHER TRANSLATIONS FROM SCHILLER, GOETHE, UHLAND, AND OTHERS. Crown 8vo, 7s. 6d.
MADONNA PIA: A TRAGEDY; AND THREE OTHER DRAMAS. Crown 8vo, 7s. 6d.
THE 'VITA NUOVA' OF DANTE. Translated with an Introduction and Notes. Fourth Edition. Small crown 8vo, 5s.
ALADDIN: A DRAMATIC POEM. By ADAM OEHLENSCHLAEGER. Fcap. 8vo, 5s.
CORREGGIO: A TRAGEDY. By OEHLENSCHLAEGER. With Notes. Fcap. 8vo, 3s.
HELENA FAUCIT (LADY MARTIN). By Sir THEODORE MARTIN, K.C.B., K.C.V.O. With Five Photogravure Plates. Second Edition. Demy 8vo, 10s. 6d. net.
POEMS AND BALLADS OF GOETHE. By Sir THEODORE MARTIN and Professor AYTOUN. Third Edition. With Introduction by Sir THEODORE MARTIN. Small crown 8vo, 6s. net.
QUEEN VICTORIA AS I KNEW HER. Square crown 8vo, 3s. 6d. net.

MARTIN, HELENA FAUCIT, LADY.
ON SOME OF SHAKESPEARE'S FEMALE CHARACTERS. By HELENA FAUCIT, LADY MARTIN. *Dedicated by permission to Her Most Gracious Majesty the Queen.* With a Portrait by Lehmann. Seventh Edition, with a new Preface. Demy 8vo, 7s. 6d.

MASSON, DAVID.
MEMORIES OF LONDON IN THE FORTIES. By DAVID MASSON. Crown 8vo, 3s. 6d. net.

MATHESON, REV. GEORGE, D.D.
CAN THE OLD FAITH LIVE WITH THE NEW? OR, THE PROBLEM OF EVOLUTION AND REVELATION. By the Rev. GEORGE MATHESON, D.D. Third Edition. Crown 8vo, 7s. 6d.
THE PSALMIST AND THE SCIENTIST; OR, MODERN VALUE OF THE RELIGIOUS SENTIMENT. Third Edition. Crown 8vo, 5s.
SPIRITUAL DEVELOPMENT OF ST PAUL. Fourth Edition. Crown 8vo, 5s.
THE DISTINCTIVE MESSAGES OF THE OLD RELIGIONS. Second Edition. Crown 8vo, 5s.
SACRED SONGS. Third Edition. Crown 8vo, 2s. 6d.

MAXWELL, GEORGE.
IN MALAY FORESTS. By GEORGE MAXWELL. Second Edition. Crown 8vo, 6s. net.

MAXWELL, RIGHT HON. SIR HERBERT, BART.
DUMFRIES AND GALLOWAY. By Right Hon. Sir HERBERT MAXWELL, Bart. Being one of the Volumes of the County Histories of Scotland. With Four Maps. Second Edition. Demy 8vo, 7s. 6d. net.
HOLYROOD, ABBEY CHURCH, PALACE, AND ENVIRONS. Crown 8vo. Paper cover, 6d. net ; cloth, 2s. 6d. net.

MEAKIN, ANNETTE M. B.
WHAT AMERICA IS DOING. Letters from the New World. By ANNETTE M. B. MEAKIN. Demy 8vo, 10s. 6d. net.

MELDRUM, DAVID S.
THE CONQUEST OF CHARLOTTE. By DAVID S. MELDRUM. Third Impression. Crown 8vo, 6s.
THE STORY OF MARGRÉDEL: Being a Fireside History of a Fifeshire Family. Cheap Edition. Crown 8vo, 3s. 6d.
GREY MANTLE AND GOLD FRINGE. Crown 8vo, 6s.

MELLONE, SYDNEY HERBERT, M.A., D.Sc.
STUDIES IN PHILOSOPHICAL CRITICISM AND CONSTRUCTION. By SYDNEY HERBERT MELLONE, M.A. Lond., D.Sc. Edin. Post 8vo, 10s. 6d. net.
LEADERS OF RELIGIOUS THOUGHT IN THE NINETEENTH CENTURY. Crown 8vo, 6s. net.
AN INTRODUCTORY TEXT - BOOK OF LOGIC. Fifth Edition, Revised. Crown 8vo, 5s.
ELEMENTS OF PSYCHOLOGY. Second Edition, Revised. Crown 8vo, 5s.
THE IMMORTAL HOPE. Crown 8vo, 2s. 6d.
FREDERICK NIETZSCHE AND HIS ATTACK ON CHRISTIANITY. Demy 8vo, paper cover, 3d.

MERZ, JOHN THEODORE.
A HISTORY OF EUROPEAN THOUGHT IN THE NINETEENTH CENTURY. By JOHN THEODORE MERZ. Vol. I. Third Impression. Post 8vo, 10s. 6d. net. Vol. II. Second Impression. 15s. net. Vol. III.
LEIBNIZ. (Philosophical Classics for English Readers.) Fcap. 8vo, 1s. net.

MEYNELL, MRS.
JOHN RUSKIN. "Modern English Writers." By Mrs MEYNELL. Third Impression. Crown 8vo, 2s. 6d.

MICKLETHWAIT, ST J. G., M.A., B.C.L.
THE LICENSING ACT, 1904. By ST J. G. MICKLETHWAIT, M.A., B.C.L., Barrister-at-Law. Crown 8vo, 2s. 6d. net.

MILL, GARRETT.
CAPTAIN GRANT'S DESPATCH. By GARRETT MILL. Crown 8vo, 6s.

MILLAR, PROFESSOR J. H.
THE MID-EIGHTEENTH CENTURY. "Periods of European Literature." By J. H. MILLAR. Crown 8vo, 5s. net.

MITCHELL, ALEXANDER F., D.D., LL.D.
THE SCOTTISH REFORMATION. Being the Baird Lecture for 1899. By the late ALEXANDER F. MITCHELL, D.D., LL.D. Edited by D. HAY FLEMING, LL.D. With a Biographical Sketch of the Author, by JAMES CHRISTIE, D.D. Crown 8vo, 6s.

MODERN ENGLISH WRITERS. In handy crown 8vo volumes, tastefully bound, price 2s. 6d. each.
MATTHEW ARNOLD. By Professor SAINTSBURY. Second Impression.
JOHN RUSKIN. By Mrs MEYNELL. Third Impression.
TENNYSON. By ANDREW LANG. Second Impression.
HUXLEY. By EDWARD CLODD.
THACKERAY. By CHARLES WHIBLEY.
BROWNING. By Professor C. H. HERFORD.

MOIR, D. M.
LIFE OF MANSIE WAUCH, TAILOR IN DALKEITH. By D. M. MOIR. With Cruikshank's Illustrations. Cheaper Edition. Crown 8vo, 2s. 6d.
—— Another Edition. Illustrated cover, 1s. ; cloth, 1s. 6d.

MOMERIE, REV. ALFRED WILLIAMS, M.A., D.Sc., LL.D.
THE ORIGIN OF EVIL; AND OTHER SERMONS. By Rev. ALFRED WILLIAMS MOMERIE, M.A., D.Sc., LL.D., late Fellow of St John's College, Cambridge. Eighth Edition, Enlarged. Crown 8vo, 5s.
PERSONALITY. The Beginning and End of Metaphysics, and a Necessary Assumption in all Positive Philosophy. Fifth Edition, Revised. Crown 8vo, 3s.

MOMERIE, REV. A. W.—*contd.*

PREACHING AND HEARING; AND OTHER SERMONS. Fourth Edition, Enlarged. Crown 8vo, 5s.

BELIEF IN GOD. Fourth Edition. Crown 8vo, 3s.

THE FUTURE OF RELIGION; AND OTHER ESSAYS. Second Edition. Crown 8vo, 3s. 6d.

THE ENGLISH CHURCH AND THE ROMISH SCHISM. Second Edition. Crown 8vo, 2s. 6d.

ESSAYS ON THE BIBLE. Crown 8vo, 3s. 6d. net.

CHARACTER. Crown 8vo, 3s. 6d. net.

MODERN SCEPTICISM AND MODERN FAITH. Crown 8vo, 3s. 6d. net.

MOMERIE, MRS.

DR ALFRED MOMERIE. His Life and Work. By Mrs MOMERIE. Demy 8vo, 12s. 6d. net.

MORICE, REV. F. D.

PINDAR. (Ancient Classics for English Readers.) By Rev. F. D. MORICE. Fcap. 8vo, 1s. net.

MORISON, SIR THEODORE, K.C.I.E., and HUTCHINSON, GEORGE P.

LIFE OF SIR EDWARD FITZGERALD LAW, K.C.S.I., K.C.M.G. By Sir THEODORE MORISON, K.C.I.E., and GEORGE P. HUTCHINSON. With portraits. Demy 8vo, 15s. net.

MUNRO, NEIL.

THE DAFT DAYS. By NEIL MUNRO. Third Impression. Crown 8vo, 6s. Uniform Edition, 3s. 6d. Cheap Edition, 1s. net.

FANCY FARM. Crown 8vo, 6s. Cheap Edition, 1s. net.

Uniform Edition Novels.

JOHN SPLENDID. The Tale of a Poor Gentleman and the Little Wars of Lorn. Sixth Impression. Crown 8vo, 3s. 6d.

CHILDREN OF TEMPEST: A TALE OF THE OUTER ISLES. Crown 8vo, 3s. 6d.

SHOES OF FORTUNE. Crown 8vo, 3s. 6d.

THE LOST PIBROCH, AND OTHER SHEILING STORIES. Fourth Impression. Crown 8vo, 3s. 6d.

DOOM CASTLE: A ROMANCE. Second Impression. Crown 8vo, 3s. 6d.

GILIAN THE DREAMER. Crown 8vo, 3s. 6d.

THE DAFT DAYS. Third Impression. Crown 8vo, 3s. 6d.

MUNRO, ROBERT, M.A., M.D., LL.D., F.R.S.E.

RAMBLES AND STUDIES IN BOSNIA-HERZEGOVINA AND DALMATIA. By ROBERT MUNRO, M.A., M.D., LL.D., F.R.S.E. Second Edition, Revised and Enlarged. With numerous Illustrations. Demy 8vo, 12s. 6d. net.

PREHISTORIC PROBLEMS. With numerous Illustrations. Demy 8vo, 10s. net.

MUNRO, WILLIAM, M.A.

ON VALUATION OF PROPERTY. By WILLIAM MUNRO, M.A., Her Majesty's Assessor of Railways and Canals for Scotland. Second Edition, Revised and Enlarged. 8vo, 3s. 6d.

MYRES, PROFESSOR JOHN L.

A MANUAL OF CLASSICAL GEOGRAPHY. By JOHN L. MYRES, M.A., Professor of Ancient History, Oxford. Crown 8vo. [*In the press.*]

NEAVES, LORD.

GREEK ANTHOLOGY. (Ancient Classics for English Readers.) By Lord NEAVES. Fcap. 8vo, 1s. net.

NEWBOLT, HENRY.

THE NEW JUNE. By HENRY NEWBOLT. Third Impression. Crown 8vo, 6s.

THE TWYMANS. Second Impression. Crown 8vo, 6s.

NICHOL, PROFESSOR.

BACON. (Philosophical Classics for English Readers.) By Professor NICHOL. Fcap. 8vo, Part I., 1s. net; Part II., 1s. net.

NICHOLSON, PROFESSOR H. ALLEYNE, and LYDEKKER, RICHARD, B.A.

A MANUAL OF PALÆONTOLOGY, for the use of Students. With a General Introduction on the Principles of Palæontology. By Professor H. ALLEYNE NICHOLSON and RICHARD LYDEKKER, B.A. Third Edition, entirely Rewritten and greatly Enlarged. 2 vols. 8vo, £3, 3s.

NICOL, REV. THOMAS, D.D.

RECENT ARCHÆOLOGY AND THE BIBLE. Being the Croall Lecture for 1898. By the Rev. THOMAS NICOL, D.D., Professor of Divinity and Biblical Criticism in the University of Aberdeen; Author of 'Recent Explorations in Bible Lands.' Demy 8vo, 9s. net.

THE FOUR GOSPELS IN THE EARLIEST CHURCH HISTORY. Being the Baird Lecture for 1907. Crown 8vo, 7s. 6d. net.

NISBET, JOHN, D.Œc.
THE FORESTER: A PRACTICAL TREATISE ON BRITISH FORESTRY AND ARBORICULTURE, FOR LANDOWNERS, LAND AGENTS, AND FORESTERS. By JOHN NISBET, D.Œc. In 2 volumes, royal 8vo, with 285 Illustrations, 42s. net.
THE ELEMENTS OF BRITISH FORESTRY. A Handbook for Forest Apprentices and Students of Forestry. Crown 8vo, 5s. 6d. net.

NOBILI, RICCARDO.
A MODERN ANTIQUE: A FLORENTINE STORY. By RICCARDO NOBILI. Crown 8vo, 6s.

NOBLE, EDWARD.
WAVES OF FATE. By EDWARD NOBLE. Crown 8vo, 6s.
FISHERMAN'S GAT: A STORY OF THE THAMES ESTUARY. Crown 8vo, 6s.

NOYES, ALFRED.
DRAKE: AN ENGLISH EPIC. By ALFRED NOYES. Books I.-III. Crown 8vo, 5s. net. Books IV.-XII. Crown 8vo, 6s. net.
—— The Complete Work in 1 vol. Crown 8vo, 7s. 6d. net.
FORTY SINGING SEAMEN. Second Impression. Crown 8vo, 5s. net.
THE ENCHANTED ISLAND, AND OTHER POEMS. Crown 8vo, 5s. net.
THE FOREST OF WILD THYME. Illustrated by Claude A. Shepperson. Small 4to, 6s. net. Velvet Calf Edition, 10s. 6d. net.
COLLECTED POEMS. 2 vols. Crown 8vo, 10s. net. Vols. sold separately, 5s. net. each.
ROBIN HOOD. Crown 8vo.

O'BRIEN, AUBREY, and BOLSTER, REGINALD.
CUPID AND CARTRIDGES. By AUBREY O'BRIEN AND REGINALD BOLSTER. With Illustrations. Demy 8vo, 10s. net. Edition for India and the Colonies, 5s. net.

"OLE LUK-OIE."
THE GREEN CURVE. By "OLE LUK-OIE." Third Impression. Crown 8vo, 6s. Cheap Edition, 1s net.

OLIPHANT, C. F.
ALFRED DE MUSSET. (Foreign Classics for English Readers.) By C. F. OLIPHANT. Fcap. 8vo, 1s. net.

OLIPHANT, LAURENCE.
PICCADILLY. By LAURENCE OLIPHANT. With Illustrations by Richard Doyle. 4s. 6d. New Edition, 3s. 6d. Cheap Edition, boards, 2s. 6d.

OLIPHANT, MRS.
ANNALS OF A PUBLISHING HOUSE. William Blackwood and his Sons; Their Magazine and Friends. By MRS OLIPHANT. With Four Portraits. Third Edition. Demy 8vo. Vols. I. and II. £2, 2s.
A WIDOW'S TALE, AND OTHER STORIES. With an Introductory Note by J. M. BARRIE. Second Edition. Crown 8vo, 6s.
KATIE STEWART, AND OTHER STORIES. New Edition. Crown 8vo, cloth, 3s. 6d. Illustrated Boards, 2s. 6d.
VALENTINE AND HIS BROTHER. New Edition. Crown 8vo, 3s. 6d.
SONS AND DAUGHTERS. Crown 8vo, 3s. 6d.
DANTE. (Foreign Classics for English Readers.) Fcap. 8vo, 1s. net.
CERVANTES. (Foreign Classics for English Readers.) Fcap. 8vo, 1s. net.
THE PERPETUAL CURATE. Illustrated boards, 2s.; cloth, 2s. 6d.
JOHN: A LOVE STORY. Illustrated boards, 2s.; cloth, 2s. 6d.
THE RECTOR and THE DOCTOR'S FAMILY. Illustrated cover, 1s.; cloth, 1s. 6d.

OLIPHANT, MRS, and TARVER, F.
MOLIÈRE. (Foreign Classics for English Readers.) By MRS OLIPHANT and F. TARVER. Fcap. 8vo, 1s. net.

OMOND, T. S.
THE ROMANTIC TRIUMPH. "Periods of European Literature." By T. S. OMOND. Crown 8vo, 5s. net.

O'NEILL, MOIRA.
SONGS OF THE GLENS OF ANTRIM. By MOIRA O'NEILL. Fourteenth Impression. Crown 8vo, 3s. 6d.

OXENDEN, MAUD.
THE STORY OF ESTHER. By MAUD OXENDEN. Crown 8vo, 6s.

PAGE AND LAPWORTH.
INTERMEDIATE TEXT-BOOK OF GEOLOGY. By Professor LAPWORTH. Founded on Dr Page's 'Introductory Text-Book of Geology.' Crown 8vo, 5s.
ADVANCED TEXT-BOOK OF GEOLOGY. New Edition. Revised and Enlarged by Professor LAPWORTH. Crown 8vo. [In the press.
INTRODUCTORY TEXT-BOOK OF PHYSICAL GEOGRAPHY. Crown 8vo, 2s. 6d.
PHYSICAL GEOGRAPHY EXAMINATOR. Crown 8vo, sewed, 9d.

PATERSON, JOHN W., Ph.D.
A MANUAL OF AGRICUTURAL BOT-
ANY. From the German of Dr A. B.
Frank, Professor in the Royal Agricul-
tural College, Berlin. With over 100
Illustrations. Crown 8vo, 3s. 6d.

PATTISON, R. P. DUNN.
HISTORY OF THE 91ST ARGYLL-
SHIRE HIGHLANDERS. By R. P.
DUNN PATTISON. With Maps and Illus-
trations. Demy 4to, 42s. net.

PAUL, SIR JAMES BALFOUR.
HISTORY OF THE ROYAL COMPANY
OF ARCHERS, THE QUEEN'S BODY-
GUARD FOR SCOTLAND. By Sir JAMES
BALFOUR PAUL, Advocate of the Scot-
tish Bar. Crown 4to, with Portraits
and other Illustrations. £2, 2s.

PEARSE, COLONEL.
MEMOIR OF THE LIFE AND MILI-
TARY SERVICES OF VISCOUNT
LAKE, BARON LAKE OF DELHI AND
LASWAREE, 1744-1808. By Colonel HUGH
PEARSE. With Portraits, &c. Demy
8vo, 15s. net.;

**PERIODS OF EUROPEAN LITERA-
TURE.** Edited by Professor SAINTS-
BURY. For List of Vols., see p. 32.

**PHILOSOPHICAL CLASSICS FOR
ENGLISH READERS.** Edited by
WILLIAM KNIGHT, LL.D., Professor of
Moral Philosophy, University of St
Andrews. Cheap Re-issue in Shilling
Volumes net. For List of Vols., see p. 32.

PIELE, LIEUT.-COLONEL S. C. F.
LAWN TENNIS AS A GAME OF
SKILL. By Lieut.-Col. S. C. F. PIELE.
Seventh Edition. Fcap. 8vo, 1s.

POLLOK, ROBERT, A.M.
THE COURSE OF TIME: A POEM. By
ROBERT POLLOK, A.M. New Edition.
With Portrait. Fcap. 8vo, gilt top,
2s. 6d.

PORTER, MARY BLACKWOOD.
JOHN BLACKWOOD, EDITOR AND
PUBLISHER. By MARY BLACKWOOD
PORTER. With Two Portraits and view
of Strathtyrum. Demy 8vo, 21s.

**POTTS, A. W., M.A., LL.D., and
DARNELL, REV. C., M.A.**
AUDITUS FACILIORES. An Easy
Latin Construing Book, with Vocabu-
lary. By A. W. POTTS, M.A., LL.D.,
Late Headmaster of the Fettes College,
Edinburgh, and sometime Fellow of St
John's College, Cambridge; and the
Rev. C. DARNELL, M.A., Late Head-
master of Cargilfield Preparatory School,
Edinburgh, and Scholar of Pembroke
and Downing Colleges, Cambridge.
1s. 6d. net.

POTTS and DARNELL—contd.
ADITUS FACILIORES GRÆCI. An
easy grade construing book. With
complete vocabulary. Fcap 8vo, 3s.

**POTTS, A. W., M.A., LL.D., and
HEARD, W. A., M.A., LL.D.**
CAMENARUM FLOSCULOS in Usum
Fettesianorum decerptos notis quibus-
dam illustraverunt A. GUL. POTTS,
M.A., LL.D.; GUL. A. HEARD, M.A.,
LL.D. New Impression. Crown 8vo,
3s. 6d.

PRESTON-THOMAS, H., C.B.
THE WORK AND PLAY OF A
GOVERNMENT INSPECTOR. By
HERBERT PRESTON-THOMAS, C.B. With
a Preface by the Right Hon. JOHN
BURNS, M.P. Demy 8vo, 10s. 6d. net.

**PRINGLE - PATTISON, A. SETH,
LL.D., D.C.L.**
SCOTTISH PHILOSOPHY. A Compari-
son of the Scottish and German Answers
to Hume. Balfour Philosophical Lec-
tures, University of Edinburgh. By
A. SETH PRINGLE - PATTISON, LL.D.,
D.C.L., Fellow of the British Academy,
Professor of Logic and Metaphysics in
Edinburgh University. Fourth Edition.
Crown 8vo, 5s.
MAN'S PLACE IN THE COSMOS, AND
OTHER ESSAYS. Second Edition, En-
larged. Post 8vo, 6s. net.
TWO LECTURES ON THEISM. De-
livered on the occasion of the Sesqui-
centennial Celebration of Princeton
University. Crown 8vo, 2s. 6d.
THE PHILOSOPHICAL RADICALS,
AND OTHER ESSAYS, including Chapters
reprinted on the Philosophy of Religion
in Kant and Hegel. Crown 8vo, 6s. net.

**PUBLIC GENERAL STATUTES
AFFECTING SCOTLAND from
1707 to 1847, with Chronological
Table and Index.** 3 vols. large 8vo,
£3, 3s. Also Published Annually, with
General Index.

"Q" (SIR A. T. QUILLER-COUCH).
HOCKEN AND HUNKEN. By "Q"
(Sir A. T. QUILLER-COUCH). Crown
8vo, 6s.

RANJITSINHJI, PRINCE.
THE JUBILEE BOOK OF CRICKET.
By PRINCE RANJITSINHJI.
Popular Edition. With 107 full-page
Illustrations. Sixth Edition. Large
crown 8vo, 6s.

REEVE, HENRY, C.B.
PETRARCH. (Foreign Classics for Eng-
lish Readers.) By HENRY REEVE, C.B.
Fcap. 8vo, 1s. net.

REYNARD, CAPTAIN F.
THE HISTORY OF THE NINTH
LANCERS FROM 1715 to 1903. By
Capt. F. REYNARD. Royal 8vo, 42s. net.

RICHARDS, H. GRAHAME.
RICHARD SOMERS. By H. GRAHAME
RICHARDS. Crown 8vo, 6s.
LUCREZIA BORGIA'S ONE LOVE.
Second Impression. Crown 8vo, 6s.

RICHARDSON, MAJOR E. H.
WAR, POLICE, AND WATCH DOGS.
By Major E. H. RICHARDSON. With
Illustrations. Crown 8vo, 5s. net.

RIVETT-CARNAC, J. H., C.I.E.
MANY MEMORIES OF LIFE IN
INDIA, AT HOME, AND ABROAD.
By J. H. RIVETT-CARNAC, C.I.E. With
Portraits. Second Impression. Demy
8vo, 10s. 6d. net.

ROBERTSON, PROFESSOR CROOM.
HOBBES. (Philosophical Classics for
English Readers.) By Professor CROOM
ROBERTSON. Fcap. 8vo, 1s. net.

ROBERTSON, JAMES, D.D.
EARLY RELIGIONS OF ISRAEL. New
and Revised Edition. Crown 8vo.
[*In the press.*
THE POETRY AND THE RELIGION
OF THE PSALMS. The Croall Lec-
tures, 1893-94. By JAMES ROBERTSON,
D.D., Professor of Oriental Languages in
the University of Glasgow. Demy 8vo,
12s.

ROBERTSON, JOHN G., Ph.D.
A HISTORY OF GERMAN LITERA-
TURE. By JOHN G. ROBERTSON,
Ph.D., Professor of German, University
of London. Demy 8vo, 10s. 6d. net.
OUTLINES OF THE HISTORY OF
GERMAN LITERATURE. Crown 8vo,
3s. 6d. net.
SCHILLER AFTER A CENTURY.
Crown 8vo, 2s. 6d. net.

RONALDSHAY, EARL OF, M.P.
ON THE OUTSKIRTS OF EMPIRE IN
ASIA. By the EARL OF RONALDSHAY,
M.P. With numerous Illustrations and
Maps. Royal 8vo, 21s. net.
SPORT AND POLITICS UNDER AN
EASTERN SKY. With numerous Il-
lustrations and Maps. Royal 8vo, 21s.
net.
A WANDERING STUDENT IN THE
FAR EAST. With Maps and 60 Illus-
trations. 2 vols. short demy 8vo, 21s.
net.
AN EASTERN MISCELLANY. Demy
8vo, 10s. 6d. net.

RUTHERFURD, J. H.
THE HISTORY OF THE LINLITH-
GOW AND STIRLINGSHIRE HUNT.
From 1775 to the present. By J. H.
RUTHERFURD. With Illustrations.
Demy 8vo, 25s. net.

RUTLAND, DUKE OF, G.C.B.
NOTES OF AN IRISH TOUR IN 1846.
By the DUKE OF RUTLAND, G.C.B.
(LORD JOHN MANNERS). New Edition.
Crown 8vo, 2s. 6d.

RUTLAND, DUCHESS OF.
THE COLLECTED WRITINGS OF
JANETTA, DUCHESS OF RUTLAND.
By the DUCHESS OF RUTLAND (LADY
JOHN MANNERS). With Portrait and
Illustrations. 2 vols. post 8vo, 15s. net.
IMPRESSIONS OF BAD-HOMBURG.
Comprising a Short Account of the
Women's Associations of Germany under
the Red Cross. Crown 8vo, 1s. 6d.
SOME PERSONAL RECOLLECTIONS
of the Later Years of the Earl of Beacons-
field, K.G. Sixth Edition. 6d.
SOME OF THE ADVANTAGES of
Easily Accessible Reading and Recrea-
tion Rooms and Free Libraries. With
Remarks on Starting and Maintaining
them. Second Edition. Crown 8vo, 1s.
ENCOURAGING EXPERIENCES of
Reading and Recreation Rooms, Aims
of Guilds, Nottingham Social Guide,
Existing Institutions, &c., &c. Crown
8vo, 1s.

ST QUINTIN, COLONEL T. A.
CHANCES OF SPORTS OF SORTS.
By Colonel T. A. ST QUINTIN. Illus-
trated. Demy 8vo, 16s. net.

SAINTSBURY, PROFESSOR.
A HISTORY OF CRITICISM AND
LITERARY TASTE IN EUROPE.
From the Earliest Texts to the Present
Day. By GEORGE SAINTSBURY, M.A.
(Oxon.), Hon. LL.D. (Aberd.), Professor
of Rhetoric and English Literature in
the University of Edinburgh. In 3
vols. demy 8vo. Vol. I.—Classical and
Mediæval Criticism. 16s. net. Vol. II.
—From the Renaissance to the Decline
of Eighteenth Century Orthodoxy. 20s.
net. Vol. III.—Nineteenth Century.
20s. net.
MATTHEW ARNOLD. "Modern Eng-
lish Writers." Second Edition. Crown
8vo, 2s. 6d.
THE FLOURISHING OF ROMANCE
AND THE RISE OF ALLEGORY
(12TH AND 13TH CENTURIES). "Periods
of European Literature." Crown 8vo,
5s. net.
THE EARLIER RENAISSANCE.
"Periods of European Literature."
Crown 8vo, 5s. net.
THE LATER NINETEENTH CEN-
TURY. "Periods of European Litera-
ture." Crown 8vo, 5s. net.
A HISTORY OF ENGLISH CRITIC-
ISM. Demy 8vo, 7s. 6d. net.

SALMON, ARTHUR L.
SONGS OF A HEART'S SURRENDER.
By ARTHUR L. SALMON. Crown 8vo, 2s.
LIFE OF LIFE, AND OTHER POEMS.
Crown 8vo, 2s. 6d.
LYRICS AND VERSES. Crown 8vo,
2s. 6d.
A BOOK OF VERSES. Crown 8vo,
2s. 6d. net.
WEST COUNTRY VERSES. Crown
8vo, 3s. net.
A LITTLE BOOK OF SONGS. Fcap.
8vo, 2s. 6d. net.
A NEW BOOK OF VERSE. Fcap. 8vo,
2s. 6d. net.

SCHOOL CATECHISM.
Issued by a CONFERENCE OF MEMBERS
OF THE REFORMED CHURCHES IN SCOT-
LAND. 18mo, ½d.

"SCOLOPAX."
A BOOK OF THE SNIPE. By
"SCOLOPAX." Illustrated. Crown 8vo,
5s. net.

SCOTT, SIR J. GEORGE, K.C.I.E.
CURSED LUCK. By Sir J. GEORGE
SCOTT, K.C.I.E. Crown 8vo, 3s. 6d.

SCOTT, MICHAEL.
TOM CRINGLE'S LOG. By MICHAEL
SCOTT. New Edition. With 19 Full-
page Illustrations. Crown 8vo, 3s. 6d.
THE CRUISE OF THE MIDGE.
Illustrated boards, 2s.; cloth, 2s. 6d.

**SCOTTISH TEXT SOCIETY PUBLI-
CATIONS.** For List of Vols., see p. 29.

SCOTTISH BANKERS MAGAZINE.
The Journal of the Institute of Bankers
in Scotland. Quarterly, 1s. net.

SCUDAMORE, CYRIL.
BELGIUM AND THE BELGIANS.
By CYRIL SCUDAMORE. With Illustra-
tions. Square crown 8vo, 6s.

SELLAR, E. M.
RECOLLECTIONS AND IMPRES-
SIONS. By E. M. SELLAR. With
Eight Portraits. Fourth Impression.
Demy 8vo, 10s. 6d. net.

SELLAR, EDMUND.
MUGGINS OF THE MODERN SIDE.
By EDMUND SELLAR. Crown 8vo, 6s.
GLENTYRE. Crown 8vo, 6s.
WHERE EVERY PROSPECT PLEASES.
Crown 8vo, 6s.

SETH, JAMES, M.A.
A STUDY OF ETHICAL PRINCIPLES.
By JAMES SETH, M.A., Professor of
Moral Philosophy in the University of
Edinburgh. Tenth Edition, Revised.
Post 8vo, 7s. 6d.

SHARPLEY, H.
ARISTOPHANES—PAX. Edited, with
Introduction and Notes, by H. SHARP-
LEY. Demy 8vo, 12s. 6d. net.

SHAW, WILLIAM.
SECURITIES OVER MOVEABLES.
Four Lectures delivered at the Request
of the Society of Accountants in Edinburgh, the Institute of Accountants
and Actuaries in Glasgow, and the
Institute of Bankers in Scotland in
1902-3. Demy 8vo, 3s. 6d. net.

SHEEPSHANKS, RICHARD.
HECTOR AND ACHILLES: A TALE
OF TROY. Illustrated by J. FINNE-
MORE. Rendered into English after the
Chronicle of Homer by RICHARD
SHEEPSHANKS. Square crown 8vo, 5s.
net.

SIME, JAMES, M.A.
SCHILLER. (Foreign Classics for Eng-
lish Readers.) By JAMES SIME, M.A.
Fcap. 8vo, 1s. net.

SIMPSON, PROFESSOR J. Y., D.Sc.
SIDE-LIGHTS ON SIBERIA. Some
Account of the Great Siberian Iron
Road: The Prisons and Exile System.
By Professor J. Y. SIMPSON, D.Sc.
With numerous Illustrations and a
Map. Demy 8vo, 16s.

SIMPSON, VIOLET A.
IN FANCY'S MIRROR. By VIOLET A.
SIMPSON. Crown 8vo, 6s.

SINCLAIR, EDITH.
HIS HONOUR AND HIS LOVE. By
EDITH SINCLAIR. Crown 8vo, 6s.

SINCLAIR, ISABEL G.
THE THISTLE AND FLEUR DE LYS.
By ISABEL G. SINCLAIR. Crown 8vo,
3s. net.

SKELTON, SIR JOHN, K.C.B.
THE HANDBOOK OF PUBLIC
HEALTH. A New Edition. Revised by
JAMES PATTEN MACDOUGALL, C.B., Advocate, Secretary to the Local Government Board for Scotland, Joint-Author
of 'The Parish Council Guide for Scotland,' and ABIJAH MURRAY, Chief Clerk
of the Local Government Board for
Scotland. 3s. 6d. net.

SKRINE, F. H.
FONTENOY, AND GREAT BRITAIN'S
SHARE IN THE WAR OF THE AUSTRIAN
SUCCESSION. By F. H. SKRINE. With
Map, Plans, and Illustrations. Demy
8vo, 21s. net.

SLATER, FRANCIS CAREY.
FROM MIMOSA LAND. By FRANCIS
CAREY SLATER. Crown 8vo, 3s. 6d. net.

SMITH, PROFESSOR G. GREGORY.
THE TRANSITION PERIOD. "Periods
of European Literature." By G.
GREGORY SMITH, M.A. (Oxon.), Pro-
fessor of English Literature, Belfast
University. Crown 8vo, 5s. net.

SPECIMENS OF MIDDLE SCOTS.
Post 8vo, 7s. 6d. net.

SNELL, F. J.
THE FOURTEENTH CENTURY.
"Periods of European Literature." By
F. J. SNELL. Crown 8vo, 5s. net.

"SON OF THE MARSHES, A."
WITHIN AN HOUR OF LONDON
TOWN: AMONG WILD BIRDS AND THEIR
HAUNTS. Edited by J. A. OWEN.
Cheap Uniform Edition. Crown 8vo,
3s. 6d.

WITH THE WOODLANDERS AND
BY THE TIDE. Cheap Uniform Edition. Crown 8vo, 3s. 6d.

ON SURREY HILLS. Cheap Uniform
Edition. Crown 8vo, 3s. 6d.

ANNALS OF A FISHING VILLAGE.
Cheap Uniform Edition. Crown 8vo,
3s. 6d.

SORLEY, PROF., Litt.D., LL.D.
THE ETHICS OF NATURALISM. By
W. R. SORLEY, Litt.D., LL.D., Fellow
of the British Academy, Fellow of
Trinity College, Cambridge, Professor
of Moral Philosophy, University of
Cambridge. Second Edition. Crown
8vo, 6s.

RECENT TENDENCIES IN ETHICS.
Crown 8vo, 2s. 6d. net.

SPROTT, GEORGE W., D.D.
THE WORSHIP AND OFFICES OF
THE CHURCH OF SCOTLAND.
By GEORGE W. SPROTT, D.D. Crown
8vo, 6s.

THE BOOK OF COMMON ORDER
OF THE CHURCH OF SCOTLAND,
Commonly known as JOHN KNOX's
LITURGY. With Historical Introduction
and Illustrative Notes. Crown 8vo,
4s. 6d. net.

SCOTTISH LITURGIES OF THE
REIGN OF JAMES VI. Edited with
an Introduction and Notes. Crown
8vo, 4s. net.

EUCHOLOGION. A Book of Common
Order. Crown 8vo, 4s. 6d. net.

**ST ANDREWS UNIVERSITY CAL-
ENDAR.** Printed and Published for
the Senatus Academicus. Crown 8vo,
2s. 6d. net.

**ST ANDREWS UNIVERSITY L.L.A.
CALENDAR.** Printed and Published
for the Senatus Academicus. Crown
8vo, 1s.

STEEVENS, G. W.
THINGS SEEN: IMPRESSIONS OF MEN,
CITIES, AND BOOKS. By the late G. W.
STEEVENS. Edited by G. S. STREET.
With a Memoir by W. E. HENLEY, and
a Photogravure reproduction of Collier's
Portrait. Memorial Edition. Crown
8vo, 6s.

FROM CAPETOWN TO LADYSMITH,
and EGYPT IN 1898. Memorial Edition. Crown 8vo, 6s.

IN INDIA. With Map. Memorial Edition. Crown 8vo, 6s.

THE LAND OF THE DOLLAR. Memorial Edition. Crown 8vo, 6s.

GLIMPSES OF THREE NATIONS.
Memorial Edition. Crown 8vo, 6s.

MONOLOGUES OF THE DEAD. Memorial Edition. Crown 8vo, 3s. 6d.

STEPHENS.
THE BOOK OF THE FARM; dealing
exhaustively with every Branch of
Agriculture. Edited by JAMES MAC-
DONALD, F.R.S.E., Secretary of the
Highland and Agricultural Society of
Scotland. With over 700 Illustrations
and Animal Portraits. In Six Divisional
Volumes at 10s. 6d. net each; or Three
Volumes of over 500 pages each, price
21s. net per Volume. Each Volume sold
separately.

LAND AND ITS EQUIPMENT. With
346 Illustrations and 8 Plans of Farm
Buildings. Royal 8vo, 21s. net.

FARM CROPS. With 354 Illustrations.
Royal 8vo, 21s. net.

FARM LIVE STOCK. With 77 Illustrations and 84 Animal Portraits. Royal
8vo, 21s. net.

STEVENSON, G. H.
THE SILVER SPOON. By G. H.
STEVENSON. Crown 8vo, 6s.

STEWART, CHARLES.
HAUD IMMEMOR. Reminiscences of
Legal and Social Life in Edinburgh
and London, 1850-1900. By CHARLES
STEWART. With 10 Photogravure Plates.
Royal 8vo 7s. 6d.

STEWART and CUFF.
PRACTICAL NURSING. By ISLA STEWART, Matron of St Bartholomew's Hospital, London; and HERBERT E. CUFF, M.D., F.R.C.S., Medical Officer for General Purposes to the Metropolitan Asylums' Board, London; late Medical Superintendent, North-Eastern Fever Hospital, Tottenham, London. Revised by H. E. CUFF; assisted by B. CUTLER, Assistant Matron of St Bartholomew's Hospital. Third Edition. Crown 8vo, 5s. net. Also in 2 volumes, each 3s. 6d. net.

STODDART, ANNA M.
LIFE AND LETTERS OF HANNAH E. PIPE. By ANNA M. STODDART. With Portraits and Illustrations. Demy 8vo, 15s. net.

STORMONTH, REV. JAMES.
DICTIONARY OF THE ENGLISH LANGUAGE, PRONOUNCING, ETYMOLOGICAL, AND EXPLANATORY. By the Rev. JAMES STORMONTH. Revised by the Rev. P. H. PHELP. Library Edition. New and Cheaper Edition, with Supplement. Imperial 8vo, handsomely bound in half morocco, 18s. net.
ETYMOLOGICAL AND PRONOUNCING DICTIONARY OF THE ENGLISH LANGUAGE. Including a very Copious Selection of Scientific Terms. For use in Schools and Colleges, and as a Book of General Reference. The Pronunciation carefully revised by the Rev. P. H. PHELP, M.A. Cantab. A New Edition. Edited by WILLIAM BAYNE. Crown 8vo, pp. 1082. 5s. net.
HANDY SCHOOL DICTIONARY, PRONOUNCING AND EXPLANATORY. Thoroughly Revised and Enlarged by WILLIAM BAYNE. 16mo, 7d. net.

SWAYNE, G. C.
HERODOTUS. (Ancient Classics for English Readers.) By G. C. SWAYNE. Fcap. 8vo, 1s. net.

SYLLABUS OF RELIGIOUS INSTRUCTION FOR PUBLIC SCHOOLS.
Issued by a CONFERENCE OF MEMBERS OF THE REFORMED CHURCHES IN SCOTLAND. 18mo, 1d.

SYNGE, M. B.
THE STORY OF THE WORLD. By M. B. SYNGE. With Coloured Frontispieces and numerous Illustrations by E. M. SYNGE, A.R.E., and Maps. 2 vols., 3s. 6d. each net.

TABLE OF FEES FOR CONVEYANCING, &c. 4to. Roxburgh, 3s. 6d.; sewed, 2s. 6d.

THACKERAY, MISS.
MADAME DE SÉVIGNÉ. (Foreign Classics for English Readers.) By Miss THACKERAY. Fcap. 8vo, 1s. net.

THEOBALD, FRED. V., M.A. (Cantab.)
A TEXT-BOOK OF AGRICULTURAL ZOOLOGY. By FRED. V. THEOBALD. With numerous Illustrations. Crown 8vo, 8s. 6d.

THOMSON, COLONEL ANSTRUTHER.
HISTORY OF THE FIFE LIGHT HORSE. By Colonel ANSTRUTHER THOMSON. With numerous Portraits. Small 4to, 21s. net.

THOMSON, DAVID.
HANDY BOOK OF THE FLOWER-GARDEN. By DAVID THOMSON. Crown 8vo, 5s.

THOMSON, WILLIAM.
A PRACTICAL TREATISE ON THE CULTIVATION OF THE GRAPE VINE. By WILLIAM THOMSON, Tweed Vineyards. Tenth Edition. 8vo, 5s.

THORBURN, S. S.
ASIATIC NEIGHBOURS. By S. S. THORBURN. With Two Maps. Demy 8vo, 10s. 6d. net.
THE PUNJAB IN PEACE AND WAR. Demy 8vo, 12s. 6d. net.
INDIA'S SAINT AND THE VICEROY. A Novel. Crown 8vo, 6s.

THURSTON, KATHERINE CECIL.
THE CIRCLE. By KATHERINE CECIL THURSTON. Ninth Impression. Crown 8vo, 6s.
JOHN CHILCOTE, M.P. Fifteenth Impression, crown 8vo, 6s. Cheap Edition, 1s. net. People's Edition, 6d.
THE MYSTICS. With Illustrations. Crown 8vo, 3s. 6d.
THE FLY ON THE WHEEL. Crown 8vo, 6s.

TIELE, PROFESSOR, Litt.D., &c.
ELEMENTS OF THE SCIENCE OF RELIGION. Part I.—Morphological. Part II.—Ontological. Being the Gifford Lectures delivered before the University of Edinburgh in 1896-98. By C. P. TIELE, Theol.D., Litt.D. (Bonon.), Hon. M.R.A.S., &c., Professor of the Science of Religion in the University of Leiden. In 2 vols. post 8vo, 7s. 6d. net each.

TIME, MARK.
A DERELICT EMPIRE. By MARK TIME. Second Impression. Crown 8vo, 6s.

TRANSACTIONS OF THE HIGHLAND AND AGRICULTURAL SOCIETY OF SCOTLAND. Published Annually, price 5s.

TRAVERS, GRAHAM (Margaret Todd, M.D.)
THE WAY OF ESCAPE. A Novel. By GRAHAM TRAVERS (Margaret Todd, M.D.) Second Impression. Crown 8vo, 6s.
WINDYHAUGH. Fourth Edition. Crown 8vo, 6s.
FELLOW TRAVELLERS. Fourth Edition. Crown 8vo, 6s.

TROLLOPE, ANTHONY.
CÆSAR. (Ancient Classics for English Readers.) By ANTHONY TROLLOPE. Fcap. 8vo, 1s. net.

TROLLOPE, HENRY M.
CORNEILLE AND RACINE. (Foreign Classics for English Readers.) By HENRY M. TROLLOPE. Fcap. 8vo, 1s. net.

TRUSCOTT, L. PARRY.
THE MARRIAGE OF AMINTA. By L. PARRY TRUSCOTT. Crown 8vo, 6s.

TULLOCH, PRINCIPAL.
PASCAL. (Foreign Classics for English Readers.) By Principal TULLOCH. Fcap. 8vo, 1s. net.

TURNER, STANLEY HORSFALL, M.A.
THE HISTORY OF LOCAL TAXATION IN SCOTLAND. By STANLEY HORSFALL TURNER, M.A. Crown 8vo, 5s. net.

VAUGHAN, PROFESSOR C. E.
THE ROMANTIC REVOLT. By Professor C. E. VAUGHAN. Crown 8vo, 5s. net.

VEITCH, PROFESSOR.
HAMILTON. (Philosophical Classics for English Readers.) By Professor VEITCH. Fcap. 8vo, 1s. net.

VERNÈDE, R. E.
AN IGNORANT IN INDIA. By R. E. VERNÈDE. Crown 8vo, 5s. net.

VOYAGE OF THE "SCOTIA," THE.
Being the Record of a Voyage of Exploration in Antarctic Seas. By THREE OF THE STAFF. Demy 8vo, 21s. net.

WADDELL, REV. P. HATELY, D.D.
ESSAYS ON FAITH. By Rev. P. HATELY WADDELL, D.D. Crown 8vo, ?s. 6d.
THOUGHTS ON MODERN MYSTICISM. Crown 8vo, 3s. 6d.

WAKE, LUCY.
LADY WAKE'S REMINISCENCES. By LUCY WAKE. With Portraits and Illustrations. Second Impression. Demy 8vo, 12s. 6d. net.

WALFORD, E.
JUVENAL. (Ancient Classics for English Readers.) By E. WALFORD. Fcap. 8vo, 1s. net.

WALLACE, PROFESSOR.
KANT. (Philosophical Classics for English Readers.) By Professor WALLACE. Fcap. 8vo, 1s. net.

WARREN, SAMUEL.
DIARY OF A LATE PHYSICIAN. By SAMUEL WARREN. Cloth, 2s. 6d.; boards, 2s.; paper cover, 1s.
NOW AND THEN. The Lily and the Bee. Intellectual and Moral Development of the Present Age. 4s. 6d.

WATSON, GILBERT.
THE SKIPPER. By GILBERT WATSON. Crown 8vo, 6s.

WATT, MACLEAN.
BY STILL WATERS. By MACLEAN WATT. 1s. 6d.; leather, 2s.

WEIGALL, ARTHUR E. P.
TRAVELS IN THE UPPER EGYPTIAN DESERTS. By ARTHUR E. P. WEIGALL. With numerous Illustrations. Crown 8vo, 7s. 6d. net
THE LIFE AND TIMES OF AKHNATON, PHARAOH OF EGYPT. Illustrated. Second Impression. Crown 8vo, 10s. 6d. net.
THE TREASURY OF ANCIENT EGYPT. Chapters on Ancient Egyptian History and Archæology. With Illustrations. Demy 8vo, 7s. 6d. net.

WENLEY, PROFESSOR, D.Sc., D.Phil.
ASPECTS OF PESSIMISM. By R. M. WENLEY, M.A., D.Sc., D.Phil., Professor of Philosophy in the University of Michigan, U.S.A. Crown 8vo, 6s.

WHIBLEY, CHARLES.
THACKERAY. "Modern English Writers." By CHARLES WHIBLEY. Crown 8vo, 2s. 6d.
WILLIAM PITT. With Portraits and Caricatures. Crown 8vo, 6s. net.
AMERICAN SKETCHES. Crown 8vo, 6s.

WHISPER, A.
KING AND CAPTIVE. By A. WHISPER. Crown 8vo, 6s.
THE SINISTER NOTE. Crown 8vo, 6s.

WHITE, REV. JAMES.
SIR FRIZZLE PUMPKIN, NIGHTS AT MESS, &c. By Rev. JAMES WHITE. Illustrated cover, 1s.; cloth, 1s 6d

WHYTE, ADAM GOWANS.
THE TEMPLETON TRADITION. By ADAM GOWANS WHYTE. Crown 8vo, 6s.
YELLOWSANDS. Crown 8vo, 6s.

WILSON, CHRISTOPHER.
THE MISSING MILLIONAIRE. By CHRISTOPHER WILSON. Crown 8vo, 6s.
THE HEART OF DELILAH. Crown 8vo, 6s.

WILSON, LADY.
LETTERS FROM INDIA. By LADY WILSON. Demy 8vo, 7s. 6d. net.

WILSON, PROFESSOR.
WORKS OF PROFESSOR WILSON. Edited by his Son-in-Law, Professor FERRIER. 12 vols. crown 8vo, £2, 8s.
THE NOCTES AMBROSIANÆ. 4 vols., 16s.
ESSAYS, CRITICAL AND IMAGINATIVE. 4 vols., 16s.
CHRISTOPHER IN HIS SPORTING-JACKET. 2 vols., 8s.
LIGHTS AND SHADOWS OF SCOTTISH LIFE, AND OTHER TALES. 4s.
ISLE OF PALMS, CITY OF THE PLAGUE, AND OTHER POEMS. 4s.

WINRAM, JAMES.
VIOLIN PLAYING and VIOLIN ADJUSTMENT. By JAMES WINRAM. Crown 8vo, 5s. net.

WORSLEY, PHILIP STANHOPE, M.A.
HOMER'S ODYSSEY. Translated into English Verse in the Spenserian Stanza. By PHILIP STANHOPE WORSLEY, M.A. New and Cheaper Edition. Post 8vo, 7s. 6d. net.

WOTHERSPOON, H. J., M.A.
KYRIE ELEISON ("LORD, HAVE MERCY"). A Manual of Private Prayers. With Notes and Additional Matter. By H. J. WOTHERSPOON, M.A., of St Oswald's, Edinburgh. Cloth, red edges, 1s. net; limp leather, 1s. 6d. net.

BEFORE AND AFTER. Being Part I. of 'Kyrie Eleison.' Cloth, limp, 6d. net.

THE SECOND PRAYER BOOK OF KING EDWARD THE SIXTH (1552), ALONG WITH THE LITURGY OF COMPROMISE. Edited by Rev. G. W. SPROTT, D.D. Crown 8vo, 4s. net.

YATE, LIEUT.-COLONEL, M.P.
KHURASAN AND SISTAN. By Lieut-Colonel C. E. YATE, C.S.I., C.M.G. With numerous Illustrations and Map. Demy 8vo, 21s.

NORTHERN AFGHANISTAN; OR, LETTERS FROM THE AFGHAN BOUNDARY COMMISSION. With Route Maps. Demy 8vo, 18s.

BLACKWOODS'
Shilling Editions of Popular Novels.

Bound in Cloth. With Coloured Illustration on Wrapper.

THE DAFT DAYS.
By NEIL MUNRO.

THE LUNATIC AT LARGE.
By J. STORER CLOUSTON.

CAPTAIN DESMOND, V.C.
By MAUD DIVER.

THE GREAT AMULET.
By MAUD DIVER.

CANDLES IN THE WIND.
By MAUD DIVER.

SARACINESCA.
By F. MARION CRAWFORD.

THE MOON OF BATH.
By BETH ELLIS.

JOHN CHILCOTE, M.P.
By KATHERINE CECIL THURSTON.

THE POWER OF THE KEYS.
By SYDNEY C. GRIER.

"PIP": A Romance of Youth.
By IAN HAY.

THE RED NEIGHBOUR.
By W. J. ECCOTT.

THE GREEN CURVE.
By OLE LUK-OIE.

THE RIGHT STUFF.
By IAN HAY.

IN HIGHLAND HARBOURS WITH PARA HANDY.
By HUGH FOULIS.

A MAN'S MAN.
By IAN HAY.

FANCY FARM.
By NEIL MUNRO.

THE ADVANCED GUARD.
By SYDNEY C. GRIER.

The Scottish Text Society.

THIS SOCIETY was founded in 1882 for the purpose of printing and editing texts in Early and Middle Scots. Two parts or volumes, extending to not less than 400 pages, are published annually; but additional parts or volumes are issued when the funds permit. They are printed in uniform style, octavo, and are issued (*a*) in paper covers, or (*b*) bound in half-leather (maroon), with cloth sides, gilt top, and gilt lettering. The Annual Subscription is £1, 1s. (One Guinea), payable in advance. Specimen Volumes may be seen at the Society's Printers, Messrs William Blackwood & Sons, 45 George Street, Edinburgh, and 37 Paternoster Row, London, or in any of the libraries in Great Britain and abroad.

Note.—The volumes have been issued in half-leather since 1897. Earlier volumes are in paper covers only; but they may be bound to the Society's pattern at the cost of 1s. 6d. per volume. Most of the back volumes are in print, and may be purchased by subscribers. Particulars of price, &c., may be had on application to the Treasurer.

LIST OF PUBLICATIONS.

The Kingis Quair, together with A Ballad of Good Counsel. By King James I. Edited by the Rev. Professor W. W. Skeat, M.A., LL.D. pp. 113 and lv.

The Poems of William Dunbar. Part I. Edited by John Small, M.A. pp. 160 and iv.

The Court of Venus, By Iohne Rolland, 1575. Edited by the Rev. Walter Gregor, M.A., LL.D. pp. 231 and xxxii.

The Poems of William Dunbar. Part II. Edited by John Small, M.A. pp. 169 and vi.

Leslie's Historie of Scotland. Part I. Translated into Scottish from the original Latin by Father James Dalrymple. Edited by the Rev. E. G. Cody, O.S.B. pp. 130 and iv.

Schir William Wallace, Knight of Ellerslie. Part I. By Henry the Minstrel, commonly known as Blind Harry. Edited by James Moir, M.A. pp. 181.

The Wallace. Part II. Edited by James Moir, M.A. pp. 198.

Sir Tristrem. With Introduction, Notes, and Glossary. Edited by G. P. M'Neill, M.A. pp. 148 and xlviii.

The Poems of Alexander Montgomerie. Part I. Edited by James Cranstoun, M.A., LL.D. pp. 176 and vii.

The Poems of Alexander Montgomerie. Part II. Edited by James Cranstoun, M.A., LL.D. pp. 160 and iv.

The Poems of Alexander Montgomerie. Part III. Edited by James Cranstoun, M.A., LL.D. pp. 96 and lvii.

Gau's Richt Vay to the Kingdome of Heuine. Edited by the Rev. Professor Mitchell, D.D. pp. 130 and lviii.

Legends of the Saints (Fourteenth Century). Part I. Edited by the Rev. W. M. Metcalfe, M.A. pp. 224 and v.

Leslie's Historie of Scotland. Part II. Edited by the Rev. E. G. Cody, O.S.B. pp. 270 and xxvi.

Niniane Winȝet's Works. Vol. I. Edited by the Rev. J. King Hewison. pp. 140 and cxx.

The Poems of William Dunbar. Part III. Introduction. By Æ. J. G. Mackay, LL.D. pp. cclxxxiii.

The Wallace. Part III. Introduction, Notes, and Glossary. By James Moir, M.A. pp. 189 and liv.

Legends of the Saints. Part II. Edited by the Rev. W. M. Metcalfe, M.A. pp. 386 and iii.

Leslie's Historie of Scotland. Part III. Edited by the Rev. E. G. Cody, O.S.B. pp. 262 and iii.

Satirical Poems of the Time of the Reformation. Part I. Edited by James Cranstoun, M.A., LL.D. pp. 220 and vi.

The Poems of William Dunbar. Part IV. Containing the first portion of the Notes. By the Rev. W. Gregor, LL.D. pp. 244.

Niniane Winȝet's Works. Vol. II. Notes and Glossary. By the Rev. J. King Hewison. pp. 203 and xxxiii.

Legends of the Saints. Part III. Edited by the Rev. W. M. Metcalfe, M.A. pp. 192 and iii.

Satirical Poems of the Time of the Reformation. Part II. Edited by James Cranstoun, M.A., LL.D. pp. 181 and lix.

Legends of tne Saints. Part IV. Completing the Text. Edited by the Rev. W. M. Metcalfe, M.A. pp. 285 and iii.

The Vernacular Writings of George Buchanan. Edited by P. Hume Brown, M.A., LL.D. pp. 75 and xxxviii.

Scottish Alliterative Poems in Riming Stanzas. Part I. Edited by F. J. Amours. pp. 187 and vi.

Satirical Poems of the Time of the Reformation. Part III. Containing first portion of Notes. By James Cranstoun, M.A., LL.D. pp. 188 and iii.

The Poems of William Dunbar. Part V. Completion of Notes and Glossary. By the Rev. W. Gregor, LL.D. And Appendix, by Æ. J. G. Mackay, LL.D. pp. 291.

Satirical Poems of the Time of the Reformation. Part IV. Completion of Notes, Appendix, Glossary, and Index of Proper Names. By James Cranstoun, M.A., LL.D. pp. 186 and xii.

Barbour's Bruce. Part I. Edited by the Rev. Professor Walter W. Skeat, M.A., LL.D. pp. 351 and iii.

Barbour's Bruce. Part II. Edited by the Rev. Professor Walter W. Skeat, M.A., LL.D. pp. 450 and viii.

Barbour's Bruce. Part III. Introduction. By the Rev. Professor Walter W. Skeat, M.A., LL.D. pp. cxi.

Leslie's Historie of Scotland. Edited by the Rev. E. G. Cody, O.S.B. Part IV. Completion of Text, with Notes, Glossary, &c. By William Murison, M.A. pp. 328 and vii.

Legends of the Saints. Part V. Notes (first portion). By the Rev. W. M. Metcalfe, D.D. pp. 256 and iv.

The Poems of Alexander Scott. Edited by James Cranstoun, M.A., LL.D. pp. 218 and xxii.

Legends of the Saints. Part VI. Completion of Notes and Glossary. By the Rev. W. M. Metcalfe, D.D. pp. 240 and l.

Scottish Alliterative Poems in Riming Stanzas. Part II. Edited by F. J. Amours. pp. 294 and xc.

The Gude and Godlie Ballatis. Edited by the Rev. Professor Mitchell, D.D. pp. 338 and cliv.

The Works of Mure of Rowallan. Vol. I. Edited by William Tough, M.A. pp. 306 and xxvii.

Works of Mure of Rowallan. Vol. II. Edited by William Tough, M.A. pp. 345 and vii.

Lindesay of Pitscottie's Historie and Cronicles. Vol. I. Edited by Æneas J. G. Mackay, LL.D. pp. 414 and clx.

Lindesay of Pitscottie's Historie and Cronicles. Vol. II. Edited by Æneas J. G. Mackay, LL.D. pp. 478 and xii.

Gilbert of the Haye's Prose MS. (1456). Vol. I. *The Buke of the Law of Armys, or Buke of Bataillis.* Edited by J. H. Stevenson. pp. 303 and cvii.

Catholic Tractates of the Sixteenth Century (1573-1600). Edited by Thomas Graves Law, LL.D. pp. 308 and lxiii.

The New Testament in Scots, being Purvey's Revision of Wycliffe's Version, turned into Scots by Murdoch Nisbet (c. 1520). Edited by Thomas Graves Law, LL.D. Vol. I. pp. 300 and xxxvii.

Livy's History of Rome: The First Five Books. Translated into Scots by John Bellenden (1533). Vol. I. Edited by W. A. Craigie, M.A. pp. 305 and xvii.

The Poems of Alexander Hume (? 1557-1609). Edited by the Rev. Alexander Lawson, B.D. pp. 279 and lxxiii.

The New Testament in Scots. Edited by Thomas Graves Law, LL.D. Vol. II. pp. 367 and ix.

The Original Chronicle of Andrew of Wyntoun (c. 1420). Printed on Parallel Pages from the Cottonian and Wemyss MSS., with the Variants of the other Texts. Edited by F. J. Amours. Vol. II. (Text, Vol. I.) pp. 351 and xix.

Livy's History of Rome: The First Five Books. Completion of Text, with Notes and Glossary. Edited by W. A. Craigie, M.A. Vol. II. pp. 408.

The New Testament in Scots. Edited by Thomas Graves Law, LL.D. Vol. III. pp. 397 and xiii.

The Original Chronicle of Andrew of Wyntoun. Edited by F. J. Amours. Vol. III. (Text, Vol. II.) pp. 497 and xiv.

The Original Chronicle of Andrew of Wyntoun. Edited by F. J. Amours. Vol. IV. (Text, Vol. III.) pp. 435 and xi.

The Poems of Robert Henryson. Edited by Professor G. Gregory Smith. Vol. II. (Text, Vol I.) pp. 327 and xxi.

The Original Chronicle of Andrew of Wyntoun. Edited by F. J. Amours. Vol. V. (Text, Vol. IV.) pp. 433 and xi.

The Original Chronicle of Andrew of Wyntoun. Edited by F. J. Amours. Vol. VI. (Text, Vol. V.) pp. 436 and xv.

The Poems of Robert Henryson. Edited by Professor G. Gregory Smith. Vol. III. (Text, Vol. II.) pp. 198 and xix.

Poems of Alexander Montgomerie, and other Pieces from Laing MS. No. 447. Supplementary Volume. Edited, with Introduction, Appendices, Notes, and Glossary, by George Stevenson, M.A. pp. 392 and lxv.

The Kingis Quair by James I. of Scotland. Edited by Rev. Walter W. Skeat, Litt.D., LL.D, D.C.L., Ph.D., F.B.A. *New Series.*

FORTHCOMING WORKS.

Lindesay of Pitscottie's Historie and Cronicles. Vol. III. Glossary.

Gilbert of the Haye's Prose MS. (1459). Vol. II. *The Buke of the Order of Chivalry,* &c. Edited by J. H. Stevenson, M.A.

The Vernacular Works of James VI., King of Scots. Edited by Oliphant Smeaton.

Specimens of Early Legal Documents in Scots. Edited by David Murray, LL.D.

The Maitland Folio MS. Edited by J. T. T. Brown. (*See* SERIES OF MS. COLLECTIONS.)

John of Ireland's Works (1490), from the MS. in the Advocates' Library.

Montgomerie's Poems, from the Laing MS. Edited by George Stevenson, M.A. [*In the press.*]

The Makculloch and Gray MSS., with Excerpts from the Chepman and Myllar Prints. Edited by George Stevenson, M.A.

Catechisms of the Reformation. Edited by William Carruthers.

The Editorial Committee has other works under consideration, including—

The Buik of the Most Noble and Valiant Conqueror Alexander the Grit. From the unique copy of Arbuthnot's print of 1580, in the possession of the Earl of Dalhousie.

J. Stewart's Abbregement of Roland Furiovs, translait ovt of Ariost, togither vith svm rapsodies of the Author, &c. From the dedication MS. copy presented to James VI., now preserved in the Advocates' Library.

Abacuk Bysset's 'Rolmentis of Courts' (1622), from the MS. in the Library of the University of Edinburgh (Laing Collection) and the MS. in the Advocates' Library.

The Poems of Gavin Douglas.

The Poems of Sir David Lyndsay.

&c. &c.

And occasional Volumes of a MISCELLANY of Shorter Pieces. (Information regarding possible contributions will be gladly received by the Committee.)

PERIODS OF EUROPEAN LITERATURE: A Complete and

CONTINUOUS HISTORY OF THE SUBJECT. Edited by PROFESSOR SAINTS-
BURY. In 12 crown 8vo vols., each 5s. net.

THE DARK AGES. By Prof. W. P. Ker.
THE FLOURISHING OF ROMANCE AND THE
RISE OF ALLEGORY. (12th and 13th
Centuries.) By Prof. Saintsbury.
THE FOURTEENTH CENTURY. By F. J. Snell.
THE TRANSITION PERIOD. By Prof. G.
Gregory Smith.
THE EARLIER RENAISSANCE. By Prof.
Saintsbury.
THE LATER RENAISSANCE. By David
Hannay.

THE FIRST HALF OF THE SEVENTEENTH
CENTURY. By Prof. H. J. C. Grierson.
THE AUGUSTAN AGES. By Prof. Oliver
Elton.
THE MID-EIGHTEENTH CENTURY. By
Prof. J. H. Millar.
THE ROMANTIC REVOLT. By Prof. C. E.
Vaughan.
THE ROMANTIC TRIUMPH. By T. S. Omond.
THE LATER NINETEENTH CENTURY. By
Prof. Saintsbury.

PHILOSOPHICAL CLASSICS FOR ENGLISH READERS.

Edited by WILLIAM KNIGHT, LL.D., Professor of Moral Philosophy
in the University of St Andrews. *Re-issue in Shilling Volumes net.*

DESCARTES . . . Prof. Mahaffy.
BUTLER . . . Rev. W. L. Collins.
BERKELEY . . Prof. Campbell Fraser.
FICHTE . . . . Prof. Adamson.
KANT . . . . Prof. Wallace.
HAMILTON . . . Prof. Veitch.
HEGEL . . . Prof. Edward Caird.
LEIBNIZ . . . John Theodore Merz.

VICO . . . . . Prof. Flint.
HOBBES . . Prof. Croom Robertson.
HUME . . . . . Prof. Knight.
SPINOZA . . . . Principal Caird.
BACON—Part I. . . . . Prof. Nichol.
BACON—Part II. . . . . Prof. Nichol.
LOCKE . . . Prof. Campbell Fraser.

FOREIGN CLASSICS FOR ENGLISH READERS. Edited by

MRS OLIPHANT. CHEAP RE-ISSUE. In limp cloth, fcap. 8vo, price 1s.
each net.

DANTE . . . . Mrs Oliphant.
VOLTAIRE General Sir E. B. Hamley, K.C.B.
PASCAL . . . Principal Tulloch.
PETRARCH . . . Henry Reeve, C.B.
GOETHE . . . A. Hayward, Q.C.
MOLIÈRE . Editor and F. Traver, M.A.
MONTAIGNE . . Rev. W. L. Collins.
RABELAIS . . Sir Walter Besant.
CALDERON . . . . E. J. Hasell.
SAINT SIMON . . . C. W. Collins.

CERVANTES . . . Mrs Oliphant.
CORNEILLE and RACINE Henry M. Trollope.
MADAME DE SÉVIGNÉ . Miss Thackeray.
LA FONTAINE AND OTHER ⎱ Rev. W. Lucas
FRENCH FABULISTS . ⎰ Collins, M.A.
SCHILLER . . . James Sime, M.A.
TASSO . . . . E. J. Hasell.
ROUSSEAU . . Henry Grey Graham.
ALFRED DE MUSSET . C. F. Oliphant.

ANCIENT CLASSICS FOR ENGLISH READERS. Edited by

the REV. W. LUCAS COLLINS, M.A. CHEAP RE-ISSUE. In limp cloth,
fcap. 8vo, price 1s. each net. *Contents of the Series—*

HOMER: ILIAD . Rev. W. Lucas Collins.
HOMER: ODYSSEY . Rev. W. Lucas Collins.
HERODOTUS . . . G. C. Swayne.
CÆSAR . . . . Anthony Trollope.
VIRGIL . . . Rev. W. Lucas Collins.
HORACE . . . Sir Theodore Martin.
ÆSCHYLUS . . . Bishop Copleston.
XENOPHON . . . Sir Alex. Grant.
CICERO . . Rev. W. Lucas Collins.
SOPHOCLES . . . C. W. Collins.
PLINY . . ⎰ Rev. A. Church and
⎱ W. J. Brodribb.
EURIPIDES . . . . W. B. Donne.
JUVENAL . . . . E. Walford.
ARISTOPHANES . Rev. W. Lucas Collins.

HESIOD AND THEOGNIS . . J. Davies.
PLAUTUS AND TERENCE Rev. W. L. Collins.
TACITUS . . . . W. B. Donne.
LUCIAN . . . Rev. W. Lucas Collins.
PLATO . . . . . C. W. Collins.
GREEK ANTHOLOGY . . Lord Neaves.
LIVY . . . Rev. W. Lucas Collins.
OVID . . . . Rev. A. Church.
CATULLUS, TIBULLUS, AND ⎱ J. Davies.
PROPERTIUS . . ⎰
DEMOSTHENES . . W. J. Brodribb.
ARISTOTLE . . Sir Alex. Grant.
THUCYDIDES . . Rev. W. Lucas Collins.
LUCRETIUS . . . W. H. Mallock.
PINDAR . . . . Rev. F. D. Morice.

WM. BLACKWOOD & SONS' EDUCATIONAL WORKS

CONTENTS.

C

EDUCATIONAL WORKS.

ENGLISH.

A History of English Criticism.

By GEORGE SAINTSBURY, M.A. (Oxon.), Hon. LL.D. (Aberd.), Professor
of Rhetoric and English Literature in the University of Edinburgh. Demy
8vo, 7s. 6d. net.

WORKS BY J. LOGIE ROBERTSON, M.A.

A History of English Literature.

For Secondary Schools. By J. LOGIE ROBERTSON, M.A., First English
Master, Edinburgh Ladies' College. With an Introduction by Professor
MASSON, Edinburgh University. Fifth Edition, revised, 3s. ; and in 3 parts,
1s. 4d. each.

Daily Chronicle.—"The exposition is fresh and independent, and high above
the level of the ordinary work of this class.......The book should prove a
great boon not only to secondary schools and colleges but also to private
students."

Outlines of English Literature.

For Young Scholars, with Illustrative Specimens. By the SAME AUTHOR.
Third Edition, revised. 1s. 6d.

Spectator.—"To sketch English literature from Beowulf down to Lord
Macaulay in a hundred and fifty pages without falling into the style of a
catalogue, is an achievement of which Mr Robertson may well be proud."

English Verse for Junior Classes.

By the SAME AUTHOR. In Two Parts. 1s. 6d. *net* each.

PART I.—Chaucer to Coleridge.
PART II.—Nineteenth-Century Poets.

School Guardian.—"Of the high literary quality of this selection there
can be no question. There is nothing here that is not classical in the
strictest sense of the word."

English Prose for Junior and Senior Classes.

By the SAME AUTHOR. In Two Parts. 2s. 6d. each.
PART I.—Malory to Johnson. | PART II.—Nineteenth Century.

Educational Times.—"We do not remember to have seen a better prose collection on the same scale, and the book should be very useful to teachers who like to work on the lines of genuine literature."

Mr R. Blair, Education Officer.—"I have to inform you that the Committee of the London County Council concerned have decided to add the book entitled 'English Exercises for Junior and Senior Classes' (J. L. Robertson, 1s.) to the Council's supplementary list of books for evening schools."

English Exercises for Junior and Senior Classes.

By the SAME AUTHOR. 1s.

Schoolmaster.—"These exercises have the high recommendation of being the gradual growth of a course of practical work in an English class-room...... The manual cannot fail to be of service even to experienced teachers."

Headmaster, Council Central Secondary School.—"As an English teacher and lecturer of long experience, I may say unreservedly that I am delighted with the book. I shall certainly use it in my classes. The suggestions under each extract are extremely good, and will be valuable to teachers and students alike."

High School Headmaster.—"The exercises are admirably drawn up, and are most suitable for classes preparing for Leaving Certificate or University examinations. I have great pleasure in adopting the book as a class-book, and intend to use it systematically throughout the session."

English Drama.

By the SAME AUTHOR. 2s. 6d.

Spectator.—"This capital selection.......Not only is it a text-book with excellent notes, but a neat and handy collection of English dramatic masterpieces."

The Select Chaucer.

Edited and Elucidated by the SAME AUTHOR. Crown 8vo, 3s. ; and in Two Parts—Part I., 2s. ; Part II., 1s. 6d.

Athenæum.—"A very successful attempt to enlarge the range of Chaucer reading in schools. We wish we could believe that the book will have the circulation it deserves."

Paraphrasing, Analysis, and Correction of Sentences.

By D. M. J. JAMES, M.A., Gordon Schools, Huntly. 1s.

Also in Two Parts :—

Passages for Paraphrasing. Verse and Prose. 6d.

Exercises in Analysis, Parsing, and Correction of Sentences. 6d.

Athenæum.—"The pieces are well calculated to improve the grammar and style of the rising generation in an age which is not distinguished for lucidity or logic."

Part I., Chaucer to Burns, cloth, 1s. net.
Part II., Wordsworth to Newbolt, cloth, 1s. net.
In One Volume complete, cloth, 2s. net.
Prize Edition, 5s.

The

School Anthology of English Verse.

A Selection of English Verse
from Chaucer to the Present Day.

EDITED BY

J. H. LOBBAN, M.A.,

Lecturer in English Literature, Birkbeck College, London;
Editor of 'The Granta Shakespeare,' &c.

Athenæum.—"We have here such poetry as rings morally sound and exalts the soundest instincts and feelings of human nature."

Guardian.—"The work is worthy of nothing less than absolutely unqualifie approval, and we cordially wish it the hearty welcome it deserves."

Journal of Education.—"One of the best small anthologies we have seen for some time. The selection is made with great good taste and care."

Elementary Grammar and Composition.

Based on the ANALYSIS OF SENTENCES. With a Chapter on WORD-BUILD-ING and DERIVATION, and containing numerous Exercises. 1s.

Schoolmaster.—"A very valuable book. It is constructive as well as analytic, and well-planned exercises have been framed to teach the young student how to use the elements of his mother-tongue."

A Working Handbook of the Analysis of Sentences.

With NOTES ON PARSING, PARAPHRASING, FIGURES OF SPEECH, AND PROSODY. New Edition, Revised. 1s. 6d.

Schoolmaster.—"The book deserves unstinted praise for the care with which the matter has been arranged, the depth of thought brought to bear upon the discussion of the subject.......One of the best and soundest productions on analysis of sentences we have met with yet."

STORMONTH'S ENGLISH DICTIONARIES,

PRONOUNCING, ETYMOLOGICAL, AND EXPLANATORY.

I. Library Edition.
Imp. 8vo, half morocco, 18s. net.

II. School and College Edition.
New Edition. Crown 8vo, 1080 pp. 5s. net.

BLACKWOOD'S
SEVENPENNY
DICTIONARY

"At such a price nothing better could be asked: good clear print, concise yet ample explanations, and accurate etymology. Just such a handy volume as schools need. Has evidently been prepared with great care. It justifies its record for reliability."—*The School Guardian.*

STORMONTH'S

HANDY SCHOOL DICTIONARY

PRONOUNCING AND EXPLANATORY

Thoroughly Revised and Enlarged by
WILLIAM BAYNE

7d. net

The George Eliot Reader.

By ELIZABETH LEE, Author of 'A School History of English Literature,' &c. With an Introduction and Portrait. 2s.

Academy.—"A fascinating little volume."

English Words and Sentences.

BOOK I. FOR THE JUNIOR DIVISION. 6d.
BOOK II. FOR THE INTERMEDIATE DIVISION. 8d.

Practical Teacher.—"These books contain numerous well-graduated exercises in English, and should be popular with teachers of the subject."

Story of the World Readers. See p. 58.

Blackwood's Literature Readers. See p. 57.

Specimens of Middle Scots.

WITH HISTORICAL INTRODUCTION AND GLOSSARIAL NOTES. By G. GREGORY SMITH, M.A., Professor of English Literature, University of Belfast. Crown 8vo, 7s. 6d. net.

English Prose Composition.

By JAMES CURRIE, LL.D. Fifty-seventh Thousand. 1s. 6d.

Short Stories for Composition.

FIRST SERIES. WITH SPECIMENS OF LETTERS, AND SUBJECTS FOR LETTERS AND ESSAYS. Seventh Impression. 112 pages. 1s.

Short Stories for Composition.

SECOND SERIES. WITH LESSONS ON VOCABULARY. Third Edition. 112 pages. 1s.

Educational News.—"These stories are fresh, short, and pithy. They possess a novelty that will arrest attention, and a kernel that will tax to some measure the thinking faculty."

Short Stories, Fables, and Pupil-Teacher Exercises for Composition.

WITH INSTRUCTIONS IN THE ART OF LETTER AND ESSAY WRITING, PARAPHRASING, FIGURES OF SPEECH, &c. 1s. 3d.

BLACKWOODS' SCHOOL SHAKESPEARE.

Edited by R. BRIMLEY JOHNSON. Each Play complete, with Introduction, Notes, and Glossary. In crown 8vo volumes. Cloth, 1s. 6d. ; paper covers, 1s. each.

The Merchant of Venice.	As You Like It.
Richard II.	Henry V.
Julius Cæsar.	Macbeth.
The Tempest.	Twelfth Night.

Other Volumes in preparation.

BLACKWOODS' ENGLISH CLASSICS.

With Portraits. In Fcap. 8vo volumes, cloth.

General Editor—J. H. LOBBAN, M.A.,

Editor of 'The School Anthology'; Lecturer in English Literature, Birkbeck College, London; Editor of 'The Granta Shakespeare,' &c.

Journal of Education.—"This Series has, we believe, already won the favourable notice of teachers. It certainly deserves to do so. Its volumes are edited with scholarly care and sound literary judgment. They are strongly and neatly bound, and extremely well printed."

Saturday Review.—"The print is good, and the introductions both short and to the point, while the notes strike a happy medium between misplaced erudition and trivial scrappiness."

School Board Chronicle.—"There are no more thorough and helpful annotated editions than those of the series of Blackwoods' English Classics."

Cowper—The Task, and Minor Poems.

By ELIZABETH LEE, Author of 'A School History of English Literature.' 2s. 6d.

Guardian.—"Miss Elizabeth Lee scores a distinct success. Her introduction is to the point and none too long; her notes are apt and adequate."

Scott—Lady of the Lake.

By W. E. W. COLLINS, M.A. 1s. 6d.

Saturday Review.—"Like some other members of this series of 'English Classics' we have noticed recently, this volume is a good piece of work."

Johnson—Lives of Milton and Addison.

By Professor J. WIGHT DUFF, D.Litt., Durham College of Science, Newcastle-upon-Tyne. 2s. 6d.

Educational News.—"A scholarly edition. The introduction contains things as good as are to be found in Macaulay's essay or Leslie Stephen's monograph."

Milton—Paradise Lost, Books I.-IV.

By J. LOGIE ROBERTSON, M.A., First English Master, Edinburgh Ladies' College. 2s. 6d.

Saturday Review.—"An excellent edition."

Macaulay—Life of Johnson.

By D. NICHOL SMITH, M.A., Goldsmith's Reader in English, University of Oxford. 1s. 6d.

Journal of Education.—"Mr Smith's criticism is sound, simple, and clear. Annotated with care and good sense, the edition is decidedly satisfactory."

Carlyle—Essay on Burns.

By J. DOWNIE, M.A., U.F.C. Training College, Aberdeen. 2s. 6d.

Guardian.—"A highly acceptable addition to our stock of school classics. We congratulate Mr Downie on having found a field worthy of his labours and on having accomplished his task with faithfulness and skill."

Goldsmith—Traveller, Deserted Village, & other Poems.

By J. H. LOBBAN, M.A., Lecturer in English Literature, Birkbeck College, London. 1s. 6d.

Literature.—"If Goldsmith touched nothing that he did not adorn, Mr Lobban and his publishers have adorned Goldsmith."

Pope—Essay on Criticism, Rape of the Lock, and other Poems.

By GEORGE SOUTAR, M.A., Litt.D., Lecturer in English Language and Literature, University College, Dundee. 2s. 6d.

Guardian.—"The selection is made with taste, and the commentary is sound, adequate, and not overburdened with superfluous information."

Hazlitt—Essays on Poetry.

By D. NICHOL SMITH, M.A., Goldsmith's Reader in English, University of Oxford. 2s. 6d.

Athenæum.—"The introduction is a capital piece of work."

Wordsworth, Coleridge, and Keats.

By A. D. INNES, M.A., Editor of 'Julius Cæsar,' &c., &c. 2s. 6d.

Academy.—"For Mr Innes's volume we have nothing but praise."

Scott—Marmion.

By ALEXANDER MACKIE, M.A., Examiner in English, University of Aberdeen; Editor of 'Warren Hastings,' &c. 1s. 6d.

Guardian.—"The volume is worthy to take its place with the best of its kind."

Lamb—Select Essays.

By AGNES WILSON, Editor of Browning's 'Strafford,' &c.; late Senior English Mistress, East Putney High School. 2s. 6d.

Athenæum.—"Miss Wilson's edition is well equipped."

Milton—Samson Agonistes.

By E. H. BLAKENEY, M.A., Headmaster, King's School, Ely. 2s. 6d.

School World.—"Everything testifies to excellent scholarship and editorial care.......The notes are a joy to the critic."

Byron—Selections.

By Professor J. WIGHT DUFF, D.Litt., Armstrong College, in the University of Durham, Newcastle-upon-Tyne. 3s. 6d.

Academy and Literature.—"Nothing has been done perfunctorily; Professor Duff is himself interested in Byron, and passes on to his reader, in consequence, some of the emotion he himself has felt."

Mr G. K. Chesterton in 'The Daily News.'—"Mr Wight Duff has made an exceedingly good selection from the poems of Byron, and added to them a clear and capable introductory study."

Professor R. Wülker in 'Englische Studien.'—"Wight Duff's Byron wird sicherlich dazu beitragen des Dichters Werke in England mehr zu verbreiten, als dies bisher geschehen ist. Aber auch in Deutschland ist das Buch allen Freunden Byron's warm zu empfehlen."

HISTORY.

A Short History of Scotland.

By ANDREW LANG. Crown 8vo, 5s. net.

LATIN AND GREEK.

Higher Latin Prose.

With an Introduction by H. W. AUDEN, M.A., Principal, Upper Canada College, Toronto; formerly Assistant-Master, Fettes College, Edinburgh; late Scholar of Christ's College, Cambridge, and Bell University Scholar. 2s. 6d.

** A Key (for Teachers only), 5s. net.

Educational Times.—"Those who are in need of a short practical guide on the subject will find Mr Auden's little work well worth a trial.......The passages chosen are well suited for translation."

School Guardian.—"This is an excellent Latin prose manual. The hints on composition are first-rate, and should be of considerable use to the student of style who has mastered the ordinary rules of prose writing.......Altogether, this is a very valuable little book."

Lower Latin Prose.

By K. P. WILSON, M.A., Assistant-Master, Fettes College, Edinburgh. 2s. 6d.

** A Key (for Teachers only), 5s. net.

Journal of Education.—"A well-arranged and helpful manual. The whole book is well printed and clear. We can unreservedly recommend the work."

Higher Latin Unseens.

For the Use of Higher Forms and University Students. Selected, with Introductory Hints on Translation, by H. W. AUDEN, M.A., Principal, Upper Canada College, Toronto; formerly Assistant-Master, Fettes College, Edinburgh; late Scholar of Christ's College, Cambridge, and Bell University Scholar. 2s. 6d.

Educational News.—"The hints on translation given by Mr Auden are the most useful and judicious we have seen in such small bulk, and they are illustrated with skilful point and aptness."

Lower Latin Unseens.

Selected, with Introduction, by W. LOBBAN, M.A., Classical Master, High School, Glasgow. 2s.

Athenæum.—"More interesting in substance than such things usually are."

Journal of Education.—"Will be welcomed by all teachers of Latin."

School Guardian.—"The introductory hints on translation should be well studied; they are most valuable, and well put."

Now issued at 1s. 6d. net to meet the requirements of the
Education Department for a Latin Translation Book suited to
pupils in the early stage of the subject. In its more expensive
form the volume has been extensively used by the greater Public
Schools, and is in its Twelfth Edition. A specimen copy will be
sent gratis to any teacher wishing to examine the book with
a view to introduction.

TWELFTH EDITION.

ADITUS FACILIORES.
AN EASY LATIN CONSTRUING BOOK,
WITH VOCABULARY.

BY

A. W. POTTS, M.A., LL.D.,
Late Head-Master of the Fettes College, Edinburgh, and sometime
Fellow of St John's College, Cambridge;

AND THE

REV. C. DARNELL, M.A.,
Late Head-Master of Cargilfield Preparatory School, Edinburgh,
and Scholar of Pembroke and Downing
Colleges, Cambridge.

Contents.

PART I.—Stories and Fables—The Wolf on his Death-Bed—Alex-
ander and the Pirate—Zeno's Teaching—Ten Helpers—The Swallow
and the Ants—Discontent—Pleasures of Country Life—The Wolf and
the Lamb—Simplicity of Farm Life in Ancient Italy—The Conceited
Jackdaw — The Ant and the Grasshopper — The Hares contemplate
Suicide—The Clever Parrot—Simple Living—The Human Hand—The
Bear—Value of Rivers—Love of the Country—Juno and the Peacock—
The Camel—The Swallow and the Birds—The Boy and the Echo—The
Stag and the Fountain—The Cat's Device—The Human Figure—The
Silly Crow—Abraham's Death-Bed—The Frogs ask for a King—The
Gods select severally a Favourite Tree—Hear the Other Side.

PART II.—Historical Extracts—THE STORY OF THE FABII : Histori-
cal Introduction—The Story of the Fabii. THE CONQUEST OF VEII :
Historical Introduction—The Conquest of Veii. THE SACRIFICE OF
DECIUS : Historical Introduction—The Sacrifice of Decius.

PART III.—The First Roman Invasion of Britain—Introduction
to Extracts from Cæsar's Commentaries—The First Roman Invasion of
Britain.

PART IV.—The Life of Alexander the Great—Historical Introduction—Life and Campaigns of Alexander the Great.

APPENDIX. VOCABULARY. ADDENDA.

*Two Maps to Illustrate the First Roman Invasion of Britain and the
Campaigns of Alexander the Great.*

First Latin Sentences and Prose.

By K. P. WILSON, M.A., late Scholar of Pembroke College, Cambridge; Assistant-Master at Fettes College. With Vocabulary. 2s. 6d. Also issued in Two Parts, 1s. 6d. each.

Saturday Review.—"This is just the right sort of help the beginner wants. ......It is certainly a book to be recommended for preparatory schools or the lower classes of a public school."

Educational Review.—"Form masters in search of a new composition book will welcome this publication."

A First Latin Reader.

With Notes, Exercises, and Vocabulary. By K. P. WILSON, M.A., Fettes College. Crown 8vo, 1s. 6d.

Tales of Ancient Thessaly.

An Elementary Latin Reading-Book, with Notes and Vocabulary. By J. W. E. PEARCE, M.A., Headmaster of Merton Court Preparatory School, Sidcup; late Assistant-Master, University College School, London. With a Preface by J. L. PATON, M.A., late Fellow of St John's College, Cambridge; Headmaster of the Grammar School, Manchester. 1s.

Guardian.—"A striking and attractive volume. Altogether, we have here quite a noteworthy little venture, to which we wish all success."

Latin Verse Unseens.

By G. MIDDLETON, M.A., Classical Master, Aberdeen Grammar School, late Scholar of Emmanuel College, Cambridge; Joint-Author of 'Student's Companion to Latin Authors.' 1s. 6d.

Schoolmaster.—"They form excellent practice in 'unseen' work, in a great variety of style and subject. For purposes of general study and as practice for examinations the book is a thoroughly useful one."

Latin Historical Unseens.

For Army Classes. By L. C. VAUGHAN WILKES, M.A. 2s.

Army and Navy Gazette.—"Will be found very useful by candidates for entrance to Sandhurst, Woolwich, and the Militia."

Stonyhurst Latin Grammar.

By Rev. JOHN GERARD. Second Edition. Pp. 199. 3s.

Aditus Faciliores Græci.

An Easy Greek Construing Book, with Complete Vocabulary. By the late A. W. POTTS, M.A., LL.D., and the Rev. C. DARNELL, M.A. Fifth Edition. Fcap. 8vo, 3s.

Camenarum Flosculos in Usum Fettesianorum decerptos Notis quibusdam illustraverunt A. GUL. POTTS, M.A., LL.D.; GUL. A. HEARD, M.A., LL.D. New Impression. Crown 8vo, 3s. 6d.

Greek Accidence.

For Use in Preparatory and Public Schools. By T. C. WEATHERHEAD, M.A., Headmaster, Choir School, King's College, Cambridge; formerly of Trinity College, Cambridge, and Bell University Scholar. 1s. 6d.

Literature.—"Not the least of its merits is the clearness of the type, both Greek and English."

Pilot.—"The most useful book for beginners we have seen."

The Messenian Wars.

An Elementary Greek Reader. With Exercises and Full Vocabulary. By H. W. AUDEN, M.A., Principal, Upper Canada College, Toronto; formerly Assistant-Master, Fettes College, Edinburgh; late Scholar of Christ's College, Cambridge, and Bell University Scholar. 1s. 6d.

Saturday Review.—"A far more spirited narrative than the Anabasis. We warmly commend the book."

Higher Greek Prose.

With an Introduction by H. W. AUDEN, M.A., Principal, Upper Canada College, Toronto. 2s. 6d. *⁎* *Key (for Teachers only)*, 5s. *net*.

Guardian.—"The selection of passages for translation into Greek is certainly well made."

Journal of Education.—"A manual of well-graduated exercises in Greek Prose Composition, ranging from short sentences to continuous pieces."

Lower Greek Prose.

By K. P. WILSON, M.A., Assistant-Master in Fettes College, Edinburgh. 2s. 6d. *⁎* *A Key (for Teachers only)*, 5s. *net*.

School Guardian.—"A well-arranged book, designed to meet the needs of middle forms in schools."

Higher Greek Unseens.

For the Use of Higher Forms and University Students. Selected, with Introductory Hints on Translation, by H. W. AUDEN, M.A., Principal, Upper Canada College, Toronto; formerly Assistant-Master, Fettes College, Edinburgh. 2s. 6d.

Educational Times.—"It contains a good selection quite difficult enough for the highest forms of public schools."

Schoolmaster.—"The introductory remarks on style and translation form eminently profitable preliminary reading for the earnest and diligent worker in the golden mine of classical scholarship."

Greek Unseens.

BEING ONE HUNDRED PASSAGES FOR TRANSLATION AT SIGHT IN JUNIOR CLASSES. Selected and arranged. With Introduction by W. LOBBAN, M.A., Classical Master, The High School, Glasgow. 2s.

This little book is designed for the use of those preparing for the Leaving Certificate, Scotch Preliminary, London Matriculation, and similar examinations in Greek. The extracts are drawn from over a score of different authors, and regard has been had in the selection to literary or historical interest, and in the arrangement to progressive difficulty.

Greek Verse Unseens.

By T. R. MILLS, M.A., Lecturer in Classics, University College, Dundee, formerly Scholar of Wadham College, Oxford ; Joint-Author of 'Student's Companion to Latin Authors.' 1s. 6d.

School Guardian.—"A capital selection made with much discretion.......It is a great merit that the selections are intelligible apart from their context."

University Correspondent.—"This careful and judicious selection should be found very useful in the higher forms of schools and in preparing for less advanced University examinations for Honours."

Greek Test Papers.

By JAMES MOIR, Litt.D., LL.D., late co-Rector of Aberdeen Grammar School. 2s. 6d.

₊ *A Key (for Teachers only)*, 5s. *net.*

University Correspondent.—"This useful book.......The papers are based on the long experience of a practical teacher, and should prove extremely helpful and suggestive to all teachers of Greek."

Greek Prose Phrase Book.

Based on Thucydides, Xenophon, Demosthenes, and Plato. Arranged according to subjects, with Indexes. By H. W. AUDEN, M.A., Editor of 'Meissner's Latin Phrase Book.' Interleaved, 3s. 6d.

Spectator.—"A good piece of work, and likely to be useful."
Athenæum.—"A useful little volume, helpful to boys who are learning to write Greek prose."
Journal of Education.—"Of great service to schoolboys and schoolmasters alike. The idea of interleaving is especially commendable."

Aristophanes—Pax.

Edited, with Introduction and Notes, by H. SHARPLEY, M.A., late Scholar of Corpus Christi College, Oxford. In 1 vol. 12s. 6d. *net.*

A Short History of the Ancient Greeks from the Earliest Times to the Roman Conquest.

By P. GILES, Litt.D., LL.D., University Reader in Comparative Philology, Cambridge. With Maps and Illustrations. [*In preparation.*

Outlines of Greek History.

By the SAME AUTHOR. In 1 vol. [*In preparation.*

A Manual of Classical Geography.

By JOHN L. MYRES, M.A., Fellow of Magdalene College ; Professor of Ancient History, Oxford. [*In preparation.*

BLACKWOODS'

ILLUSTRATED

CLASSICAL TEXTS.

GENERAL EDITOR—H. W. AUDEN, M.A.

Principal of Upper Canada College, Toronto; formerly Assistant-Master at Fettes College; late Scholar of Christ's College, Cambridge, and Bell University Scholar.

Literature.—"The best we have seen of the new type of schoolbook."

Academy.—"If the price of this series is considered, we know not where to look for its equal."

Public School Magazine.—"The plates and maps seem to have been prepared regardless of cost. We wonder how it can all be done at the price."

BLACKWOODS' CLASSICAL TEXTS.

Cæsar—Gallic War, Books I.-III.

By J. M. HARDWICH, M.A., Assistant-Master at Rugby; late Scholar of St John's College, Cambridge. With or without Vocabulary. 1s. 6d.

Cæsar—Gallic War, Books IV., V.

By Rev. ST J. B. WYNNE WILLSON, M.A., Headmaster, Haileybury College; late Scholar of St John's College, Cambridge. With or without Vocabulary, 1s. 6d. Vocabulary separately, 3d.

Cæsar—Gallic War, Books VI., VII.

By C. A. A. DU PONTET, M.A., Assistant-Master at Harrow. With or without Vocabulary. 1s. 6d.

Virgil—Georgic I.

By J. SARGEAUNT, M.A., Assistant-Master at Westminster; late Scholar of University College, Oxford. 1s. 6d.

Virgil—Georgic IV.

By J. SARGEAUNT, M.A., Assistant-Master at Westminster; late Scholar of University College, Oxford. 1s. 6d.

BLACKWOODS' CLASSICAL TEXTS—*continued*.

Virgil—Æneid, Books V., VI.
By Rev. St J. B. Wynne Willson, M.A., Headmaster, Haileybury College. 1s. 6d.

Ovid—Metamorphoses (Selections).
By J. H. Vince, M.A., late Scholar of Christ's College, Cambridge, Assistant-Master at Bradfield. 1s. 6d.

Ovid—Elegiac Extracts.
By R. B. Burnaby, M.A. Oxon. ; Classical Master, Trinity College, Glenalmond. 1s. 6d.

Arrian—Anabasis, Books I., II.
By H. W. Auden, M.A., late Scholar of Christ's College, Cambridge ; Principal of Upper Canada College, Toronto ; formerly Assistant-Master at Fettes College. 2s. 6d.

Homer—Odyssey, Book VI.
By E. E. Sikes, M.A., Fellow and Lecturer of St John's College, Cambridge. 1s. 6d.

Homer—Odyssey, Book VII.
By E. E. Sikes, M.A., Fellow and Lecturer of St John's College, Cambridge.   [*In preparation.*

Demosthenes—Olynthiacs, 1-3.
By H. Sharpley, M.A., late Scholar of Corpus College, Oxford ; Assistant-Master at Hereford School. 1s. 6d.

Horace—Odes, Books I., II.
By J. Sargeaunt, M.A., late Scholar of University College, Oxford ; Assistant-Master at Westminster. 1s. 6d.

Horace—Odes, Books III., IV.
By J. Sargeaunt, M.A., Assistant-Master at Westminster. 1s. 6d.

Cicero—In Catilinam, I.-IV.
By H. W. Auden, M.A., late Scholar of Christ's College, Cambridge ; Principal of Upper Canada College, Toronto ; formerly Assistant-Master at Fettes College. 1s. 6d.

Cicero—De Senectute and De Amicitia.
By J. H. Vince, M.A., Assistant-Master at Bradfield.
[*In preparation.*

Cicero—Pro Lege Manilia and Pro Archia.
By K. P. Wilson, M.A., late Scholar of Pembroke College, Cambridge ; Assistant-Master at Fettes College. 2s. 6d.

BLACKWOODS' CLASSICAL TEXTS—*continued.*

Cicero—Select Letters.

By Rev. T. NICKLIN, M.A., Assistant-Master at Rossall. 2s. 6d.

Cicero—Pro Caecina.

By Rev. J. M. LUPTON, M.A. Cantab., Assistant-Master at Marlborough College. [*In preparation.*

Tacitus—Agricola.

By H. F. MORLAND SIMPSON, M.A., late Scholar of Pembroke College, Cambridge; Rector of Aberdeen Grammar School. [*In preparation.*

Xenophon—Anabasis, Books I., II.

By A. JAGGER, M.A., late Scholar of Pembroke College, Cambridge; Head-master, Queen Elizabeth's Grammar School, Mansfield. 1s. 6d.

Sallust—Jugurtha.

By I. F. SMEDLEY, M.A., Assistant-Master at Westminster; late Fellow of Pembroke College, Cambridge. 1s. 6d.

Euripides—Hercules Furens.

By E. H. BLAKENEY, M.A., Headmaster, King's School, Ely. 2s. 6d.

Livy—Book XXVIII.

By G. MIDDLETON, M.A., Classical Master in Aberdeen Grammar School; and Professor A. SOUTER, D.Litt., Yates Professor of New Testament Greek, Mansfield College, Oxford. 1s. 6d.

Livy—Book IX.

By J. A. NICKLIN, B.A., late Scholar of St John's College, Cambridge; Assistant-Master at Liverpool College. [*In preparation.*

Nepos—Select Lives.

By Rev. E. J. W. HOUGHTON, D.D., Headmaster of Rossall School.
[*In the press.*

MODERN LANGUAGES.

FRENCH.

Historical Reader of Early French.

Containing Passages Illustrative of the Growth of the French Language from the Earliest Times to the end of the 15th Century. By HERBERT A. STRONG, LL.D., Officier de l'Instruction Publique, Professor of Latin, University College, Liverpool; and L. D. BARNETT, M.A., Litt.D. 3s.

Guardian.—"A most valuable companion to the modern handbooks on historical French grammar."

D

The Tutorial Handbook of French Composition.

By ALFRED MERCIER, L.-ès-L., Lecturer on French Language and Literature in the University of St Andrews. 3s. 6d.

Educational Times.—"A very useful book, which admirably accomplishes its object of helping students preparing for examinations.......It is on rather novel lines, which commend themselves at once to any one who has had to teach the subject."

French Historical Unseens.

For Army Classes. By N. E. TOKE, B.A. 2s. 6d.

Journal of Education.—"A distinctly good book.......May be unreservedly commended."

A First Book of "Free Composition" in French.

By J. EDMOND MANSION, B.-ès-L., Headmaster of Modern Languages in the Royal Academical Institution, Belfast. 1s.

School World.—"We recommend it warmly to all teachers of French, and trust that it will have a wide circulation."

French Test Papers for Civil Service and University Students.

Edited by EMILE B. LE FRANÇOIS, French Tutor, Redcliff House, Winchester House, St Ives, &c., Clifton, Bristol. 2s.

Weekly Register.—"Deserves as much praise as can be heaped on it....... Thoroughly good work throughout."

All French Verbs in Twelve Hours (except Defective Verbs).

By ALFRED J. WYATT, M.A. 1s.

Weekly Register.—"Altogether unique among French grammatical helps, with a system, with a *coup d'œil*, with avoidance of repetition, with a premium on intellectual study, which constitute a new departure."

The Children's Guide to the French Language.

By ANNIE G. FERRIER, Teacher of French in the Ladies' College, Queen Street, Edinburgh. 1s.

Schoolmaster.—"The method is good, and the book will be found helpful by those who have to teach French to small children."

GERMAN.

A History of German Literature.

By JOHN G ROBERTSON, Ph.D., Professor of German in the University of London. 10s. 6d. net.

Times.—"In such an enterprise even a tolerable approach to success is something of an achievement, and in regard to German literature Mr Robertson appears to have made a nearer approach than any other English writer."

Outlines of the History of German Literature.

For the Use of Schools. By the SAME AUTHOR. Crown 8vo, 3s. 6d. net.

DR LUBOVIUS' GERMAN SERIES.

A Practical German Grammar, Reader and Writer.

By LOUIS LUBOVIUS, Ph.D., German Master, Hillhead High School, Glasgow; Lecturer on German, U.F.C. Training College; Examiner for Degrees in Arts, University of Glasgow.

Part I.—Elementary. 2s.
Part II. 3s.

Lower German.

Reading, Supplementary Grammar with Exercises, and Material for Composition. With Notes and Vocabulary, and Ten Songs in Sol-Fa Notation. By LOUIS LUBOVIUS, Ph.D. 2s. 6d.

Athenæum.—"The volume is well designed."
Preparatory Schools Review.—"A capital reading-book for middle forms."

Progressive German Composition.

With copious Notes and Idioms, and FIRST INTRODUCTION TO GERMAN PHILOLOGY. By LOUIS LUBOVIUS, Ph.D. 3s. 6d.

Also in Two Parts:—

Progressive German Composition. 2s. 6d.

*** A Key (for Teachers only), 5s. net.**

First Introduction to German Philology. 1s. 6d.

Journal of Education.—"The passages for translation are well selected, and the notes to the passages, as well as the grammatical introduction, give real assistance.......The part of the book dealing with German philology deserves great praise."

A Compendious German Reader.

Consisting of Historical Extracts, Specimens of German Literature, Lives of German Authors, an Outline of German History (1640-1890), Biographical and Historical Notes. Especially adapted for the use of Army Classes. By G. B. BEAK, M.A. 2s. 6d.

Guardian.—"This method of compilation is certainly an improvement on the hotch-potch of miscellaneous passages to be found in many of the older books."

Spartanerjünglinge. A Story of Life in a Cadet College.

By PAUL VON SZCZEPAŃSKI. Edited, with Vocabulary and Notes, by J. M. MORRISON, M.A., Master in Modern Languages, Aberdeen Grammar School. 2s.

Scotsman.—"An admirable reader for teaching German on the new method, and is sure to prove popular both with students and with teachers."

A German Reader for Technical Schools.

By EWALD F. SECKLER, Senior Language Master at the Birmingham Municipal Day School; German Lecturer, Birmingham Evening School; French Lecturer, Stourbridge Technical School. 2s.

SPANISH.

A Spanish Grammar.

With Copious Exercises in Translation and Composition; Easy reading Lessons and Extracts from Spanish Authors; a List of Idioms; a Glossary of Commercial Terms (English-Spanish); and a copious General Vocabulary (Spanish-English). By WILLIAM A. KESSEN, Teacher of Spanish, Hillhead High School, Glasgow. 3s. 6d.

Investors' Review.—"To the student who wishes to master the Spanish language for commercial or literary purposes this admirable little book will prove invaluable."

Commerce.—"Contains practically all that is necessary for the acquirement of a working knowledge of the language."

MATHEMATICS.

Arithmetic.

With numerous Examples, Revision Tests, and Examination Papers. By A. VEITCH LOTHIAN, M.A., B.Sc., F.R.S.E., Mathematical and Science Lecturer, E.C. Training College, Glasgow. *With Answers.* 3s. 6d.

Guardian.—"A work of first-rate importance.......We should find it hard to suggest any improvement.......We venture to predict that when the book becomes known, it will command a very wide circulation in our public schools and elsewhere."

Practical Arithmetical Exercises.

FOR SENIOR PUPILS IN SCHOOLS. Containing upwards of 8000 Examples, consisting in great part of Problems, and 750 Extracts from Examination Papers. Second Edition, Revised. 364 pages, 3s. *With Answers*, 3s. 6d.

JAMES WELTON, Esq., *Lecturer on Education, and Master of Method, Yorkshire College.*—"Your 'Practical Arithmetic' seems to me the most complete collection of exercises in existence. Both idea and execution are excellent."

Elementary Algebra.

The Complete Book, 288 pp., cloth, 2s. *With Answers*, 2s. 6d. *Answers* sold separately, price 9d. Pt. I., 64 pp., 6d. Pt. II., 64 pp., 6d. Pt. III., 70 pp., 6d. Pt. IV., 96 pp., 9d. *Answers* to Pts. I., II., III., each 2d. *Answers* to Pt. IV., 3d.

Educational News.—"A short and compact introduction to algebra.......The exercises are remarkably good, and the arrangement of the subject-matter is on the soundest principles. The work is, on the whole, to be commended as being at once inexpensive and scholarly."

Handbook of Mental Arithmetic.

With 7200 Examples and Answers. 264 pp. 2s. 6d. Also in Six Parts, limp cloth, price 6d. each.

Teachers' Monthly.—"The examples are mainly concrete, as they should be, are of all varieties, and, what is most important, of the right amount of difficulty.'

Educational News.—"This is, as a matter of fact, at once a handbook and a handy book. It is an absolute storehouse of exercises in mental computations. ......There are most valuable practical hints to teachers."

Modern Geometry of the Point, Straight Line, and Circle.

An Elementary Treatise. By J. A. THIRD, D.Sc., Headmaster of Spier's School, Beith. 3s.

Schoolmaster. — "Each branch of this wide subject is treated with brevity, it is true, and yet with amazing completeness considering the size of the volume. So earnest and reliable an effort deserves success."

Journal of Education. — "An exceedingly useful text-book, full enough for nearly every educational purpose, and yet not repellent by overloading."

Educational News. — "A book which will easily take rank among the best of its kind. The subject is treated with complete thoroughness and honesty."

Mensuration.

128 pp., cloth, 1s. Also in Two Parts. Pt. I., Parallelograms and Triangles. 64 pp. Paper, 4d.; cloth, 6d. Pt. II., Circles and Solids. 64 pp. Paper, 4d.; cloth, 6d. *Answers* may be had separately, price 2d. each Part.

Educational Times. — "The explanations are always clear and to the point, while the exercises are so exceptionally numerous that a wide selection is offered to the students who make use of the book."

Higher Arithmetic.

For Ex-Standard and Continuation Classes. 128 pp. Paper, 6d.; cloth, 8d. With *Answers*, cloth, 11d. *Answers* may be had separately, price 3d.

GEOGRAPHY.

Fifty-Fifth Thousand.

Elements of Modern Geography.

By the Rev. ALEXANDER MACKAY, LL.D., F.R.G.S. Revised to the present time. Pp. 300. 3s.

Schoolmaster. — "For senior pupils or pupil-teachers the book contains all that is desirable.......It is well got up, and bears the mark of much care in the authorship and editing."

One Hundred and Ninety-Sixth Thousand.

Outlines of Modern Geography.

By the SAME AUTHOR. Revised to the present time. Pp. 128. 1s.

These 'Outlines'—in many respects an epitome of the 'Elements'—are carefully prepared to meet the wants of beginners. The arrangement is the same as in the Author's larger works.

One Hundred and Fifth Thousand.

First Steps in Geography.

By the SAME AUTHOR. 18mo, pp. 56. Sewed, 4d.; in cloth, 6d.

A Manual of Classical Geography.
By JOHN L. MYRES, M.A., Professor of Ancient History, Oxford.
[In preparation.

CHEMISTRY AND POPULAR SCIENCE.

Forty Elementary Lessons in Chemistry.
By W. L. SARGANT, M.A., Headmaster, Oakham School. Illustrated. 1s. 6d.

Glasgow Herald.—"Remarkably well arranged for teaching purposes, and shows the compiler to have a real grip of sound educational principles. The book is clearly written and aptly illustrated."

Inorganic Tables, with Notes and Equations.
By H. M. TIMPANY, B.Sc., Science Master, Borough Technical School, Shrewsbury. Crown 8vo, 1s.

Things of Everyday.
A Popular Science Reader on Some Common Things. With Illustrations. 2s.

Guardian.—"Will be found useful by teachers in elementary and continuation schools who have to conduct classes in the 'science of common things.'......Well and strongly bound, and illustrated by beautifully clear diagrams."

GEOLOGY.

An Intermediate Text-Book of Geology.
By Professor CHARLES LAPWORTH, LL.D., University, Birmingham. Founded on Dr PAGE's 'Introductory Text-Book of Geology.' With Illustrations. 5s.

Educational News.—"The work is lucid and attractive, and will take high rank among the best text-books on the subject."
Publishers' Circular.—"The arrangement of the new book is in every way excellent, and it need hardly be said that it is thoroughly up to date in all details.......Simplicity and clearness in the book are as pronounced as its accuracy, and students and teachers alike will find it of lasting benefit to them."
Education.—"The name of the Author is a guarantee that the subject is effectively treated, and the information and views up to date."

PALÆONTOLOGY.

A Manual of Palæontology.
For the Use of Students. With a General Introduction on the Principles of Palæontology. By Professor H. ALLEYNE NICHOLSON, Aberdeen, and RICHARD LYDEKKER, B.A., F.G.S. &c. Third Edition. Entirely rewritten and greatly enlarged. 2 vols. 8vo, with 1419 Engravings. 63s.

PHYSICAL GEOGRAPHY.

Fifteenth Edition, Revised.

Introductory Text-Book of Physical Geography.

With Sketch-Maps and Illustrations. By DAVID PAGE, LL.D., &c., Professor of Geology in the Durham College of Science, Newcastle. Revised by Professor CHARLES LAPWORTH. 2s. 6d.

Athenæum.—"The divisions of the subject are so clearly defined, the explanations are so lucid, the relations of one portion of the subject to another are so satisfactorily shown, and, above all, the bearings of the allied sciences to Physical Geography are brought out with so much precision, that every reader will feel that difficulties have been removed and the path of study smoothed before him."

PSYCHOLOGY AND LOGIC.

An Introductory Text-Book of Logic.

With Numerous Examples and Exercises. By SYDNEY HERBERT MELLONE, M.A. (Lond.), D.Sc. (Edin.); Examiner in Philosophy in the University of Edinburgh. Fifth Edition, Revised. Crown 8vo, 5s.

Scotsman.—"This is a well-studied academic text-book, in which the traditional doctrine that has been handed down from Aristotle to the university professors of to-day is expounded with clearness, and upon an instructive system which leads up naturally to the deeper and different speculations involved in modern logic.......The book, in fine, is an excellent working text-book of its subject, likely to prove useful both to students and to teachers."

Elements of Psychology.

By SYDNEY HERBERT MELLONE, M.A. (Lond.), D.Sc. (Edin.), and MARGARET DRUMMOND, M.A. (Edin.) Second Edition, Revised. Crown 8vo, 5s.

Scotsman.—"Thoroughness is a feature of the work, and, treating psychology as a living science, it will be found fresh, suggestive, and up-to-date."

Education. — "The authors of this volume have made satisfactory use of accredited authorities; in addition, they have pursued original investigations and conducted experiments, with the result that great freshness of treatment marks their contribution to the teaching of psychology."

A Short History of Logic.

By ROBERT ADAMSON, LL.D., Late Professor of Logic in the University of Glasgow. Edited by W. R. SORLEY, Litt.D., LL.D., Fellow of the British Academy, Professor of Moral Philosophy, University of Cambridge. Crown 8vo, 5s. net.

"There is no other History of Logic—short or long—in English, and no similar short work in any other language."

FORESTRY.

The Elements of British Forestry.

A Handbook for Forest Apprentices and Students of Forestry. By JOHN NISBET, D.Œ., Professor of Forestry at the West of Scotland Agricultural College, Author of 'The Forester.' Crown 8vo, 5s. 6d. net.

Forest Entomology.

By A. T. GILLANDERS, Wood Manager to His Grace the Duke of Northumberland, K.G. Second Edition, Revised. With 351 Illustrations. Demy 8vo, 15s. net.

ELEMENTARY SERIES.
BLACKWOODS'
LITERATURE READERS.

Edited by JOHN ADAMS, M.A., LL.D.,
Professor of Education in the University of London.

BOOK I. . . . . . Pp. 228. Price 1s.
BOOK II. . . . . . Pp. 275. Price 1s. 4d.
BOOK III. . . . . . Pp. 303. Price 1s. 6d.
BOOK IV. . . . . . Pp. 381. Price 1s. 6d.

NOTE.

This new Series would seek to do for Literature what has already been done by many series of School Readers for History, Geography, and Science. Many teachers feel that their pupils should be introduced as soon as possible to the works of the great writers, and that reading may be learnt from these works at least as well as from compilations specially written for the young. Because of recent changes in Inspection, the present is a specially suitable time for the introduction of such a series into Elementary Schools. In the Preparatory Departments of Secondary Schools the need for such a series is clamant.

It is to be noted that the books are not manuals of English literature, but merely Readers, the matter of which is drawn entirely from authors of recognised standing. All the usual aids given in Readers are supplied; but illustrations, as affording no help in dealing with Literature, are excluded from the series.

"The volumes, which are capitally printed, consist of selected readings of increasing difficulty, to which notes and exercises are added at the end. The selected pieces are admirably chosen, especially in the later books, which will form a beginning for a really sound and wide appreciation of the stores of good English verse and prose."—*Athenæum.*

"The selected readings......are interesting, and possessed of real literary value. The books are well bound, the paper is excellent, and the unusual boldness and clear spacing of the type go far to compensate for the entire absence of pictorial illustrations."—*Guardian.*

"A very excellent gradus to the more accessible heights of the English Parnassus......The appendices on spelling, word-building, and grammar are the work of a skilful, practical teacher."—*Pall Mall Gazette.*

"If we had the making of the English Educational Code for Elementary Schools, we should insert a regulation that all boys and girls should spend two whole years on these four books, and on nothing else."—*Bradford Observer.*

"The books are graded with remarkable skill."—*Glasgow Herald.*

" Absolutely the best set of all the history readers that have hitherto been published."—*The Guardian.*

THE STORY OF THE WORLD.

FOR THE CHILDREN OF THE BRITISH EMPIRE. (In Five Books.)

By M. B. SYNGE.

With Coloured Frontispieces and numerous Illustrations by E. M. Synge, A.R.E., and Maps.

BOOK I. ON THE SHORES OF THE GREAT SEA. 1s. 4d.

Colonial Edition, 1s. 6d.

THE Home of Abraham—Into Africa—Joseph in Egypt—The Children of Israel—The First Merchant Fleet—Hiram, King of Tyre—King Solomon's Fleet—The Story of Carthage—The Story of the Argonauts—The Siege of Troy—The Adventures of Ulysses—The Dawn of History—The Fall of Tyre—The Rise of Carthage—Hanno's Adventures—The Battle of Marathon—King Ahasuerus —How Leonidas kept the Pass—Some Greek Colonies—Athens—The Death of Socrates—The Story of Romulus and Remus—How Horatius kept the Bridge—Coriolanus—Alexander the Great—King of Macedonia—The Conquest of India—Alexander's City—The Roman Fleet—The Adventures of Hannibal—The End of Carthage—The Triumph of Rome—Julius Cæsar—The Flight of Pompey—The Death of Cæsar.

BOOK II. THE DISCOVERY OF NEW WORLDS. 1s. 6d.

THE Roman World—The Tragedy of Nero—The Great Fire in Rome—The Destruction of Pompeii—Marcus Aurelius—Christians to the Lions—A New Rome—The Armies of the North—King Arthur and his Knights—How the Northmen conquered England—The First Crusade—Frederick Barbarossa—The Third Crusade—The Days of Chivalry—Queen of the Adriatic—The Story of Marco Polo—Dante's Great Poem—The Maid of Orleans—Prince Henry, the Sailor—The Invention of Printing—Vasco da Gama's Great Voyage—Golden Goa—Christopher Columbus—The Last of the Moors—Discovery of the New World—Columbus in Chains—Discovery of the Pacific—Magellan's Straits—Montezuma—Siege and Fall of Mexico—Conquest of Peru—A Great Awakening.

BOOK III. THE AWAKENING OF EUROPE. 1s. 6d.

Colonial Edition, 1s. 9d.

STORY of the Netherlands—The Story of Martin Luther—The Massacre of St Bartholomew—The Siege of Leyden—William the Silent—Drake's Voyage round the World—The Great Armada—Virginia—Story of the Revenge—Sir Walter Raleigh—The 'Fairy Queen'—First Voyage of the East India Company—Henry Hudson—Captain John Smith—The Founding of Quebec—The Pilgrim Fathers—Thirty Years of War —The Dutch at Sea—Van Riebeek's Colony —Oliver Cromwell—Two Famous Admirals—De Ruyter—The Founder of Pennsylvania—The ' Pilgrim's Progress '—William's Invitation—The Struggle in Ireland—The Siege of Vienna by the Turks—The Story of the Huguenots—The Battle of Blenheim—How Peter the Great learned Shipbuilding --Charles XII. of Sweden—The Boyhood of Frederick the Great—Anson's Voyage round the World—Maria Theresa—The Story of Scotland.

THE STORY OF THE WORLD—*continued.*

BOOK IV. THE STRUGGLE FOR SEA POWER. 1s. 9d.

THE Story of the Great Mogul—Robert Clive—The Black Hole of Calcutta—The Struggle for North America—George Washington—How Pitt saved England—The Fall of Quebec—"The Great Lord Hawke"—The Declaration of Independence—Captain Cook's Story—James Bruce and the Nile—The Trial of Warren Hastings — Maria Antoinette — The Fall of the Bastile — Napoleon Bonaparte—Horatio Nelson—The Adventures of Mungo Park—The Travels of Baron Humboldt—The Battle of the Nile—Copenhagen — Napoleon — Trafalgar — The Death of Nelson—The Rise of Wellington—The First Australian Colony—Story of the Slave Trade—The Defence of Saragoza—Sir John Moore at Corunna—The Victory of Talavera—The Peasant Hero of the Tyrol—The "Shannon" and the "Chesapeake"—Napoleon's Retreat from Moscow—Wellington's Victories in Spain—The Fall of the Empire—Story of the Steam Engine—Waterloo—The Exile of St Helena.

BOOK V. GROWTH OF THE BRITISH EMPIRE. 2s.

How Spain lost South America—The Greek War — Victoria, Queen of England — The Great Boer Trek—The Story of Natal—The Story of Canada—The Winning of the West —A Great Arctic Expedition—Discoveries in Australia—The Last King of France—Louis Kossuth and Hungary—The Crimean War—The Indian Mutiny—King of United Italy —Civil War in America—The Mexican Revolution—Founding the German Empire—The Franco-German War—The Dream of Cecil Rhodes — The Dutch Republics in South Africa—Livingstone's discoveries in Central Africa—China's Long Sleep—Japan, Britain's Ally—Russia—The Annexation of Burma — The Story of Afghanistan — The Empire of India — Gordon, the Hero of Khartum—The Redemption of Egypt—The Story of British West Africa—The Story of Uganda — The Founding of Rhodesia — British South Africa — The Dominion of Canada — Australia — The New Nation — Freedom for Cuba—Reign of Queen Victoria —Welding the Empire—Citizenship.

Also in 2 volumes, at 3s. 6d. each net, suitable as prize books.

Uniform with this Series.

THE WORLD'S CHILDHOOD.

With numerous Illustrations by Brinsley Le Fanu.

I. STORIES OF THE FAIRIES. 10d.

CONTENTS

1. Lit-tle Red Ri-ding Hood.
2. The Three Bears.
3. The Snow-Child.
4. Tom Thumb.
5. The Ug-ly Duck-ling.
6. Puss in Boots.
7. The Lit-tle Girl and the Cats.
8. Jack and the Bean-Stalk.
9. Gol-dy.
10. Cin-der-el-la—Part I.
11. Cin-der-el-la—Part II.
12. The Lost Bell.
13. Jack the Gi-ant Kill-er.
14. Star-bright and Bird-ie.
15. Beau-ty and the Beast.
16. Peach-Dar-ling.
17. In Search of a Night's Rest.
18. Dick Whit-ting-ton and his Cat.
19. The Sleep-ing Beau-ty.

II. STORIES OF THE GREEK GODS AND HEROES. 10d.

CONTENTS.

1. A-bout the Gods.
2. The Names of the Gods.
3. Turn-ed in-to Stone.
4. The Shin-ing Char-i-ot.
5. The Laur-el Tree.
6. A Horse with Wings.
7. The Cy-press Tree.
8. The Fruits of the Earth.
9. Cu-pid's Gold-en Ar-rows.
10. Pan's Pipe.
11. A Long Sleep.
12. The Re-ward of Kind-ness.
13. At-a-lan-ta's Race.
14. The Stor-y of Al-ces-tis.
15. The Snow-White Bull.
16. The Spi-der and his Web.
17. I-o—the White Cow.
18. The Three Gold-en Ap-ples.
19. The Ol-ive Tree.
20. A Boy Her-o of Old.
21. The Thread of Ar-i-ad-ne.
22. The Boy who tried to Fly.
23. The Gold-en Harp.
    Teacher's Appendix.

"If history can be given a form likely to make it palatable to young folks, "F" has succeeded in doing so in these 'Stories of the English.' It is no exaggeration to say that the book represents not only *a masterpiece in literature for children*, but a work of no slight value for the national good."—*Scotsman.*

STORIES OF THE ENGLISH
FOR SCHOOLS.

By F.

FOR JUNIOR SCHOLARS.

VOL. I.—FROM THE COMING OF THE ENGLISH TO THE ARMADA. — **1s. 6d.**

CONTENTS.—The coming of the White Horse—The coming of the Cross—The Fight with the Raven—Alfred the Great—Edward the Confessor—William the Conqueror—The Kings of the Golden Broom—Richard Lion-Heart—King John and Magna Charta—Earl Simon the Righteous—Edward the Englishman—Bannockburn and Berkeley—The Lions and the Lilies—A King dethroned—Prince Hal—King Harry—The Wars of the Roses—Henry VIII. and the Revolt from Rome—Edward VI. and Mary—Elizabeth, the Great Queen : (1) English Adventurers and the Cruise of the *Pelican* ; (2) Mary, Queen of Scots ; (3) Papist Plots and the Massacre of Saint Bartholomew ; (4) The Armada.

ILLUSTRATIONS.—Dover Castle—The Pharos, Dover—Norsemen—Homes of our Ancestors—Château Gaillard—Tomb of a Crusader (Gervase Alard), Winchelsea Church—Carnarvon Castle—Coronation Chair, Westminster Abbey—Knights of the Fourteenth Century—Edward the Third—The Battle of Cressy—Tomb of Edward the Third, Westminster Abbey—Tomb of the Black Prince, Canterbury Cathedral—Richard II. on his voyage to Ireland—Jerusalem Chamber, Westminster Abbey—Henry V. with Military Attendants—Henry V. addressing his Army—Joan of Arc—The Crowning of Henry VII. on Bosworth Field—Henry VIII.—Wolsey—Sir Thomas More taking leave of his Daughter—Calais during the Sixteenth Century—Queen Elizabeth—The Armada—Drake—Mary, Queen of Scots—Drake playing Bowls with his Captains—Sir Walter Raleigh.

FOR SENIOR SCHOLARS.

VOL. II.—THE STRUGGLE FOR POWER AND GREATER ENGLAND.—**1s. 6d.**

CONTENTS.—The First of the Stuarts—The Struggle for Power—The Puritan Tyranny—The Second Struggle for Power : Charles II.—The Revolution—The Fight with France : The Dutch King—Queen Anne and Marlborough—Greater England—The Story of Anson—The Story of Wolfe—The Story of Captain Cook—The Story of Clive—The War of American Independence—The great French War—The Story of Nelson—The Story of the Great Duke—The End of the Stories.

ILLUSTRATIONS.—James I.—Bacon—Charles I.—A Cavalier—Oliver Cromwell—The Great Fire of London—The Seven Bishops going to the Tower—Landing of William of Orange in England—Marlborough—Gibraltar—Chatham—Fight between the *Centurion* and the Manila Ship—General Wolfe—The Death of Captain Cook—Washington—Pitt—Napoleon Bonaparte—Nelson—H.M.S. *Victory*, Portsmouth Harbour—Duke of Wellington—Napoleon on board the *Bellerophon.*

Moira O'Neill, Author of 'Songs of the Glen of Antrim,' writing to Mr Blackwood, says : "F.'s 'Stories of the English' was written for my little daughter Susan. The child is quite fascinated by it, but equally so are all the grown-up friends to whom I have shown it. I lent it once to a sailor uncle, and he sat up to all hours of that night with it, and afterwards told me that he could hardly believe that such an account of Nelson's great battles had been written by a woman, because it was technically accurate. And a soldier friend and critic used about the same words about the account of Marlborough's campaigns. F. is the most patient and faithful student of history that I know. She has such a strong literary sense that she simply could not write anything except in a literary form, and combined with it she has that rare thing, a judicial mind. This, I think, gives her work a quite peculiar value."

Standard Readers.

Revised Edition. With Supplementary Pages, consisting of "Spelling Lists," "Word-Building," "Prefixes and Suffixes," &c. Profusely Illustrated with Superior Engravings.

BOOK I.	40 Lessons	. . . .	8d.
BOOK II.	40 Lessons	. . . .	9d.
BOOK III.	60 Lessons	. . . .	1s. 0d.
BOOK IV.	60 Lessons	. . . .	1s. 3d.
BOOK V.	60 Lessons	. . . .	1s. 4d.
BOOK VI.	60 Lessons	. . . .	1s. 6d.

Schoolmaster.—"We strongly recommend these books.......Children will be sure to like them; the matter is extremely suitable and interesting, the print very distinct, and the paper a pleasure to feel."

Infant Series.

FIRST PICTURE PRIMER. . Sewed, 2d. ; cloth, 3d.
SECOND PICTURE PRIMER . . Sewed, 2d. ; cloth, 3d.
PICTURE READING SHEETS.

1ST SERIES. | 2ND SERIES.

Each containing 16 sheets, unmounted, 3s. 6d. Mounted on 8 boards with cloth border, price 14s. ; varnished, 3s. 6d. per set extra.

Or the 16 sheets laid on linen, varnished, and mounted on a roller, 17s. 6d.

THE INFANT PICTURE READER. With numerous Illustrations. Cloth, limp, 6d.

Educational News.—"Teachers will find these Primers a useful introduction to the art of reading. We consider them well adapted to their purpose."

Geographical Readers.

With numerous Maps, Diagrams, and Illustrations.

GEOGRAPHICAL PRIMER. (For Stand. I.) 96 pp.		9d.
BOOK I. (For Stand. II.) 96 pp.	. .	9d.
BOOK II. (For Stand. III.) 156 pp.	.	1s. 0d.
BOOK III. (For Stand. IV.) 192 pp.	.	1s. 3d.
BOOK IV. (For Stand. V.) 256 pp.	.	1s. 6d.
BOOK V. (For Stand. VI.) 256 pp.	.	1s. 6d.
BOOK VI. (For Stand. VII.) 256 pp.	.	1s. 9d.

Schoolmaster.—"This is a really excellent series of Geographical Readers. The volumes have, in common, the attractiveness which good paper, clear type, effective woodcuts, and durable binding can present ; whilst their contents, both as to quality and quantity, are so graded as to be admirably adapted to the several stages of the pupil's progress."

Historical Readers.

With numerous Portraits, Maps, and other Illustrations.

SHORT STORIES FROM ENGLISH
 HISTORY . . . . . 160 pp. 1s. 0d.
 FIRST HISTORICAL READER . . . 160 pp. 1s. 0d.
 SECOND HISTORICAL READER . . . 224 pp. 1s. 4d·
 THIRD HISTORICAL READER . . . 256 pp. 1s. 6d.

Schoolmaster.—"These new Historical Readers have been carefully compiled. The facts are well selected; the story is well told in language most likely to impress itself in the memory of young children; and the poetical pieces are fitting accompaniments to the prose."

School Board Chronicle.—"The treatment is unconventional, but always in good taste. The volumes will meet with much favour generally as lively, useful, high-toned Historical Readers."

Standard Authors.

Adapted for Schools.

HAWTHORNE'S TANGLEWOOD TALES. With Notes and Illustrations. 160 pp. 1s. 2d.

Aytoun's Lays of the Scottish Cavaliers.

With Introduction, Notes, and Life of the Author, for Junior Classes.

EDINBURGH AFTER FLODDEN . 32 pages, 2d. ; cloth, 3½d.
THE EXECUTION OF MONTROSE . 32 pages, 2d. ; cloth, 3½d.
THE BURIAL-MARCH OF DUNDEE 32 pages, 2d. ; cloth, 3½d.
THE ISLAND OF THE SCOTS . . 32 pages, 2d. ; cloth, 3½d.

Teachers' Aid.—"Capital annotated editions.......Beautifully clear and painstaking; we commend them heartily to our brother and sister teachers."

Educational News.—"Useful issues of well-known poems.......The notes are exceedingly appropriate, and leave nothing in doubt. For class purposes we can specially recommend these little books."

School Recitation Books.

BOOK I. 32 pages . . . . 2d.
BOOK II. 32 pages . . . . 2d.
BOOK III. 48 pages . . . . 3d.
BOOK IV. 48 pages . . . . 3d.
BOOK V. 64 pages . . . . 4d.
BOOK VI. 64 pages . . . . 4d.

Schoolmistress.—"These six books are a valuable contribution to school literature. The poems for each standard are judiciously chosen, the explanatory notes and questions at the end of every lesson are very suitable."

Grammar and Analysis.

BOOK II.	24 pages	.	. Paper, 1½d. ; cloth, 2½d.
BOOK III.	24 pages	.	. Paper, 1½d. ; cloth, 2½d.
BOOK IV.	48 pages	.	. Paper, 2d. ; cloth, 3d.
BOOK V.	64 pages	.	. Paper, 3d. ; cloth, 4d.
BOOK VI.	64 pages	.	. Paper, 3d. ; cloth, 4d.
BOOK VII.	64 pages	.	. Paper, 3d. ; cloth, 4d.

Schoolmaster.—"This is a series of good practical books whose merits ought to ensure for them a wide sale. Among their leading merits are simplicity in definitions, judicious recapitulation, and abundance of well-selected exercises for practice."

Teachers' Aid.—"For thoroughness, method, style, and high-class work, commend us to these little text-books.......A practical hand has impressed every line with individuality.......We are determined to use them in our own department."

Arithmetical Exercises.

BOOK I.	.	.	. Paper, 1½d. ; cloth, 2½d.
BOOK II.	.	.	. Paper, 1½d. ; cloth, 2½d.
BOOK III.	.	.	. Paper, 2d. ; cloth, 3d.
BOOK IV.	.	.	. Paper, 2d. ; cloth, 3d.
BOOK V.	.	.	. Paper, 2d. ; cloth, 3d.
BOOK VI.	.	.	. Paper, 2d. ; cloth, 3d.
BOOK VII.	.	.	. Paper, 3d. ; cloth, 4d.

HIGHER ARITHMETIC for Ex-Standard and Continuation Classes. 128 pp. . . Paper, 6d. ; cloth, 8d.

* *ANSWERS may be had separately, and are supplied direct to Teachers only.*

Schoolmaster.—"We can speak in terms of high praise respecting this series of Arithmetical Exercises. They have been carefully constructed. They are well graduated, and contain a large and varied collection of examples.......We can recommend the series to our readers."

Schoolmistress.—"Large quantity, excellent quality, great variety, and good arrangement are the characteristics of this set of Arithmetical Exercises."

Elementary Grammar and Composition.

Based on the ANALYSIS OF SENTENCES. With a Chapter on WORD-BUILDING and DERIVATION, and containing numerous Exercises. New Edition. 1s.

Schoolmaster.—"A very valuable book. It is constructive as well as analytic, and well-planned exercises have been framed to teach the young student how to use the elements of his mother-tongue.......A junior text-book that is calculated to yield most satisfactory results."

Educational Times.—"The plan ought to work well.......A decided advance from the old-fashioned practice of teaching."

Grammar and Analysis.

Scotch Code.

STANDARD II. 24 pages. Paper, 1½d. ; cloth, 2½d.
STANDARD III. 32 pages. Paper, 1½d. ; cloth, 2½d.
STANDARD IV. 56 pages. Paper, 2½d. ; cloth, 3½d.
STANDARD V. 56 pages. Paper, 2½d. ; cloth, 3½d.
STANDARD VI. 64 pages. Paper, 3d. ; cloth, 4d.

Teachers' Aid.—"These are thoughtfully written and very practically conceived little helps.......They are most exhaustive, and brimming with examples."

New Arithmetical Exercises.

Scotch Code.

STANDARD I. 32 pages . Paper, 1½d. ; cloth, 2½d.
STANDARD II. 32 pages . Paper, 1½d. ; cloth, 2½d.
STANDARD III. 56 pages. Paper, 2d. ; cloth, 3d.
STANDARD IV. 64 pages . Paper, 3d.; cloth, 4d.
STANDARD V. 80 pages . Paper, 4d. ; cloth, 6d.
STANDARD VI. 80 pages . Paper, 4d. ; cloth, 6d.
HIGHER ARITHMETIC for Ex-Standard and Continuation Classes 128 pages . Paper, 6d. ; cloth, 8d.

* ANSWERS may be had separately, and are supplied direct to Teachers only.

Educational News.—"The gradation of the exercises is perfect, and the examples, which are very numerous, are of every conceivable variety. There is ample choice for the teacher under every head. We recommend the series as excellent School Arithmetics."

Merit Certificate Arithmetic.

96 pp. Paper cover, 6d. ; cloth, 8d.

Mensuration.

128 pp., cloth, 1s. Also in Two Parts. Pt. I., Parallelograms and Triangles. 64 pp. Paper, 4d.; cloth, 6d. Pt. II., Circles and Solids. 64 pp. Paper, 4d. ; cloth, 6d. *Answers* may he had separately, price 2d. each Part.

Educational Times.—"The explanations are always clear and to the point, while the exercises are so exceptionally numerous that a wide selection is offered to the students who make use of the book."

A First Book on Physical Geography.

For Use in Schools. 64 pp. 4d.

Journal of Education.—"This is a capital little book, describing shortly and clearly the geographical phenomena of nature."

Manual Instruction—Woodwork. DESIGNED TO MEET THE
REQUIREMENTS OF THE MINUTE OF THE SCIENCE AND ART DEPARTMENT
ON MANUAL INSTRUCTION. By GEORGE ST JOHN, Undenominational
School, Handsworth, Birmingham. With 100 Illustrations. 1s.

Blackwoods' Simplex Civil Service Copy Books.

By JOHN T. PEARCE, B.A., Leith Academy. Price 2d. each.

CONTENTS OF THE SERIES.

No. 1. Elements, Short Letters, Words.
   " 2. Long Letters, Easy Words.
   " 3. Capitals, Half-line Words.
   " 4. Text, Double Ruling, Sentences.
   " 5. Half-Text, Sentences, Figures.
   " 6. Intermediate, Transcription, &c.
   " 7. Small Hand, Double Ruling.
   " 8. Small Hand, Single Ruling.

The Headlines are graduated, up-to-date, and attractive.

Blackwoods' Universal Writing Books.

Have been designed to accompany the above series, and teachers will find it
advantageous to use them as Dictation Copies, because by them the learner
is kept continually writing at the correct slope, &c. No 1. is adapted for
LOWER CLASSES, No. 2 for HIGHER CLASSES. Price 2d. each.

Practical Teacher.—"Our readers would do well to write for a specimen of
this book, and of the blank exercise-books ruled on the same principle. They
are worth careful attention."

School World.—"Those teachers who are anxious to train their pupils to
write in the style associated with Civil Service Competitions should find the
copy-books designed by Mr Pearce very useful. The writing is certainly simple;
it may, in fact, be reduced to four elements, in which the pupil is rigorously
exercised in the earlier books before proceeding in later numbers to continuous
writing."

Schoolmaster.—"Those of our readers in search of new books should see
these."

Journal of Education.—"Aids the eye and guides the hand, and thus
checkmates any bias towards error in the slope."

UNIVERSITY CALENDARS.

St Andrews University Calendar.

Printed and Published for the Senatus Academicus. Crown 8vo, 2s. 6d. net.

St Andrews University L.L.A. Calendar.

Printed and Published for the Senatus Academicus. Crown 8vo, 1s.

WILLIAM BLACKWOOD & SONS, EDINBURGH AND LONDON.

9/12.

CPSIA information can be obtained
at www.ICGtesting.com
Printed in the USA
LVHW090329171221
706462LV00004B/272